# LAND LAW AND POLICY IN ISRAEL

PERSPECTIVES ON ISRAEL STUDIES
S. Ilan Troen, Natan Aridan, Donna Divine, David Ellenson,
Arieh Saposnik, and Jonathan Sarna, *editors*

# LAND LAW AND POLICY IN ISRAEL

*A Prism of Identity*

Haim Sandberg

INDIANA UNIVERSITY PRESS

This book is a publication of

Indiana University Press
Office of Scholarly Publishing
Herman B Wells Library 350
1320 East 10th Street
Bloomington, Indiana 47405 USA

iupress.org

© 2022 by Haim Sandberg

All rights reserved
No part of this book may be reproduced or utilized in any form or by any means, electronic or mechanical, including photocopying and recording, or by any information storage and retrieval system, without permission in writing from the publisher. The paper used in this publication meets the minimum requirements of the American National Standard for Information Sciences—Permanence of Paper for Printed Library Materials, ANSI Z39.48-1992.

Manufactured in the United States of America

First printing 2022

Cataloging information is available from the Library of Congress.

ISBN 978-0-253-06044-0 (hardback)
ISBN 978-0-253-06045-7 (paperback)
ISBN 978-0-253-06047-1 (ebook)

# CONTENTS

*Acknowledgments* vii

*Notes on Translation and Internet Hyperlinks* ix

Introduction: Land Law and Land Policy: A Prism of Identity   1

1  The Fingerprints of History in Land Inventory   14

2  Culture, Nation, and Socialism in the Administration of Public Lands   45

3  Privatization of Public Lands: A Slow Maturation Process   72

4  National Land Planning in a Small Country: Challenges and Innovation   95

5  Jewish and Democratic: Land Policy and the Arab Minority   130

6  Creative Judiciary: Equitable and Constitutional Safeguards to Property Rights   175

Epilogue: Identity in Flux   203

*Bibliography*   211

*Index*   245

# ACKNOWLEDGMENTS

THIS BOOK IS BASED ON MY RESEARCH, TEACHING, and legal consulting activities over the past twenty-five years. I am indebted to my students in the property law classes I teach in the law faculties of the College of Management, the Hebrew University of Jerusalem, and Tel Aviv University, which have helped me, sometimes unknowingly, to formulate the ideas expressed in this book. I am indebted to a long chain of scholars, colleagues, judges, and practitioners that laid the foundation to Israel's real estate law and its academic research. The book is intended to honor their great and rich work. Special thanks to Prof. Joshua Weisman, who was a pioneer in the study of property law in Israel and from whom I learned the basics of the field. In 2019 he passed away, and this book is dedicated to his memory.

The book would not have been published without the constant support and encouragement of Prof. Ilan Troen, who heads the Editorial Committee of the Indiana University Press's Perspectives on Israel Studies series. His patience, guidance, good advice, and insights through the long journey of the publication process were invaluable. Thanks also to the two anonymous readers of the manuscript whose comments helped me to improve and refine it. Special thanks to Betsy Rosenberg for the wonderful touch her linguistic skills has contributed to both the fluency and comprehension of the text.

I thank Gary Dunham and the staff of Indiana University Press for their dedicated and professional handling of the book's publishing.

Finally, I thank my dear and beloved family—my wife, Haya, and my daughters, Noya, Yael, Lilach, and Keren, for endlessly embracing me with love and support, without which this project could not have come to fruition.

Jerusalem,
September 2021

# NOTES ON TRANSLATION AND INTERNET HYPERLINKS

1. Names of Hebrew resources were translated to English by the author and, with few exceptions, were not transliterated. After each such resource, the word *Hebrew* has been added in parenthesis (Hebrew).
2. All Hebrew quotations were translated by the author, except where there is a reference in notes to other publicly available English translations.
3. The years in the formal names of Israeli laws and bills of law are officially mentioned according to the counts of both the Hebrew (5XXX) and the Gregorian calendars. I referred to the Hebrew calendar year only in the first reference to each law or bill of law, but in later references to the same item, as well as in the bibliography, I used only the Gregorian year.
4. All internet hyperlinks were last accessed on September 9, 2021, unless explicitly stated otherwise.

LAND LAW AND POLICY IN ISRAEL

# INTRODUCTION

## Land Law and Land Policy: A Prism of Identity

> What is Man but the earth of his small domain, The imprint of his native land.
> Shaul Tchernichovsky

A NATION'S LAND LAWS AND POLICIES HAVE FAR-REACHING consequences that shape its identity. Revealing them allows researchers to reverse engineer the character and fundamental problems of a given society and to uncover its history, economy, social fabric, and political regime. While this is true of every human society, it is especially evident when it comes to the State of Israel. Israeli land law and policy reflect some of the country's most pronounced identity problems: its struggles as an independent state to overcome the burdens of history; its transition from socialism to a capitalist-style free market economy; its small size and dense population; its championing of creativity and innovation despite its scarcity of natural resources; its aspiration to be both Jewish and democratic; its ability to maintain pride in an independent and creative judiciary while grumbling that the courts have too much power.

Israel's land law and land policy create a unique prism for understanding these aspects of identity. They help clarify subtle nuances in Israel's present and the difficult challenges that lie ahead. The aim of the book, then, is to offer a fresh perspective on the relationship between seemingly mundane land laws and the distinctive identity of the State of Israel. In this introduction we shall consider the broader meaning of *identity* and *national identity* in the context of land and land law. We shall explore Israel's paradigmatic value in the study of land law and policy and then offer a brief structural overview of the book at hand.

### Land, Land Law, and Identity

#### The Meaning of 'Identity'

The term *identity* is often used in the discourse of the social sciences—psychology, anthropology, sociology, political science, or international relations—and in the field of legal philosophy.[1] Nevertheless, the word carries various meanings and lacks a single, generally accepted definition.[2] Its broadest commonality finds in a single object or group of objects one or more similarities (characteristics that are the "same") that define them and their differences from other objects.[3] An identity object can be a thing, a person or group, a nation, or a state. Identity can be a single attribute or a set of attributes. A collection of features that are not unique to an object may nonetheless be unique to its identity. The evaluation of uniqueness may vary according to the viewpoint of the person defining it.[4] Thus, there may be an attempt to define an objective identity—to describe features of the object as they are in reality. Certain areas of research explore the ways in which an object of identity perceives the components of its own identity.[5] Our use of the term here will refer to its most conspicuous elements, with a focus on those that can be distinguished by studying the land laws and policies of the State of Israel.

## The Role of Land in Individual Identity

Land is key in the life of all species, and their end purpose is to gain control of a particular habitat in order to secure nourishment, shelter, and reproductive advantage. The connection between the land and its flora and fauna, whether endemic or invasive,[6] reflects their unique characteristics. Thus, the observation of territorial behavior provides researchers with a wealth of information and a commonly accepted means of formulating, defining, and cataloging biological identity.[7]

Human activity utilizes the many different components of the land, from its surface and subsurface areas to its bodies of water, minerals, and so forth. People may occupy or acquire land, adapt it to their purposes, and fight over the right to use it as they choose. The relationship to land and especially the attachment to one's home environment or native town are charged with emotion.[8] There is an interdisciplinary field of research dedicated to the study of such "place attachment," the ways in which people express their sense of belonging to a particular place.[9] This widespread psychological phenomenon reflects the tendency to hold on to something in one's possession (loss aversion) and to ascribe particular importance to possessions (the endowment effect).[10]

Although all populations exhibit an attachment to land, their relationships may differ. Cain was a farmer; Abel, a shepherd.[11] The country mouse eats the crops; the town mouse enjoys the city life. Some people feel an affinity for a specific place, while others feel it for multiple places (their place of birth, place of residence, etc.).[12] An examination of an individual's relationship to the land allows an observer to learn much about the important components of that individual's identity and lifestyle. Since the sixteenth century, philosophers and legal theorists have considered the relationship to property in general and land in particular to be an important component of personality perspective in liberal democracies. The liberal conception considers the legal protection of assets to be of fundamental importance to personal liberty.[13]

### The Importance of Land in Forming a Collective or National Identity

Land is an important determinant in collective patterns of habitation, occupation, procreation, government administration, and family organization. Religious beliefs too are connected to land and are often centered on temple sites and sacred spaces. There is a group advantage to the use and defense of territory, as this affords an evolving sense of continuity.[14]

The memory of a historical territory may at times become so ingrained in a faith or culture that it acquires an autonomous existence, persisting even after the nation is cut off from its territory. Sometimes this emotional link evolves into an abstract spiritual affinity to the land that has nothing to do with material needs. The connection to the land in such cases embodies the group's psychological attachment to what the land symbolizes or evokes: a yearning for the past or hope for the future, a sense of group cohesion and evolutionary continuity even when the territorial advantage does not exist in actuality.[15] An obvious example of this would be the Jewish and Zionist yearnings for the Holy Land.[16] "By the rivers of Babylon we sat and wept when we remembered Zion," chanted the exiled Jews who mourned for their homeland.[17] Similarly, the protagonist of the Polish-Lithuanian poet Adam Mickiewicz's work laments: "Lithuania, my country, thou art like health; how much thou shouldst be prized only he can learn who has lost thee."[18] The pairing of the words *my land* is *my pride* can be found in the languages of many different nationalities.[19] A spiritual relationship to territory plays an important role in the identity of indigenous peoples,[20] and its memory "from time immemorial" forms an important component of their cultures.[21] Even imaginary communities may develop an affinity to a particular territory,[22] one that represents the foundational concept of a state in international law.[23] Land is thus inherent to the identity of most world nations.[24]

## How Does Land Influence Identity?

The connection between land and identity is a complex one, affected by physical borders and parameters, topography, natural resources, and climate.[25] Sometimes it is shaped by the history of its inhabitants or by other factors unrelated to territorial dimensions and physical features. Some countries have a long, unbroken history of rule over a specific territory, while others have undergone frequent changes in government or conducted territorial wars. National identity may consist of socioeconomic, cultural, demographic, or territorial features,[26] and issues of land may penetrate ideologies and worldviews. Nations have long recognized private ownership of land. In the contemporary world, most Western countries espouse a market economy and the right to private property. Individually owned real estate is a notable type of private property. Nevertheless, we of the modern world have witnessed the emergence of theories that deny private land ownership and advocate communitarianism or the conservation of land and its natural resources for future generations. Thus, the allocation and distribution of land and its resources is an added feature of a nation's economic identity.[27]

Technological advances like cybersecurity, information systems, and the sharing economy model likewise define the role of land in identity[28] and the perception of the world as a global village is now shaping a multinational approach to natural resources.[29] All such factors may be brought to bear on the landscape and influence the place of land in the identity of individuals and nations. Hence, land law and land policies reflect the role of land in national identity.

## The Relationship between Land Law and National Identity

The relationship between law and national identity is not unique to land law. However, since laws derive from national identity and contribute to it,[30] this profound relationship accounts for the powerful connection between identity and land law. Let us observe some examples.

As mentioned above, the cultural importance attributed to land may stem from a nation's history of subjugation, liberation, territorial struggles, and so forth. Implicit to it may be national ownership of the land, its reserves, and the shape of its administration, as, for example, in Venezuela's constitutional protection of national land ownership. The fact that it is one of the only such nations in the world demonstrates the importance of territory to the national identity of Venezuela, stemming from many historical border disputes.[31]

When the aspiration for territorial independence occupies a significant place in a nation's identity, it may uproot earlier legal implants and reshape its system of laws. Implants that are not removed indicate that the past has not been eradicated but is still imprinted in the identity of the state.[32]

Since land is an economic resource, land regulation reflects a country's unique economic identity. Thus, for example, one of the most striking characteristics of socialist states is their preservation of national land ownership, whereas countries with free market economies are characterized by private ownership.[33] In countries undergoing economic transformation, much can be discerned from the management of public lands in relation to national identity.[34]

Geography has as great an impact on land laws as it has on national identity. For example, countries with a significant coastline and marine heritage are more likely to develop maritime law and policy.[35] Small and crowded urban areas strongly emphasize land law in high-rise construction and condominium law.[36] Geography has greatly influenced the identity of indigenous nations.[37] Some live in maritime neighborhoods, which make marine territories an important component of their traditional land laws.[38] Land disputes in Canada reveal the importance of hunting and fishing in the identity and legal traditions of the indigenous nations of British Columbia.[39]

Problematic social stratification is manifest in the informal and unregistered land rights of South America and various third-world nations.[40] Racial discrimination in the United States is reflected in urban renewal projects that sometimes came to be known as urban removal.[41] In countries where freedom is an important value, the degree of private property protection afforded by the state is a major criterion of identity, one that reveals the social role of the courts in the protection of this freedom. A prominent historical example is the role of the courts of equity in the protection of private property in English society.[42] The central role of the US Constitution and its courts in national identity is reflected in the rulings of the Supreme Court with regard to the protection of private property.[43] In the same way, the rulings of the European Union and the European Court of Human Rights with regard to private rights to land indicate the status of personal liberty in the national identity of those nations.⁴⁴

The study of land law and land policy can thus serve as a litmus test for the predominant features of any given society, allowing the researcher to reverse engineer its characteristics and fundamental problems. Of course, identity is reflected variously in a nation's culture and social institutions, its politics, legal system, and so forth. Land law and policy, on the other hand, are regarded as a collection of obscure regulations, the purview of a select few. Indeed, the famous British property law scholar Frederick Lawson wrote that the concepts of real property law "seem to move among themselves according to the rules of a game which exists for its own purposes," creating "a world of pure ideas from which everything physical or material is entirely excluded."⁴⁵ Yet land law is not and should not be the exclusive purview of legal experts. It is an important concern in the study and decoding of a society's identity, and it plays a substantial role in the lives of individuals. In many respects, land policy and the "real [e]state" of a country's affairs are reflective of real problems that plague it as opposed to a theoretical discussion of what is or ought to be. Land laws and land policies are indicative of practical dilemmas. The actual code to a society's identity is cached amid the details and directives of the law.

## Exploring Israel's Identity through Land Law and Land Policy

Land law and land policy constitute an important medium for understanding Israel's identity. As part of the biblical Holy Land, Israel epitomizes a territorial domain that constitutes a central component of religious, ethnic, and national identities. Ever since "The Land" was promised to Abraham in the Bible, the Land of Israel has represented a core element of Jewish identity. In the nineteenth century, the Zionist movement adopted it as the locus of self-determination and its national home.⁴⁶ The same territory is closely bound to Christian and Muslim identity.⁴⁷ Given this historical background, the territory of the "Land of Israel" and its laws are particularly interesting.

Pre-state Israel was ruled first by the Ottoman Empire and later was administered by the British Mandate; hence, the country's land law resonates with historical struggles.⁴⁸ The challenge of bridging the gap between the national aspirations of the Jewish majority and the Arab minority is deeply rooted in Israel's land policies.⁴⁹ Israel has, in the few decades since its establishment, transitioned from a centralized socialist economic system to a free market economy. The process has led, inter alia, to the privatization of land.[50] Israel has one of the most active and creative judicial systems in the world, and the role of its judiciary in land-related issues reveals much about the national values of liberty and private property, as well as judicial independence.[51]

Because Israel is one of the smallest and most densely populated countries in the world, problems related to identity in terms of land are particularly intense. Global phenomena—urban sprawl, loss of open spaces, and inequality between center and periphery—have spread more swiftly and acutely in Israel than elsewhere. Creative planning solutions were thus urgently needed, and Israel's planning laws are among the prominent features of both its national identity and its striving for excellence in entrepreneurship and technological innovation.[52]

This book presents a fascinating land law model of immense value in the realms of political, social, and economic science. Indeed, Israel has long been the recipient of far more international attention than one might expect for such a small Middle Eastern state. This is due primarily to the Israeli-Arab conflict in its various aspects. Israel's identity is indeed affected by the conflict, as are its land laws and policies, yet other aspects of comparable value have so far been neglected. Moreover, the book uncovers sources largely inaccessible to non-Hebrew speakers. Although *The Land Law of Palestine*, by Frederic Goadby and Moses Douchan, was published in Tel Aviv in 1935,[53] in the eighty-five years since then, during which the State of Israel was established and its land laws and land policies have undergone considerable change, not a single comprehensive book on the different facets of Israel's land laws and policies has appeared in English. In light of the comparative value of research on Israel, this deficiency must be corrected. The present book tells the comprehensive story of Israel's land law and policy and its evolving identity at the dawn of the third millennium.

## The Structure of This Book

Each chapter will focus on a specific aspect of Israel's identity as reflected in its land law and land policy within the legal boundaries recognized today, excluding the West Bank (Judea and Samaria) and Gaza. The conflicts regarding the status of those territories are significant for contemporary Israeli identity and comprise many aspects of land law and land policy, but international interest on the subject has attracted abundant interest and generated countless political and academic disputes.[54] The issue is vast and merits a separate work.

Chapter 1 offers an explanation as to how the composition of the private and public land inventory in Israel reflects an attempt to be rid of past influences and demonstrate legal independence. While these tendencies are important components of Israel's identity, the enduring imprint of history is still evident in the shape of its land inventory. Thus, Ottoman rule, the British Mandate, the Zionist vision, and the Israeli-Arab conflict are all manifest in the daily lives of every Israeli and continue to disrupt the Israeli real estate market in the twenty-first century.

Chapter 2 reveals how the administration of the Israel's public land inventory attests to three basic tenets: most of Israel's territory is kept as public lands, symbolizing the return of the Jewish people to their ancient home; the transfer of ownership to foreigners is therefore difficult; according to the socialist worldview of the nation's founders, government should retain land ownership to advance equality and social justice. An analysis of these three tenets in terms of public land administration will provide a new perspective on Israel's current identity. Through the prism of ideological change, we shall observe the decline in Israel's adherence to public ownership as it is stimulated by land privatization.

Chapter 3 takes a closer look at the privatization process in the realm of public land. This process has been long and gradual. Privatization undergoes a slow maturation process in which the legal and administrative frameworks confront a changing reality and informal privatization anticipated formal privatization. This chapter attempts to analyze the steps taken toward privatization over the past decades in two important categories, urban and agricultural lands. It sheds light on the difficult transition from a socialist administration to a market economy and the gradual formal nature of the shift it brought to Israel's identity.

Chapter 4 discusses two policies in Israel's land planning that relate to national identity: first, despite being a small country, Israel is an entrepreneurial powerhouse; and second, because it is one of the most densely populated countries in the world, Israel has unique land needs that pose extraordinary challenges to planning. To cope with the shortage of land and the abundance of needs, Israel must exercise creativity and innovation. The notions of being small and of being a creative and innovative nation find expression in Israel's land planning.

Chapter 5 analyzes how land policy addresses the Arab minority. Israel aspires to be the nation-state of the Jewish people while ensuring full equality for all its citizens. Israeli land law reflects this paradox in its treatment of the impact of the War of Independence on land ownership and in allocation policies. In both areas the law is conflicted: should land be returned to its owners, or should the owners be compensated? Should the segregation of different populations be encouraged, or should they be encouraged to assimilate in mixed neighborhoods? These dilemmas present a fundamental paradox to Israeli identity and to Israel's land policies.

Chapter 6 will analyze how land law reflects the status of the Israeli judicial system. While Israel is blessed with a proudly independent and universally recognized judiciary, its creativity has been at the center of a heated public debate over the limits of judicial authority. One of the most controversial debates in Israeli society over the past decades has revolved around the role of the judicial branch in Israel's identity as a democracy. This aspect of Israel's identity manifests in land law by way of two prominent activities engaged in by the judiciary branch in democratic countries: the development of equitable rights in land and the constitutional protection of private property. This chapter will analyze the activities of the Israeli judicial system in these areas and draw conclusions about the extent to which the Israeli judiciary merits approval or criticism for its independence and creativity.

The epilogue will summarize what Israel's land law and policy reveal about the identity of Israel and the underlying themes of constant flux and conflict: the struggle for independence and the difficulties of disengaging from the past; the drift toward privatization in the face of Israel's socialist foundations; creative land development notwithstanding geographic and demographic limitations; the Jewish character of Israel vis-à-vis democratic values; and the value of an independent and creative legal system and the opposition it arouses.

The reader is invited to join the search for the code to Israel's identity through the directives of its "real [e]state" laws and policies.

### Notes

1. Joseph Raz, "The Identity of Legal Systems," 59 *California Law Review* (1971): 795–15.
2. Rawi Abdelal et.al, "Identity as a Variable," in *Measuring Identity: A Guide for Social Scientists*, ed. Rawi Abdelal et al. (Cambridge: Cambridge University Press, 2009), 17, 17–18;

Rogers Brubaker and Frederick Cooper, "Beyond 'Identity,'" 29 *Theory and Society* (2000): 1; James D. Fearon, "What Is Identity (as We Now Use the Word)?" (unpublished manuscript, November 3, 1999), Stanford University, https://web.stanford.edu/group/fearon-research/cgi-bin/wordpress/wp-content/uploads/2013/10/What-is-Identity-as-we-now-use-the-word-.pdf.

3. "Identity," Oxford English Dictionary, accessed June 29, 2020, https://www.oed.com/view/Entry/91004?redirectedFrom=identity#eid; Harold Noonan and Ben Curtis, "Identity," in *The Stanford Encyclopedia of Philosophy*, ed. Edward N. Zalta (The Metaphysics Research Lab Center for the Study of Language and Information, Stanford University, Summer 2018 Edition), https://plato.stanford.edu/archives/sum2018/entries/identity.

4. Richard Kiely et al., "The Markers and Rules of Scottish National Identity," 49 *Sociological Review* (2001): 33, 42–47.

5. See resources supra note 2.

6. Herbert H. T. Prins and Iain J. Gordon, "Testing Hypotheses about Biological Invasions and Charles Darwin's Two-Creators Rumination," in *Invasion Biology and Ecological Theory: Insights from a Continent in Transformation*, ed. Herbert H. T. Prins and Iain J. Gordon (Oxford: Oxford University Press, 2014), 1, 1–2.

7. Robert Ardrey, *The Territorial Imperative*, 1969 reprint (London: Collins, 1966), 3–7; Luca Giuggioli and V. M. Kenkre, "Consequences of Animal Interactions on Their Dynamics: Emergence of Home Ranges and Territoriality," 2 *Movement Ecology* (2014): 1; H. Jochen Schenk et al., "Spatial Root Segregation: Are Plants Territorial?," 28 *Advances in Ecological Research* (1999): 145, 145–46, 162–68.

8. M. Carmen Hidalgo and Bernardo Hernandez, "Place Attachment: Conceptual and Empirical Questions," 21 *Journal of Environmental Psychology* (2001): 273, 273–75, 278.

9. Setha M. Low and Irwin Altman, "Place Attachment: A Conceptual Inquiry," in *Place Attachment*, ed. Irwin Altman and Setha M. Low (New York: Plenum, 1992), 1, 1–6.

10. Daniel Kahneman et al., "Anomalies: The Endowment Effect, Loss Aversion, and Status Quo Bias," 5 *Journal of Economic Perspectives* (1991): 193, 194, 205; Eyal Zamir, *Law, Psychology, and Morality: The Role of Loss Aversion* (Oxford: Oxford University Press, 2015), 15–22.

11. Genesis 4:2.

12. Kiely, "Markers and Rules," supra note 4, at 42–43, 45.

13. Margaret Jane Radin, "Property and Personhood," 34 *Stanford Law Review* (1982): 957, 991–96.

14. Ohad David and Daniel Bar-Tal, "A Sociopsychological Conception of Collective Identity: The Case of National Identity as an Example," 13 *Personality and Social Psychology Review* (2009): 354, 367.

15. Anthony Douglas Smith, *National Identity* (Reno: Nevada University Press, 1991), 9, 22–23, 49, 127.

16. Ardrey, *Territorial Imperative*, supra note 7, at 305–7; see resources in note 46 below.

17. Psalms 137:1.

18. Adam Mickiewicz, *Pan Tadeusz: The Last Foray in Lithuania*, trans. George Rapall Noyes (London: J. M. Dent & Sons, 1917); reprint: Semicentennial Publications of the University of California, https://archive.org/stream/pantadeuszorlastoomickuoft/pantadeuszorlastoomickuoft_djvu.txt.

19. Gordon H. Hills, *Native Libraries: Cross-cultural Conditions in the Circumpolar Countries* (Lanham, MD: Scarecrow, 1997), 165; Richard T. Antoun, "Civil Society, Tribal Process, and Change in Jordan: An Anthropological View," 32 *Int. J. Middle East Stud.* (2000): 441, 460; Honaida Ghanim, "Poetics of Disaster: Nationalism, Gender, and Social

Change among Palestinian Poets in Israel after Nakba," 22 *International Journal of Politics, Culture, and Society* (2009): 23, 33–36.

20. United Nations Declaration on the Rights of Indigenous Peoples 2007, §25, GA Res 61/295 UN GAOR 61st Sess., Supp. No. 49, Vol. III, UN Doc. A/61/ 49 (2008), 15; Jérémie Gilbert, *Indigenous Peoples' Land Rights under International Law: From Victims to Actors* (Leiden: Brill Nijhoff, 2016), 192–97.

21. A. St. J. J. Hannigan, "Native Custom, Its Similarity to English Conventional Custom and Its Mode of Proof," 2 *Journal of African Law* (1958): 101, 104–6; Daniel G. Kelly, "Indian Title: The Rights of American Natives in Lands They Have Occupied since Time Immemorial," 75 *Colum. L. Rev.* (1975): 655, 660–61; Shaunnagh Dorsett, "Since Time Immemorial: A Story of Common Law Jurisdiction, Native Title and the Case of Tanistry," 26 *Melb. U. L. Rev.* (2002): 32, 36–43.

22. Benedict Anderson, *Imagined Communities: Reflections on the Origin and Spread of Nationalism* (London: Verso, 2006), 53–55.

23. David B. Knight, "Identity and Territory: Geographical Perspectives on Nationalism and Regionalism," 72 *Annals of the Association of American Geographers* (1982): 514, 519; John G. Sprankling, *The International Law of Property* (Oxford: Oxford University Press, 2014), 5.

24. Colin Williams and Anthony D. Smith, "The National Construction of Social Space," 7 *Progress in Geography* (1983): 502, 504–12; David and Bar-Tal, "Sociopsychological Conception," supra note 14.

25. Guntram H. Herb, "Identity and Territory," in *Nested Identities: Nationalism, Territory, and Scale*, ed. Guntram H. Herb and David H. Kaplan (Oxford: Rowman & Littlefield, 1999), 9, 17; Anssi Paasi, "The Institutionalization of Regions: A Theoretical Framework to Understanding the Emergence of Regions and the Constitution of Regional Identity," 164 *Fennia* (1986): 105, 120–21.

26. Knight, "Identity and Territory," supra note 23, at 517.

27. Stuart Elden, "Land, Terrain, Territory," 34 *Prog. Hum. Geogr.* (2010): 799, 810–11; Gregory S. Alexander and Eduardo M. Peñalver, *An Introduction to Property Theory* (Oxford: Oxford University Press, 2010), 11, 57; Gregory S. Alexander, *Property and Human Flourishing* (Oxford: Oxford University Press, 2018), 82–95.

28. Nestor M. Davidson and John J. Infranca, "The Sharing Economy as an Urban Phenomenon," 34 *Yale Law and Policy Review* (2016): 215, 236–37; Haim Sandberg, "Real Estate E-conveyancing: Vision and Risks," 19 *Information & Communications Technology Law* (2010): 101, 103; Victoria L. Lemieux, "Evaluating the Use of Blockchain in Land Transactions: An Archival Science Perspective," 6 *European Property Law Journal* (2017): 392, 392–93, 440; Nicolás Nogueroles Peiró and Eduardo J. Martinez García, "Blockchain and Land Registration Systems," 6 *European Property Law Journal* (2017): 296, 317–18.

29. Amnon Lehavi, "Land Law in the Age of Globalization and Land Grabbing," in *Comparative Property Law: Global Perspectives*, ed. Michele Graziadei and Lionel Smith (Cheltenham, UK: Edward Elgar, 2017), 290, 290–91; Sprankling, *International Law of Property*, supra note 23, at 18–20.

30. Hugh Collins, "European Private Law and the Cultural Identity of States," 3 *European Review of Private Law* (1995): 353; Menachem Mautner, *Law and the Culture of Israel* (Oxford: Oxford University Press, 2011), 32, 41.

31. Constitution of the Bolivarian Republic of Venezuela §13, https://venezuelanalysis.com/constitution/title/2; Allan R. Brewer-Carías, "Guyana-Venezuela Border Dispute," in *Max Planck Encyclopedia of Public International Law*, ed. R. Wolfrum, online ed. (Oxford:

Oxford University Press, 2006); Michael J. Strauss, *The Leasing of Guantanamo Bay* (Westport, CT: Praeger Security International, 2009), 32.

32. William David McIntyre, *British Decolonization 1946–1997* (London: Macmillan, 1998), 31–33.

33. Joseph L. Sax, "The Legitimacy of Collective Values: The Case of the Public Lands," 56 *University of Colorado Law Review* (1985): 537–38.

34. M. R. Jepsen et al., "Transitions in European Land-Management Regimes between 1800 and 2010," 49 *Land Use Policy* (2015): 53, 61.

35. Sandy Kerr et al., "Planning at the Edge: Integrating across the Land Sea Divide," 47 *Marine Policy* (2014): 118, 120–23.

36. Anne Haila, "Real Estate in Global Cities: Singapore and Hong Kong as Property States," 37 *Urban Studies* (2000): 2241, 2241–42; Amnon Lehavi, "Law, Collective Action and Culture: Condominium Governance in Comparative Perspective," 23 *Asia Pacific Law Review* (2015): 5, 19–26; Lei Chen and Mark D. Kielsgard, "Evolving Property Rights in China: Patterns and Dynamics of Condominium Governance," 2 *Chinese Journal of Comparative Law* (2014): 21–24.

37. Ramy Bulan, "Indigenous Identity and the Law," 25 *Journal of Malaysian and Comparative Law* (1998): 127, 165; see also resources supra note 21.

38. Rutgerd Boelens et al., "Contested Territories: Water Rights and the Struggles over Indigenous Livelihoods," 3 *International Indigenous Policy Journal*, no. 3, article 5 (January 2012): 1–15; Nonie Sharp, *Saltwater People: The Waves of Memory* (Toronto: University of Toronto Press, 2002), 121–29.

39. Tsilhqot'in Nation v. British Columbia (2007) BCJ No. 2465 (Par 7, 23 to J. D. H. Vickers); Emily Jane Davis and Maureen G. Reed, "Governing Transformation and Resilience: The Role of Identity in Renegotiating Roles for Forest-Based Communities of British Columbia's Interior," in *Social Transformation in Rural Canada: Community, Cultures, and Collective Action*, ed. John R. Parkins and Maureen G. Reed (Vancouver: University of British Columbia Press, 2013), 249, 253–54, 261–63.

40. Hernando De Soto, *The Mystery of Capital* (London: Black Swan, 2001), 96–106; Gregory S. Alexander, "Culture and Capitalism: A Comment on De Soto," in *Hernando De Soto and Property in a Market Economy*, ed. D. Benjamin Barros (Abingdon: Routledge, 2016; first published 2010, Ashgate Publishing, Farnham), 41, 43–47.

41. Kelo v. City of New London 545 US 469, 521–22 (2005) (J. Thomas).

42. A. H. Marsh, *History of the Court of Chancery* (Toronto: Carswell, 1890), 2–17; John McGee (ed.), *Snell's Equity*, 32nd ed. (London: Sweet & Maxwell, 2010), 387.

43. Michael Kammen, "The Right of Property and Property in Rights: The Problematic Nature of Property in the Political Thought of the Founders and the Early Republic," in *Liberty, Property, and the Foundations of the American Constitution*, ed. Ellen Frankel Paul and Howard Dickman (New York: SUNY Press, 1989), 1.

44. Hendrik D. Ploeger and Daniëlle A. Groetelaers, "The Importance of the Fundamental Right to Property for the Practice of Planning: An Introduction to the Case Law of the European Court of Human Rights on Article 1, Protocol 1," 15 *European Planning Studies* (2007): 1423, 1436–37.

45. Frederick H. Lawson, *The Rational Strength of English Law* (London: Stevens & Sons, 1951), 79.

46. Boaz Newman, *Land and Desire in Early Zionism*, trans. Haim Watzman (Waltham, MA: Brandeis University Press, 2011), 78–82; Anita Shapira, *Land and Power: The Zionist*

*Resort to Force 1881–1948* (Stanford, CA: Stanford University Press, 1999), 6, 9–10; Emanuele Ottolenghi, "A National Home," in *Modern Judaism: An Oxford Guide*, ed. Nicholas De Lange and Miri Freud-Kandel (Oxford: Oxford University Press, 2005), 54, 56–57.

47. Glenn Bowman, "Christian Ideology and the Image of a Holy Land: The Place of Jerusalem Pilgrimage in the Various Christianities," in *Contesting the Sacred: The Anthropology of Christian Pilgrimage*, ed. John Eade and Michael J. Sallnow (Urbana: University of Illinois Press, 2000; first published 1991, Routledge, London), 98, 98–106; Jacob Lassner, *Medieval Jerusalem: Forging an Islamic City in Spaces Sacred to Christians and Jews* (Ann Arbor: University of Michigan Press, 2017), 60–62.

48. Daniel Friedmann, "Independent Development of Israeli Law," 10 *Israel Law Review* (1975): 515, 536–37; see chap. 1 and 6 in this book.

49. See chap. 1, 2, and 5 in this book.

50. Ronen Mandelkern and Amir Paz-Fuchs, "Privatizing Israel: An Introduction," in *The Privatization of Israel: The Withdrawal of State Responsibility*, ed. Amir Paz-Fuchs et al. (New York: Palgrave Macmillan, 2018), 1, 1–3, 6–10; Rachelle Alterman, "National-Level Planning in Israel: Walking the Tightrope between Government Control and Privatization," in *National-Level Planning in Democratic Countries: An International Comparison of City and Regional Policy-Making*, ed. Rachelle Alterman (Liverpool: Liverpool University Press, 2001), 257, 268–70; see chap. 2 and 3 in this book.

51. Shimon Shetreet, "The Critical Challenge of Judicial Independence in Israel," in *Judicial Independence in the Age of Democracy: Critical Perspectives from Around the World*, ed. Peter H. Russell and David M. O'Brien (Charlottesville: University Press of Virginia, 2001), 233, 233–35; Eli Salzberger, "Judicial Activism in Israel," in *Judicial Activism in Common Law Supreme Courts*, ed. Brice Dikson (Oxford: Oxford University Press, 2008), 217; Yoav Dotan, "Judicial Accountability in Israel: The High Court of Justice and the Phenomena of Judicial Hyperactivism," 8 *Israeli Affairs*, no. 4 (2002): 87–106; see chap. 1 and 6 in this book.

52. See chap. 4 in this book.

53. Frederic Goadby and Moses Doukhan, *The Land Law of Palestine* (Tel Aviv: Shoshany's, 1935).

54. Just a few recent representative publications in this area: Abraham Bell and Eugene Kontorovich, "Palestine, *uti possidetis juris* and the Borders of Israel," 58 *Arizona Law Review* (2016): 633, 686–92; Orna Ben-Naftali et al., *The ABC of the OPT: A Legal Lexicon of the Israeli Control over the Occupied Palestinian Territory* (Cambridge: Cambridge University Press, 2018); Elisha Efrat, *The West Bank and Gaza Strip: A Geography of Occupation and Disengagement* (Abingdon: Routledge, 2006).

# 1

## THE FINGERPRINTS OF HISTORY IN LAND INVENTORY

THE GOVERNMENT OF A NEWLY ESTABLISHED STATE OFTEN faces dilemmas posed by the older regime. Resentment at bygone evils and the aspiration to independence may motivate the new regime to cast off the legacy of the past, while efficiency and equity considerations and the search for continuity may permit the past to influence the present and the future. The formulation of Israel's land inventory reflects three such dilemmas: First, the Israeli government had to decide whether to discard land laws created by centuries of Ottoman rule and thirty years under the British Mandate and transform them into an independent legal system consistent with the independent Jewish-Zionist character of their newly established state or to preserve the legacy of the past to maintain stability and avoid infringement of existing property rights. Second, the State of Israel had to contend with tremendous demographic changes brought about by the War of Independence, which left hundreds of Palestinian villages and towns uninhabited. The question of whether assets should be returned arose, along with the problem of what to do with them until a final determination could be reached. Third, the shift from land purchase under foreign rule to a situation in which the Jewish state holds the full inventory of government land raised the issue of whether the Jewish National Fund (JNF), which during the British Mandate was the Zionist movement's central arm for the purchase of land and Zionist settlement, had a valid reason to exist following the establishment of the state and, if so, what role it should play in the management of its large inventory.

In principle, Israel chose to abolish the Ottoman and Mandatory heritage, to deny the return of the refugees and the transfer of their assets, to take over the management of the JNF's assets, and to convert the fund's purpose from "redeeming the land" to "redeeming the wilderness."[1] These matters were not resolved all at once. The legacy of the Ottoman and British past, the refugee problem, and the redemption of JNF land are on Israel's agenda to this day and continue to exert significant influence on the structure of state land reserves. The long reach of legal history is still disrupting the Israeli real estate market in the twenty-first century.

The chapter before us will examine how each of the three dilemmas left a prominent fingerprint on Israel's land inventory and how they reveal the impact of the past in the identity of the State of Israel.

## The Dead Hand of the Ottoman Legacy

### The Ottoman Heritage Dilemma

In 1982, Professor Joshua Weisman, an eminent scholar of land law in the State of Israel, published an article entitled "How Long Will the Ottoman Land Laws Govern Us?"[2] The article criticized Israel's legal system for a failure to disengage from the Ottoman land laws a decade after their formal annulment and for its laxness in transforming them into an independent Israeli system. The gradual process of abolishing Ottoman land laws began with the appointment of a professional committee to "amend the land laws." The committee, headed by then district court judge and later Supreme Court president Moshe Landau, submitted its opinion in January 1950,[3] but the process apparently ended in 1969 with the Knesset's enactment of Land Law, 5729–1969, and its nearly complete annulment of the Ottoman land laws.[4]

Supporters of the annulment believed that Ottoman land laws reflected an obsolete system that was essentially irrelevant to the State of Israel. Thus, for example, immediately after the enactment of the law, Justice Landau's wife, Leah, herself an expert in real estate law, wrote that most of the provisions in Ottoman legislation "were necessities of the economic and social reality of the Ottoman Empire that struggled with backwardness and neglect and the remnants of a feudal social order."[5]

Little more than a decade after the formal annulment of the Ottoman laws, Professor Weisman was surprised to discover the extent to which Ottoman land laws still affected the lives of Israelis. Although Ottoman land laws have disappeared almost entirely from Israeli law in the three decades since then, they still affect the structure of the country's public and private land inventory. Indeed, more than a century after the end of Ottoman rule and seventy years since the establishment of the State of Israel, the long arm of the Ottoman administration, with help from the British Mandate, reaches into the future. Let us try to understand how this miracle occurred.

## Principles of Ottoman Land Laws

The Ottoman legal system was based primarily on the Muslim land laws in force across the entire Ottoman Empire. Thus, Israel's land inventory is similar in structure to those found in other countries that were under Ottoman control.[6] The normative system that affected the constitution of Israel's land inventory was a product of the last fifty years in four centuries of Ottoman rule. Its main component was the Ottoman Land Code of 1858.[7] This was mostly a codification of preexisting laws, yet it also initiated a number of reforms. While the land code's main concern was defining the status of, and administrative procedures for, government land, it also laid the foundation for the privatization of those lands.[8] The Ottoman system defined land status as either private or public on the basis of its nature and use. Built-up lots in urban or village settings were regarded as privately owned (*mulq, waqf*) while urban areas intended for public use were regarded as publicly owned municipal lands (*matruka*). There were two classes of open land: first, smaller, cultivated or cultivable plots (*miri*) surrounding developed land that were formally owned (*raqabe*) by the regime inasmuch as agriculture was the main source of income for both the ruler and his subjects; and second, a more common class of government-owned land that was rural but non-agrarian and that was located in outlying areas (*mewat*).[9] Figure 1.1 illustrates the definitions of private and public ownership under Ottoman law.

## Privatization of Governmental Land: The Ottoman Version

Toward the end of the Ottoman Empire, government-owned lands underwent a process of privatization. Individuals were primarily granted only limited rights to cultivable lands (*miri*), including rights of possession and use (*tassaruf*), which could be neither transferred nor inherited and which had to be returned to the government if the owner departed or ceased to cultivate the land (*mahlul*).[10] By the end of the nineteenth century, a deeper gradual process of privatizing cultivated land had begun, and full ownership rights to *miri* lands were slowly transferred from the government to private hands.[11] From a legal standpoint, the process led to a blurring of

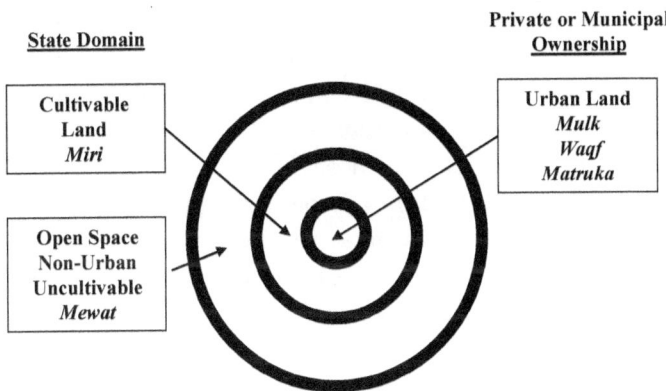

Fig. 1.1 Private and Public Ownership under the Ottoman Law

distinctions between ownership and usage rights: usage rights could now be commercially traded, and the government did not always enforce the obligation to return land that was left uncultivated. The British Mandate government and then the State of Israel registered full ownership to those who had cultivated lands for more than a decade or in certain cases for fifteen and even twenty-five years.[12] Israel had completed this process early in its third decade with the formulation of Land Law 5729–1969, which states that "the ownership of immovable property which . . . belonged to the Miri category shall be under full ownership."[13]

The other avenue for privatization, in force until 1921, pertained to uncultivable government lands (*mewat*) on the outskirts of settlements. The Ottoman Land Code recognized the possibility of reviving such lands (*ihya*; "Revival").[14] During the British Mandate, the court decided that revival constituted "conversion from the unfruitful to the productive"[15] and, as such, turned those lands into *miri* land, which led to the privatization of the "revived" areas. Two famous cases of revival of *mewat* land toward the end of the Ottoman period involved the sand dunes west of the settlement of Rishon Le-Zion (with the permission of the governor, Jamal Paha)[16] and the sand dunes south of Jaffa.[17] In 1921, the British abolished the option of acquiring *mewat* lands through "revival"[18] to retain ownership of the full inventory of wastelands, thereby meeting the obligation in article 6 of the Mandate for Palestine, granted by the League of Nations, which required them "[to] encourage . . . close settlement by Jews on the land, including State lands and waste lands not required for public purposes."[19]

The State of Israel did not change the British ordinance forbidding the revival of *mewat* lands but ordered registration of these lands as state lands.[20] Today, some Israeli Bedouin are attempting to substantiate litigation, suing for ownership of lands in the northern Negev, on the basis of their claim that they revived those lands before 1921.[21] Israel's Supreme Court has thus far adopted the approach that the Negev is *mewat* land, rejecting claims of revival.[22] In any event, the accumulation of "dead" land as governmental land was frozen in 1921. Most of the undeveloped territory in British Mandate Palestine became governmental land that year, thus making it impossible to acquire private ownership via revival.

### The Registration of the Ottoman Heritage during the British and Israeli Eras

Ottoman rule in Palestine officially ended in 1917, but Ottoman law remained in force for many years thereafter. The British Mandate government adopted the majority of Ottoman laws, including the Ottoman Land Code of 1858 (excluding the above-mentioned changes in the *mewat* category).[23] The British Mandate's most important contribution to the development of Israel's inventory of public and private lands was its institution of a modern land title registration mechanism. Although land records did exist during the Ottoman period, they lacked demarcation and documented only a tiny percentage of lands, both public and private.[24] The British filled in the gaps by instituting a systematic process of land title registration and by opening a modern land title registry based on the Torrens system. According to this system, every plot of land went through legal examination: if a private owner proved ownership to the plot of land, the government registered the land in the name of this owner. If no one proved ownership for a given plot of land, the government registered it as state owned. Registration of rights in the land registry was a product of a mapping and surveying (cadastre) that clearly and precisely established the borders of each plot. The court decided ownership in cases of legal disputes, and its decisions granted in rem rights. New registration was final and nearly indefeasible.[25]

The land title registration process started with the legislation of the Land (Settlement of Title) Ordinance, 1928, and continues to this day.[26] The British managed to register rights for only 5,500 square kilometers of land, of which only 5,000 were included in the territory of the State of Israel in 1949. The settled territory was spread out along the coast in the shape of the letter N, from Khan Yunis to Nahariya, eastward across the valleys through

Bet She'an, and northward from there, via the Jordan valley and the northern valleys, to Metula. Most of this land was agricultural and cultivated, and most of it was, at the time, privately owned.[27] The British Mandate government managed to register only a small amount of its territory (about 1,500 square kilometers). The British Mandate government evaluated about 12,577 square kilometers of the "Be'er Sheva desert" as *mewat* or uncultivated *miri* land, making these areas (with the exception of not more than 2,000 square kilometers) government owned according to Ottoman law. Yet, as a matter of fact the British government did not register these lands.[28]

The State of Israel continued the process of registration in the Galilee, the Negev, the inner Shefela region, and urban areas. Ownership of most state lands, including most of the Negev, was then settled and registered.[29] The State of Israel continued with land title registration efforts in areas in which Israeli law was implemented after 1967—in other words, East Jerusalem[30] and the Golan Heights.[31]

In sum, the process of title registration initiated by the British Mandate government and still in force today is responsible for the registration of the land inventory as either private or public, as it was developed by Ottoman law. In this way the inherited principles of Ottoman land law were translated into the extracts of land registration and ultimately shaped Israel's land inventory.

## The Long Reach of Ottoman Heritage Today: State Land and Private Land

The new State of Israel gradually limited the application of Ottoman land laws.[32] In 1970, the Knesset voided the Ottoman law almost entirely while retaining earlier rights created through it.[33] Although Ottoman law is applicable in only 2.2 percent of the country's territory today,[34] it succeeded in defining the vast majority of Israel's private and public lands before 1970. Ottoman law, then, has had a decisive and lasting influence over the distribution of these types of ownership in Israel.

Most of the territory in Ottoman-era Palestine belonged to the *mewat* category. *Mewat* included all nonurban and uncultivated lands not adjacent to villages or built-up areas. The League of Nation's Mandate vested this great volume of government-held land to the British high commissioner, in trust "for the Government of Palestine."[35] When the British Mandate came to an end, Israeli law transferred all of this government-held land to the State of Israel.[36] Thus, the nascent state inherited ownership of *mewat* lands

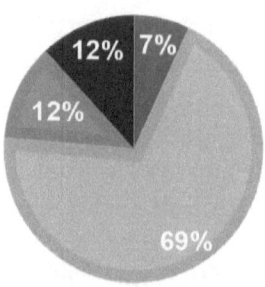

Fig. 1.2 Israel's Private and Public Land Inventory

from its predecessors, as well as *miri* lands—fit for cultivation but as of yet uncultivated—that had not been transferred to private hands prior to 1970. If the Ottoman law had not been voided, most state land would be *mewat* land today. As a direct result of these steps, Israel's government land inventory currently comprises about 14,885 square kilometers, covering nearly 69 percent of its territory (see fig. 1.2).[37]

According to data, 74 percent of state-owned lands produce only 35 percent of the public land inventory income, a relatively low value in comparison to other components of the public inventory and privately owned lands.[38] Gauging the distance of state land from settled areas is a historical outgrowth of Ottoman classification. Figure 1.3 shows that the proportion of state lands in the total land inventory is especially large in the open and undeveloped peripheral regions in the south and north of Israel. The proportion of this component is significantly smaller in the settled, urban regions of central Israel, where the proportion of private lands is greater.[39]

Ottoman law is similarly the source of Israel's private land ownership inventory. As mentioned above, Ottoman law recognized two kinds of private ownership: ownership of built-up lands in cities and villages (*mulq*) and acquired ownership of cultivable lands (*miri*) by way of continuous cultivation over long periods of time. These mechanisms produced a private inventory of built-up and cultivated lands that lasted to the end of the British Mandate period. Only about 1,486 square kilometers of these lands, about 7 percent of Israel's sovereign territory, remain private to this day (see fig. 1.2). Most of this inventory was created in accordance with

## The Fingerprints of History in Land Inventory | 21

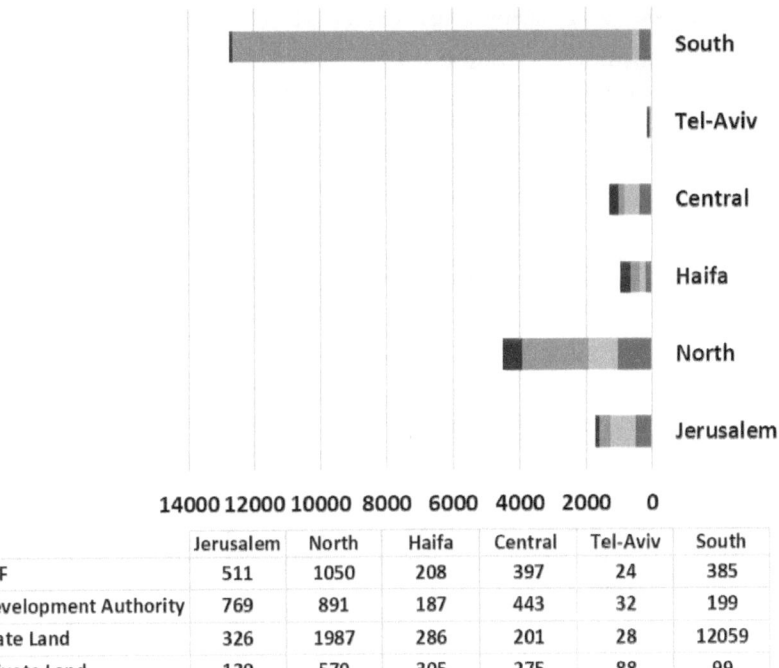

Fig. 1.3 Distribution of Land Inventory in Israel by Districts (Sq. Km.)

Ottoman law in neighborhoods that existed prior to the establishment of the State of Israel.

This historical backdrop to the inventory of private lands influenced both its geographical location and its value. Most private land in Israel is located in cities or villages that existed during Ottoman and British rule and that survived after the founding of the state. Hence, a large proportion of privately owned land is located in older cities, such as Jerusalem, Tel Aviv, or Haifa, in settlements that were established between the advent of Zionism and the establishment of the state, and in Arab cities and villages that remained intact after Israel's establishment. These are the State of Israel's core areas, and lands there are highly valuable.

On the other hand, it is quite rare to find privately owned land in localities established in peripheral areas after the founding of the state, considered *mewat* lands under Ottoman law. A move toward privatization in such areas, a small proportion of all public lands, has only recently begun and has not changed the scale and internal composition of the inventory in

Table 1.1. The Distribution of Private and Public Land in Selected Urban Textures (km²).

| Total | Unsettled Ownership | Private Land | Israel Lands (Public) | Urban Texture |
|---|---|---|---|---|
| | | Arab Villages Existing before and after 1948 | | |
| 30.257 | (1%) 0.166 | (64%) 19.360 | (35%) 10.731 | Sakhnin |
| 40.794 | (1%) 0.425 | (59%) 24.148 | (40%) 16.221 | Shefa-Amr |
| 27.413 | (1%) 0.285 | (44%) 12.102 | (55%) 15.026 | Umm al-Fahm |
| | | Jewish (or Mixed) Cities Established before 1948 | | |
| 31.204 | (0%) 0.102 | (63%) 19.534 | (37%) 11.568 | Hadera |
| 132.792 | (37%) 49.526 | (24%) 32.282 | (38%) 50.984 | Jerusalem |
| 97.096 | (2%) 2.113 | (55%) 53.654 | (43%) 41.329 | Tel Aviv Metropolitan Area—South |
| 56.603 | (1%) 0.463 | (54%) 30.634 | (45%) 25.506 | Tel Aviv Metropolitan Area—North |
| 47.266 | (0.5%) 0.207 | (46%) 21.949 | (53%) 25.110 | Petah Tikva |
| 100.861 | (0.5%) 0.523 | (46%) 46.701 | (54%) 54.683 | Rishon Le-Zion |
| 134.651 | (5%) 6.198 | (41%) 54.551 | (55%) 73.902 | Haifa and Krayot |
| | | Jewish Cities Established after 1948 | | |
| 45.531 | (3%) 1.433 | (22%) 9.957 | (75%) 34.141 | Beit-Shemesh |
| 34.866 | (0%) 0.032 | (19%) 6.775 | (81%) 28.059 | Modi'in |
| 29.177 | (0%) 0.002 | (8%) 2.293 | (92%) 26.882 | Kiryat Gat |
| | | Cities Populated by Absentees before 1948 | | |
| 45.511 | (5%) 2.211 | (22%) 9.861 | (73%) 33.439 | Ramla-Lod |
| 45.367 | (0.5%) 0.257 | (21%) 9.387 | (79%) 35.723 | Ashkelon |
| 24.416 | (3.8%) 0.935 | (18.9%) 4.60 | (77.3%) 18.881 | Tiberias |

a significant way, nor is it expected to do so in the near future. See the distribution of private and public land in selected urban textures in table 1.1.[40]

In summary, although from a legal standpoint the State of Israel is already free of Ottoman land restrictions, Ottoman law has left a significant mark on the geography of the country's real estate market. Although Israel made efforts to abolish the Ottoman legacy, it failed, or perhaps it did not fully intend to erase the Ottoman fingerprint from its land inventory. It should be noted that a similar process is taking place today in Judea and Samaria (the West Bank), which are outside the official borders of the State of Israel as they are recognized today and therefore beyond the scope of the present book, although the situation does merit special attention.[41]

# Fingerprints of the Refugee Problem in Israel's Land Inventory

## The Palestinian Refugee Dilemma

The War of Independence was the bloodiest and most difficult of Israel's wars. By the time it ended, hundreds of thousands of Palestinians had become refugees. The demographic and geographic consequences of the war have had a critical effect on Israel's public land inventory and on the identity of the state and every one of its citizens. The present chapter will focus on the effects of the transfer of Palestinian property to the Israeli administration, the first prominent change in the structure of Israel's land inventory. Palestinian refugees had left behind their houses and cultivated lands in hundreds of villages and several cities. According to Ottoman law, these assets remained the refugees' private property.

Estimates of the volume of private property abandoned by the refugees vary because many of them had not listed their property in the land registry before their departure and because property ownership was based on interpretations of Ottoman law and the identification of land usage (urban or agricultural).[42] For instance, one evaluation presented to the United Nations Conciliation Commission for Palestine (UNDOP), which was established soon after the creation of the refugee problem to examine possible solutions, reported that the refugees left behind 14 square kilometers of built-up land in villages and 4,590 square kilometers of land fit for various levels of cultivation.[43] According to an Israeli evaluation presented to UNDOP, Palestinians abandoned only 3,980 square kilometers in total.[44] At the heart of earlier evaluations lay a report on the breadth of cultivable territory undertaken by the British in 1945.[45] In 1952, the Israeli Ministry of Finance organized a review that found the breadth of cultivable territory to be much smaller.[46] As a result of this review, the total amount of rural land, both cultivated and built-up, came to 3,290 square kilometers. The amount of abandoned urban territory was assessed at about 25 square kilometers.[47]

When the war ended, Palestinian refugees lost the opportunity to administer their assets. The State of Israel blocked their return to their property on principle and began settling the millions of Jewish refugees from European and Arab countries who began pouring into the country.

Palestinian property was also used to expand extant urban settlements and to establish new ones.[48]

Israel never could have done so had it not legally transferred refugee property titles to itself. Yet, as we shall see below, this transfer retained most of the former Palestinian private inventory as an independent category of land, which seemingly points to a political meaning: that the refugee problem has not been resolved and that Israel is still in a dilemma over it. Let us first describe the metamorphosis of the refugee inventory from private to public land. Then we shall attempt to discover the fingerprints of the problem in the design and current management of this public inventory.

### Transferring Palestinian Refugee Lands to the Public Administration

The state's first step toward legalizing the transfer of refugee lands was to define them as absentees' property and transfer their administration to a custodian of absentees' property.[49] But this was insufficient because the control of property by a "custodian" was, from a legal point of view, a temporary measure on behalf of actual owners, the beneficiaries, so the state transferred ownership of absentees' property on a permanent basis to a new government body created specifically for this purpose: the Development Authority.[50] Ownership of refugee property was transferred to the Development Authority over two parallel channels. First, in 1953, the custodian of absentees' property sold all absentee lands under his authority, including any he would receive in the future, to the Development Authority.[51] In addition, the Land Acquisition (Validation of Acts and Compensation) Law, 5713–1953, authorized the finance minister to grant all abandoned property designated or in use for "necessary development needs, settlement or security" to the Development Authority.[52] Most of the property transferred over the latter channel was located in abandoned villages already under the control of the custodian of absentees' property and the Development Authority.[53]

The main purpose of these double expropriations was to ratify the process of seizing the abandoned property of Palestinian refugees who remained Israeli citizens ("present absentees"). Although their property in the abandoned villages had already become "absentee property," they were Israeli citizens, so it was utterly inexcusable for the state not to compensate them after the seizure of their lands. The Acquisition Law was principally intended to grant refugees with Israeli citizenship the right to compensation.[54] The finance minister granted the Development Authority a total of 1,225 square kilometers of land. Yet the legal focus of the land of "present absentees" was of a far smaller magnitude, roughly 239 square kilometers under private Palestinian ownership, 66 square kilometers of *waqf* land, and 0.101 square kilometers of church property.[55]

In 1960, the Israeli Parliament vested the administration of all Development Authority land in the Israel Lands Administration (ILA), a body created that year to centralize the management of all public lands.[56] After that time, the Development Authority was subsumed under the Israel Lands Administration and no longer functioned as an independent body with its own management.[57] While the Development Authority does not function anymore, it still exists from a perspective of legal formalism and is still listed in the land registry as the owner of 2,500 square kilometers of land, accounting for about 12 percent of Israel's sovereign territory (see figs. 1.2 and 1.3). Furthermore, while the scale of Development Authority land comes to only 12 percent of the public land inventory in Israel, its yield between 2000 and 2013 was 30 percent of all profits from public land. The reason for this disparity is that these lands comprise a high proportion of what had been privately owned land. The profits officially accrue to the Development Authority and are then transferred to the Finance Ministry as a loan on an annual basis.[58] Why, then, does this formal separation between Development Authority assets and all other state assets persist?

### *Fingerprints of the Refugee Problem: Why Does the Development Authority Still Exist?*

This question was raised as far back as 1960, when the Knesset deliberated over the enactment of the legislation that vested the administration of the Development Authority with the Israel Lands Administration. Knesset Member Menachem Begin, then head of the opposition party and later prime minister, suggested including the Development Authority's lands with all other state lands. Then Attorney General Haim Cohn, who later went on to become a Supreme Court justice, responded that he opposed "this suggestion for an inherently politically reason. We could have dispensed with the Development Authority and transferred its assets to the state. We intentionally created a separate authority. And we intend to use this separate body and the fact of it being separate from the state in negotiations that we hope will one day be conducted."[59] Cohn further stated that the government was willing to accept the risk of this separation being interpreted as willingness to negotiate the future return of Development Authority assets.[60]

Are all these considerations still relevant today? At least superficially, the Development Authority's continued independent existence appears to confirm the idea that the seizure of absentees' lands and their transfer to the authority were meant to be temporary. The Supreme Court has stated that this situation will last "until the formulation of political arrangements between Israel and its neighbors, in which the fate of the property will be decided on the basis of reciprocity between the countries."[61] However, the State of Israel's consistent stance in international forums has been that the refugees' assets will not be returned to their original owners.

Former attorney general and Supreme Court justice Elyakim Rubinstein testified that "at the Camp David Summit in 2000, I was a member of the Israeli delegation and chaired the subcommittee that dealt with the subject of the refugees, and there was no doubt in Israel's position (which was also supported by the USA) that denied the very basis of that right [of return] as being 'national suicide.'"[62] It seems, then, that the separation of Development Authority lands from other state lands does not indicate that Israel plans to return refugee lands to their original owners. So, what is the explanation for this separation?

One explanation may be the designation of profits yielded by those assets to serve at some future time for the funding of a solution to the refugee problem. It may also be that Israel fears a further change in the status of Development Authority lands might be met with both international and domestic opposition and reawaken claims meant to bring about the return of the lands to the absentees. Such claims—at least for the present absentees (i.e., refugees who retained Israeli citizenship)—appear in *The Future Vision of the Palestinian Arabs in Israel*.[63] Various organizations have made it their mission to see that the assets are returned,[64] and they are still filing lawsuits today.[65] International claims for the refugees' right of return and right to their assets continue unabated.[66] It would seem that political sensitivity to this issue prevents the complete dissolution of the Development Authority and the transfer of its lands to the state. Indeed, such a transfer would have very little practical meaning. Yet simply allowing the status quo to continue carries political implications as well.

In summary, the structure and separate management of lands in the Development Authority reveal Israel's ambivalence toward the refugee problem, which will probably continue for years to come.

## JNF Fingerprints in Israel's Land Inventory

### The JNF Dilemma

The transfer of Jewish National Fund (JNF) lands to the government administration constituted another major change in the public land inventory following Israel's establishment. Today, the JNF's land is administered by the Israel Lands Authority, a governmental agency. JNF's land inventory includes 2,574 square kilometers, or 12 percent, of the sovereign territory of Israel (see fig. 1.2). Around 1,000 square kilometers were purchased during the pre-state period, and more than 1,000 square kilometers, mostly belonging to Palestinian absentees, were sold to the JNF after Israel's founding.[67] The JNF lands are in areas that were part of the private land inventory in the pre-state period. Some of these areas have since become well-established settlements, and some are in or near densely populated areas. This is the most reasonable explanation for the fact that the JNF's lands yielded 35 percent of the profits from all public lands between 2000 and 2013, even though they accounted for only 12 percent of Israeli public lands.[68]

Why is such a large and important inventory of real estate managed by the state instead of by its owner, and what does it mean that the state preserves the separate ownership of the JNF in this inventory? As we shall see below, the shaping of this special relationship reflects deep and ongoing doubts about the justification for the existence of the fund and its role. It reflects an attempt to bridge the commitment of the State of Israel to the Jewish people, on the one hand, and to the citizens of Israel, on the other. In the following section, we will analyze the historical background of these developments and the manner in which the management of the JNF's land continues to reflect these dilemmas.

### The JNF after 1948: Is Its Existence Still Justified?

The JNF was founded in 1907 and was registered as a private company. During the Mandate period, it functioned as the World Zionist Organization's arm for purchasing land property in the Land of Israel.[69] The money used to fund these purchases came from donations collected from Jews throughout the world and profit yields from the JNF's assets and real estate transactions.[70] The JNF focused its land purchases on private owners, mostly Arabs, who had gained ownership through Ottoman law. Most of the lands were agricultural, cultivated, or at least cultivable. They were generally located on the periphery of existing Arab villages, and the fund used them to establish new Jewish settlements or neighborhoods. Representatives of the Arab National Movement vehemently opposed the JNF's activity, both because they were politically opposed to Zionism and because they viewed that activity as a way of dispossessing Arabs of their land. As a result, the Mandate government implemented the "White Papers," which set limits on Jewish purchase of Arab land,[71] but the newly founded State of Israel immediately voided these limits.[72] The JNF had successfully purchased just under 1,000 square kilometers of land during the Mandate period,[73] during which these lands were categorized as private. Now the government of Israel controlled more than 80 percent of the sovereign territory of the state and could use this huge inventory to create settlements and take in great waves of immigrants. It seemed there was no need for the JNF to purchase more land, yet the fund had grown so powerful that it convinced the government to sell it, via the Development Authority, more than 1,000 square kilometers of Palestinian refugee assets, and this boosted the scale of the JNF's land inventory to its current size.[74]

These transactions, however, did not remove the question of the JNF's continued existence, in light of the major land inventory held by a Zionist, Jewish government. This question arose, first and foremost, within the Israeli government. Prime Minister Ben-Gurion did not want the JNF to become "a state within a state." He believed that all public lands should be administered by a single government body that treats all citizens as equals.[75] Even the heads of the JNF wondered why it still existed when there was no longer a need to "redeem the land." Joseph Weitz, one of the heads of the JNF, wrote that it was a "to be or not to be" question.[76] The effects of such doubt were also felt in the limited funds that the JNF managed to raise. At a certain point, the JNF did not have the resources to purchase the thousands of square kilometers of land it had almost convinced the government to sell it.[77] These difficulties prompted heads of the JNF and the government to search for a new purpose for the JNF and to restructure the administration of the lands it had already purchased.

### From "Redeeming the Land" to "Redeeming the Wilderness"

In 1957, Prime Minister Ben-Gurion tasked a committee (hereafter: the Eshkol Committee), headed by then finance minister Levi Eshkol, with "clarifying the Jewish National Fund problem."[78] The other committee members were Agriculture Minister Kadish Luz, Trade and Industry Minister Pinhas Sapir, former minister of agriculture Peretz Naftali, general manager of the

Ministry of Agriculture Hayim Gvati, and JNF representative Joseph Weitz. The committee made several recommendations: that all JNF lands be transferred to the administration of the government while the JNF retained ownership over them; that JNF representatives be involved in the administrative mechanisms of all public lands; and that a principle of not transferring ownership of government lands, including JNF lands, be anchored in a Basic Law, granting it special legal and constitutional status. The committee also suggested that the JNF focus its activities on "redeeming the wilderness" rather than "redeeming the land." In that respect, it would serve as the government contractor responsible for afforestation and reclamation of all public lands, including JNF land, state land, and Development Authority land. It would continue its education and fundraising activities throughout the Jewish world. The committee also recommended that the state and the JNF create accounting mechanisms through which the state would receive administrative fees and the JNF would receive the profits from its land and payment for its afforestation and foundation-laying efforts. The committee advocated a relationship defined by a "covenant" between the government and the JNF that would be signed by both bodies.[79] The committee members believed that their recommendations would justify the JNF's continued existence "for at least the next 50 years," as Pinhas Sapir suggested.[80] Committee chair Levi Eshkol proclaimed that "if we were to bring about the JNF's end, I would see it as a tragedy and a great loss."[81] He predicted that the recommendations would hold for "10, maybe 20 generations."[82]

## Legal Relationships between the State and the JNF since the 1960s

The Eshkol Committee's recommendations were accepted in full and have constituted the working arrangement for the administration of JNF land to this day. In 1960, the Knesset enacted the Basic Law: Israel Lands. It coined the eponymous term for the full inventory of the State of Israel's public lands: "Israel Lands."[83] This term refers to three separate categories of land: land owned by the state, land owned by the Development Authority, and land owned by the JNF. The Basic Law's first clause establishes that "the ownership of Israel lands . . . shall not be transferred either by sale or in any other manner." In that same year, the Knesset further enacted the Israel Lands Administration Law, which created a new body, the Israel Lands Administration (ILA), and charged it with the administration of all Israel lands, including JNF lands.[84] The law's third clause established the "Israel

Lands Council" and directed it to "lay down the land policy in accordance with which the Administration shall act, shall supervise the activities of the Administration and . . . shall approve the draft of its budget." Six out of fourteen Israel Lands Council members are JNF representatives, despite upheavals within the structure of the council over the past few years.[85]

Prior to the enactment of these laws, the government and the directorate of the JNF had already approved a version of a covenant between the bodies, which was finally signed on November 21, 1961.[86] The covenant defined the relationship between them in consonance with the recommendations of the Eshkol Committee. Clauses 17–19 describe the procedures for ending the covenant's force. In accordance with clause 10, the JNF serves as the government's agent for "the reclamation and afforestation of Israel lands" to this day. The JNF has performed the majority of its activities in this area on state and Development Authority lands.[87] The fund also works to rehabilitate streams and create water reservoirs.[88] As clause 16 dictates, the JNF will continue "to operate, as an independent agency of the World Zionist Organization, among the Jewish public in Israel and the Diaspora, raising funds for the redemption of land from desolation and conducting informational and Zionist-Israel educational activities." This aside, the scale of JNF land purchasing has shrunk, as expected. Although the fund continues to purchase lands beyond Israel's borders (in the West Bank) and in East Jerusalem, the scale of this activity is miniscule.[89]

### New Difficulties in the Relationship between the JNF and the State

In recent years the governmental administration of JNF lands faced problems that reignited public discussion about the fund's future. To start with, the JNF has dedicated significant resources to its organizational survival—the management of its bureaucratic mechanisms and pension obligations.[90] Furthermore, most of the JNF's income is earned from its governmentally administered lands. In 2016, for example, 92 percent of the fund's income came from such lands while only 5 percent came from donations.[91] Donations have also been meager relative to expenditures for afforestation and other purposes, and JNF can definitely not sustain its present breadth of activity by donations alone.[92] Over the past few years, this state of affairs engendered sharp public criticism of the JNF's management,[93] and the fund was forced to agree to Israel state comptroller oversight[94] and to earmark part of its revenue for uses decided by the government.[95] Some of these steps incited the JNF to threaten that it would end its working relationship with the government and take over the administration of its own land.[96]

The steps taken toward privatization of urban public lands, which will be discussed in the upcoming chapters, presented another challenge to the administration of JNF land by the Israel Lands Authority. The transfer of ownership of JNF lands stands in opposition to the JNF statute in two ways: First, the JNF opposes transferring ownership of its assets. As far as it is concerned, its assets must remain in an eternal charitable trust for the Jewish people. Moreover, it is strongly opposed to the transfer of its lands to non-Jewish owners, as the JNF was established to serve the Zionist cause.[97] On the other hand, the Israel Lands Authority, which administers the JNF's lands, is a government body, obligated by both statutory and case law to treat all Israeli citizens equally.[98] As will be elucidated in the coming chapters, since 2000 the government's policy has been to work toward privatizing all Israel lands that are built up and urban, which has created the potential for a serial contradiction between the JNF's stance of rejecting the transfer of ownership and the government's policy of supporting privatization. Privatization efforts have forced both sides to come up with a permanent solution to this problem, reigniting the debate about the purpose of the current arrangement and its continuation.

## *The Future of JNF Land: Nationalization or Return?*

Three solutions to the problem of privatizing JNF land have been promulgated in Israeli public discourse: nationalizing JNF lands and permanently transferring them to government administration (henceforth: "nationalization"); returning the administration of JNF land to JNF auspices (henceforth: "return"); and swapping JNF lands in the desired regions set for privatization with other state lands (henceforth: "swap"). We will now elaborate on each of the three suggestions.

Nationalization has been called for principally by nonprofit organizations and politicians who represent Israel's Arab minority. Supporters claim that nationalization is crucial to enabling the government to administer JNF lands equally with respect to all citizens. Nationalization also reflects a historical criticism sounded by the representatives of the Arab minority against the sale of refugee assets to the JNF.[99] Unfortunately, this option undermines the JNF's private property and requires an inventory that has accumulated over generations from money Diaspora Jewry donated toward the goals of the Zionist movement to be expropriated and used for the needs of all of Israel's citizens. Nationalization is likely to bring about the end of the JNF, as it will attack the body's main source of funds. It will put an end to JNF's afforestation and reclamation activities, its areas of expertise, its educational activities, its advocacy, and its active relationship with Diaspora Jewry. It is safe to assume that nationalization will also spell the end of the JNF's fundraising activities and of the modest land purchasing that it still engages in outside of Israel's borders. The JNF, then, does not support this option, nor have any of Israel's governments made a formal decision toward that option up to now.[100]

The heads of the JNF have recently considered demanding the return of its lands to its own auspices. In 2014 they went so far as to put their intention into writing and presented it to Prime Minister Benjamin Netanyahu.[101] The supporters of this alternative, some of whom are politicians from right-wing parties, backed up their stance with three main claims. One is that the JNF must continue working to fulfill the goals of Zionism and that hence there is no justification for using JNF lands in ways that violate its statute—its assets should be used exclusively for the purpose of actualizing the goals of the Zionist movement.[102] This claim seems to constitute a criticism of certain liberal views adopted by the state toward its non-Jewish citizens. It reflects a lack of trust in the Jewish state's ability to fulfill the Zionist vision and to sustain this vision alongside Israel's democratic character. The second claim is that the return of JNF land to its own administration will contribute to the growth of property market competition with the Israel Lands Administration, which controls most of the state's territory.[103] The problem with this claim is that the JNF is officially a not-for-profit that, over the past few years, as noted above, has faced sharp criticism over its financial management. This casts doubt on the degree to which return will actually lead to an improvement in administrative efficiency and competition in the land market. The third claim in support of return, which is probably also the main motivation for the demand, is that the heads of the JNF are dissatisfied with state intervention in the use of their income. The plan for return was announced, not in anger, but as a conscious decision to put pressure on the state and make it renege on its plan to intervene in the management of the JNF's monetary resources.[104]

The State of Israel has not supported return so far. There is also some legal doubt surrounding the possibility of the option. Return is not applicable without a change in legislation. Whatever the status of the covenant with the JNF, it does not have the power to force the Israeli Parliament to make a legislative change that the Parliament itself is not interested in.[105]

The third possible solution to the problem of JNF lands is to swap them with those of the state. The current arrangement, in which the Israel Lands Authority administers the JNF land, would remain intact. The JNF would retain ownership of its land but would sell its urban properties, meant for privatization, to the state, which would in turn grant the JNF ownership of alternative lands in the country's geographical periphery. A financial accounting between the sides would also be conducted. This option would enable the government to apply its privatization policy equally to all of the land it administers, and to unburden itself of the limitations placed on it by the JNF. At the same time, the swap would enable the JNF to preserve its principles through the new land inventory it would acquire. A land exchange would essentially allow both sides to continue enjoying the advantages of the current arrangement. The JNF would retain the size of its land inventory, would continue to serve as the government's contractor for "redeeming the wilderness," and would continue to fundraise and receive income for its educational and advocacy activities. The state would continue to administer the JNF's land inventory as part of the full public land inventory and would continue, with the JNF's consent, to increase the transparency of its financial management and keep the JNF vulnerable to public criticism.

The advantages of a land exchange led the state and the JNF to adopt it in June 2009, after bumpy negotiations that were compounded by changes in the government. Prime Minister Ehud Olmert put together an agreement in principle for its implementation,[106] but the JNF was delayed in approving it because of legal objections to the validity of the agreement, probably influenced by the political shocks that occurred around that time.[107] The proceedings were canceled at the JNF's initiative a few years later, following the fund's decision to abandon its plans to implement swap.[108] This decision was reached after the creation of a new government, led by Benjamin Netanyahu, and the sharpening of political confrontations between various government components. Then finance minister Yair Lapid, head of the centrist Yesh Atid (lit. "There is a Future") party, supported the submission of the JNF to public oversight and to state intervention with its financial management. The right-wing HaBayit HaYehudi [lit. "The Jewish Home"] party, charged with the responsibility of managing the Israel Lands Administration, supported a plan for separation and return.[109] However, beginning in 2013, the Israel Lands Administration decided to grant long-term renters of JNF lands all the economic benefits bound up with the transfer of ownership, even before it received the JNF's agreement to such a transfer.[110] At the end of 2015, after a new government was formed and the management of the Israel Lands Authority was entrusted to new finance minister Moshe Kahlon, head of the centrist Kulanu [lit. "All of Us"] party, the JNF and the state, with the mediation of Minister Avi Gabay, then of the Kulanu party, agreed to accept the terms of the 2009 agreement in principle for conducting a land swap. The parties also agreed to negotiate by 2021 the wish of the JNF to cancel the covenant and return its lands to its independent management.[111]

Representatives of Israel's Arab minority claimed that the agreement was illegal and petitioned the Supreme Court with an opposition to a component regarding the number of JNF representatives on the Israel Lands Council.[112] The court rejected the petition on the grounds that the partnership between the fund and the state in the management of Israel lands is legitimate and that it does not violate the principle of equality because all members of the council, including representatives of the JNF, are subject to it.[113]

The state has begun the implementation of the land swap. In 2015 it announced that 1.5 kilometers of JNF-owned land with thirteen thousand housing units in central Israel had been located for the purpose of swapping it for state land in the western Negev.[114] In 2016–17 the JNF exchanged ownership of 36.24 square kilometers of land in different areas of Israel.[115] The implementation of the agreement was fully completed in 2018.[116] The swaps that have been executed seem to have made minimal changes to the scale of the JNF's land inventory.

## The Administration of the JNF Inventory and Israel's Identity: Summary

In summary, ever since the founding of the State of Israel, JNF land policies have served as the litmus test for the justification of its existence. While the JNF continues to represent the Jewish people and the Zionist movement and to manage its inventory to this end, the actual need for such an institution is uncertain. Though Israel sees itself as the state of the Jewish people, its primary commitment is to all its citizens, Jewish and non-Jewish alike. Can the two perspectives be bridged? This is one of Israel's existential dilemmas, and it has caused public debate on the future of the JNF.

Practical arrangements for the management of the JNF land inventory by the state reflect both the difficulties and the determination to solve this dilemma. The state and the JNF are still dancing a tango. The state manages the JNF's lands for all its citizens and, if necessary, exchanges lands with the JNF. The JNF, for its part, invests the profits for the Jewish people as well as for public projects that serve all the citizens of Israel. When there is disagreement over these investments, both sides threaten to stop the joint dance, respectively, either by completely nationalizing the JNF's inventory or by retaking control of its administration. So far, they have reached a compromise.

## Public Land Inventory and National Identity: Conclusion and Comparative Remarks

Has the State of Israel succeeded in overcoming the identity crisis created by its establishment? In this chapter, we have attempted to derive the answer through an analysis of the process of creating the land inventory and its components. The conclusion of this analysis is that, despite attempts to disengage from the past, history is deeply ingrained in the State of Israel and affects the structure and management of its land inventory.

Although Ottoman land laws no longer apply in Israel, most of the territory of the State of Israel today is still owned by the state. Most owners of private land in Israel should thank the Ottomans for having granted them that ownership and also thank the British for creating a mechanism for its registration. Ottoman land laws have reached far into the current millennium and are responsible for the fact that from Jerusalem and Tel Aviv to Nazareth and Sakhnin, there is a large concentration of privately owned land, while in the periphery there is only government land. The State of Israel accepted this influence and has so far not attempted to change it.

The transfer of the lands of Palestinian refugees to the control of the State of Israel occurred back in the 1950s. As we shall see in chapter 5, the issue of refugee rights was not handed down from the state agenda, but at least in Israel's internal discourse, it now occupies a more marginal place. However, the fingerprints of the refugee land inventory are still etched in the Israeli public land inventory as a kind of silent reminder that the problem still hovers over the public agenda. Most of the refugee land is still registered with the Development Authority, a formal body that is no longer active but that has not been divested of its formal ownership. Does the continued existence of this entity and the continued registration of approximately 2,500 square kilometers in its name reflect an intention to negotiate the return of the inventory to its owners one day or to share its revenues? Do the billions of shekels that this fictitious body has lent the state testify to such political intention? In any event, the State of Israel has never attempted to take the refugees' assets from the Development Authority and to merge them with the rest of its land. This situation indicates that doubts surrounding the proper solution to the refugee problem still remain.

A third question constantly hovers over both the identity of the State of Israel and its land inventory: that of the role of the Jewish National Fund. Did the establishment of the State of Israel make unnecessary the continued existence of a body established to acquire land under British rule? Can the Israeli government, which currently manages the JNF land, combine its commitment to all of its citizens with its commitment to manage the JNF land inventory for the benefit of the Jewish people? At the end of the 1950s, a committee headed by Levi Eshkol created a brilliant, positive solution to both questions. This solution leaves the ownership of the fund in its hands but imposes the fund's inventory management on the state. The state adopted this arrangement in the 1960s, but recently both sides have begun to question its logic. Even if both sides sometimes threaten to break the rules, the arrangement has held for nearly sixty years. However, no one knows whether Levi Eshkol's prediction that it would last for "10, maybe 20 generations"[117] will come to pass.

Weighty questions of national identity are expressed in the composition of the State of Israel's land inventory, as we have seen, and similar conclusions can be drawn from the analysis of the formation of any country's real estate inventories. In fact, land inventory is one of the most prominent areas in which history has a real long-term impact. The land inventory reflects both historical upheavals and waves of privatization, as is apparent in the land inventory of the United States.[118] In Germany, the land inventory reflects past revolutions and twentieth-century regime changes.[119] The public land inventory of England reflects the changes in the status of its royal house.[120]

An analysis of land inventory reveals latent dilemmas that may underlie national identity. It also shows how historical processes affect real estate far into the future. Such are the unique insights that emerge from this type of analysis and serve as a litmus test of national identity.

## Notes

1. See note 79 below.
2. Joshua Weisman, "How Long Will the Ottoman Land Laws Govern Us?," 12 *Mishpatim—Hebrew University of Jerusalem Law Review* (1982) (Hebrew): 3.

3. Land Law Amendment Committee, *Final Report* (submitted to the minister of justice, January 25, 1950) (Hebrew) (copy preserved by the author).

4. "Land Law 5729-1969," 5 *Israel Law Review* (1970): 292, 320–21 (§158) (Hereafter: Land Law 1969).

5. Leah Doukhan-Landau, "The Land Law, 5729-1969 at First Sight," 26 *Hapraklit—Israel Bar Law Journal* (1971) (Hebrew): 101, 107.

6. Justice Middleton, "Sketch of the Ottoman Land Code for Cyprus," 2 *Journal of the Society of Comparative Legislation* (1900): 141–50; Bernard Lewis, "Ottoman Land Tenure and Taxation in Syria," 50 *Studia Islamica* (1979): 109.

7. Frederick Ongley, *The Ottoman Land Code Translated from the Turkish*, H. E. Miller revised (London: William Clowes and Sons, 1892); R. C. Tute, *The Ottoman Land Laws—with a Commentary on the Ottoman Land Code of 7th Ramadan 1274* (Jerusalem: Greek Conv. Press, 1927).

8. Haim Gerber, *The Social Origins of the Modern Middle East* (Boulder: Lynne Reinner, 1987), 67; E. Attila Aytekin, "Agrarian Relations, Property and Law: An Analysis of the Land Code of 1858 in the Ottoman Empire," 45 *Middle Eastern Studies* (2009): 935, 946.

9. Frederic Goadby and Moses Doukhan, *The Land Law of Palestine* (Tel Aviv: Shoshany's Printing, 1935), 17–68; Joshua Weisman, "The Land Law, 1969: A Critical Analysis," 5 *Israel Law Review* (1970): 379, 381, 396–97; Joshua Weisman, *Principle Features of the Israel Land Law 1969* (London: British Institute of International and Comparative Law, 1972), 1–3.

10. The Ottoman Land Code 1858, §1, 3, 68.

11. Ruth Kark, "Changing Patterns of Landownership in Nineteenth-Century Palestine: The European Influence," 10 *Journal of Historical Geography* (1984): 357, 359–62; Ruth Kark, "Consequences of the Ottoman Land Law: Agrarian and Privatization Processes in Palestine, 1858–1918," in *Societies, Social Inequalities and Marginalization*, ed. Raghubir Chand et al. (Cham, Switzerland: Springer International AG, 2017), 101, 102–6, 116.

12. The Ottoman Land Code 1858, §78; Haim Sandberg, *Land Title Settlement in Eretz-Israel and the State of Israel* (Jerusalem: JNF's Land Use Research Institute and Sacher Institute, Hebrew University of Jerusalem, 2001) (Hebrew), 239–44; Alexandre Kedar, "The Legal Transformation of Ethnic Geography: Israeli Law and the Palestinian Landholder 1948-1967," 33 *N.Y.U. J. Int'l L. & Pol.* (2001): 923, 935.

13. Land Law 1969, §153.

14. The Ottoman Land Code 1858, §103.

15. CA 65/40 Habibi v. Government of Palestine (1940) 1 SCJ 168, 170–71.

16. "Decision of the Administrative Council of Jerusalem regarding the Improvement (or Revival) of the 'Mahlul' Sand Dunes by the Rishon-le-Zion People and an Official Announcement by the High Commissioner of Palestine" (August 23, 1921), Israel State Archive (ISA) 22nd Division, Box M/3497, File GP/2/35a; Sandberg, *Land Title Settlement*, supra note 12, at 123.

17. "Jaffa Land Dunes" (1947), ISA, 22nd Division, Box 3508, File SD 12(19); Sandberg, *Land Title Settlement*, supra note 12, at 126–28; Goadby & Doukhan, *Land Law of Palestine*, supra note 9, at 48.

18. Land (Mewat) Ordinance 1921, *Palestine Gazette*: 6.

19. Emphasis added. The Mandate for Palestine (July 24, 1922), Israeli Foreign Ministry, http://www.mfa.gov.il/mfa/foreignpolicy/peace/guide/pages/the%20mandate%20for%20palestine.aspx: §6.

20. Land Law 1969, §155.

21. Havatzelet Yahel, "Land Disputes between the Negev Bedouin and Israel," 11 *Israel Studies* (2006): 1, 8; Noa Kram, "The Naqab Bedouins: Legal Struggles for Land Ownership Rights in Israel," in *Indigenous (In)justice: Human Rights Law and Bedouin Arabs in the Naqab/Negev*, ed. Ahmad Amara et al. (Cambridge, MA: Human Rights Program at Harvard Law School, 2012), 127, 129–30; Seth J. Frantzman, "The Politization of History and the Negev Bedouin Land Claims: A Review Essay on Indigenous (In)justice," 19 *Israel Studies* (2014): 48, 51; Alexandre Kedar et al., *Emptied Lands: A Legal Geography of Bedouin Rights in the Negev* (Stanford: Stanford University Press, 2018), 66–74.

22. CA 4220/12 Al-Uqbi v. State of Israel (Nevo, 14.5.2015) (Hebrew), official English translation: https://supremedecisions.court.gov.il/Home/Download?path=EnglishVerdicts\12\200\042\v29&fileName=12042200.V29&type=5; F.D. 3751/15 Al-Uqbi v. State of Israel (Nevo, 19.7.2015) (Hebrew); PCA 3094/11 Al-Qi'an v. State of Israel, §21-23 Justice Rubinstein (Nevo, 5.5.2015), English translation: VERSA: Opinions of the Supreme Court of Israel, Translated Opinions, http://versa.cardozo.yu.edu/sites/default/files/upload/opinions/Al-Qi%27an%20v.%20State.pdf.

23. The Palestine Order in Council 1922, §46, United Nations Information System on the Question of Palestine (UNISPAL), https://unispal.un.org/DPA/DPR/unispal.nsf/0/C7AAE196F41AA055052565F50054E656; Goadby & Doukhan, *Land Law of Palestine*, supra note 9, at 1.

24. Goadby & Doukhan, *Land Law of Palestine*, supra note 9, at 298; Ruth Kark and Haim Gerber, "Land Registry Maps in Palestine during the Ottoman Period," 21 *Cartographic Journal* (1984): 30, 30; Ruth Kark and Dov Gavish, "The Cadastral Mapping of Palestine 1858–1928," 159 *Cartographic Journal* (1993): 70, 71; Sandberg, "Land Title Settlement," supra note 12, at 134–55.

25. Goadby & Doukhan, *Land Law of Palestine*, supra note 9, at 271–93; Sandberg, "Land Title Settlement," supra note 12, at 196, 209–31; Kedar, *Legal Transformation*, supra note 12, at 938.

26. 1928 *Palestine Gazette*: 260 (May 30, 1928); Land (Settlement of Title) Ordinance (New Version), 5729–1969, *Diney Meinat Israel-Nosah Hadash* (New Version) (Hebrew), 293.

27. Sandberg, "Land Title Settlement," supra note 12, at 335; Dov Gavish, *A Survey of Palestine under the British Mandate, 1920–1948* (Abingdon: Routledge, 2005), 199; "Proposal to End Land Settlement Operations (Surveying and Mapping) in the Entire Country," appendix to Letter from Head of the Land Registration Division to State Comptroller (April 24, 1960) (Hebrew), ISA Division 74, Box 5733, file 3520/7.

28. Government of Palestine, *Survey of Palestine—Prepared in December 1945 and January 1946 for the Information of the Anglo-American Committee of Inquiry* (Palestine: Government Printer, 1946), 1:257–58.

29. Sandberg, "Land Title Settlement," supra note 12, at 343–46, 357–59; Haim Sandberg, "Land Title Settlement in Jerusalem—Legal Aspects," 23 *Journal of Israeli History* (2004): 216, 217–18; Yahel, "Land Disputes," supra note 21, at 11–12.

30. Law and Administration Order (No. 1), 5727–1967, *Kovetz HaTakanot* (Israeli Regulations) 2690 (Hebrew); Jerusalem Declaration (Expansion of the Municipal Area), 5727–1967, *Kovetz HaTakanot* 2694 (Hebrew); "Basic Law: Jerusalem, Capital of Israel, 1980," 34 The Laws of the State of Israel (LSI) 209 §5, as amended in Basic Law: Jerusalem, Capital of Israel (Amendment), 5761–2000, *Sefer Ha-Hukim* (The Book of Laws) 28 (Hebrew); Unofficial updated translation by Dr. Susan Hattis Rolef, Knesset, https://main.knesset.gov.il/EN

/activity/Documents/BasicLawsPDF/BasicLawJerusalem.pdf; Ruth Lapidoth and Moshe Hirsch (eds.), *The Jerusalem Question and Its Resolution: Selected Documents* (Dordrecht: Martinus Nijhoff, 1994), 167, 322 (Translation of the 1967 Enactments and Map); Sandberg, *Land Title Settlement in Jerusalem*, supra note 29, at 219–22.

31. The Golan Heights Law, 5742–1981, *Sefer Ha-Hukim* 6 (Hebrew), 36 LSI 7; Land Settlement Order 5743–1983 (March 1, 1983), *Yalkut Pirsumim* (Collection of Publications of Official Orders) 1433 (Hebrew); CA 7340/13 State of Israel v. Al-Sha'ar (Nevo, 11.10.2015) (Hebrew).

32. Prescription Law, 5718–1958 §5, 22, 12 LSI 129–33. Available also at Geocities.ws, http://www.geocities.ws/savepalestinenow/israellaws/fulltext/prescriptionlaw.htm.

33. Land Law 1969, §152–59.

34. Land Law 1969, §162; Israel Land Administration, *Report on Activities for the 2011 Budget Year* (2012) (Hebrew), 53, https://land.gov.il/doclib5/dochshnati_2011.pdf (Reports 494.157 km² of unregistered land).

35. The Palestine Order in Council 1922, §2, 12; Goadby & Doukhan, *Land Law of Palestine*, supra note 9, at 60.

36. State Property Law 5711–1951, §2, 3, 5 LSI 45.

37. Israel Land Administration, *Report on Activities for the 2012 Budget Year* (2013) (Hebrew), 72, https://land.gov.il/doclib5/dochshnati_2012.pdf.

38. Haim Sandberg, *Basic Law: Israel Lands—Commentary*, Commentary on The Basic Laws Series, ed. Izhak Zamir (Jerusalem: Sacher Institute, Hebrew University of Jerusalem, 2016) (Hebrew), 285–87.

39. Sandberg, *Basic Law*, supra note 38.

40. Urban textures are areas designated as urban land according to Israel National Outline Plan for Construction, Development and Conservation No. 35 (November 27, 2005). The data are taken from the texture cards of these areas, as published by Beery Cohen et al., *National Outline Plan 35: Follow-up and Updating Guidance, Expansion to the Report Stage B—Texture Cards* (Israel Ministry of the Interior, Planning Administration, 2009) (Hebrew).

41. Haim Sandberg, "The Politics of 'Over-victimization': Palestinian Proprietary Claims in the Service of Political Goals," 19 *Israel Affairs* (2013): 488, 490–92; Geremy Forman, "A Tale of Two Regions: Diffusion of the Israeli '50 Percent Rule' from the Galilee to the Occupied West Bank," 34 *Law and Social Inquiry* (2016): 671, 694–95.

42. Michael R. Fischbach, *The Peace Process and Palestinian Refugee Claims: Addressing Claims for Property Compensation and Restitution* (Washington: US Institute for Peace Press, 2006), 19–50; UN Conciliation Commission for Palestine, *15th Progress Report, Covering Period 1 Jan 1955–30 Sep. 1956*, A/3199 (October 4, 1956), UNISPAL, https://unispal.un.org/DPA/DPR/unispal.nsf/0/9D94E9A17FBEB1F58525610200738D67: §3–10.

43. "Valuation of Abandoned Arab Land in Israel" (Hereafter: "Berncastle Report") 17 (August 14, 1951), Central Zionist Archive (CZA), Joseph Weitz Archive, Section 246A, File 199; Michael R. Fischbach, *Records of Dispossession: Palestinian Refugee Property and the Arab-Israeli Conflict* (New York: Columbia University Press, 2003), 405n67.

44. Berncastle Report, supra note 43, at 8.

45. Government of Palestine, *Village Statistics* (Jerusalem, 1945), the National Library of Israel, http://web.nli.org.il/sites/nli/Hebrew/library/Pages/BookReader.aspx?pid=856390.

46. Ministry of Finance, "Custodian of Absentees' Property, Report on the Use of Absentees' Lands in Completely Abandoned Villages by the End of 1952" (February 22, 1953) (Hebrew), CZA, Joseph Weitz Archive, Section 246A.

47. "Agreement between the Custodian of Absentees' Property and the Development Authority" (A copy of unsigned draft, dated September 29, 1953) (Hebrew), CZA, Joseph Weitz Archive, Section 246A, File 275 (Hereafter: "Absentees' Property Sale Agreement"), appendixes A, B, C.

48. Benny Morris, *The Birth of the Palestinian Refugee Problem Revisited* (Cambridge: Cambridge University Press, 2004), xi, xii; Jacob Tovy, *Israel and the Palestinian Refugee Issue: The Formulation of Policy 1948–1956* (Abingdon: Routledge, 2014), 13–36; Fischbach, *Records of Dispossession*, supra note 43, at 1–13; Arnon Golan, "Jewish Settlement of Former Arab Towns and Their Incorporation into the Israeli Urban System," in *The Israeli Palestinians: An Arab Minority in the Jewish State*, ed. Alexander Bligh (London: Frank Cass, 2003), 149, 149–50, 154.

49. Absentees' Property Law 5710-1950, §1, 4, in *Sefer Ha-Hukim* 86 (20.3.1950) (Hebrew); 4 LSI 68; Eyal Benvenisti and Eyal Zamir, "Private Claims to Property Rights in the Future Israeli-Palestinian Settlement," 89 *Am. J. Int'l L.* (1995): 295, 300.

50. Development Authority (Transfer of Property) Law 5710-1950 §2, 3, *Sefer Ha-Hukim* 278 (Hebrew); 4 LSI 151.

51. "Absentees' Property Sale Agreement," supra note 47; Fischbach, *Records of Dispossession*, supra note 43, at 55–56; Government of Israel, *Government Year Book* 5716 (Jerusalem: Government Printer, 1956) (Hebrew), 58–59.

52. §2, *Sefer Ha-Hukim* 58 (Hebrew); 7 LSI 43.

53. Haim Sandberg, *The Lands of Israel: Zionism and Post-Zionism* (Jerusalem: Sacher Institute, Hebrew University of Jerusalem, 2007) (Hebrew), 155–70.

54. Sandberg, *Post-Zionism*, supra note 53, at 83; Benvenisti & Zamir, "Private Claims to Property," supra note 49, at 301; Yitzhak Oded, "Land Losses among Arab Villagers," 65 *New Outlook* (1964): 10, 21.

55. Sandberg, *Post-Zionism*, supra note 54, at 78–80; Israel Land Administration, *Report on Activities for the 1964–1965 Budget Year* (1965) (Hebrew), 165–66; Joseph Weitz, "Summary of Actions for the Realization of the Land Acquisition (Validation of Acts and Compensation) Law, 5713–1953" (April 12, 1954), CZA, Section 246A, File 275.

56. Israel Lands Administration Law 5720-1960, §2(a), *Sefer Ha-Hukim* 57 (Hebrew); 14 LSI 50.

57. Sandberg, *Basic Law*, supra note 53, at 180–83.

58. Sandberg, *Basic Law*, supra note 53, at 182–83, 285–88.

59. Author translation. Minutes of Session No. 22 of the Constitution, Law and Justice Committee of the Fourth Knesset 2 (March 21, 1960) (Hebrew), http://fs.knesset.gov.il//4/Committees/4_ptv_417526.PDF; Yossi Katz, *The Land Shall Not Be Sold in Perpetuity: The Jewish National Fund and the History of State Ownership of Land in Israel* (Berlin: De Gruyter, 2016), 103–4.

60. Minutes of Session No. 22 of the Constitution, Law and Justice Committee of the Fourth Knesset 2; Katz, *Land Shall Not Be Sold*, supra note 59.

61. HCJ 4713/93 Golan v. Special Committee under Section 29 of the Absentees' Property Law, PD 48(2) 638, 644 (1994) (Hebrew), as cited and translated at HCJ 5931/06 Hussein v. Cohen, Par. 16 J. Grunis (Nevo, 15.4.2015) (Hebrew); English translation: VERSA: Opinions of the Supreme Court of Israel, Translated Opinions, https://versa.cardozo.yu.edu/sites/default/files/upload/opinions/Hussein%20v.%20Cohen.pdf.

62. HCJ 5931/06 Hussein v. Cohen, supra note 61, at 43; Joel Singer, "Point/Counterpoint: No Palestinian 'Return' to Israel," 8 *Human Rights Brief*, no. 2 (Winter 2001): 5–8.

63. The National Committee for the Heads of the Arab Local Authorities in Israel, *The Future Vision of the Palestinian Arabs in Israel* (Nazareth: National Committee for the Heads of the Arab Local Authorities in Israel, 2006), 11, 15, https://www.adalah.org/uploads/oldfiles/newsletter/eng/dec06/tasawor-mostaqbali.pdf.

64. Adalah, *Inequality Report: The Palestinian Arab Minority in Israel* (Haifa: Adalah—Legal Center for Arab Minority Rights in Israel, 2011), 9, https://www.adalah.org/uploads/oldfiles/upfiles/2011/Adalah_The_Inequality_Report_March_2011.pdf; "Our Vision," Zochrot, accessed June 5, 2020, http://zochrot.org/en/content/17.

65. HCJ 840/97 Sbeit v. Government of Israel, PD 57(4) 803, 815 (2003) (Hebrew) (Ikrit and Biram villages); CA 4067/07 Jabareenn v. State (Nevo, 3.1.2010) (Hebrew), English translation in "The Nakba Files," http://nakbafiles.org/nakba-casebook/jabareen-v-state-of-israel-ca-406707/ (Al-Lajun village).

66. Yaffa Zilbershats and Nimra Goren-Amitai, *Position Paper: Return of Palestinian Refugees to the State of Israel*, ed. Ruth Gavison (Jerusalem: Metzilah Center for Zionist, Jewish, Liberal and Humanist Thought, 2011), 49–77, http://din-online.info/pdf/mz7.pdf (Critical discussion of the claims of the right of return under international law); Sandberg, "Over-victimization," supra note 41, at 496–500 (The effect of a demand for a return on arrangements for the rehabilitation of refugees in Syria before the civil war).

67. See resources in notes 73–74.

68. Sandberg, *Basic Law*, supra note 53, at 191, 285–88.

69. Yossi Katz, *The Battle for the Land* (Jerusalem: Hebrew University Press, 2005), 28; Haim Sandberg, "From JNF to Viva Palestina—UK Policy towards Zionist and Palestinian Charities," 22 *Trust & Trustees* (2016): 195, 197–98.

70. Katz, *Battle*, supra note 69, at 239, 263; Yoram Bar-Gal, "The Blue Box and JNF Propaganda Maps 1930–1947," 8 *Israel Studies* (2003): 1.

71. Katz, *Battle*, supra note 69, at 163–204, 275–87.

72. Law and Administration Ordinance (No. 1) 5708–1948, §13(b), *Official Gazette* 2 (May 21, 1948), 1 LSI 1.

73. Katz, *Battle*, supra note 69, at 352–53.

74. Fischbach, *Records of Dispossession*, supra note 43, at 63–67; Yifat Holzman-Gazit, *Land Expropriation in Israel: Law, Culture and Society* (Aldershot: Ashgate, 2007), 71; Yifat Holzman-Gazit, "Law as a Status Symbol: The Jewish National Fund Law of 1953 and the Struggle of the Fund to Maintain Its Status after Israel's Independence," 26 *Iyuney-Mishpat—Tel Aviv University Law Review*, no. 2 (2002) (Hebrew): 601, 621–24, 635–37; Sandberg, *Post-Zionism*, supra note 54, at 73–75; Sandberg, *Basic Law*, supra note 53, at 192n5.

75. Joseph Weitz, *The History of the Covenant between the Government of Israel and the Jewish National Fund* (Jerusalem: Central Bureau of the Jewish National Fund, 1960) (Hebrew), 4; Holzman-Gazit, "Law as a Status Symbol," supra note 74, at 620.

76. Author translation. Weitz, *History of the Covenant*, supra note 75, at 4.

77. Weitz, *History of the Covenant*, supra note 75, at 5; Holzman-Gazit, "Law as a Status Symbol," supra note 74, at 635–37; Ben-Eliyahu Committee, *The Committee for Examining the Separation of the Management of JNF Assets from the Administration of the Israel Land Administration* (2009) (Hebrew), 49.

78. Minutes of the Committee for Clarifying the Problem of the Jewish National Fund, CZA Section 246A, File 107 (Hebrew). The committee held four meetings, but only the minutes of the first (August 19, 1957), second (August 26, 1957), and fourth (October 23, 1957)

meetings were found in that file; Weitz, *History of the Covenant*, supra note 75, at 8; Sandberg, *Basic Law*, supra note 53, at 194–95.

79. Minutes of the Eshkol Committee (October 23, 1957), supra note 78, at 2–3; Weitz, *History of the Covenant*, supra note 75, at 11–17.

80. Minutes of the Eshkol Committee (October 23, 1957), supra note 78, at 12.

81. Minutes of the Eshkol Committee (October 23, 1957), supra note 78, at 5.

82. Minutes of the Eshkol Committee (October 23, 1957), supra note 78, at 14–15.

83. Basic Law: Israel Lands, 5720–1960, *Sefer Ha-Hukim* 56 (Hebrew), 14 LSI 48; Katz, *Land Shall Not Be Sold*, supra note 59, at 87.

84. Israel Lands Administration Law 5720–1960, *Sefer Ha-Hukim* 57 (Hebrew), 14 LSI 50.

85. §4a(a1) Israel Lands Administration Law 5720–1960, as amended with §6 Israel Lands Administration (Amendment No. 7), 5769–2009, *Sefer Ha-Hukim* 318 (Hebrew); see hereafter discussion accompanying footnotes 112–113.

86. Covenant between the State of Israel and Keren Kayemeth LeIsrael (JNF) (signed November 28, 5722–1961), *Yalkut HaPirsumim* 5728–1968 (7.6.1968), 1597 (formal Hebrew text), translated to English at Jewish National Fund, http://www.kkl-jnf.org/about-kkl-jnf/kkl-jnf-id/kkl-jnf-israeli-government-covenant/; Weitz, *History of the Covenant*, supra note 75, at 16–18 (indicates that the text of the convention was approved by the fund on January 14, 1959, and by the government on February 8, 1959).

87. Ben-Eliyahu Committee, supra note 77, at 29; "Forestry and Ecology," accessed June 5, 2020, http://www.kkl-jnf.org/forestry-and-ecology/.

88. Ben-Eliyahu Committee, supra note 77, at 30; "Water of Israel," JNF, accessed June 5, 2020, http://www.kkl-jnf.org/water-for-israel/.

89. Ben-Eliyahu Committee, supra note 77, at 28, 30.

90. "Transparency in the JNF: JNF Budgets and Annual Financial Reports," JNF, accessed June 5, 2020 (Hebrew), http://www.kkl.org.il/about-us/organizational-transparency/.

91. "Jewish National Fund Financial Statements as of December 31, 2016," 5, JNF, accessed June 5, 2020 (Hebrew), http://www.kkl.org.il/files/HEBREW_FILES/odotenu/financial-report-2016.pdf.

92. "Jewish National Fund Financial Statements," supra note 90.

93. Shuki Sadeh, "JNF Accused of Squandering Your Generosity," *Haaretz*, April 3, 2014, http://www.haaretz.com/israel-news/business/.premium-1.583680.

94. Roi Yanovsky, "State Comptroller Issues Scathing Report on KKL," *Ynet*, January 8, 2017, http://www.ynetnews.com/articles/0,7340,L-4909566,00.html.

95. Decision No. 2047 of the 33rd Government "Regulation of the Budget Transferred to the Jewish National Fund for Development and Housing," October 7, 2014 (Hebrew), https://www.gov.il/he/Departments/policies/2014_dec2047; Agreement between the Government of Israel on Behalf of the State of Israel and the Jewish National Fund Dated November 18, 2015 §3, 5–8 (Hebrew) (copy reserved by the author) (Hereafter: "2015 Agreement"); Jewish National Fund, Minutes of the Board of Directors' Meeting (December 23, 2015) (Hebrew), 19, http://www.kkl.org.il/files/HEBREW_FILES/protocols/board-of-directors/board-of-directors-23dec2015.pdf.

96. Letter of JNF Board Members to Prime Minister Benjamin Netanyahu (October 23, 2014) (Hebrew) (copy reserved by the author); Jewish National Fund, "A Verbal Report for 2014," 14, JNF, 2015, accessed June 5, 2020 (Hebrew), http://www.kkl.org.il/files/HEBREW_FILES/odotenu/financial-report-2014-explanation.pdf.

97. Katz, *Land Shall Not Be Sold*, supra note 59, at 1–8; Haim Sandberg, "From JNF to Viva Palestina," supra note 69, at 97.

98. HCJ 6698/95 Kaadan v. Israel Lands Administration PD 54(1) 258 (2000) (Hebrew), formal English translation: https://supremedecisions.court.gov.il/Home/Download?path= EnglishVerdicts\95\980\066\a14&fileName=95066980_a14.txt&type=5; VERSA: Opinions of the Supreme Court of Israel, Translated Opinions, http://versa.cardozo.yu.edu/opinions /ka%E2%80%99adan-v-israel-land-administration; HCJ 9205/04 Adalah—The Legal Center for Arab Minority Rights in Israel v. Israel Lands Administration (Nevo, January 28, 2016) (Hebrew); HCJ 9205/04 Adalah—The Legal Center for Arab Minority Rights in Israel v. Israel Lands Administration (Nevo, September 28, 2008) (Hebrew).

99. *Future Vision*, supra note 63, at 17–18; Proposed Bill Law for the Abolition of National Institutions (Legislative Amendments), 2014, Private Bill of MK Jamal Zahalka, Hanin Zoabi, and Basel Ghattas, No. 2271/19 (March 10, 2014) (Hebrew). Similar bills were laid down by Knesset members of the Balad party for the Eighteenth (P / 18/314), Seventeenth (P / 351/17), Sixteenth (P / [832]), and Fifteenth Knesset (p / 830) (Hebrew); Haim Sandberg, "Distributive Justice vs. the Denial of the Jewish Nation State," in *Land, Democracy and the Relations of the Majority-Minor*, ed. Yitzhak Schnell et al. (Tel Aviv: Walter Lebach Institute, Tel Aviv University, 2013) (Hebrew), 23, 26, 32–34.

100. Ben-Eliyahu Committee, supra note 77, at 32.

101. Letter to PM Netanyahu, supra note 96.

102. Ben-Eliyahu Committee, supra note 77, at 10; Proposed Basic Law: Israel Lands (Amendment—Cancellation of Linkage to the Jewish National Fund), 5765–2005, Private Bill of MK Shaul Yahalom No. 3245 (February 28, 2005) (Hebrew); Proposed Basic Law: Israel Lands (Amendment—Cancellation of Linkage to the Jewish National Fund), 5767–2006, Private Law Proposal of MK Zevulun Orlev No. 1545/17 (October 16, 2006) (Hebrew).

103. Yael Darel, "It's Over: Jewish National Fund and Israel Finally Agree to Part Ways," *Ynet*, February 1, 2015, http://www.ynetnews.com/articles/0,7340,L-4620833,00.html; Nimrod Bousso, "After 52 Years, Jewish National Fund Divorcing Israel Lands Administration," *Haaretz*, June 30, 2013, http://www.haaretz.com/israel-news/business/.premium-1.532730; Ben-Eliyahu Committee, supra note 77, at 76; Minutes of the Ninth Meeting of the Economics Committee of the Nineteenth Knesset (May 8, 2013) (Hebrew).

104. Minutes of the Ninth Meeting of the Economics Committee of the Nineteenth Knesset 41–42 (May 8, 2013) (Hebrew); Nimrod Bousso, "Everyone Is Going to Lose from the Separation between JNF Lands and the State," *Marker*, July 6, 2013 (Hebrew), https://www .themarker.com/realestate/1.2064095 (KKL-JNF Land Administration, Alex Hefetz: "The JNF is pushed out by the Minister").

105. Sandberg, *Basic Law*, supra note 53, at 198–204.

106. Principles of the Agreement between the State and the JNF (May 26, 2009) (Hebrew) (copy preserved by the author).

107. Ron Freidman, "JNF Assembly Approves Land Swap in Disputed Vote," *Jerusalem Post*, June 23, 2009, http://www.jpost.com/Israel/JNF-assembly-approves-land-swap-in -disputed-vote; PCA 6382/09 Keren Kayemeth Le Israel (JNF) v. Diamant (Nevo, June 1, 2009) (Hebrew).

108. OM (JM Dist. C.) 8304/09 Viderman v. Keren Kayemeth LeIsrael (Nevo, June 25, 2013) (Hebrew).

109. Resources in supra note 103; Niv Elis and Sharon Udasin, "Lapid Calls to Nationalize 'Corrupt' KKL-JNF," *Jerusalem Post*, February 11, 2015, http://www.jpost.com/Israel-News /Lapid-calls-to-nationalize-corrupt-KKL-JNF-390652.

110. §2 Decision 1185 of the Israel Lands Council "Reform in the Administration of Israel Lands," (December 28, 2009) (Hebrew); Decision 3264 of the Executive Board of Israel Land

Administration "Implementation of a Uniform Policy between State and Development Authority Tenants and JNF Tenants regarding Council Resolution 1185" (August 21, 2012) (Hebrew); Land Administration Report, supra note 37, at 2012 budget year 72.

111. §4 "2015 Agreement," supra note 95; Decision No. 563 of the 34th Government of Israel "An Outline of an Arrangement with the Jewish National Fund" (October 11, 2015) (Hebrew), https://www.gov.il/he/departments/policies/2015_dec563.

112. Association for Civil Rights in Israel (ACRI), "Annul JNF Representation on the Israel Land Council," ACRI, August 23, 2016, https://www.acri.org.il/en/2016/08/23/annul-jnf-representation-on-the-israel-land-council/.

113. HCJ 6411/16 The National Committee for the Heads of the Arab Local Authorities in Israel v. Knesset Israel, J. Solberg at par. 42 (Nevo, June 19, 2018) (Hebrew); Editorial, "The Israeli High Court's Strange Views about Equality: A Panel Actually Ruled That an Entity That Declares That It Discriminates Can Be among Israel's Decision-Makers," *Haaretz*, July 4, 2018, https://www.haaretz.com/opinion/the-israeli-high-court-s-strange-views-about-equality-1.6242391.

114. Israel Land Authority, *Report on Activities for the 2015 Budget Year* (2016) (Hebrew), 66, http://land.gov.il/doclib5/doch_2015.pdf.

115. Israel Land Authority, *Report on Activities for the 2017 Budget Year* (2018) (Hebrew), 59, http://land.gov.il/DocLib5/doch_2017.pdf; Israel Land Authority, *Report on Activities for the 2016 Budget Year* (2017) (Hebrew), 57, http://land.gov.il/doclib5/doch_2016.pdf.

116. Israel Land Authority, *Report on Activities for the 2018 Budget Year* (2019) (Hebrew), 65, https://land.gov.il/doclib5/doch_2018.pdf.

117. Minutes of the Eshkol Committee (October 23, 1957), supra note 78, at 14–15.

118. US Department of the Interior, Bureau of Land Management, *Public Land Statistics 2012* (2013), 1, 5, https://www.blm.gov/sites/blm.gov/files/pls2012-web.pdf.

119. Heather M. Stack, "The 'Colonization' of East Germany? A Comparative Analysis of German Privatization." 46 *Duke L. J.* (1997): 1211, 1220; Rainer Frank, "Privatization in Eastern Germany: A Comprehensive Study," 27 *Vand. J. Transnat'l L.* (1994): 809, 838.

120. "Our History," Crown Estate, accessed June 17, 2019, https://www.thecrownestate.co.uk/en-gb/our-business/our-history/.

# 2

## CULTURE, NATION, AND SOCIALISM IN THE ADMINISTRATION OF PUBLIC LANDS

> The Jubilee year ... [is] an ancient institution set up by our Teacher Moses ... to ensure the ends of social justice ... our methods serve the purpose none the less. The increases in land values accrue not to the individual owner, but to the public.
>
> Theodore Herzl, *Old New Land (Altneuland)*

THE PUBLIC LAND INVENTORY IN ISRAEL COVERS 93 percent of the territory of the State of Israel, most of it uninhabited desert or other expanses and a valuable amount of agricultural and urban land in the heart of the country. The guiding principle in the government's management of this large inventory is centralized control, enacted in the 1960 Basic Law: Israel Lands.[1] The first clause of the Basic Law, "Prohibition of transfer of ownership," establishes that "the ownership of Israel Lands ... shall not be transferred by sale or in any other manner."

For several reasons, the determination of such a principle in a Basic Law indicates its importance. First, Israel's Basic Law has a special constitutional status. The laws it encompasses are intended as chapters of the constitution, and their legal status, as ruled by the Israeli Supreme Court, trumps that of regular legislation enacted by the Knesset.[2] Likewise, it specifically confirms, albeit with less finality, the constitutional status of Basic Law: Israel Lands.[3] Second, this Basic Law, the second Basic Law enacted by the Knesset, was legislated far earlier than the twelve that followed, dealing with weighty topics like government, the IDF, and human rights. Third, anchoring the prohibition of transferring ownership of government-owned lands in the constitution is quite exceptional. The constitutions of most Western countries—and even those of not very liberal Middle Eastern countries, such as Iran[4] and Egypt[5]—emphasize the protection of private property, not the preservation of public ownership.

The enactment of this legislation to prohibit the transfer of government-owned lands in the Basic Law at such an early stage is another indication of its importance. But how and to what extent did this singular prohibition survive in the Basic Law of a country that views itself as a modern Western state in the second decade of the twenty-first century?

The principle that governs the control of the public land inventory progresses from three ideological motives. The first, cultural and symbolic, establishes a connection between Jewish tradition and the return of the Jewish people to their homeland. The second, national and historical, impedes the transfer of land ownership to non-Jews or foreigners. The third, economic and consistent with a socialist worldview, places an imperative on the government to retain lands to advance equality and social justice. The three motives sparkled through the visions of the founders of the Zionist movement and were taken up by Zionist leaders from the British Mandate era till the end of the 1970s. An analysis of the three motives from the perspective of public land administration will reveal how deeply rooted socialist ideology is in Israel's public land policy.

## The Cultural and Symbolic Motive

### *The Zionist Vision of the Land of Israel*

A close relationship to the Land of Israel (*Eretz Israel*) is one of the pillars of Jewish faith. God's promise of the land to Abraham is central to the biblical covenant between God and Abraham's descendants.[6] The "redemption of the land" and the return to *Eretz Israel* have been prominent themes in Jewish prayer since the days of the destruction of the Second Temple and the exile in the Diaspora.[7] These themes are fundamental to Zionism and inform the ethos of most Zionist and Israeli leaders, both religious and secular. Yet notwithstanding, Zionism is a secular, national, and political movement, and the religious longing for the redemption of the land differs from its secular correlate. While religious believers may regard the redemption of the land as a biblical commandment, secular Jews view it mainly as an aspiration of their nationality, culture, or ideology.[8] The view of Judaism as both a religion and a national culture allows for a shifting impact on national life. The effect of this ambivalence on the identity of Jews and Zionists raises vexing questions in many areas of Israeli life today.[9] Such questions even reached Israel's Supreme Court, which was asked to recognize the existence of a separate Israeli identity/status as opposed to a Jewish identity/status or Israeli citizenship, a determination it was careful to avoid.[10] However, there is no doubt that religious concepts have an impact on Jewish nationalism, even according to the secular Zionist worldview. The prohibition of the transfer of Israeli lands is an excellent example of the cultural role played by religion in the shaping of secular national principles. In the following paragraphs, we shall analyze the role of the biblical Jubilee laws in shaping the prohibition.

## *The Biblical Commandment of Jubilee*

According to the laws of the Jubilee Year (*Shnat haYovel*), as they are described in Jewish scripture, possession of a plot of land must be returned to its original owners every fifty years. This commandment appears in Leviticus: "In the Year of Jubilee ye shall return every man to his possession,"[11] and "The fiftieth year shall be a jubilee for you."[12] Leviticus provides a religious explanation for this commandment—the Holy Land belongs to God: "The land shall not be sold in perpetuity, for the land is mine, for ye are strangers and settlers with me."[13] The book of Numbers gives a social explanation of the commandment: "So shall no inheritance of the children of Israel remove from tribe to tribe; for the children of Israel shall cleave everyone to the inheritance of the tribe of his fathers."[14] The book further commands, "Notwithstanding the land shall be divided by lot; according to the names of the tribes of their fathers they shall inherit."[15]

In a patriarchal society with a tribally based social structure, the retention of land in perpetuity within the patrilineal ancestor's tribe is of prime importance. In such societies land is not merely a central source of income for the family or tribe but a crucial component of its continued existence as a social unit.[16] Allowing outsiders to take possession of land, whether by way of sales or inheritance, weakens not only the economy but the very fabric of society.[17] This way of thinking is preserved in rural societies like traditional Arab villages.[18]

The ancient heritage of the Jubilee informed the legislation of the Basic Law, and the Israeli judiciary, legal scholars, and historians often quote the biblical background of the prohibition of transferring ownership of Israel lands in explaining the Basic Law.[19] However, it would be erroneous to suggest that Israeli legislators implemented the biblical account of the Jubilee precisely as presented in the Bible. Most of the legislators involved with this Basic Law were secular Jews not guided by religious faith or *Halakhah*. Moreover, stringent adherence to religious law as such could not have been the basis for the prohibition in the Basic Law because the biblical prohibition refers not to public lands but to privately owned lands apportioned by lot. Furthermore, the Jubilee cycle has not been applied since the destruction of the First Temple, and Maimonides, one of the most authoritative interpreters of Jewish Law, wrote that the Jubilee will only be reinstated when the Messiah comes.[20] Thus, the repeated references to the biblical Jubilee as a justification for the imperative of retaining land ownership in Israel do not point to religious adherence but to an alternate motive.

### *The Bible as Cultural-National Inspiration*

The laws of Jubilee did in fact serve as a cultural and symbolic inspiration for the legislators of the prohibition of the transfer of land ownership. The evocation of biblical sources emphasized Israel's cultural link to the heritage of the Jews as a people.[21] The Jubilee year and its agricultural principles were meant to tie the Jewish people to their land through toil, sweat, and the "redemption" of the wilderness.[22] Former chief justice of the Israeli Supreme Court Dorit Beinish explained the underlying principle of the Basic Law prohibiting public land transfer to private ownership (in the Dror case of 2012) thus: "We view the traditions of the Jewish People as a nation and a society as profoundly meaningful and multidimensional, symbolizing the return of the people to their homeland."[23]

Jubilee laws may also support modern conceptions of equality. As will be shown later on, these conceptions had a definitive impact on the prohibition of the transferal of land ownership. Zionist thinkers of a secular-nationalist disposition were overjoyed to use the Jewish tradition as a stimulus for their modern social ideas. The biblical parameter that guided land division among the tribes was equality in proportion to their numbers: "To a larger group give a larger inheritance, and to a smaller group a smaller one; each is to receive its inheritance according to the number of those listed."[24] This biblical message of equality inspired Theodor Herzl, seer of the Jewish state, to base his economic vision on the Jubilee laws. In *Altneuland*, published about fifty years before the founding of the state, Herzl proclaimed through his protagonist, David, that "the Jubilee year . . . [is] an ancient institution set up by our Teacher Moses," the purpose of which was "to ensure the ends of social justice."²⁵ As Herzl admitted, "We indeed arranged it a bit differently. The land now reverts back to the New Society,"²⁶ and the "increases in land value accrue not to the individual owner, but to the public."²⁷

There are many other examples of the use of this inspiration in Zionist thought,²⁸ among them two embodiments of different political and philosophical backgrounds: the founder of the Revisionist movement, Ze'ev Jabotinsky, whose writings articulate Israel's political right-wing manifesto, anchored his ideas in the biblical Jubilee laws and supported their adoption by the Jewish state so as to bring about "social reconstruction" that would periodically repair the distortions of the free market and restore the division of property to its initial point of balance;²⁹ and Aaron David Gordon, one of the intellectual ideologues of practical Zionism and Labor Zionism, who wrote that "our main requirements, for example, working the land and forging a nation through labor, can be acceptable even to the ultra-Orthodox: 'The land must not be sold in perpetuity, because the land is mine...' says the Torah."³⁰

The Israel land regulations drew concepts and terminology from the Jubilee laws. For example, the standard land lease period was set at forty-nine years and ended in the fiftieth year, the Jubilee.³¹ The end of a lease period is referred to as the "lease Jubilee" [*Yovel*] in the Israel lands regulations.³²

The cultural-symbolic background of the Jubilee is enacted in the law and in the declarative value of preserving ownership of land in the State of Israel. Religious imperatives such as striving for equal allotment of resources helped modern leaders justify the ban on transferring public ownership. Yet it is doubtful that a historical-cultural source of inspiration was reason enough to convince the state to adopt the operative policy of ownership retention and to cling to it for so many years. There were different reasons—stronger and more practical—for the state's preservation of the policy. The legacy of the biblical Jubilee in the legislative structure of public land management in Israel reflects both the importance and the limitations of the religious background of Israel's Zionist identity.

## The National and Historic Motive

### *The Fears of an Arab or Foreign Takeover*

A central tenet of Zionism is that Jews, whether as individuals or as a collective, cannot maintain an orderly and honorable religious, national, or cultural lifestyle within a host country or society. According to this assumption, the concentration of Jews within an independent political framework will enable them to shape their national and cultural life freely and to realize the goal of self-determination in an optimal manner.[33] The Zionist national movement's aspiration for independence encountered Arab and Palestinian resistance from the start. The struggle against Arab resistance is likewise reflected in the issue of land. Before the establishment of the state, Zionism fought for the right to purchase land. After the War of 1948, the struggle focused on resistance to the return of assets to Palestinian refugees and on the administration of public land (chap. 5 will elaborate on these two topics). The fear of imperiling Israel's political independence is reflected in numerous areas of life and shared by many Jewish Israeli citizens; thus it may be viewed as a characteristic element in the identity of Israeli Jews.[34] Did this fear affect the prohibition in Israel of land ownership transference and, if so, to what extent?

In academic literature, claims abound that the State of Israel instituted this prohibition in order to prevent the transfer of land ownership to its non-Jewish citizens.[35] Critics may raise such arguments to indicate the inequality or dispossession that is inherent in the prohibition. In the following paragraphs, I will argue that the weight ascribed to this factor as a reason for the Basic Law's enactment is greatly overestimated. The fear of a foreign takeover did exist in the background of the legislative process, but it did not really guide the framers of the prohibition. The fear of foreigners remained a dormant complex that has arisen in recent years in light of the privatization trend with regard to Israel's land, on the one hand, and the growing interest of non-Jewish foreign investors in the Israeli land market, on the other.

### *Transferring Rights to Non-Jewish Citizens*

Indeed, the fear of ownership transfer to non-Jews characterized the JNF's policy regarding the lands it had acquired during the British Mandate period. At the time, the JNF served as the only source of land supply for the Jewish minority in Palestine. It was a period of national struggle toward establishing a Jewish state while under foreign British rule, which opposed Jewish purchase of lands. The JNF feared that, were it not to retain ownership over the lands it had acquired with huge sums of money and under difficult circumstances, those lands would revert to non-Jewish hands.[36]

This fear ceased to guide Israel's government after the establishment of the Jewish state. The government now had at its disposal a huge inventory of public lands, which included, as explained in the previous chapter, tens of thousands of square kilometers of state-owned and Development Authority lands. Now in the minority, the non-Jewish population of Israel seemed powerless to lead an economic struggle over the purchase of lands. In its Declaration of Independence, the State of Israel assured this minority that it would have total equality of civil rights and would not suffer from discrimination.[37] Hence, Israel could not prevent minority citizens from acquiring ownership rights to Israeli land.

As early as 1949, when the government was deliberating the idea of limited transfer of land ownership, Prime Minister David Ben-Gurion declared: "We are now dealing with a State. . . . There is no comparison between our situation when lands were purchased by the JNF and our current situation."[38] In a cabinet meeting, Finance Minister Eliezer Kaplan stated: "Regarding the Arabs . . . either we seriously think that that small number of Arabs who live here will have equal rights, or else we don't really mean that. . . . In any event, we cannot enact [such] restrictions because there are Arabs living in Israel."[39]

During the process of legislating the Basic Law, toward the end of the State of Israel's first decade, lawmakers gave no weight to the fear that land rights would be transferred to the state's Arab minority. The starting assumption of the ministerial committee that penned the Basic Law, chaired by Minister Levi Eshkol, was that with the establishment of the state, the JNF had changed its purpose "from redeeming the land from foreign rule, to redeeming the wilderness."[40] The explanatory remarks on the Basic Law Bill stated that "the purpose of JNF and the State lands (including those belonging to the Development Authority) is one and the same: to serve the needs of the State *and its residents*."[41] The chair of the Knesset's Constitution, Law and Justice Committee, MK Zerach Warhaftig, clarified that "any law we pass is for the good of *all* who reside in the State."[42] MK Yohanan Bader, one of the leaders of the right-wing *Heirut* party, opposed instituting the ban, noting that "the fathers of Zionism . . . intended to ensure that the land which the JNF was to purchase would not pass from Jewish hands to foreign ownership . . . *this purpose is no longer relevant*."[43] MK Ya'acov Hazan, member of the left-wing, socialist *Mapa"m* party and supporter of the Basic Law, testified that in the committee of which he was a member, a consensus was reached to prepare a law saying that the Israel Lands Administration would need to oversee the land rights of "Jewish and Arab citizens alike."[44]

Concerns about the sale of land to Arabs were not discussed in Knesset deliberations leading up to the enactment of the Basic Law. There was no formal reason for such concern. Moreover, in and of itself, the Basic Law's ban on transferring land ownership did not prevent the transfer of other proprietary land rights to non-Jewish citizens. Since the founding of the state, there has never been a ban on leasing Israel's land to non-Jewish citizens; the state does indeed lease land to these citizens.[45]

Only the JNF clung to the prohibition, established in Mandate times, of transferring land ownership or even leasing lands to non-Jews. The much-discussed legislative steps taken toward the enactment of the Basic Law were apparently meant to preserve that ban on land transfer,[46] and the JNF viewed its adoption as a victory that preserved its principle of retaining state lands.[47] The Israel Lands Administration, however, found ways to avoid discriminating against non-Jewish citizens in the allotment of JNF lands, by exchanging lands given to non-Jews for lands belonging to the state or to the Development Authority.[48] Moreover, today, when urban Israel lands are privatized, their ownership is transferred equally to anyone who has held the lease rights to them, without regard to national or religious affiliation. The attorney general reiterated before the Supreme Court that he would do so with JNF lands as well, and he promised equality in their leasing.[49] This setup also applies to JNF lands in light of a general agreement on the exchange of lands, which it signed with the state, as described in the previous chapter. There are indeed claims that the allotment policy for Israel lands to non-Jews is discriminatory. Chapter 5 will examine these claims. Yet it is undisputed that a ban on transferring rights to non-Jewish citizens does not exist. The desire to prevent the transfer of land ownership to Israel's non-Jewish citizens could not have been, and never was, a motive for the general prohibition of transferring ownership of Israel lands.

## *Transferring Rights to "Foreigners"*

In contrast to concerns about the transfer of Israel lands to citizens of the state, the general prohibition seemed more reasonable when applied to concerns about land falling into the hands of "foreigners." The War of Independence and the creation of the "refugee problem" elicited a concern that the Palestinian refugees, their representatives, or forces in Arab states would purchase Israel lands as a step toward actualizing the right of return. Preventing such purchases may be the purpose of the legal ban. Yet in practice, the concern that foreign bodies would purchase lands did not seem to trouble the legislators of the Basic Law. This attitude might have stemmed from Israel's success at the time in effectively quashing attempts of return.[50]

MK Bader, the prominent right-wing politician who opposed the Basic Law, was the only one to explicitly reference this concern during the legislation process, a concern he dismissed out of hand: "The risk that we will sell our land to foreigners in an Israeli State—that could happen with a dunam or half a dunam—is no longer possible."[51]

Years after the Basic Law was enacted, the concern that foreigners would purchase lands was invoked as an explanation for prohibiting the transferal of ownership of Israel lands. Four later developments had led to this.

First, in 1967, Israel gained control of territories in the West Bank and the Gaza Strip, and the possibility that refugees in those territories would return and attempt to purchase their lands within the official state borders became more tangible. As a result, a new law was legislated, banning certain agricultural land transactions and constituting "divergent use" of the lands as a criminal offense.[52] MKs claimed that one of the unstated but driving reasons for the law was the desire to prevent transactions with former refugees.[53] Yet during the 1960s and 1970s, very few complaints were lodged with the Israel Lands Administration regarding informal subleasing of agricultural Israel lands to Arabs.[54]

Second, at the beginning of the 1980s, Israel's government removed its monetary oversight of foreign currency. This generated the concern that the state would no longer be able to control a flow of resources intended for the purchase of rights over Israel lands from hostile entities. In an effort to quell these concerns, the government suggested enacting a new law, for the purpose of "preventing the possibility of granting land to [foreign] hostile or unwanted bodies."[55] The Beth-El communities' land purchases provided another catalyst for this suggestion. Beth-El comprised Protestant Christian communities in Zichron Ya'akov and other locations throughout the country, headed by the German nun Emma Berger.[56] During their deliberations, MKs casually brought up a general fear of purchases by Saudi Arabia or via "Petro-dollars," which seemed to reflect concerns about future eventualities rather than consequences of actual phenomena.[57] Although that bill and similar others did not pass, in 1982, the Israel Lands Council, responsible for the Israel lands policy, decided for the first time since its inception to place restrictions on the granting of rights to foreigners.[58] In this decision and a series of later decisions based on it, *foreigner* was defined as anyone who is neither a resident nor a citizen of Israel, nor entitled to move to Israel through the Law of Return. This policy was meant to prevent only non-Jewish outsiders from purchasing lands.[59]

The third development that raised concern about transferring Israel lands to foreigners was the privatization of urban lands. Some opposed privatization because of the fear that privatized lands would seep through to hostile entities.[60] As a result, the Israel Lands Council reiterated its dedication to the ban on transfer to foreigners.[61]

It was not until 2011 that the prohibition of transferring both leasing rights and ownership of Israel lands to foreigners found its way to a formal parliamentary legislation.[62] The new legislation did not ban ownership transfer to foreigners but conditioned it on the approval of the defense and foreign ministers and required its main consideration to be "the good of the public and its security."[63] As stated in the bill, the legislation was meant "to prevent the spread of foreign entities, including hostile bodies, across the State's land."[64] During the time leading up to the enactment of this law, Israeli media outlets published investigations that raised suspicions that foreign entities stood behind the purchase of privately owned Jewish lands.[65] Knesset members from right-wing parties who supported the legislative amendments used these publications to support their stance,[66] but supporters of the law from center and left-wing parties also intimated that a real danger existed.[67] However, statistics provided by the Israel Lands Administration during the legislation process showed that in the preceding years only a few dozen requests to transfer Israel Lands to foreign ownership had been filed,[68] and most of them—mainly from foreign companies—were approved.[69]

The fourth and latest development that raised interest in banning land ownership transfer to foreigners was the advent of globalization, which heightened concern about land purchases by foreign countries and multinational companies.[70] Globalization created an opening in Israel for major companies to purchase lands, as when the Chinese food giant, Bright Food (Group), owned by the Chinese government, purchased the Israeli food company T'nuva. This transaction prompted sharp public and political criticism that focused on the claim that the Chinese government would now control 3.3 hectares of land, worth 1.4 billion new Israeli shekels. The criticism, however, did not prevent the sale.[71]

Hostile entities' initiatives to purchase lands in Israel likely encounter problems of accessibility, elevated prices, and economic limitations stemming from regulations against money laundering.[72] Therefore, the likelihood of such purchases occurring on a wide scale is minimal. No reliable research on the scale of the phenomenon has yet been published. However, such bans are common in other countries.[73] Whatever the viability of land sales to foreigners may be, justification of the ban on this basis is doubtless a result of developments that came after the legislation of the Basic Law. The idea of banning the transfer of land to nonresident foreigners did not guide the authors of the Basic Law; it drew attention many years after the law's enactment.[74] However, continuing discussions of the issue and the development of laws to halt it evidence an existential fear of foreign takeover rooted in the identity of the State of Israel.

## The Economic and Socialist Motive

### Israel's Economic Identity: Socialist or Capitalist?

The socialist worldview that guided the leadership of the Jewish settlement (*Yishuv*) in the decades leading up to and following the establishment of the state supported state control over all government-allotted means of production in order to advance equality. Alternating between suspicion of private ownership and outright hostility, this perspective accorded well with a general ban on the transfer of land ownership. It allowed the government to distribute land resources, oversee their usage, and enjoy their increase in value for the good of the population as a whole. The strongest motive driving the adoption of the prohibition of transferring ownership of Israel lands was this socialist worldview, favored by a majority of Israel's leaders during the 1960s.

Israel's economic orientation is an important component of its identity. The history of the law prohibiting the transference of land ownership in Israel reveals the deeply rooted socialism of its framers, as attested by the fact that it is still in force. Like China[75] and Cuba,[76] the State of Israel is one of a few countries where such a prohibition still exists. Yet since the late 1970s, Israel has been led by a political party with a right-wing worldview that encourages market forces and privatization. Israel's legislators began to reduce the scope of the prohibition and initiate the privatization of small but valuable parts of the inventory. And nevertheless, as we shall see below, the ban on the transfer of land ownership points to a significant socialist component of Israel's identity.

### "Profiteering" versus "Equality": The Historical Socialist Background

From its very inception, the Zionist movement fostered a socialist worldview. Socialism was a new and popular idea at the time and was especially appealing to the Jewish leaders and supporters who were concerned about

Jewish poverty.[77] On the whole, members of the Zionist movement and the Jewish community tolerated diverse viewpoints, some more radical than others.[78] Most viewed the national ownership of land as a central economic principle. Theodor Herzl, for example, wrote in his utopian novel *Altneuland* that the public should retain ownership of lands "to ensure the ends of social justice. . . . The increases in land values accrue not to the individual owner, but to the public."[79] In other words, leaving land ownership in its own hands allows the public to enjoy the increase of land value. Most leaders of the *Yishuv* in Palestine during the British Mandate were socialist leaning and thus deeply repelled by the idea of private land ownership.[80] They fiercely attacked "profiteering" and "speculation," derogatory terms for purchasing land not to use it but to turn a profit by reselling it at a higher price. In December 1933, David Ben-Gurion, who was at that time the leader of the *Yishuv*, wrote, "A terrible disease has struck us—profiteering from bartered lands so that it becomes nearly impossible to purchase any."[81] Then head of the JNF, Avraham Granovsky wrote in 1940 that "it is of utmost importance to erect a legal governmental block against the phenomenon of land profiteering in the Hebrew State."[82] Otherwise, he warned, "we should fear anarchy in the real-estate market and the speculative rise of land costs."[83] Socialist worldviews were particularly relevant when it came to agricultural lands, the main objective in the Zionist movement's land purchases in its early days. Influential Zionist thinkers took the socialist stance that the preservation of land ownership is necessary to protect farmers from the risks of agricultural work, to preserve equality in the allotment of agricultural plots, and to prevent "speculative" land use by farmers.[84]

The socialist stream continued to direct the State of Israel after its establishment. Many leaders, particularly the representatives of workers' parties, continued to justify public land ownership with similar reasoning. In this worldview, state ownership of land is the proper tool for economic development, while the transfer of lands to holders of capital will lead perforce to "profiteering." This was the predominant view among those who justified the prohibition of ownership transfer during the deliberations that took place over the ban on state and Development Authority assets in the early 1950s,[85] as well as in the late 1950s before the legislation of the Basic Law.[86] In the final deliberation, Finance Minister Levi Eshkol noted that the foundation of the Basic Law is "a socialist worldview regarding the means of production."[87]

These socialist views encountered liberal-capitalist opposition to government monopoly and support of privatization and free initiative.[88] For example, MK Yohanan Bader, leader of the legislative opposition on the right, argued that government control of most of the state's territory would deter investors and that a property owner who sells his property is not a "profiteer."[89] He argued further that retention of land ownership in perpetuity would be like the dead controlling the living, "Manus mortua," "a curse for industry and the nation," and "a blocking of all development."[90] MK Shne'or Zalman Abramov, the theoretician of Israel's Liberal Party, claimed that the principle of state ownership of land is "an attempt to revolt against hoped-for development" and "an anachronism."[91] Yet in the encounter between these opposing views, the socialist approach came out on top.

### The Socialist Justification in the Israeli Supreme Court

In recent decades the socialist view gained renewed support from Supreme Court judgments. In the Ka'adan case,[92] which examined the state's authority to allot Israel lands through a "separate but equal" policy based on national affiliation, Chief Justice Aharon Barak reviewed the purposes of governmental land administration. The starting point of his analysis was the original purpose for the legislation of the Basic Law.[93] Here the court listed the goal as the prevention of "speculative trade in State land."[94] The message that the preservation of ownership was meant to advance equality was emphasized in the New Discourse case,[95] which ruled against the granting of special benefits to lessees of agricultural Israel lands because the purpose of retaining public ownership is "the realization of distributional justice and land allotment" and its goal is "the just social division of resources."[96] Justice Barak even claimed that "law plays an important role in everything relating to the oversight of decisions about the division of wealth in society."[97] In the Avi-ezer case, the court ruled that the allotment of agricultural plots to industrial entities is inconsistent with "principles of social justice."[98] In the Workers' Society case, the court ruled that public lessees, such as the General Workers' Organization ("*HaHistadrut*"), could not "yield profits for themselves from State lands allocated to them for public purposes."[99] In the Independent Cities Forum case, which dealt with the allotment of benefits to lessees of agricultural Israel lands, the court ruled that the government must give considerations of social justice "significant weight when making decisions about rights and uses of Israel Lands."[100] In the Dror case, the court criticized legislation that allows privatization of urban lands. The court quoted, and in part accepted, the petitioners' claims that there is "concern over the transfer of large areas of land, all developed, to the hands of 'land barons', as they define them, who might create 'islands' of private lands, and control them for the purpose of yielding profit."[101]

In these rulings, the Supreme Court sided with the original views that influenced the principle of ownership retention. Yet, as we shall presently see, the timing of these rulings belied changes in the air beyond the court walls. The court felt compelled to emphasize and underscore the distributional reasons behind the prohibition of land transfer at the time, specifically because of the steps toward privatization at its threshold seeking judicial review. A more far-fetched explanation is that the court wanted to preserve the waning elitist values of the "previous liberal hegemonies."[102]

Yet, at the end of the day, the Supreme Court's general approach to the principal of ownership transfer did not prevent steps toward the privatization of certain components of Israel lands. The court refused to acknowledge the claim that privatizing lands infringes on "the public's property rights."[103] In the Independent Cities Forum, Justice Arbel ended her ruling with the statement that "years have passed, the State has been established, and with the passage of time, needs have changed, preferences have changed, and the ethos has changed . . . we must consider the changing reality, the economic changes."[104] In the coming sections, we will describe those changes of "ethos" in the policy of Israel's public lands inventory.

### The Changing Ethos: From Socialism to Market Economy

In the decades that have passed since Basic Law: Israel Lands was legislated, the political map has changed, and the socialist parties have lost power. Since 1977, a right-wing, liberal economic worldview has guided the parliamentary majority in both the Knesset and the succeeding governments. Israeli society has slowly become a more competitive, Western-style, free market society.[105] In the past, representatives of the agricultural settlement movements, which control the majority of agricultural Israel lands, stood at the forefront of the supporters of ownership retention; in the new century, some have served as popular representatives of privatization demands. A prime example of this is the statement made by the representative of the NGO *Admati* ("My Land"), which represents 147 communal settlements (*Kibbutzim*) that were founded before the state, during a Knesset deliberation over the privatization of Israel lands: "I have stopped fighting for equality. I will now move forward and discuss ownership transfer. We ask, we demand, equality between homes on a *kibbutz* or *moshav* and homes in the city."[106] Preserving ownership did not prove itself economically, either. The policy led to the establishment of a large, inefficient bureaucratic mechanism, the Israel Lands Administration, which struggled to deal with the huge inventory for which it was responsible and experienced many points of tension with citizens.[107] In 2009, a new body called the Israel Lands Authority was formed for the purpose of making the inventory's administration more efficient and improving it according to accepted business standards.[108] Its subsequent absorption into the government apparatus met with obstacles, and the state comptroller expressed doubts about whether it had—or would in the future—realize its purpose.[109] Moreover, though the government struggled for decades to produce the expected economic profits from the ownership retention mechanisms, it gradually dispensed with a significant portion of them (chap. 3 will discuss this process). Over time, corruption and acts of favoritism increased.[110] The governmental mechanism did not manage to supply land demand, and as a result, property prices have quickly shot up, especially in recent years.[111] The benefit of public ownership in urban areas became a burden. It did not yield the expected economic profits for the public. All of this led to a weakening of the socialist justifications for banning ownership transfer. It did not lead to the voiding of the Basic Law or of the principle embodied in that law, but it did lead to changes in legislation and policy steps that limited the application of the principle and advanced Israel land privatization.

In 2009, for the first time, primary legislation set out the goals of the new Israel Lands Authority, created to administer Israel lands more efficiently. These goals reflect the change that has swept over the traditional distributive view. While the first goal of the administration of Israel lands is "for the good of the public" and "for public needs," it is accompanied by goals that reflect a new, contradictory outlook: "the advancement of competition in the land market" and "the prevention of concentrated control of lands."[112] Comments on the bill explained that transfer of ownership to lessees must be enabled because "preserving ownership . . . interferes with market efficiency."[113] The change that has occurred in the views of Israel's leadership is evident in the Knesset discourse surrounding the extended powers of privatization. Socialist views that support the principle of ownership retention were heard, but they reflected only the minority opinion opposing privatization.[114]

## The Narrow Justification of Public Ownership

Another change occurred with respect to the definition of *public needs*, in whose name the Israel Lands Authority was supposed to retain ownership of public lands. If in the past these public needs included almost all types of land usage, the narrower view of recent years defined ownership retention as necessary mainly in the case of lands used for the governmental supply of public goods or for the preservation of resources for future generations. This view lends justification to continued public ownership of natural resources and of as-yet-unused Israel lands, but it allows the privatization of developed lands meant for other usages, principally urban ones. We will now explain some basic terms of this limiting approach.

*Public good* means that consumption by one party does not deprive another of the ability to consume it and that consumption by others may not be prevented by or made conditional on payment. The inability to prevent consumption neutralizes any motivation for private production of the good, as others who did not invest in its production will benefit equally from it. The governmental supply of a public good is one way to handle market failure. Prominent examples of such goods are security and public order.[115]

Lands are not a public good, being a finite resource whose use by one precludes that of another and whose owner can prevent its use by others. Yet land serves as a medium for the production of public goods. As such, military training grounds, for example, "produce" security for the state's residents; forests and nature reserves "produce" environmental quality and improve quality of life; and an antiquities site "produces" cultural and historical heritage. If private owners were to use their land to produce security, environmental quality, or cultural heritage, they could not prevent other people from using those goods without paying for them and hence would have no reason to produce those public goods on their private land. They would prefer to designate their land for the production of nonpublic goods, in exchange for which they could charge money. It is possible that some of those goods would themselves contribute to the production of public goods, yet their contribution would be less than needed and would continue to decrease. Therefore, so long as the production of these public goods is essential for society, the government must ensure their production on public lands through the retention of government ownership.[116] This is the common justification for the retention of government ownership of lands used as parks, nature reserves, beaches, antiquity sites, sites of historical importance, forests, open landscape areas, and military training territory.[117] Similarly, the allotment of the full inventory of private lands in this generation would likely ignore the needs and desires of future generations. The present generation would produce greater benefits and externalize negative impacts (creating shortages and damage) onto future generations.[118] This line of reasoning can also be used to justify public ownership of natural resources or of unexploited land inventory.[119]

The 2009 legislative amendments explicitly state these new ideas and guide the authorities to administer Israel lands not only "as a resource for the development of the State of Israel and for the good of the public" but also for "*the environment, and future generations.*"[120] Retaining ownership of the land for the good of future generations was emphasized several times in the Israel Lands Authority Law, stating that "enough land *reserves* [must be left] for the needs and the development of the State *in the future*"[121] and for "the preservation of land *reserves* for public needs."[122] The draft of the State of Israel's final constitution, prepared in 2006 by a special Knesset committee, suggested that the general principle of prohibiting ownership transfer of Israel Lands should be replaced by a simple clause indicating a general obligation to preserve lands and natural resources for future generations.[123] This suggestion has yet to be accepted.

In recent years, the Supreme Court has considered the needs of future generations to be a justifiable reason for the policy of land ownership retention. Thus, for example, in the Dror case, the court ruled that urban lands should be privatized "sparingly and in line with the needs stemming from the natural growth rate of the population."[124] In the Independent Cities Forum case, Justice Arbel approved steps toward the privatization of structures in agricultural areas but warned that "extended construction in open areas will hurt future generations, whose needs we must take into account as well," and that "there is room to take into account long-term considerations, relating to consequences of a given distributional decision on future generations."[125]

In practice, most Israel lands do include undeveloped areas. The total land reserved for development in Israel, including privately owned areas, stands at 1,729 square kilometers, which is only about 8 percent of the country's territory. The area that has already been developed stands at 988.5 square kilometers, which is another 4.5 percent of the state's territory. The remaining territory includes mainly open land (87.5%);[126] rocky territory, brush, and excavated lands (64.7%); threshed forests and parks

(7.3%); agricultural lands (20%);[127] army training territory (30%); IDF and Ministry of Security and Security Industries structures and camp territory (5%);[128] national parks and nature reserves (23%);[129] and twenty-two thousand antiquity sites,[130] all of which may overlap at times. Most Israel lands, then, serve for the production of public goods such as landscape, security, nature, heritage, and the preservation of reserves for future generations. The general principle of retaining public ownership still applies to most of Israel's territory.

## Concluding and Comparative Remarks

The constitutional prohibition of transferring ownership of public land in Israel derives from three different ideological motives and reflects prominent characteristics of Israel's identity: the cultural-symbolic motive meant to establish a connection between Jewish tradition and the return of the Jewish nation to its homeland; the national-historical motive of making the transfer of ownership to either non-Jews or to foreigners a difficult undertaking; and the third and decisive socialist-economic motive. The prohibition is consistent with a socialist worldview that places an imperative on the government to retain ownership of its lands in order to advance equality and social justice.

Yet the State of Israel has undergone a far-reaching ideological transformation since the original formation of the principle of retaining ownership of Israel lands. The leftist, socialist worldview that informed the design of the prohibition was exchanged for a more liberal version. While this did not void the principle, it did lead to changes in application. An ever-expanding policy of privatization replaced the strict policy of ownership retention.

The transition between these policies is not unique to Israel. Similar changes have taken place in other historically socialist countries that underwent liberalization, such as Russia, whose constitution obliges it to preserve lands and natural resources but does not impose a general obligation to preserve public ownership.[131] This is the common approach in the West as well. In its Millennium Development Goals of 2012, the World Bank allowed for any use of natural resources, including lands, that is efficient and sustainable.[132] The central goal of the Bureau of Land Management's (BLM) administration of the United States' federal land inventory is to ensure the accessibility of natural resources (quarries, forests, landscapes, parks) and assets of historical and cultural value to the general public.[133] According to the Federal Land Policy and Management Act 1976 (FLPMA),[134] land may be privatized only once a plan has been set for it; the guiding principles of such plans are environmental protection and consideration of potential for use and long-term benefit.[135] In England, on the other hand, the Crown Estate Commissioners, whose authorities are defined in the Crown Estate Act 1961 (CEA 1961),[136] have been criticized for their inadequate consideration of wider public interests.[137] As a result, the commissioners declared that they would not limit their focus exclusively to future profit yields but would seek to advance sustainability and social and environmental benefits as well.[138]

In sum, while most Israel lands are undeveloped territories or territories used to produce public goods, the balancing point in Israeli governmental land administration gradually shifted away from the socialist end of the political-ideological scale toward a more capitalist privatization. (This privatization trend will be discussed in the next chapter.) Yet, as we have shown here, the socialist basis of Israeli society is still deeply embedded in the administration of its public land inventory.

## Notes

1. Basic Law: Israel Lands, 5720–1960, *Sefer Ha-Hukim* 56 (Hebrew), 14 LSI 48.

2. CA 6821/93 United Mizrahi Bank Ltd. v. Migdal Cooperative Village (1995), PD 49(4): 221 (Hebrew), official English translation: https://supremedecisions.court.gov.il/Home/Download?path=EnglishVerdicts\93\210\068\z01&fileName=93068210_z01.txt&type=4; VERSA: Opinions of the Supreme Court of Israel, Translated Opinions, http://versa.cardozo.yu.edu/opinions/united-mizrahi-bank-v-migdal-cooperative-village; Suzie Navot, *The Constitution of Israel: A Contextual Analysis* (Oxford: Hart, 2014), 49–51.

3. HCJ Tnua'at 729/10 Dror Israel v. State of Israel, par. 42, 44 J. Beinisch (Nevo, May 24, 2012) (Hebrew) (Hereafter: Dror); Haim Sandberg, *Basic Law: Israel Lands—Commentary*, Commentary on the Basic Laws Series, ed. Izhak Zamir (Jerusalem: Sacher Institute, Hebrew University of Jerusalem, 2016) (Hebrew), 244–46.

4. Islamic Republic of Iran Constitution § 22, §31, https://www.wipo.int/edocs/lexdocs/laws/en/ir/ir001en.pdf.

5. Egypt Constitutional Declaration 2011 §5, http://www.egypt.gov.eg/english/laws/constitution/.

6. Genesis 15:1–15.

7. Shmuel Almog, "Redemption in Zionist Rhetoric," in *Redemption of the Land of Eretz-Israel: Ideology and Practice*, ed. Ruth Kark (Jerusalem: Yad Ben-Zvi, 1990) (Hebrew), 13, 13–14; Henry Near, "Redemption of the Soil and of Man: Pioneering in Labor Zionist Ideology, 1904–1935," in *Redemption of the Land of Eretz-Israel*, 33, 43–44; Boaz Newman, *Land and Desire in Early Zionism*, trans. Haim Watzman (Waltham, MA: Brandeis University Press, 2011), 16–17.

8. Near, "Redemption of the Soil and of Man," supra note 7, at 41–44; Almog, "Redemption in Zionist Rhetoric," supra note 7, at 14–17; Newman, *Land and Desire in Early*

*Zionism*, supra note 7, at 20–25; Zeev Sternhell, *The Founding Myths of Israel*, trans. David Maisel (Princeton, NJ: Princeton University Press, 1998), 16; Yoram Bar-Gal, *Propaganda and Zionist Education: The Jewish National Fund, 1924–1947* (Rochester: University of Rochester & University of Haifa Press, 2003), 170–77; Haim Sandberg, "From JNF to Viva Palestina—UK Policy towards Zionist and Palestinian Charities," 22 *Trust & Trustees* (2016): 195, 196–98.

9. Asher Cohen and Bernard Susser, *Israel and the Politics of Jewish Identity: The Secular-Religious Impasse* (Baltimore: Johns Hopkins University Press, 2000), 33; Gila Stopler, "National Identity and Religion–State Relations: Israel in Comparative Perspective," in *Israeli Constitutional Law at a Crossroads*, ed. Gideon Sapir et al. (Oxford: Hart, 2013), 503, 510–16.

10. CA 8573/08 Ornan v. Ministry of Interior (Nevo, October 6, 2013), VERSA: Opinions of the Supreme Court of Israel, Translated Opinions, https://versa.cardozo.yu.edu/opinions/ornan-v-ministry-interior; CA 630/70 Tamrin v. State of Israel (1972), PD 26(1): 197.

11. Leviticus 25:13; JPS Tanakh 1917.

12. Leviticus 25:11.

13. Leviticus 25:23.

14. Numbers 36:7; Benjamin Porat, "Social Justice as Embodied in the Law of the Jubilee Year," 13 *Akdamot* (2003) (Hebrew): 77, 87.

15. Numbers 26:55.

16. Numbers 26:53.

17. Numbers 27:1–11; Numbers 36:1–12; Henry Schaffer, *Hebrew Tribal Economy and the Jubilee* (Leipzig: J. C. Hinrichs'sche Buchhandlung, 1922), 98–99; Jeffrey A. Fager, *Land Tenure and the Biblical Jubilee* (Sheffield: Sheffield Academic Press, 1993), 27–34; John Sietze Bergsma, *The Jubilee from Leviticus to Qumran: A History of Interpretation* (Leiden: Brill, 2007), 8–12.

18. Haim Sandberg and Adam Hofri-Winogradow, "Arab Israeli Women's Renunciation of Their Inheritance Shares: A Challenge for Israel's Courts," 8 *International Journal of Law in Context*, no. 2 (June 2012): 253, 255; Rassem Khamaisi, *Between Customs and Laws: Planning and Management of Land in Arab Localities in Israel* (Jerusalem: Floersheimer Institute for Policy Studies, 2007) (Hebrew), 28.

19. Yossi Katz, *The Land Shall Not Be Sold in Perpetuity: The Jewish National Fund and the History of State Ownership of Land in Israel* (Berlin: De Gruyter, 2016), 4–5; Menachem Elon, *Jewish Law: History, Sources, Principles*, trans. Bernard Auerbach and Melvin J. Sykes (Philadelphia: Jewish Publication Society, 1994), 4: 1651–52.

20. "Yovel" (Jubilee), 22 *Talmudic Encyclopedia* (HaShut Project's ed., 2011) (Hebrew), §2, 7; Maimonides, *Melachim uMilchamot* (The Laws of Kings and Their Wars), 11:1.

21. Menachem Mautner, *Law and the Culture of Israel* (Oxford: Oxford University Press, 2011), 32, 41; Elon, *Jewish Law*, supra note 20, at 1918–19; Yifat Holzman-Gazit, *Land Expropriation in Israel: Law, Culture and Society* (Aldershot: Ashgate, 2007), 56–57.

22. Almog, "Redemption in Zionist Rhetoric," supra note 7, at 16; Katz, *Land Shall Not Be Sold*, supra note 19, at 3–6. See generally the resources in notes 7–8.

23. Author translation. Dror, supra note 3, J. Beinisch par. 26.

24. Numbers 26:54.

25. Theodore Herzl, *Old New Land: (Altneuland)*, trans. David Simon Blondheim, 1916 (Berlin: Contumax, 2015; first printed 1902, Leipzig), 77.

26. Herzl, *Altneuland*, supra note 25, at 77.

27. Herzl, *Altneuland*, supra note 25, at 77.

28. Katz, *Land Shall Not Be Sold*, supra note 19, 1–12.

29. Porat, "Social Justice," supra note 14, at 87.
30. Author translation. Aharon David Gordon, "To My Friends in the Spirit of Defeat," Ben Yehuda Project, 1919 (Hebrew), https://benyehuda.org/gordon_ad/victis_amicis_spiritu.html#_ftn1.
31. Decision No. 1 of the Israel Land Council "Land Policy in Israel" (May 17, 1965), Section 3A, 4B (Hebrew).
32. Decision No. 166 of the Israel Lands Council "Jubilee Lease—Rules for Extending the Land Lease Contract for Urban Housing and Businesses, Workshops and Municipal Industrial Enterprises" (February 23, 1976) (Hebrew).
33. Chaim Gans, "The Palestinian Right of Return and the Justice of Zionism," 5 *Theoretical Inquiries in Law* (2004): 269, 272–73; Shlomo Avineri, *The Making of Modern Zionism: The Intellectual Origins of the Jewish State* (New York: Basic Books, 1981; first published 1981, Perseus Books, Philadelphia), 247.
34. Sammy Smooha, *Still Playing by the Rules: Index of Arab-Jewish Relations in Israel 2015* (Haifa: Pardes, 2017), 33–34.
35. Hussein Abu Hussein and Fiona McKay, *Access Denied: Palestinian Land Rights in Israel* (London: Zed Books, 2003), 143; Alexandre Kedar, "The Legal Transformation of Ethnic Geography: Israeli Law and the Palestinian Landholder 1948–1967," 33 *NYU J. Int'l L. & Pol.* (2001): 923, 947.
36. Yossi Katz, *The Battle for the Land* (Jerusalem: Hebrew University Press, 2005), 163–204, 275–87.
37. Provisional Government of Israel, The Declaration of the Establishment of the State of Israel, 1 *Official Gazette* 1, May 14, 1948 (Hebrew), official English translation, Knesset: https://www.knesset.gov.il/docs/eng/megilat_eng.htm.
38. Author translation. Michal Oren-Nordheim, "And the Land Will Not Be Sold in Perpetuity," 16 *Studies in the Geography of the Land of Israel* (2003) (Hebrew): 146, 159.
39. Author translation. Oren-Nordheim, "And the Land," supra note 38, at 161.
40. Minister of Finance Levi Eshkol to the Knesset, *Divrei Ha-Knesset*, vol. 28, col. 675 (1960) (Hebrew).
41. Emphasis added. Bill of Basic Law: The Land of the People 5719–1959, *Hatzaot-Hok* (Bills of Law) 272 (Hebrew).
42. Emphasis added. MK Zerah Warhaftig to the Knesset, *Divrei Ha-Knesset*, vol. 28, col. 1920, 1925 (1960) (Hebrew).
43. Emphasis added. MK Yohanan Bader to the Knesset, *Divrei Ha-Knesset*, vol. 28, col. 680 (1960).
44. MK Ya'acov Hazan, *Divrei Ha-Knesset*, vol. 28, col. 689 (1960) (Hebrew).
45. Rassem Khamaisi, "Centrifugal and Centripetal Factors' Influence on the Structure of the Arab Settlement," in *The Arab Community in Israel: Geographic Processes*, ed. David Grossman and Avinoam Meir (Bar Ilan: Ben Gurion and Hebrew University Press, 1994) (Hebrew), 114, 122; Rassem Khamaisi, *Planning and Housing among Arabs in Israel* (Tel Aviv: International Center for Peace in the Middle East, 1990) (Hebrew), 144–47, 216–19.
46. Minister of Finance Levi Eshkol to the Knesset, *Divrei Ha-Knesset*, vol. 28, col. 708 (1960) (Hebrew); MK Joseph Serlin, *Divrei Ha-Knesset*, vol. 28, Col. 693; MK Eliyahu Meridor, *Divrei Ha-Knesset*, vol. 29, col. 1921 (1960) (Hebrew); MK Shneor Zalman Abramov, *Divrei Ha-Knesset*, vol. 28, col. 1921; MK Moshe Sneh, *Divrei Ha-Knesset*, vol. 28, col. 1921–22.
47. Katz, *Land Shall Not Be Sold*, supra note 19, at 80.

48. The Jewish National Fund, Minutes of the Board of Directors' Meeting (May 27, 2009) (Hebrew); The Jewish National Fund, "Response to Petitions for an Order Nisi and Requests for an Interim Injunction," in HCJ 9205/04 Adalah—the Legal Center for Arab Minority Rights in Israel v. Israel Lands Administration § 92–94 (filed on December 9, 2004) (Hebrew) (copies of these two documents are reserved by the author).

49. HCJ 9205/04 Adalah—the Legal Center for Arab Minority Rights in Israel v. Israel Land Administration (Nevo, September 28, 2008) (Hebrew):

> In the previous hearing, the Attorney General's counsel noted that . . . [in] any case in which a non-Jew wins the land in the tender, the ILA will make a land swap with the JNF and provide land to the JNF in areas that are not developed and are not intended for marketing. Today, the State Attorney announced that the arrangement that currently stands as an interim arrangement will also apply to rights in land transferred by the current holder to the next holder, that is, it will then be possible to sell apartments and to transfer and register them. . . . There is no doubt that this issue must be permanently resolved. We assume that the position of the Attorney General regarding the application of the principle of equality to the marketing of land held by the Israel Lands Administration and its management will be borne by the subjects and negotiators.

50. Benny Morris, *The Birth of the Palestinian Refugee Problem Revisited* (Cambridge: Cambridge University Press, 2004), 341–82; Arnon Golan, *Wartime Spatial Changes: Former Arab Territories within the State of Israel, 1948–1950* (Sde Boker: Ben Gurion Heritage Center, Ben Gurion University of the Negev, 2001) (Hebrew), 236, 243.

51. MK Yohanan Bader to the Knesset, *Divrei Ha-Knesset*, vol. 28, col. 680 (1960) (Hebrew).

52. Agricultural Settlement (Restrictions on the Use of Agricultural Land and Water) Law, 5727–1967, *Sefer Ha-Hukim* 108 (Hebrew).

53. MK Shlomo Rosen, *Divrei Ha-Knesset*, vol. 47, col. 160 (1967) (Hebrew); MK Uri Avnery, *Divrei Ha-Knesset*, vol. 47, col. 165; MK Tawfik Taubi, *Divrei Ha-Knesset*, vol. 47, col. 168.

54. Shmuel Soler, "Head of the Givat Ada Council: 'They Allocated Land to People Who . . . Went Abroad,'" *Ma'ariv*, November 4, 1962 (Hebrew) (explains that the head of the Givat Ada Regional Council denied "false rumors" about the sublease of JNF lands to Arabs from Nazareth but confirmed that over the years workers who shared winter crops cultivated these lands); Davar Staff, "Jews Lease Land and Sub-lease It to the Arabs," *Davar*, July 13, 1975 (Hebrew) (complaint by the mayor of Or Yehuda to the head of the Israel Lands Council); Aharon Priel, "A Public Committee Will Try to Prevent Sublease of Land," *Ma'ariv*, September 30, 1980 (Hebrew) (explains that the Israel Land Council is concerned about reports of subleasing to "Arab farmers," including "farmers beyond the Green Line").

55. Proposed Bill Land Law (Granting Rights to Foreigners), 5741–1981, *Hatzaot-Hok* 16 (Hebrew); Minister of Justice Moshe Nissim to Knesset, *Divrei Ha-Knesset*, vol. 90, col. 60 (1981) (Hebrew).

56. MKs Toubi, Shilansky, Gross, Sheinman, Tamir, and Hashay, *Divrei Ha-Knesset*, vol. 90, col. 63, 68, 70, 78, 79, 80 (1981) (Hebrew); Zvi Lavi, "Laws for the Protection of State Lands from Invaders and Strangers—Approved," *Davar*, January 16, 1980 (Hebrew); Israel Landers, "The Emma Berger Law," *Davar*, October 15, 1980 (Hebrew); Baruch Meiri, "A New Law Will Prevent the Sale of Land in Israel to Foreigners," *Ma'ariv*, September 16, 1980 (Hebrew).

57. MKs Hausner, Tamir, *Divrei Ha-Knesset*, vol. 90, col. 71, 79 (1981) (Hebrew).

58. Decision No. 259 of the Israel Lands Council "Granting Land Rights to Foreigners" (June 29, 1982) (Hebrew).

59. Decision No. 1148 of the Israel Lands Council "Granting Land Rights to Foreigners and Those Entitled to Immigrate to Israel under the Law of Return, 5710–1950" (March 9, 2008) (Hebrew). Previous versions: Decisions No. 1111 (May 21, 2007), No. 371 (February 16, 1988), No. 342 (November 11, 1986).

60. Minutes of Session No. 36 of the Economics Committee of the Eighteenth Knesset 9 (June 23, 2009) (Hebrew); MK Mula, Kadima feared that "some rich man from Iran [would] come and buy all the lands of Israel."

61. Decision No. 1185 of the Israel Lands Council, "Reform in the Administration of Israel Lands" § 3.8.2 (December 28, 2009) (Hebrew); Decision No. 1144 of the Israel Lands Council, "Allocation of Land Ownership for Industrial and Commercial Purposes" §2 (March 9, 2008) (Hebrew); Article 1.3 of Decision No. 1066 of the Israel Lands Council, "Reforming the Land of Israel" §1.3 (January 11, 2006) (Hebrew).

62. The Israel Lands Law (Amendment No. 3), 5771–2011, *Sefer Ha-Hukim* 754 (Hebrew); Amended §2a of the Israel Lands Authority Law, 5720–1960 and §4(19)(c) of the Israel Lands Authority Law, 5720–1960 (previously named Israel Lands Administration Law) (Hebrew).

63. Israel Lands Law, §2a(b)(4)(a).

64. Proposed Bill Land Law (Amendment No. 3) Restriction on the Purchase or Transfer of Rights in Real Estate to Foreigners, 5771–2011, *Hatzaot-Hok Knesset* 43 (Hebrew).

65. Ayala Hasson, "A Dunam Here and a Dunam There," *Weekly Diary Program, Channel 1*, May 7, 2010 (Hebrew), http://www.youtube.com/watch?v=N3p7ysvPo3E (report on the purchase of land in Rosh Pina by Arab citizens of Israel: first it was claimed that the purchase was financed by foreigners, but the claim was later denied. The program also reported an attempt to purchase land in Yavne'el by Arabs); Chen Shalita, "Nof Zion Buyer Believed to Be Bashir Al-Masri, *Jerusalem Post*, December 16, 2010 (Hebrew), http://www.jpost.com/Business/Globes/Nof-Zion-buyer-believed-to-be-Bashar-al-Masri.

66. MK Yaakov Katz to the Knesset, Minutes of Session No. 205 of the Eighteenth Knesset, (January 18, 2011) (Hebrew), 43–41; MK Aryeh Eldad, Minutes of Session No. 205 of the Eighteenth Knesset, 50; MK Nissim Ze'ev, Minutes of Session No. 205 of the Eighteenth Knesset, 53.

67. MK Nachman Shay to the Knesset, Minutes of Session 205 of the Eighteenth Knesset (January 18, 2011) (Hebrew), 40; MK Sheli Yehimovich, Minutes of Session 205 of the Eighteenth Knesset, 52; MK Shay, Minutes of Session No. 142 of the Eighteenth Knesset (June 9, 2010) (Hebrew), 73.

68. Attorney Yahalom Shara'abi, Israel Lands Administration, Minutes of Session No. 367 of the Constitution, Law and Justice Committee of the Eighteenth Knesset (March 16, 2011) (Hebrew), 10, 29.

69. Mr. Yaron Bibi, Director of the Israel Lands Administration, Minutes of Session No. 19 of the Economics Committee of the Eighteenth Knesset (June 3, 2009) (Hebrew), 6.

70. Testimony of Prof. Yossi Katz, Minutes of Session No. 19 of the Economics Committee of the Eighteenth Knesset, supra note 69, at 30. Economist Staff, "Buying Farmland Abroad: Outsourcing's Third Wave," *Economist*, May 21, 2009, https://www.economist.com/international/2009/05/21/outsourcings-third-wave; the map shows the distribution of investments in the purchase of agricultural land in the world in 2006–9. Fatmata S. Kabia, "Behind the Mirage in the Desert: Customary Land Rights and the Legal Framework of Land Grabs," 47 *Cornell Int'l L. J.* (2014): 709, 710; American, Chinese, and Saudi companies invest huge sums in purchasing land for agriculture, mainly in Africa. Elizabeth R. Gorman,

"When the Poor Have Nothing Left to Eat: The United States' Obligation to Regulate American Investment in the African Land Grab," 75 *Ohio St. L. J.* (2014): 199, 205; the acquisitions stem from expectations of an increase in food prices and the need for land for the production of biofuels.

71. Niv Elis, "Israeli Politicians Protest China's Bright Foods Purchase of Tnuva," *Jerusalem Post*, May 23, 2014, http://www.jpost.com/Business/Business-News/Israeli-politicians-protest-Chinas-Bright-Foods-purchase-of-Tnuva-353153.

72. Ruth Plato-Shinar, "Israel: The Impact of the Anti-money Laundering Legislation on the Banking System," 7 *Journal of Money Laundering Control* (2004): 18–37.

73. Joshua Weisman, "Restrictions on the Acquisition of Land by Aliens," 28 *Am. J. of Comp. Law* (1980): 39–66.

74. Katz, *Land Shall Not Be Sold*, supra note 19, at 145.

75. Constitution of the People's Republic of China (full text after amendment on March 14, 2004) §10, http://www.npc.gov.cn/zgrdw/englishnpc/Constitution/2007-11/15/content_1372963.htm.

76. Constitution of the Republic of Cuba 1992 §15, http://www.cubanet.org/htdocs/ref/dis/const_92_e.htm.

77. Yehuda Mirsky, "What Is a Nation State?," in *Defining Israel: The Jewish State, Democracy, and the Law*, ed. Simon Rabinovitch (Cincinnati: Hebrew Union College Press, 2018), 299, 300–301; Sandberg, "From JNF to Viva Palestina," supra note 8, at 198.

78. See resources in note 8 above.

79. Herzl, *Altneuland*, supra note 25.

80. Oren-Nordheim, "And the Land," supra note 38, at 148–49.

81. Author translation. David Ben-Gurion, *Memories* (Tel-Aviv: Am Oved, 1971) (Hebrew), 1:209–10.

82. Author translation. Abraham Granovsky, *The Battle for the Land* (Jerusalem: JNF Press, 1940) (Hebrew), 28.

83. Granovsky, *Battle for the Land*, supra note 82, at 31; Abraham Granovsky, *Land Policy in Palestine* (New York: Bloch, 1940), 84–85.

84. Abraham Granovsky [Granot], *Behitnahel Am (Settlement of a People)* (Jerusalem: JNF Press by Dvir Press, 1951) (Hebrew), 40; Granovsky, *Land Policy*, supra note 84, at 108–9.

85. Katz, *Land Shall Not Be Sold*, supra note 19, at 39; Oren-Nordheim, "And the Land," supra note 38, at 152, 155–58, 166–67; MK Aharon Zisling to the Knesset, *Divrei Ha-Knesset*, vol. 3, col. 298, (1949) (Hebrew); MK Yechiel Duvdevani, *Divrei Ha-Knesset*, vol. 3, col. 301; MK Avraham Herzfeld, *Divrei Ha-Knesset*, vol. 3, col. 302; MK Zerah Verhaftig, *Divrei Ha-Knesset*, vol. 3, col. 303; MK Moshe Sneh, *Divrei Ha-Knesset*, vol. 8, col. 890 (1951) (Hebrew); MK Shmuel Dayan, *Divrei Ha-Knesset*, vol. 8, col. 970.

86. MK Avraham Herzfeld, *Divrei Ha-Knesset*, vol. 28, col. 683 (1960) (Hebrew); MK Michael Hazani, *Divrei Ha-Knesset*, vol. 28, col. 686; MK Ya'acov Hazan, *Divrei Ha-Knesset*, vol. 28, col. 688; MK Nahum Nir, *Divrei Ha-Knesset*, vol. 28, col. 692; MK Shmuel Shoresh, *Divrei Ha-Knesset*, vol. 28, col. 694; MK Moshe Sneh, *Divrei Ha-Knesset*, vol. 28, col. 696–97; MK Amos Dgani, *Divrei Ha-Knesset*, vol. 28, col. 701; MK Kesse, *Divrei Ha-Knesset*, vol. 28, col. 703.

87. *Divrei Ha-Knesset*, vol. 28, col. 707 (1960) (Hebrew).

88. *Divrei Ha-Knesset*, vol. 3, col. 300, 305–6, 309 (1949) (Hebrew); *Divrei Ha-Knesset*, vol. 6, col. 2377–78 (1950) (Hebrew); *Divrei Ha-Knesset*, vol. 7, col. 195 (1951) (Hebrew); *Divrei Ha-Knesset*, vol. 28, col. 699 (1960) (Hebrew); Oren-Nordheim, "And the Land," supra note 38, at 167–68

89. *Divrei Ha-Knesset*, vol. 3, col. 301 (1949).
90. *Divrei Ha-Knesset*, vol. 28, col. 680 (1960) (Hebrew).
91. *Divrei Ha-Knesset*, vol. 29, col. 1918 (1960) (Hebrew).
92. HCJ 6698/95 Ka'adan v. Israel Land Administration (2000), PD 54(1): 258, 282 (Hebrew); formal English translation, Barak J. Par. 31: https://supremedecisions.court.gov.il/Home/Download?path=EnglishVerdicts\95\980\066\a14&fileName=95066980_a14.txt&type=5; VERSA: Opinions of the Supreme Court of Israel, Translated Opinions, http://versa.cardozo.yu.edu/opinions/ka%E2%80%99adan-v-israel-land-administration.
93. Ka'adan, Barak J. Par. 14.
94. Ka'adan, Barak J. Par. 19.
95. HCJ 244/00 The New Discourse Organization for a Democratic Discourse in Israel v. The Minister of National Infrastructures (2002), PD 56(6): 25, 38, 64 (Hebrew).
96. New Discourse Organization, 64.
97. New Discourse Organization, 66.
98. CA 1257/01 Avi-ezer v. State of Israel (2003), PD 57(5): 625, 643 (Hebrew).
99. HCJ 11087/05 General Cooperative Workers Company in Palestine Ltd. v. State of Israel, Naor J. Par. 1–2 (Nevo, August 21, 2012) (Hebrew).
100. HCJ 1027/04 Independent Cities Forum v. Israel Lands Council, Arbel J. par. 50 (Nevo, June 9, 2011) (Hebrew).
101. Dror, supra note 3, J. Beinisch par. 47–48.
102. Mautner, *Law and the Culture*, supra note 22, at 103.
103. Dror, supra note 3, J. Beinisch par. 45.
104. Independent Cities Forum, supra note 100, J. Arbel, par. 148.
105. Mautner, *Law and the Culture*, supra note 21, at 115; Arye Naor, "The Political System: Government, Parliament and the Court," in *Israel since 1980*, ed. Guy Ben-Porat et al. (Cambridge: Cambridge University Press, 2008), 69, 73; Guy Ben-Porat, "Political Economy: Liberalization and Globalization," n *Israel since 1980*, ed. Guy Ben-Porat et al. (Cambridge: Cambridge University Press, 2008), 91, 91, 97, 115; Eliezer Ben Rafael, *Crisis and Transformation: The Kibbutz at Century's End* (New York: SUNY Press, 1997), 127; Ronen Mandelkern and Gideon Rahat, "Parties and Labour Federations in Israel," in *Left-of-Centre Parties and Trade Unions in the Twenty-First Century*, ed. Elin Haugsgjerd Allern and Tim Bale (Oxford: Oxford University Press, 2017), 149, 166.
106. Minutes of Session No. 36 of the Economics Committee of the Eighteenth Knesset 36–35 (June 23, 2009) (Hebrew).
107. *Report of the Committee for Reform of the Israel Lands Policy* (Ronen Committee) 15 (1997) (Hebrew).
108. Proposed Bill The Economic Efficiency (Legislative Amendments for Implementing the Economic Plan for 2009 and 2010) Law, 5769–2009, *Hatzaot-Hok* 348, at 515; Israel Land Administration, *Report on Activities for the 2012 Budget Year* (2013) (Hebrew), 5.
109. Israel State Comptroller, *Annual Report No. 64C for 2013 and for the Financial Year 2012* (2014) (Hebrew), 321–22.
110. Criminal Case (Tel Aviv District Court) 10291–01-12 State of Israel v. Cherney, J. Rosen paras. 430, 440 (Nevo, March 31, 2014) (Hebrew) (Suspicion of receiving bribes); Sharon Pulwer, "Supreme Court Clears Ehud Olmert of Main Corruption Charge in Holyland Case; Cuts Jail Term," *Haaretz*, December 29, 2015, http://www.haaretz.com/israel-news/1.694309 (Yaakov Efrati, the head of the Israel Land Administration, was acquitted); Criminal Case (Tel Aviv District Court) 23843–06-10 State of Israel v. Ida (Nevo, April 28, 2011) (Hebrew)

(Head of the Contracts Section of the Israel Lands Administration was convicted of taking bribes); Criminal Case (Tel Aviv Magistrate Court) 8438/03 State of Israel v. Oded (Nevo, September 9, 2008) (Hebrew) (Conviction of district director in Israel Lands Administration of bribery and breach of trust).

111. Arik Mirovsky, "Israel Tops World in Increase in Housing Prices," *Haaretz*, March 13, 2017, http://www.haaretz.com/israel-news/1.776849; Tamir Agmon, *The Rise of Housing Price in Israel: Implications and Ways of Coping* (Knesset Research and Information Center, November 5, 2009), http://knesset.gov.il/mmm/data/pdf/mo2354.pdf (Hebrew) (The low contribution of public initiative to the number of housing starts until 2009 is one of the reasons for the increase in prices in the following period); Minutes of Session No. 9 of the Economics Committee of the Nineteenth Knesset "The Israel Land Authority's Monopoly and the Implications on Housing Prices" (May 8, 2013) (Hebrew).

112. §1a Israel Lands Authority Law as amended by §3 Israel Lands Administration (Amendment No. 7) Law, 5769–2009, *Hatzaot-Hok* 318 (Hebrew).

113. Proposed Bill The Economic Efficiency 2009, supra note 111, at 515.

114. Minutes of Session No. 36 of the Economics Committee of the Eighteenth Knesset 9–10, 15, 17–18, 57, 60 (June 23, 2009) (Hebrew); Minutes of Session No. 240 of the Sixteenth Knesset 55 (March 29, 2005) (Hebrew).

115. David K. Whynes and Roger A. Bowles, *The Economic Theory of the State* (New York: St. Martin's, 1981), 66; Stanley Fischer et al., *Economics*, 2nd ed. (New York: McGraw Hill, 1988), 64.

116. Richard D. Auster and Morris Silver, *The State as a Firm: Economic Forces in Political Development* (Boston: Martinus Nijhoff, 1979), 56.

117. Rachelle Alterman, "National-Level Planning in Israel: Walking the Tightrope between Government Control and Privatization," in *National-Level Planning in Democratic Countries: An International Comparison*, ed. Rachelle Alterman (Liverpool: Liverpool University Press, 2001), 257, 268; Douglass B. Lee Jr., "Land Use Planning as a Response to Market Failure," in *The Land Use Policy Debate in the United States*, ed. Judith Innes de Neufville (New York: Plenum, 1981), 149, 161.

118. William R. Lowry, *Preserving Public Lands for the Future: The Politics of Intergenerational Goods* (Washington, DC: Georgetown University Press, 1998), 3; John Rawls, *A Theory of Justice* (Cambridge, MA: Harvard University Press, 1971), 284–93.

119. Rachelle Alterman, "Who Can Retell the Exploits of the Israel Lands Authority? From the Aspects of Justifying the Continuation of Local Ownership of Land," 21 *Iyuney-Mishpat—Tel-Aviv University Law Review* (1998) (Hebrew): 535, 551; Daphne Barak-Erez and Oren Perez, "Planning in State-Owned Land in Israel: Toward Sustainable Development," 7 *Mishpat Umimshal* (Law and Government)—*Haifa University Law Review* (2004) (Hebrew): 865, 892; Yossi Dahan, "Who Owns This Land? On the Rights and Concepts of Distributive Justice," 8 *Mishpat Umimshal* (Law and Government)—*Haifa University Law Review* (2005) (Hebrew): 223, 235.

120. Emphasis added. §1a (1) Israel Lands Authority Law.

121. Emphasis added. §1a (1) Israel Lands Authority Law.

122. Emphasis added. §1a (1) Israel Lands Authority Law.

123. The Constitution, Law and Justice Committee of the Sixteenth Knesset, sitting as the Committee for the Preparation of a Constitution by Broad Consensus, Explanatory Version of Proposals of Constitution 11, 23 (2006), http://main.knesset.gov.il/Activity/Constitution/Documents/huka_for_print.pdf (Hebrew).

124. Dror, supra note 3, J. Beinisch par. 39.

125. Independent Cities Forum, supra note 100, J. Arbel, par. 49–50.

126. Ministry of the Interior, Planning Administration, *NOP 35 Follow-Up and Update: Phase III Report*, ed. Ari Cohen et al. (2010) (Hebrew), 11–12.

127. Israel Bureau of Statistics, *Israel in Figures: Selected Data from the Statistical Abstract of Israel* 5 (2019), https://www.cbs.gov.il/he/publications/DocLib/isr_in_n/isr_in_n19e.pdf.

128. Amiram Oren and Rafi Regev, *Land in Uniform: Territory and Defence in Israel* (Jerusalem: Carmel, 2008) (Hebrew), 11, 481.

129. "Nature Reserves and Declared Parks 1964–2019," Nature and Parks Authority, accessed June 6, 2020 (Hebrew), https://static.parks.org.il/wp-content/uploads/2018/06/5ccfdc961af7d.pdf.

130. "Information to the Public," Israel Antiquities Authority, accessed June 6, 2020 (Hebrew), http://www.antiquities.org.il/bestsitesmap_heb.asp.

131. The Constitution of the Russian Federation §9, http://www.constitution.ru/en/10003000-02.htm; Jane Henderson, "The Politics of the Emergence of Private Landholding in Russia," 7 *Journal of Comparative Law* (2012): 157, 169–70.

132. World Bank, *Global Monitoring Report 2012: Food Prices, Nutrition, and the Millennium Development Goals* (2012), xi, 24, https://openknowledge.worldbank.org/bitstream/handle/10986/6017/681710PUB0EPI00SE00NLY090Box367902B.pdf?sequence=1&isAllowed=y.

133. US Department of the Interior, Bureau of Land Management, *Public Land Statistics 2012* (2013), 1-2, 199–200, https://www.blm.gov/sites/blm.gov/files/pls2012-web.pdf.

134. 43 USC §1701 (1976).

135. 43 USC §1712(c) (1976).

136. Crown Estate Act 1961, 10 Eliz 2, c.55 (English).

137. House of Commons Treasury Committee, *The Management of the Crown Estate, 8th Report of Session 2009–2010* (2010), 1:11, 14, https://publications.parliament.uk/pa/cm200910/cmselect/cmtreasy/325/325i.pdf.

138. The Crown Estate, *Annual Reports and Account 2014* (2014), 10–11, https://assets.publishing.service.gov.uk/government/uploads/system/uploads/attachment_data/file/325139/TCE_2014_FINAL.PDF; Crown Estate, *Integrated Annual Report and Accounts 2018/19* (2019), 3, https://assets.publishing.service.gov.uk/government/uploads/system/uploads/attachment_data/file/811393/The_Crown_Estate_Annual_report_and_Accounts.pdf.

# 3

## PRIVATIZATION OF PUBLIC LANDS

*A Slow Maturation Process*

Following the political upheaval of the late 1970s, Israel drew away from its socialist foundations. Its leaders began to accelerate the economic march in a more right-wing, capitalist direction toward an unfettered free market, increased competition, and privatization. Privatization was fast becoming part of Israel's economic identity.

While the vast majority of Israel lands remained untouched by privatization, the process reached two very central and valuable components of the inventory: urban lands and agricultural lands. However, this did not occur overnight. Decisions regarding the transfer of public lands were preceded by a slow and lengthy turnover of government ownership to private individuals. The informal processes had begun years before the enactment of a formal policy on the privatization of public lands. Israeli scholars have diagnosed these informal channels of privatization as "camouflaged," "sprawling," or "gradual."[1]

Why didn't privatization occur overnight? As we saw in the previous chapter, the motives for governmental control of public land were mixed, and it took time for leaders and administrators to internalize the practical meaning of the ideological shift in Israel's economic orientation. The actual transition from centralized socialist control to privatization was accompanied by internal political dilemmas and conflicts.

Privatization, then, is not just an ideological change. It is a slow maturation process in which the legal and administrative frameworks confront a changing reality. This chapter will try to analyze this gradual shift in the economic identity of Israel toward free market economy through the prism of public land privatization. First, we shall review the mechanism that administers land privatization in Israel and then examine the steps to privatization in the two important categories of public lands, urban and agricultural.

## Administering Public Lands

### Israel Lands Council

The Israel Lands Council, established in 1960, is the governmental body responsible for drafting the principles and administrative policies of Israel's public lands inventory. The council's main authority is to "institute a land policy in accordance with which the Administration shall act."[2] It has also the authority to "supervise the activities of the Administration and approve its draft budget plan."[3] The council has shaped the State of Israel's land policies by making more than 1,600 decisions since its inception. These decisions have the status of secondary legislation. Practically speaking, then, Israel's land policies are primarily shaped by a governmental body and not through primary parliamentary legislation.

The Israeli Supreme Court has sharply criticized this state of affairs, claiming that it is the mission of Knesset legislators to establish the principles of Israel lands policy.[4] The court has further claimed that the extensive authority to shape Israel lands policy given by the Knesset to the council, a government body, amounted to "lazy legislation."[5] Yet the attempt to entrust the Israel lands policy-making authority to a government body was not a result of "laziness" but a fully intentional, calculated move by the legislature. The majority in every Israeli Parliament purposefully preserves the power to shape land policy for itself. The Israel Lands Council makes policy decisions in an internal, governmental, bureaucratic framework. The government appoints all council members, and the head of the council is always a minister.[6] No Israeli politician, from any end of the political spectrum, has ever welcomed the idea of relinquishing the power vested by the government to control the Israel Lands Council or the responsibility of outlining the state's land policies. Holding this power has traditionally been one of the most highly sought perks in the negotiations to building governments; this has certainly been the case over the past few decades. For that reason, the ministry under whose auspices the council operates undergoes continual change, in tandem with whoever wins control of the ministry (agriculture, housing, infrastructure, treasury, and the prime ministry).[7] It is the lot of the politically powerful to be granted control of the council, and that control generates even more political power. Over the past several decades, two prime ministers (Ariel Sharon and Ehud Olmert) served as council chair before becoming head of state; both capitalized on their position to enact reforms and changes in land policy.[8] During the 2015 negotiations over the thirty-fourth government, led by Benjamin Netanyahu, Treasury Minister Moshe Kahlon, head of the Kulanu party, demanded that any coalition agreement commit to appointing him chairman of the Israel Lands Council. He did indeed get his wish.[9]

As far back as the 1960s, politicians consciously and intentionally preferred keeping the charge of creating land policy in the hands of the council. They insisted on it, not just vis-à-vis marginal and technical issues one would not expect Parliament to deal with but also with regard to central issues of national land policy. For example, the bill that preceded Basic Law: Israel Lands proposed that "control of Israel Lands not be transferred in any way other than leasing or license-granting."[10] In deliberations over the Knesset's Constitution, Law and Justice Committee, disagreement arose regarding the proper length for leasing periods, and it was eventually decided that the clause be stricken from the law altogether and that the Israel Lands Council eventually be tasked with creating legislation as regards leasing.[11] Sixty years have passed since then, and no such legislation has ever made its way to the Knesset. The Israel Lands Council articulated the policy for transferring land control in its central compendium of regulation, and the ministers who chaired the council over the years had critical say in its formation.

## Formal and Informal Privatization

Because of the extent of the authority that the legislature placed in the hands of the Israel Lands Council, in order to obtain a complete picture of the privatization process, it is not enough to examine the main legislation. Ideological or interest struggles over privatization are conducted at lower levels. Much of the prominent privatization in Israel was not the result of informed Knesset decisions or of organized, top-down policy guidelines. These undertakings began at the bottom, in semi-administrative decisions made by the Israel Lands Council. The nontransferability of ownership was, and remains, the guiding legal principle in the administration of Israel lands. In effect, however, many so-called technical policy decisions have permitted deviations that eroded the principle and gradually created the reality of privatization. In this way, different aspects of the Israel lands have been undergoing an *informal* process of privatization. This means that the government retains formal land ownership while dispensing with its main practical application.

Such a process anticipates formal privatization. The government's insistence on ownership of lands, despite having dispensed with any external signs of it, is akin to closing the stable doors after the horses have bolted. There is no reason to retain formal ownership once the essential aspects of ownership are gone. What's more, it becomes increasingly difficult for politicians to conduct unpopular policy moves, such as high fee collection from hundreds of thousands of people who occupy Israel lands or the evacuation of thousands of those who do not manage to uphold their contracts with the state. The political profit produced by granting discounts and other benefits to that population is, in stark contrast, immediate and clear.

Therefore, informal privatization processes are expected to culminate in formal privatization. In Israel, formal privatization tends to occur only after the government has waived any long-term economic advantages to ownership. It functions as the closing act in the process of privatization, not the opening one. Therefore, the informal processes that precede it are of far greater importance. We will now elaborate on these insights by analyzing two types of Israel lands that are currently undergoing privatization: urban land and agricultural land.

## Privatizing Urban Land

### Formal Retention of Ownership and Leasing Policy

Although the government retained ownership of most of its developed urban lands until the start of the new millennium, it rented urban land and other real estate to private hands through leasing contracts, in a system that came to be known as "the public leasehold system."[12] Israel Lands Council's Decision 1 formulated the policy for transferring both urban and agricultural lands via leasing, and it is still in effect today. The decision established that urban lands "shall be transferred through lease only" and that the lease period "shall not exceed 49 years." At the end of said period, "the leasing rights may be extended for another period of 49 years, at the request of the lessee."[13] The leasing system reflected the policy of Israel lands ownership retention as expressed in the Basic Law. Leasing properties gives private bodies the right of usage and control for a defined period. It allows the lessor to enjoy rent and other payments and to update them in accordance with changes in the property's value. Essential aspects of ownership remain in the lessor's hands: the right to end the contract at the end of the leasing period, the right to predicate contract renewal on certain conditions and payments, the right to oppose the transfer of the leasing rights, and rights to change the property and types of usage it may serve. The government may use these tools to attain the goals of the socialist worldview behind Herzl's vision and the Basic Law: using the ownership of Israel lands for the good of the entire public.

Indeed, the possibility of privatizing urban Israel lands is mentioned in clause 2 of Basic Law: Israel Lands, entitled "Permission by Law." It stipulates that "Section 1 [which prohibits the transfer of ownership] shall not apply to classes of lands and classes of transactions determined for that purpose by law." In accordance with this allowance, the Israel Lands Law, 5720–1960 was enacted.[14] This law, lower in legal status than the Basic Laws, specified in clause 2, entitled "Permission to Transfer Ownership," the types of ownership that could be transferred. The clause allowed mostly for internal land transfers between different owners of Israel lands or for the exchange of public land for private land. The most prominent allowance for privatization was limited to no more than 100 square kilometers, to privatize Israel lands "for the purpose of non-agricultural development" and for "the transfer of the ownership of lands . . . which are urban lands."[15] Legislation regarding Development Authority assets had already provided a similar allowance in the 1950s.[16] The concern that foreign investors would hesitate to invest in urban projects if they were not to gain full ownership of the lands was the main reason for this exception to the rule.[17]

However, until the beginning of the new millennium, only about 60 square kilometers of public land were formally transferred to private ownership.[18] This amounted to less than a quarter of the then 251 kilometers of all built-up Israel lands.[19] Most of the lands that underwent privatization were urban assets that proved burdensome for the responsible bodies.[20] The majority of the public urban lands remained Israel lands.

## The Informal Privatization Milestones

Over the years, the government leased hundreds of thousands of housing units, business spaces, and other urban structures built on Israel lands to Israeli citizens. As the number of leased housing units increased, it became clear that the government would have to create a bureaucratic mechanism to actualize all leasing benefits by signing and renewing contracts, conducting and updating land assessments, collecting payments, granting permits, and listing transfers and other transactions in a registry. Meanwhile, the burden on the government and the lessees was becoming significant, and steps were undertaken to reduce their constant friction. Nevertheless, although they appeared to constitute merely technical and administrative matters not aimed at the transfer of land ownership to lessees, these steps were precisely what led to informal privatization and the creation of an irreversible reality. This process occurred first through the gradual unraveling of the government-owner's economic advantages and then through the sense of ownership it created among the lessees, which in turn created an expectation that the state would not reclaim its property ownership rights. The process virtually camouflaged the informal privatization of urban Israel lands[21] so that while the lands remained formally and legally under government ownership, the content and character of ownership trickled down to the lessees. We will now proceed to describe the important milestones in this informal privatization process of urban Israel lands.

The *first* milestone occurred during the 1970s, as expressed in the implementation of a policy allowing urban lessees to make a one-time, lump-sum requisite payment to the Israel Lands Administration at the time of signing. This payment, due at the start of the lease, replaced the combination of annual payments and payments in the event that the lessee wished to transfer the lease rights to someone else.[22] The new system applied exclusively to lessees of housing units in "houses containing at least four apartments on two floors."[23] This seemed to be a technical decision, meant to obviate the need for constant and periodic evaluation and collection. Concentrating payments at the beginning of the contract period ensured that the lessor and the lessee would have no need for one another during the extended lease period.[24] This progression was a sort of waiving of potential payments for the government in the event of significant increases in the value of lands not accounted for in the lump sums paid in advance. Loss of other income was caused by the significant discounts given to those who opted for the advance lump-sum lease payments, meant to encourage the lessees to take that option.[25] Strengthening bureaucratic efficiency seemed to offset these income losses. Yet this course of action had certain side effects that made it irreversible. The fact that lessees were making one large payment for a property, rather than smaller annual ones, blurred their experience as renters and encouraged a feeling of ownership. The lessees repressed the thought that at the end of the lease period they would have to pay a large, updated sum to hold on to the property for a new lease period. "From a psychological point of view," wrote Professor Joshua Weisman, this requirement could "seem like exploitation."[26] The lump sum affected the psychology of the lessees, allowing them to ignore the possibility that the rights acquired would not last forever.[27]

The politicians responsible for the administration of Israel lands did not overlook the sense of ownership that developed among Israel lands lessees. That is what led to the *second* milestone in the informal privatization process: the formulation of rules guiding the lease Jubilee, establishing the conditions for extending the initial lease period of forty-nine years for an additional forty-nine years. Work on the formulation of these rules began in the 1970s and stabilized in the mid-1980s. The main innovation was the decision not to collect initial leasing payments for the second lease period (80% of the land value). If the lessee were to opt for paying the advance lump sum when signing the renewed lease contract, he or she would then receive a significantly discounted price. Similar conditions, without discounts on capitalization, applied to annual lease payments of urban lands intended for commercial, manufacturing, and other industrial uses rather than for housing.[28] Although these decisions appeared to be technical and did not seem to interfere with the formal ownership of Israel lands, they involved the government's waiving of a certain amount of income that would otherwise have accrued to it as the owner of the public lands. The serial renewal of lease contracts for additional periods at discounted prices, effectively deferred the time when the government would actually see significant income from the lands and amplified the lessees' feelings that they would never have to return the lands to their formal owner.

Contributing to lessees' feelings of ownership was the fact that they paid for the building of structures on the plots and shouldered the expenses of development and taxes. Since the land's value was the result of the lessees' building investments, it seemed unfair to charge them rent for those buildings. For this reason, the Israel Lands Council decided that rental rates for urban property would be calculated according to the value of the land only, without regard to the value of fixtures that might be attached to it.[29] The lessees' significant contribution to the lands' value ended up greatly affecting the likelihood that they would return land to the state at the end of the lease period, since by then the state would probably be unable to afford to compensate them for their investments. The alternative, demanding that the lessees destroy whatever they had built on their plots before returning them to the state, seemed unfair in many cases, as well as economically unreasonable. The state would probably not have been able to implement such a policy without significant opposition from the public.[30] It should be noted that in the United Kingdom, legislation supported by the European Court for Human Rights decreed that in certain circumstances, long-term investments by lessees in leased properties would justify the transfer of ownership to them.[31]

## Switching to Formal Privatization

The changes described above created a clear contradiction between the government's stated policy of retaining property ownership and the practical disintegration of most of the advantages of ownership. Ownership turned into a formal burden with no practical utility. In an attempt to solve this problem, once every decade the government appointed a public committee, which made increasingly determined suggestions to extend the lease period of urban lands to 196 years or in perpetuity.[32] The central reasons given seemed technical: restricting "friction" with lessees and freeing the Israel Lands Administration from the burden of administering those lands.[33] Yet behind these suggestions was a desire to transfer ownership to the lessees, leading critics to brand them as nothing more than "a sleight of hand."[34]

Finally, the State of Israel came to the conclusion that there was no reason to continue with the "sleight of hand" and, at the turn of the millennium, began implementing a policy of immediate transfer of *formal* ownership to all lessees of urban lands who paid the discounted, lump-sum, advance rent payments for ninety-eight years. Such was the start of full, formal privatization of public urban lands for lessees. The state determined this process in several stages. First, the management of the Israel Lands Administration decided to start transferring ownership within the framework of the limited quota of urban lands that the 1960 law had already authorized.[35] In 2006, the Knesset amended that law and increased the maximum amount of urban lands for privatization to two hundred square kilometers. At that stage, privatization was limited to buildings containing at least four housing units.[36] In 2009, the Knesset further amended legislation, adopting a general privatization policy for *all* urban lands, including every kind of housing construction. The possibility of transferring ownership also applied to lessees of "business" structures, including "industry, handicrafts, offices, commerce, tourism or hospitality."[37] However, the council required certain lessees to pay the value of future development rights before transferring ownership.[38] The council's decisions enabled future privatization of structures in communal or agricultural rural settlements.[39] As of today, the Israel Lands Authority is working toward privatizing all developed public land, leased for housing and for business. In 2009, urban Israel lands were leased to about 800,000 lessees: about 63 percent for apartments in saturated buildings, about 32 percent for apartments in low construction buildings with fewer than four apartments, and the rest, about 5 percent, for commercial use.[40] From 2011 to 2018, the ownership of 631,000 properties was transferred. Lessees of tens of thousands of additional properties whose ownership could not be registered for technical reasons received letters of eligibility for ownership.[41]

With the present policy of privatization, government is actually waiving its claim to future income, which seems to contradict the constitutional principle of retaining ownership of Israel lands. Moreover, the quota of Israel lands that the law authorizes for privatization—about 800 square kilometers as of 2009—is three times as large as the complete 251 square kilometers of urban Israel lands that have already been leased.[42] In principle, this quota gives the government the option of transferring ownership of lands that have yet to undergo urban development. Concern over the loss of future public income has led a unique coalition of politicians and nongovernmental organizations (NGOs) from across the political spectrum to file a petition with the Supreme Court against the privatization of urban land. While the Supreme Court did validate the constitutionality of the privatization process, it warned that "transferring the lands must be done in proper measure, in accordance with the needs of natural population growth."[43] This warning implies that if the government should implement a "squandering" policy of superfluous privatization of its lands, the court would view it as a deviation from the constitutional framework allowed by the Basic Law.

The process of privatization of urban public lands in Israel has already passed from the informal stage of conceding economic advantages to the formal stage of transferring ownership to lessees. The process is moving forward but is currently limited to urban lands that have already been developed. Neither the government nor the Supreme Court are eager to expand the process to include nonurban or undeveloped lands, where the idea of public land administration still dominates. However, as we shall see, here too informal privatization processes have begun.

## Privatizing Agricultural Land

### Formal Retention of Ownership

Unlike urban Israel lands, agricultural Israel lands have not been affected by legislation allowing formal ownership transfer, and thus there is no formal privatization process over such lands. The scope of agricultural Israel lands is several times greater than that of urban lands. An area of about 4,400 square kilometers, or around 20 percent of all state land, is suitable for agricultural work.[44] Another 4,000 square kilometers are used for pasture.[45] Most of the agricultural territory and all pasture regions are Israel lands, administered by the government.[46] Decision 1 of the Israel Lands Council established that these lands, similar to urban lands, may only be transferred via leases for periods not exceeding forty-nine years.[47] Contracts for pasturelands never exceed one year.[48] As mentioned in chapter 2, the agricultural land, historically, was the natural target for efforts to retain government ownership because of the great importance that Zionism and the State of Israel ascribed to agricultural work in the process of renewing their hold on the Land of Israel. Retaining ownership of agricultural lands also fits with the narrower rationale of guaranteeing the production of public goods, as agriculture can affect public food safety, environmental protection, development of rural areas, and the strengthening of security in border areas. Retaining ownership of agricultural lands ensures the provision of these public goods in case of a political crisis. It also subsidizes agricultural work and protects it from factors that affect its stability, such as seasonal production, difficulties in matching supply and demand, high fluctuations in supply and prices, and dependence on the ever-changing provision of water. The State of Israel still views the protection and development of agriculture as supremely important.[49] Privatizing agricultural lands may endanger these goals and lead private owners to abandon agriculture in favor of nonagricultural endeavors. To avoid this, the state does not allow policies of formal privatization for agricultural Israel lands.

### Urban Pressure over Agricultural Land

Despite this refusal of formal privatization, agricultural Israel lands have confronted an informal privatization process, largely because of the ever-increasing demand to use agricultural lands for more profitable enterprises, such as housing, commerce, tourism, and industry. Israel is a small state with a limited inventory of lands in desirable areas and with steadily expanding needs, as we shall discuss in chapter 4. Increasing demands have led in practice, if not in law, to the lessening of Israel's agricultural impressiveness. Retaining the agricultural purpose of its lands has become, especially in the center of the country, secondary to immediately utilizing nonagricultural components or changing the designation to more profitable urban purposes.[50] This is the case both for the lessees who hold the land and for the Israel Lands Authority, which owns it. The continuation of the land's agricultural designation is a bargaining chip for the lessees in the battle over profits gleaned from designating agricultural land as urban. This battle is precisely what has delayed the designation change in areas where such change is crucial, and it is likewise a factor contributing to the price hike in Israel's more desirable areas.[51]

The declining appeal of agricultural lands is evident in the symbolic difference between the Israel Lands Administration's logo and that of the Israel Lands Authority, which took over the lands' administration in 2009. The administration's logo sketches wide swaths of land with dark-green lines, reminiscent of agricultural or pastureland; there is no representation of urban lands. The authority's new logo, on the other hand, gives more prominence to urban lands: the logo has only one green line, on a downward-facing bias, with a brown line beneath it representing the soil, a soaring blue line, and above these lines, seven black squares of differing sizes clearly representative of urban lands.[52]

### The Battle over the Profits of Urbanization: Cooperative Settlements

By the end of the 1990s, a public battle between the government and the representatives of the agricultural community erupted over the size of the share of profits the latter would receive from the changed designation of lands. While farmers claimed that they deserved relatively large shares, the government sought to restrict them as far as possible. This conflict led to a sharp division in public opinion, which has apparently become less sympathetic toward farmers than it was in the past.

The start of the battle was marked by a petition filed with the Supreme Court in the late 1990s by a social movement called the Eastern Democratic Arc and officially known as New Discourse: For the Sake of Democratic, Multicultural Discourse in Israel (hereon: the New Discourse case).[53] The petition was aimed at the new policy decisions regarding the change in designation of agricultural lands, known later as the Boeing Decisions because their serial number in the council's list of decisions happened to resemble the model numbers of Boeing planes.[54] The decisions had granted agricultural settlements two economically valuable benefits in the event of designation changes of agricultural lands for urban purposes: preemptive rights to receive properties without applying for tender in a new designation and the right to receive these properties for nonagriculture use at a discount. The discount was to be calculated on the basis of the new evaluation of the property, which would grow with the desirability of the area in which it was located. The Democratic Arc movement petitioned to void these decisions.[55]

The movement's founders claimed that the state should not give benefits to the farming community because doing so infringes on equality. Since the farming community was a well-off minority descended from the "founders" of the state who had emigrated from Eastern Europe, there could be no justification for giving them preferential treatment over weaker populations whom the movement saw itself as representing, such as "immigrants" from Arab countries and "native" Arab citizens.[56] The attorney general joined the petitioners in claiming that the court should void the decisions, but for different reasons. He based his stance on the claim that the discounts "are not suitable to the reality of lands today . . . therefore, they are unreasonable."[57]

The court accepted the petition and voided the decisions.[58] The ruling did not refer to the petitioners' sociological observations concerning "founders," "immigrants," and "natives," and it even praised the agricultural community's great, historical contribution "to the Land of Israel and the State of Israel."[59] The court based its ruling on the claim that the Israel Lands Council's decisions granted farmers exaggerated, unreasonable benefits arbitrarily defined by the value of the lands, thereby infringing on the principles of equality and distributive justice.[60]

Since the New Discourse case, the battle over the profits from designation changes have taken many different forms. The government formulated a "leaner" benefits policy for farmers who wished to change the designation of agricultural land: they would have to return the land to the Israel Lands Authority, in exchange for compensation of its agricultural value alone. The government is prepared to grant a middling additional sum for the return of land on the basis of the amount of time a given farmer has occupied it. It is even prepared to grant additional benefits at times, such as partnership in low percentages of urban projects to be built on the lands after their return.[61] The farmers, for their part, did not consider these incentives to be sufficient compensation and were in no hurry to relinquish their lands. A senior official at the Israel Lands Authority testified at the Knesset in 2014 that before the New Discourse case, "the agreements were relatively simple and the desire of the rights-holders of the lands to return them was much simpler. Today, it is much more complex."[62] A year later, he testified before the Israel Lands Council that "since [New Discourse] we are trying to create a new order regarding the return of lands following designation changes."[63]

Without strong enough incentives to leave the land, both sides simply sit around, preparing for the expected eviction. This, then, has become the main informal process of privatization: on the one hand, farmers stick to the agricultural usage of their current contracts and hold steadfastly to the land by flashing their Zionism, and on the other, because of the growing cost of land, they anticipate that the agricultural land will eventually be designated as urban land. Their adherence to the agricultural use of their properties serves the farmers as bargaining chips. At the end of the day, farmers hope to yield profits from the change in the land use. The state is gradually increasing incentives for voluntary eviction but, at the same time, threatening to terminate contracts and expand the eviction authority it already possesses.[64]

### The Mehadrin Case: A Metaphor for the Battle over the Profits of Urbanization

The above process is taking place in the context of agricultural land held by both cooperative settlements (moshavim and kibbutzim) and private commercial lessees of public agricultural land. A perfect example for this process is the Mehadrin case.[65] In the 1950s, the state leased to the Mehadrin company lands for planting orchards and groves.[66] The original contract did not include an express clause allowing owners to terminate the contract in the event that they needed the land for a different purpose. When the time came to renew the lease, the Israel Lands Administration conditioned the renewal on the inclusion of such a clause, under the assumption that one day they would need the land for nonagricultural purposes. The company opposed the addition of the clause and insisted upon its right to continue the agricultural designation of the lease according to the original terms.[67] The company claimed that it was interested in continuing its agricultural work and not in engaging in "economic land speculation."[68]

Although the company's main activity was growing and marketing agricultural products, the company's shares were traded on the Tel Aviv stock market as securities under the Real Estate and Construction category. It even has a growing department of profitable real estate assets. Its shareholders were major investment and real estate companies in the Israeli market.[69] In 2012, the Tel Aviv Regional Court accepted the company's stance that the new clause insisted upon by the state should not be included in the new contract.[70]

As a result, the company's 2013 report to its investors stated: "The company estimates that over the course of the next two decades, the designation of many hundreds of dunams of land leased to the company will be changed from agricultural to a different designation. The group's rights in those lands, including the level of compensation it is to receive (if at all) and its ability to continue holding the land with its new designation, whether through exemption from tender or otherwise, depend, among other things, on the lease contract that will be in force at that time."[71] The company's report makes it clear that it took into account the economic utility that could result from the designation change.

The state appealed the ruling, and the Supreme Court accepted the appeal, rejecting the company's opposition to the inclusion of a stipulation in the contract that the owner could repossess the land in the event of a designation change.[72] Justice Rubinstein noted that the appellants "do not adequately take into account the limited national need for agricultural land compared to the past" and that, in summary, "developing the land—yes, speculation—no, so it is for the Administration and so it is for the lessees."[73] Yet the court's instructions regarding the implementation of the authority to retract lands only encouraged the farmers to cleave to their control of the lands in their agricultural form, though neither side had any further interest in agriculture. Justice Rubinstein ordered the Israel Lands Authority to examine "seriously" and "carefully" the degree of necessity in changing a designation for the good of the public and to consider "the appellees' continued agricultural work on the land."[74] These guidelines may well strengthen the firm's dedication to agricultural work and need not eradicate all hope of making a fortune from it.

Indeed, only a short time after the court handed down its ruling, the controlling shareholders of Mehadrin (87%) approached the company's public shareholders (13%) with an offer to purchase stock at a price higher than in the stock market.[75] The public investors rejected the offer.[76] The explanation both for the offer and for its rejection may be that despite the Supreme Court's ruling, all sides continued to cling to positive speculations about the future of the land and the profits that would stem from continued control of it. All sides continued to "sit on the fence" following the rejection of the proposal, and the company's stock appeared on the Tel Aviv exchange's list of minimally traded securities between June 2015 and February 2017.[77] The scope of the stock's trade increased in anticipation of the May 2017 signing of an agreement that gave the company the right to high compensation for relinquishing control of certain agricultural lands it leased, which would revert to the Israel Lands Authority. The contract also granted the company percentages of a large residential project to be built on that land, without the need to apply to a public tender. The company of course reported this to its investors immediately.[78] The wait paid off. The company won a portion of the profits of the change in designation.

### Privatization of Agricultural Land Used for Residential Purposes

Another informal privatization process that took effect vis-à-vis agricultural Israel lands was the transfer of property rights very similar to ownership from the Israel Lands Authority to farmers at highly discounted prices for leasing as residences. This process appears to be a direct and natural continuation of the privatization processes in play over urban lands. The informal character of the process stems from the allocation system of most agricultural lands known as the "*Nahalot* (Estates) System."[79] This system allocates around 3,000 square kilometers of agricultural Israel lands to settlements of a collective nature, meaning *moshavim* (32,508 estates) and *kibbutzim* (35,402 estates).[80] The estate (*Nahala*), which is the system's most basic unit of allotment, includes as a single unit land used for agriculture and components used for other purposes, such as buildings used as the farmers' homes and other structures used for any and all production needs.[81] When the government enters into a lease contract of an agricultural estate, it is essentially leasing land used for many purposes, some more urban than agricultural.

The formulators of the land policy in the 1950s believed that the main use of the land was agricultural and that other uses were secondary or incidental. This outlook had three operative consequences: First, splitting up the different components of the estate was prohibited, as it was believed that together they formed a unit that served the land's agricultural purpose. Second, in exchange, farmers paid symbolic rental fees for their rights over all estates. Finally, the extension of the contract was contingent upon the farmer's continued use of the land for agriculture and residence on the property. A farmer who ceased cultivating the estate or who left it was obliged to return every component of it to the government so it could be allotted to someone else.[82] This policy suited the socialist-Zionist worldview of those who designed the system, with its emphasis on encouraging agriculture and subsidizing it. One of the main achievements of this system was that most of the estates are still being cultivated today.[83]

Despite this, reality has made the system dangerous and inefficient both for land holders and for the government because of the increasing demand for a more profitable use of agricultural land. In many areas, the value of the land's nonagricultural components, especially its residential component, significantly affects the value of the estate. Capital holders who desire to live in a large home on a pleasant estate are willing to pay sums anywhere between $1.5 million and $9 million.[84] The obligation to maintain the estate's agricultural use might seem like a small burden to bear. Yet the high price of estates, because of the residential component, actually prevents their purchase by those who are interested specifically in agricultural work, since the chances that agricultural activity will pay a return on the investment are extremely low.[85] Many of the long-term lessees of agricultural estates continue to hold on to the estates because of the nonagricultural advantages that they provide or that may come about in the future.[86] The fear of losing these advantages is the only thing that has prevented the abandonment of the agricultural lands thus far, but it also includes a risk of eviction for older farmers. The government also sees a disadvantage in this setup. The connection between different components of the estate has a negative effect on the commercial value of built areas on agricultural land, restricts their development, and amplifies the increase in the price of housing.

For these reasons, various public committees suggested long-term anchoring of the farmers' residential rights.[87] The state was concerned that if it permitted the separation of residential rights from the estate and protected them separately, it would weaken the incentive to continue tilling the agricultural areas and lead to exaggerated suburban development.[88] Ultimately, through a series of decisions, the Israel Lands Council formulated a policy granting farmers leasing rights identical to those of their urban counterparts in the residential component of their estates, in exchange for lump-sum payments of only 33 percent of the land value and the rights to it. Farmers were further granted the right to split off residential structures from the agricultural estate and to trade them, on the condition that at least one residential unit should remain on the estate and that the estate would continue to be used for agricultural purposes.[89] Several petitions appealed to the Supreme Court against this policy. Farmers claimed that the price was too high and did not take their investment in the properties into account. The Union for Distributive Justice claimed that the price for the benefits was too low and gave farmers an advantage over the urban population.[90] The Forum of the Heads of Israel's Large Cities joined the opposition, claiming that urbanizing rural areas would create competition with established cities and threaten their proper urban development.[91]

The Supreme Court rejected all the petitions. Justice Arbel summarized her ruling with the finding that the Israel Lands Council "gives proper weight to a complex reality, to the past as well as the present, to agricultural settlement as well as urban settlement, to the great efforts invested and the proper exchange that ought to be given for them, for change as well as renewal."[92]

In light of these developments, the fate of residential areas within agricultural settlements has now been determined. Although the Israel Lands Council has yet to decide on the question of formal ownership transfer to the farmers, essentially, the farmers already hold most owner's privileges.

## Concluding and Comparative Remarks

Privatization processes are clear expressions of a political movement to the right. International experience indicates that a democratic process of privatization does not occur at once. This was the case with the general privatization initiatives in the United Kingdom under the Thatcher government,[93] as well as with the privatization of public services in Israel.[94] The informal privatization of land rights has usually preceded formal privatization in China as well.[95] Urban and agricultural public lands in Israel have been undergoing a similar process. Privatization began with the gradual relinquishment of the state's economic rights as landlord, and only then did formal processes of privatization ensue. Israel's urban lands are already undergoing formal privatization. The agricultural land, whose area and potential profit is greater, is still at a stage of minor informal concessions to public rights.

Privatization reflects a deep ideological change in the country's economic orientation. However, an examination of the privatization process shows that such changes are gradual. They require adaptation and assimilation. The bottom-up reality triggers change more than policy dictated from the top down. At the forefront of privatization are bureaucrats rather than legislators. The privatization of Israel's land is therefore part of the State of Israel's maturation process. It is not easy to abandon the cultural, national, and economic motives of Zionism, which created the principle of preserving government ownership of the inventory. Yet the pioneers and dreamers, with ideals of equality, were slowly replaced by bureaucrats. The series of bureaucratic decisions that led to privatization points to the internal change in the values and worldviews of Israeli society in recent decades. This is another prism through which to view the changes in the economic identity of the state.

## Notes

1. Gilat Benchetrit and Daniel Czamanski, "The Gradual Abolition of the Public Leasehold System in Israel and Canberra: What Lessons Can Be Learned?," 21 *Land Use Policy* (2004): 45, 48; Rachelle Alterman, "The Land of Leaseholds: Israel's Extensive Public Land Ownership in an Era of Privatization," in *Leasing Public Lands: Policy Debates and International Experiences*, ed. Steven C. Bourassa and Yu-Hung Hong (Cambridge, MA: Lincoln Institute of Land Policy, 2002), 115, 116; Rachelle Alterman, *Planning in the Face of Crisis: Land Use, Housing and Mass Immigration in Israel* (Abingdon: Routledge, 2002), 52–54; Joshua Weisman, "Camouflaged Privatization of Land in Israel," 21 *Iyuney-Mishpat—Tel-Aviv Law Review* (1998) (Hebrew): 525, 527–28; Rachelle Alterman, "Who Can Retell the Exploits of the Israel Lands Authority? From the Aspects of Justifying the Continuation of Local Ownership of Land," 21 *Iyuney-Mishpat—Tel-Aviv University Law Review* (1998) (Hebrew): 535, 546; Daphna Barak-Erez, "An Acre Here, an Acre There: Israel Land Administration in the Vise of Interest Groups," 21 *Iyuney-Mishpat—Tel-Aviv University Law Review* (1998) (Hebrew): 613, 614–17.
2. §3 Israel Lands Administration Law 5720–1960, *Sefer Ha-Hukim* 57 (Hebrew), 14 LSI 50.
3. §3 Israel Lands Administration Law 5720–1960.
4. HCJ 244/00 The New Discourse Organization for Democratic Discourse in Israel v. The Minister of National Infrastructures (2002), PD 56(6): 25, 87–88 (Hebrew) (Hereafter "New Discourse case").
5. New Discourse case, 65–66.
6. §4a Israel Lands Administration Law 5720–1960 as amended by §3 Israel Lands Administration (Amendment) Law 5755–1995, *Sefer Ha-Hukim* 111 (Hebrew); §6 Israel Lands Administration (Amendment No. 7) Law, 5769–2009, *Hatzaot-Hok* 318 (Hebrew).
7. Changes in the definition of *minister*, Israel Lands Administration Law.
8. The identity of the chairpersons of the council can be monitored according to their signatures on council decisions. Ariel Sharon served as the head of the council 1990–92, 1996–99, and during part of his tenure as prime minister 2002–3. Ehud Olmert served as the council's chairperson in 2003–6.

9. Moran Azulay, "Kahlon Demands Israel Land Administration Portfolio," *Ynet-News*, January 12, 2015, https://www.ynetnews.com/articles/0,7340,L-4614404,00.html; §14.1 "A Coalition Agreement for the Establishment of the 34th Government of the State of Israel between the Likud Faction in the 20th Knesset and Our Entire Faction Headed by Moshe Kahlon in the 20th Knesset," April 29, 2015 (Hebrew), http://main.knesset.gov.il/mk/government/documents/Coalition2015_1.pdf; Moti Basok, "Government Approved the Transfer of Israel Lands Authority and the Planning Administration to the Treasury," *Marker*, May 19, 2015 (Hebrew), https://www.themarker.com/news/1.2640198.

10. §4 Proposed Bill Basic Law: Israel Lands 5720–1960, *Hatzaot-Hok* 34 (Hebrew).

11. Minutes of Session No. 25 of the Constitution, Law and Justice Committee of the Fourth Knesset 3–4 (March 30, 1960) (Hebrew), http://fs.knesset.gov.il//4/Committees/4_ptv_417532.PDF; Yossi Katz, *The Land Shall Not Be Sold in Perpetuity: The Jewish National Fund and the History of State Ownership of Land in Israel* (Berlin: De Gruyter, 2016), 104.

12. Alterman, "Land of Leaseholds," supra note 1, at 128.

13. §B1, B4 Decision 1 of Israel Lands Council, "Land Policy in Israel" (May 17, 1965).

14. Israel Lands Law, 5720–1960, *Sefer Ha-Hukim* 56 (Hebrew), LSI 49.

15. §2(7) Israel Lands Law 1960; Alterman "Land of Leaseholds," supra note 1, at 125–26.

16. Development Authority (Transfer of Property) Law 5710–1950, *Sefer Ha-Hukim* 278 (Hebrew), 4 LSI 151; State Property Law, 5711–1951, *Sefer Ha-Hukim* 52 (Hebrew), 5 LSI 45.

17. Minister of Finance Eliezer Kaplan, MK Yohanan Bader to the Knesset, *Divrei Ha-Knesset*, vol. 3, col. 309 (1949) (Hebrew); MK Yohanan Bader to the Knesset, *Divrei Ha-Knesset*, vol. 3, col. 301.

18. Ronen Committee, *Report of the Committee for the Reform of the Israel Lands Policy* (1997) (Hebrew) (Hereafter: "Ronen Committee 1997"), 18.

19. HCJ 729/10 Tnua'at Dror Israel v. State of Israel, Par. 18 J. Beinisch (Nevo, May 24, 2012).

20. Israel Lands Administration, *Report on the Activities of the Israel Lands Administration for the 1972/73 Budget Year* (1973) (Hebrew), 36; Israel Lands Administration, *Report on the Activities of the Israel Lands Administration for the 1989/90 Budget Year* (1990) (Hebrew), 110; Israel Lands Administration, *Report on the Activities of the Israel Lands Administration for the 1992/93 Budget Year* (1994) (Hebrew), 80.

21. Alterman, "Land of Leaseholds," supra note 1, at 131–32; Weisman, "Camouflaged Privatization," supra note 1, at 531; Joshua Weisman, "Long Term Lease as a Substitute for Ownership," in *Memorial Book for Gad Tedeschi: Essays in Civil Law*, ed. Yitzhak Englard et al. (Jerusalem: Sacher Institute, Hebrew University of Jerusalem, 1996) (Hebrew), 211, 224.

22. Decision 130 of Israel Lands Council, "Changes in the Conditions of Leasing Land to Saturated Public Housing" (September 10, 1973) (Hebrew); Alterman "Land of Leaseholds," supra note 1, at 132, 135–37; Benchetrit and Czamanski, "Gradual Abolition," supra note 1, at 49; Ravit Hananel, "The Land Narrative: Rethinking Israel's National Land Policy," 45 *Land Use Policy* (2015): 128, 130–31.

23. §6 Decision 130.

24. §2 Decision 130.

25. Alterman, "Land of Leaseholds," supra note 1, at 132, 135–37; Amir Kaminetzki, *Long-Term Lease* (Tel Avivi: Bursi, 2011) (Hebrew), 475–76, 482, 535.

26. Joshua Weisman, *Property Law—General Part* 255 (Jerusalem: Sacher Institute, Hebrew University of Jerusalem, 1993) (Hebrew).

27. Weisman, *Property*, supra note 26, at 248; Kaminetzki, *Long-Term Lease*, supra note 25, at 534–35; Alterman, "Land of Leaseholds," supra note 1, at 136.

28. §1–§2.1–2.2 Decision 146 of Israel Lands Council "Jubilee Lease—Rules for Extending the Lease Contract—Land for Urban Housing" (February 3, 1975) (Hebrew); Decision 269 of Israel Lands Council "Jubilee Lease—Rules for Extending the Lease Contract for Urban Land" (August 22, 1983) (Hebrew); Decisions 282, 537, 689, 714, 851, 968, 1061, 1090 of Israel Lands Council—Amendments to the Former Decisions (Hebrew); Alterman, "Land of Leaseholds," supra note 1, at 131–32; Benchetrit and Czamanski, "Gradual Abolition," supra note 1, at 48–49.

29. §B.3 Decision 1; Ministry of Justice, Land Appraisal Division, *Guidelines: Special Issues in the Appraisals Carried Out for the Israel Lands Administration* (April 3, 2011) (Hebrew).

30. Alterman, "Land of Leaseholds," supra note 1, at 129, 131.

31. James v. United Kingdom, 96 Eur. Ct. H. R Ser. A 67 (1986), para. 49.

32. Goldenberg Committee, *Report of the Public Committee to Examine Land Policy Goals* (1986) (Hebrew); Tzaban Commission, *Report of the Committee to Examine New Urban Land Reorganization* (1995) (Hebrew); Ronen Committee 1997, supra note 18; Gadish Committee, *Report of the Public Committee for Reform in the Israel Land Administration* (2005) (Hebrew) (Hereafter: "Gadish Committee"); Alterman, "Land of Leaseholds," supra note 1, at 130; Benchetrit and Czamanski, "Gradual Abolition," supra note 1, at 48–49.

33. Ronen Committee 1997, supra note 18, at 15.

34. Joshua Weisman, "A Lease That Is Renewed Permanently: A Miracle Drug or Deceit," 29 *Karka (Land)—Journal of the JNF Land Policy and Land Use Research Institute* (1987) (Hebrew): 2, 11; Weisman, "Camouflaged Privatization," supra note 1, at 527–28; Weisman, *Property*, supra note 26, at 220.

35. Israel Lands Administration, *Report on the Activities of the Israel Lands Administration for 1999/2000 Budget Year* (2000) (Hebrew), 50.

36. §11, 12 The Arrangements in the State Economy (Legislative Amendments for Achieving Budget and Economic Policy Goals for the 2006 Fiscal Year) Law, 5766–2006, *Sefer Ha-Hukim* 306 (Hebrew); §4(17) Israel Land Authority Law.

37. §1, 2(7) Israel Lands Law, 5720–1960 as amended in Section 13 of the Israel Lands Administration Law (Amendment 7), 5769–2009, *Sefer Ha-Hukim* 318 (Hebrew).

38. §4(17) Israel Lands Authority Law; Decision 1370 Israel Lands Council, "Reform in the Administration of Israel Lands" (June 22, 2014) (Hebrew).

39. § 3.9 Decision 1370 Israel Lands Council, "Reform," supra note 38.

40. Data provided by former Israel Lands Administration director-general Yaron Bibi to the Knesset. Minutes of the 19th Meeting of the Economics Committee of the Eighteenth Knesset (June 3, 2009) (Hebrew).

41. Israel Land Authority, *Report on the Activities of the Israel Lands Authority for the Budget Year 2018* (2019) (Hebrew), 64–65.

42. §2(7) Israel Lands Law, as amended in 2009; see also supra note 19.

43. Dror case, supra note 19, J. Beinisch at par. 39.

44. Israel Bureau of Statistics, *Israel in Figures: Selected Data from the Statistical Abstract of Israel* 5 (2019), https://www.cbs.gov.il/he/publications/DocLib/isr_in_n/isr_in_n19e.pdf.

45. Ministry of Agriculture and Rural Development, "Pasture Authority" (Hebrew), accessed October 23, 2017, http://www.moag.gov.il/yhidotmisrad/technun_calcali/rashut _miree/Pages/default.aspx.

46. Data provided by the Israel Lands Administration to the Committee for Examination of the Land Policy for the Management of Agricultural Land, which is included in the Israeli

Lands Law and was appointed by the government of Israel in October 2010. The author was a member of this committee. Author's record dated January 20, 2011, July 21, 2011 (Hebrew).

47. §A3 Decision 1.

48. Ministry of Agriculture and Rural Development, "Pasture Authority," supra note 45.

49. Ministry of Agriculture and Rural Development, "Ministry Vision and Goals for 2017," accessed June 9, 2020, http://www.moag.gov.il/en/About%20the%20Ministry/Pages/Ministry_Vision.aspx.

50. Yoav Gal and Efrat Hadas, "Land Allocation: Agriculture vs. Urban Development in Israel," 31 *Land Use Policy* (2013): 498, 500–502.

51. Haim Sandberg, *Basic Law: Israel Lands—Commentary*, Commentary on the Basic Laws Series, ed. Izhak Zamir (Jerusalem: Sacher Institute, Hebrew University of Jerusalem, 2016) (Hebrew), 124–28; Daniel Felsenstein and Ziv Rubin, "Supply Side Constraints in the Israeli Housing Market: The Impact of State Owned Land," 65 *Land Use Policy* (2017): 266, 268, 274–75.

52. Israel Lands Administration, *Report on Activities for the 2012 Budget Year* (2013) (Hebrew), 1, https://land.gov.il/doclib5/dochshnati_2012.pdf; Israel Land Authority, *Report on Activities for the 2013 Budget Year* (2014) (Hebrew), 1, https://land.gov.il/doclib5/dochshnati_2013.pdf.

53. New Discourse case, supra note 4.

54. Decision 717 of the Israel Lands Council "Long-Leasing of Land for Factories of Kibbutzim, Collective Moshavim, Moshavim and Cooperative Villages"(June 20, 1995) (Hebrew); Decision 727 of the Israel Lands Council "Agricultural Land Whose Purpose Was Changed under the Israel Lands Administration Law, 5720-1960" (July 3, 1995) (Hebrew); Decision 737 of the Israel Lands Council "Expansion of Residential Units in Agricultural Settlements That Are Workers' Moshav, Cooperative Village, Cooperative Moshav, Kibbutz or Agricultural Cooperative Society" (December 17, 1995) (Hebrew); Ravit Hananel, "Zionism and Agricultural Land: National Narratives, Environmental Objectives, and Land Policy in Israel," 27 *Land Use Policy* (2010): 1160, 1167.

55. New Discourse case, supra note 4.

56. Hananel, "Zionism and Agricultural Land," supra note 54, at 1164; Daphna Barak-Erez, "The Administrative Process as a Domain of Conflicting Interests," 6 *Theoretical Inquiries in Law* (2005): 193, 205; Benchetrit and Czamanski, "Gradual Abolition," supra note 1, at 51; §59, 102, 115 "The Petitioner's Petition in the New Discourse Case" (Hebrew) (a copy reserved with the author).

57. New Discourse Case, supra note 4, at 54.

58. New Discourse Case, supra note 4, at 84.

59. New Discourse Case, supra note 4, at 64.

60. New Discourse Case, supra note 4, at 70–79.

61. Decisions of Israel Lands Council (Consolidated) §8.18 (April 2019) (Hebrew).

62. Testimony of Mr. Ilan Dgani, Director of the Marketing Department of the Israel Lands Authority, Minutes of Session No. 268 of the Internal Affairs and Environment Committee of the Nineteenth Knesset (April 29, 2014) (Hebrew).

63. Testimony of Mr. Ilan Dgani, Director of the Marketing Department of the Israel Lands Authority, Israel Land Council, in "Transcript of the Israel Land Council 29 June 2015 Meeting" (June 29, 2015), Israel Land Authority, accessed June 9, 2020 (Hebrew), https://land.gov.il/land_policy/landcouncil/doclib/protocolm_29062015.pdf.

64. §4A of the Public Land (Land Evacuation) Law, 5741-1981, as amended in Section 4 of the Public Land Law (Removal of Invaders) (Amendment), 5765–2005, *Sefer Ha-Hukim*

106 (Hebrew); §29A–29I of Promotion of Constructions in Preferred Housing Compounds (Temporary Order) Law, 5764–2014, as amended in the Promotion of Construction in Preferred Housing Compounds (Temporary Order) (Amendment No. 3), 5766–2016, *Sefer Ha-Hukim* 682 (Hebrew) and Promotion of Constructions in Preferred Housing Compounds (Temporary Order) (Amendment No. 4), 5767–2017 *Sefer Ha-Hukim* 1162 (Hebrew).

65. CA 8325/12 State of Israel Israel Lands Administration v. Mehadrin Ltd. (Nevo, June 5, 2014) (Hebrew) (Hereafter "Mehadrin case").
66. Mehadrin case, Justice Rubinstein at section 1–3.
67. Mehadrin case, Justice Rubinstein at section 9.
68. Mehadrin case, Justice Rubinstein at section 58.
69. "Mehadrin Ltd.," Tel Aviv Stock Exchange, accessed June 9, 2020 (Hebrew), http://maya.tase.co.il/company/686.
70. (Tel Aviv District Court) 1523/07 Mehadrin Ltd. v. Israel Lands Administration (Nevo, September 27, 2012) (Hebrew).
71. Author's translation. "Mehadrin Ltd., Periodic Report for 2013" 52 (March 2, 2014), Tel Aviv Stock Exchange, accessed June 9, 2020 (Hebrew), http://mayafiles.tase.co.il/RPdf/881001-882000/P881766-00.pdf.
72. Mehadrin case, supra note 65, Justice Rubinstein at section 41, 49; Justice Barak Erez at section 1.
73. Mehadrin case, Justice Rubinstein at section 52.
74. Mehadrin case, Justice Rubinstein at section 51.
75. "Mehadrin Ltd., Details of a Full Tender Offer," 9–6 (June 1, 2014), Tel Aviv Stock Exchange, accessed June 9, 2020 (Hebrew), http://mayafiles.tase.co.il/RPdf/900001-901000/P900744-00.pdf.
76. "Delek Group, Unaudited Financial Statements as of June 30, 2014," 4 (August 28, 2014), Tel Aviv Stock Exchange, accessed June 9, 2020 (Hebrew), http://maya.tase.co.il/bursa/report.asp?report_cd=917640
77. "Mehadrin Ltd., Condensed Financial Statements as of March 31, 2015," 11 (May 12, 2015), Tel Aviv Stock Exchange, accessed June 9, 2020 (Hebrew), https://maya.tase.co.il/reports/details/965739/2/0.
78. "Mehadrin Ltd., An Immediate Report on an Event or Matter Deviating from the Corporation's Ordinary Business—The Signing of a Land Restitution Agreement with the Israel Land Authority" (May 4, 2017), Tel Aviv Stock Exchange, accessed June 9, 2020 (Hebrew), http://maya.tase.co.il/reports/details/1095835.
79. §A.4.a Decision 1.
80. Data provided by the Israel Lands Administration to the Committee for Examination of the Land Policy for the Management of Agricultural Land, which is included in the Israeli Lands Law, which was appointed by the government of Israel in October 2010. The author was a member of the committee. Author's record dated January 20, 2011 (Hebrew).
81. §A.1, A.7 Decision 1.
82. §A5–A9 Decision 1; Decision 427 of the Israel Lands Council "Lease Fees for Agricultural Land under the Israel Lands Administration Law, 5719–1960" (August 3, 1989) (Hebrew).
83. Data provided by the Ministry of Agriculture (Mr. Shay Dotan) to the Committee for Examination of the Land Policy for the Management of Agricultural Land, included in the Israeli Lands Law, which was appointed by the government of Israel in October 2010. The author was a member of the committee. Author's record dated February 3, 2011 (Hebrew).

84. Nimrod Bousso, "The Transformation of the Moshav: From Chicken Coops to Mansions," *Haaretz*, June 26, 2015, http://www.haaretz.com/israel-news/business/real-estate /.premium-1.663002; Ministry of Justice, Land Appraisal Division, *Guidelines: Preparation of Appraisals for the Calculation of Consent Fees in "Nahala" (Estate)* (December 2007) (Hebrew).

85. Gideon Vitkon, "Agricultural Land Management Policy in Israel," 11 *Mekarkein* (Real Estate) (2012) (Hebrew): 103–4.

86. Larisa Fleischmann et al., *Changes in the Nature of Agriculture and the Farmland: Attitudes of Residents of the Rural Area in the Central Region* (Jerusalem: Jerusalem Institute for Policy Research, 2009) (Hebrew), 39.

87. Ronen Committee 1997, supra note 18, at 20–31; Milgrom Committee, *Report of the Inter-ministerial Team to Examine All Aspects of Changing the Designation of Agricultural Land* (2000) (Hebrew), 52–56; Gadish Committee, supra note 32, at 16; Haber Committee, *Report of the Committee to Examine the Rights in the Residential Area of the Agricultural Communities* (2005) (Hebrew), 35–36.

88. HCJ 1027/04 Independent Cities Forum v. Israel Lands Council, J. Arbel at par. 9 (Nevo, June 9, 2011) (Hebrew).

89. Decision 979 of the Israel Lands Council, "Determination of Rights in the Residential Plot in Agricultural Settlements That Are Moshavim, Cooperative Village, Cooperative Moshav, Kibbutz or Agricultural Cooperative Association" (March 27, 2007). Several changes have occurred in this decision since it was adopted. Its updated and integrated versions are now expressed in regulations 8.3.40–8.3.54 (Moshav) and 8.4.13–8.4.47 (Kibbutz) in the Decisions of Israel Lands Council (Consolidated) (April 2019) (Hebrew).

90. Independent Cities Forum, supra note 88, J. Arbel at par. 18, 21, 25.

91. Independent Cities Forum, supra note 88, J. Arbel at par. 19.

92. Author translation, Independent Cities Forum, supra note 88, J. Arbel at par. 148.

93. PBS Staff, "Public Interview," *Public Broadcasting Service (PBS)*, January 19, 2000, https://www.pbs.org/wgbh/commandingheights/shared/minitext/int_kennethbaker.html (an interview with Lord Kenneth Baker, minister for industry and information technology in Margaret Thatcher's first Conservative government).

94. Yoav Dotan, "Informal Privatization and Distributive Justice in Israeli Administrative Law," 36 *Hamline Law Review* (2014): 27, 30–33.

95. Ruoying Chen, "Informal Sales of Rural Housing in China: Property, Privatization and Local Public Finance," (Dr. Juris. diss., University of Chicago, 2010), 3–4.

# 4

## NATIONAL LAND PLANNING IN A SMALL COUNTRY

*Challenges and Innovation*

> It is small, our land, and how great are its troubles.
> Shmuel Yosef Agnon, *Only Yesterday*

ISRAEL IS A SMALL, DENSELY POPULATED COUNTRY CONSTRAINED by geographic and demographic limitations. Belonging to this small country is part of the Israeli ethos. As a popular Israeli song expresses it, "A little country with a moustache, half a pin on the world map."[1] Nevertheless, human capital, Israel's most valuable resource, has overcome natural limitations, and Israelis are rightly proud of their innovativeness and originality. Indeed, in recent years Israel has become an entrepreneurial powerhouse in many fields.[2] The tension between restriction and pride in entrepreneurship and innovation is a common characteristic of Israel's current identity.

In this chapter we examine how the notion of being small and the idea of being an innovative nation are both expressed in Israel's land planning. We follow this with an analysis of the planning challenges Israel has faced owing to its unique geographic and demographic situation, and the ways in which the principles that guide its planning institutions try to overcome these challenges. We shall then focus briefly on two innovative projects stemming from Israel's scarcity of land: the development of underground and maritime space.

## Israel's Planning Challenges

### *Small, Long, and Narrow*

Israel is a small country, one of the smallest in the region and in the world, spread over a mere 22,072 square kilometers.[3] It is larger in territory than city-states like Singapore and Monaco, principalities like Andorra and Lichtenstein, Mediterranean islands like Cyprus and Malta, and even Bahrain, Lebanon, Qatar, and Kuwait. It is significantly smaller than the rest of its neighbors in the Middle East, including Jordan, Syria, Egypt, Saudi Arabia, Iraq, and Iran. In Europe, only Montenegro and Slovenia are smaller than Israel, and in South America, only El Salvador.[4]

Israel is not simply a small country. It is long and narrow, about 500 kilometers from north to south, but its population is mainly concentrated in a narrow strip of about 200 kilometers along the western coastline and center of the country. The farther one travels from the narrow center and the Tel Aviv metropolis area, the sparser the population.[5] Israel's periphery accounts for most of its territory, and aside from some smaller and less economically established cities, the periphery comprises mostly agricultural, open, green, and desert lands. Most of the country's territory, uninhabited desert, lies in the South (the Negev and the Judean Desert).[6] Israel's continental borders with Lebanon, Syria, Jordan, Egypt, the West Bank, and the Gaza Strip adjoin the peripheral territories. Because these neighboring countries are largely hostile to Israel, even in times of peaceful relations, the border regions remain vulnerable to security threats. Settling in the periphery generally and the border areas specifically has always been considered one of the most important ways of maintaining state sovereignty.[7]

### *Crowding*

Israel's population growth rate is one of the highest in the world, with an average of 3.7 percent per year 1960–2016. Few countries reached such levels during that period, and those that did were mostly city-states (Singapore, Hong Kong, Andorra) and a few neighboring countries (Jordan, Kuwait, Qatar, and the United Arab Emirates).[8] While the current population growth rate, as measured in 2016, has slowed to 2 percent, it remains on the high end of population growth the world over and above the average rate for OECD member states and countries in North America, East Asia, Latin America, and Europe. It is on a par with average growth rates in most countries in the Arab world but lower than those in Jordan, Lebanon, Saudi Arabia, the Persian Gulf states, sub-Saharan countries, and the Palestinian territories of the West Bank and the Gaza Strip. This growth rate generally characterizes countries where the per-person income fluctuates between low (2.7%) to lower middle (1.4%).[9]

Israel is already an extremely crowded country. In 2017, its population density reached 395 per square kilometer, more than double the 1961 average of 161 per square kilometer. This is a population density higher than that of any Western country, with the exception of the Netherlands, at 505 per square kilometer. In the Middle East, only the Gaza Strip and West Bank (756 per square kilometer), Lebanon (587 per square kilometer), and Bahrain (1,848 per square kilometer) have a higher population density. Compared to the most highly populated countries farther away, Bangladesh, South Korea, Rwanda, Burundi, and India, the city-states of Hong Kong, Singapore, Monaco, and Macao, and the island states of Bermuda, the Maldives, Malta, and Mauritius, Israel's population is less dense.[10] In the next fifty years, Israel's population is expected to increase somewhere between 54 percent (1.08% annually) and 170 percent (3.4% annually).[11] If this prediction proves correct, Israel's population density in 2059 will reach between 501 and 880 per square kilometer and, with the exception of the city-states, it will have the highest population density in the developed world.[12]

## *Urban Spread*

Israel is also an urban country. According to the World Bank's indices in undeveloped countries, there is a high rate of rural populations, while in developed countries the population resides mainly in cities.[13] Israel is, in this regard, a typical developed country. The percentage of its urban population among the entire population is one of the highest in the world (around 90%).[14] This, however, is lower than the typical rate in city-states (e.g., Hong Kong, Monaco, or Singapore), some Persian Gulf states (Kuwait, Bahrain, and Qatar) and Belgium, Malta, Iceland, Venezuela, and Uruguay. Yet it has a higher rate than the vast majority of Western countries and neighboring Middle Eastern countries, including the Palestinian Authority and the Gaza Strip.[15]

In 2003, the average density in Israel's residential regions was at 7,700 per square kilometer, which was a 6.6 percent increase from 1998 (7,200 per square kilometer).¹⁶ When compared to the World Bank's findings of population density, measured in ninety cities across the world in 2000, Israel fit with the average population density for developing countries (8,000 per square kilometer). Its density is higher than the average in more developed countries (United States, Canada, Japan, and Australia—2,300 people per square kilometer) and in Europe (4,345 people per square kilometer) but lower than the average for Southeast Asia (16,495 people per square kilometer), Central Asia (13,720 people per square kilometer), and North Africa (9,250 people/square kilometer).[17]

The gap between the country's center and its peripheral areas is also evident in their respective densities. Cities in the center of the country have a population density ranging from 8,000 to 25,000 individuals per square kilometer. Of those, cities with a large concentration of ultra-Orthodox Jews, having a high birth rate, are the most densely populated. The farther cities are from the center, the less densely populated they are.[18]

Israel's developed and urban lands are growing at a relatively fast pace. Analysis of data collected in 2003 with geographic information systems (GIS) and aerial photos measured the total developed land area at 1,224 square kilometers, and the data from 2007 measured it at 1,300 square kilometers, constituting between 5.5 percent and 6 percent of Israel's territory. Approximately 70 percent of these (4% of Israel's total territory) were residential (about 840 square kilometers in 2003 and 900 square kilometers in 2007). The other 30 percent included industrial and commercial buildings, quarries, tourist sites, army camps, and roads.[19] The cumulative growth rate of developed lands was 4.6 percent from 1998 to 2003 (48.4 square kilometers) and 7.8 percent from 1998 to 2007 (83 square kilometers).[20] The annual growth rate of these lands in those years was 0.92 percent and 0.87 percent, respectively. This is a higher rate than that measured in Europe in the 1990s, based on a sample of fifteen major cities (0.75%).[21] According to research conducted by the World Bank, the average growth rate of developed lands in the greater Tel Aviv metropolis, which constitutes the majority of the settled lands in Israel's center, was significantly higher than the global standard, reaching 5.76 percent from 1987 to 2000 (from 166.5 square kilometers in 1987 to 340.31 square kilometers in 2000).[22] The average growth rate during those years, as measured in ninety sample cities around the world, was 3.2 percent, ranging from 7.2 percent in Central and South Asia to 2 percent in Europe and East Asia. High urban growth rates tend to characterize less developed countries, while more developed countries tend to have a slower urban growth rate.²³ Israel's growth rate was closer to those of underdeveloped countries.

The fast expansion of urban territory, especially in the state's core areas, may endanger the reserves of land meant for development and have a troubling effect on their degradation rate. For example, an average growth rate of 1 percent will exhaust 1,500 square kilometers of land in a hundred years. The same amount of land will be exhausted in half that time with an average growth rate of 2 percent. The ability to control and restrict these growth rates is, quite literally, an existential necessity for the State of Israel.

## Shortage of Land Reserves

Unique characteristics limit Israel's potential for urban spread. First, its long structure means that most of its land reserves are in peripheral areas, while the reserves in the state's center are continually shrinking. Already today, built-up land covers 64 percent of the Tel Aviv region, while that percentage shrinks as distance from the center of the country grows (5.95% in the North and 1.9% in the South).²⁴ Second, Israel has faced security threats from its neighbors ever since its founding, and restrictions have been placed on urban development as a result. Army training grounds cover about 30 percent of the total territory of the state, military building restrictions are in place in 11 percent of the country, and army and the Ministry of Defense compounds use another 5 percent.²⁵ Third, a sizeable portion of the state's open lands serve public purposes, including forest and park territories (7.3%) and agricultural lands (20%).²⁶ In a state with thousands of years of history, antiquity sites and ancient urban quarters further restrict urban expansion.²⁷

Widespread urban crawl may infringe on agricultural territories, lands used for security needs, and parks and nature reserves, although there is already pressure to restrict these areas. Infringing on those lands may have far-reaching economic, social, and environmental consequences. Specifically in Jerusalem, Israel's capital, additional political limitations delay the eastward urban expansion.²⁸ All of this has resulted in limited reserves of land for urban development, especially in the sought-after, core areas of the country. A survey conducted on behalf of the Israel Lands Administration in 2004 estimated the land inventory for development to be only 1,500 square kilometers, 7 percent of the state's total territory. At that time, planning for around 73 percent of the inventory, 1,095 square kilometers, was already underway.²⁹

Even optimistic scenarios for urban renewal and the actualization of capping plans show open lands for residential use running out no later than 2046, according to current assessments by the National Economy Council.[30] The council has further cautioned that "without urban renewal on a significantly larger scale, we will be faced with a planning catastrophe in which all open lands meant for development in the center of the country will run out."[31] Professor Alon Tal warns that "if the land is full now, with twice as many people it will be intolerable."[32] The State of Israel faces a significant challenge in determining how most efficiently to capitalize on its limited land resources while maneuvering between various conflicting public needs.

## Natural Resources and Natural Hazards

The continental area of Israel is blessed with a number of natural resources. The Dead Sea, with its southern end spreading across 265 square kilometers inside the country's borders, provides a valuable quarry reservoir, especially for potash and bromine.[33] In the southern Negev, there are also reserves of phosphate, clays and silica sand, limestone, and oil shales.[34] Using these resources has led to environmental problems. Exploiting the resources of the Dead Sea has recently caused parts of the sea to dry up and levels to rise because of the settling of salt high enough to reach beachfront hotels. Withdrawal of the water line has created sinkholes near the water's edge.[35] Phosphate mining in the Barir field in the Negev has raised concerns about potential health and environmental hazards.[36] The discovery a few years ago of large natural gas reservoirs in Israel's Exclusive Economic Zone (EEZ) of the Mediterranean Sea has enabled the state to achieve energy independence[37] but has raised concerns about pollution during the gas-production process.[38]

Israel enjoys many days of sunshine throughout the year, and the government means to increase the scale of electricity production from renewable energy sources, such as thermo-solar and photovoltaic, to 13 percent of all energy consumption by 2025.[39] One of Israel's fundamental problems is a chronic lack of water, which has afflicted the state and its agriculture since its establishment. The 1950s saw the construction of Israel's National Water Carrier to send fresh water from the Sea of Galilee in the North of the country to the South. Global weather changes over the past few years have made the water problem even more acute. In response, six of the world's largest and most sophisticated seawater desalination plants were built along the Mediterranean coast.[40] As the prime minister of Israel declared before the United Nations General Assembly, Israel has become a "global water power."[41] The Israeli planning system was required to provide solutions for these unique enterprises, including an allotment of land for infrastructure facilities and means of transportation, whether overland or within the country's maritime space.

Apart from its natural resources, Israel, with its borders along the Syrian-African fault line, is under constant threat of an earthquake. Seismological activity in the region has led to some strong quakes in the past and will undoubtedly produce more in the future. Until the 1970s, construction standards in Israel did not provide a sufficient engineering response to this danger. Many buildings erected prior to that time do not meet necessary structural standards. Coping with the threat of an earthquake is yet another challenge with which Israel's planning apparatus has dealt intensively over the past several years.[42]

## Summary of Challenges

The geography and demography of the State of Israel present its government with unique challenges. Israel, one of the smallest countries in the region and in the world, is long and narrow, with a densely populated center and a sparsely populated periphery. Its population growth over the past fifty years has been one of the highest in the world, and its projected growth rate over the next fifty years lags closely behind only the very poorest nations. Half a century on, at the current rate of population growth, Israel will become the most crowded of the developed countries in the world. Typically for developed countries, Israeli society is urban, and the majority of its population lives in cities. Since population density in the cities has already surpassed that of other developed nations, Israel has already fallen to the level of a developing nation. Its land development is increasing at the rate of undeveloped countries, while its land reserves are dwindling fast, particularly in the most sought-after areas. Security and environmental needs likewise restrict urban expansion. Israel has a plethora of natural resources to exploit in a unique environment and a heritage it desires to preserve.

In sum, Israel is facing many singular planning challenges. It must balance the natural attraction of the central areas with an endeavor to nurture and strengthen the periphery. It must deal with population growth and density, an increasing demand for real estate in the center, and the need to preserve "green lungs" and land reserves for the future. It must develop infrastructure and respond to nature's blessings and curses. Although Israel is not the only country with such problems, certain factors intensify the problems to unparalleled levels and require a degree of creativity and innovation on the part of the planning system. Brené Brown's famous statement that "vulnerability is the birthplace of . . . creativity"[43] is somewhat reflective of Israel's situation.

In the coming sections, we will examine the planning mechanisms for meeting the challenges listed above, the main policy principles that guide the planning system, and some of the creative and innovative long-term responses Israel is developing.

## Responding to Challenges: The Planning System

### *Planning Institutions*

Israel's planning authorities are the institutions responsible for providing an appropriate response to planning challenges. Ideally, the response should be swift and efficient and should meet the needs of both central and local governments. Israel's planning and building system is thus torn between the two ideals and must also sort through a veritable thicket of bureaucracy.

The foundation for Israel's planning and building laws was set down during the British Mandate period.[44] Only in 1965 did Israel's legislature enact its own planning law: the Planning and Building Law, 5725–1965.[45] Israel's planning and building system is hierarchical and consists of three levels: national, regional, and local. Government-approved "National Outline Plans" (NOPs) establish national-level policy principles.[46] The National Council for Planning and Building (NCPB), the highest planning institution in Israel, is responsible for preparing the plans for government approval.[47] The minister of finance or the minister of the interior, is the chair of the council, and the rest of its members, most of whom are appointed by the government or by government ministers, represent various plan-related interests and include senior civil servants, representatives of local government, and representatives of other public stakeholders.[48]

Over the years, the law established additional national-level planning bodies, often infringing on the National Council's authorities. Their establishment generally reflected a desire to support a particular planning interest. Two such independent committees are responsible for protecting agricultural land[49] and the coastal environment,[50] respectively. Since 1995, the former has also been responsible for the protection of open spaces.[51] In 2002, the law transferred the responsibility for planning national infrastructure to another body, the National Committee for the Planning and Building of National Infrastructure (National Infrastructure Committee, or NIC). This smaller body was charged with planning and licensing for national infrastructure plants.[52] In 2014, it tasked a new body, the National Committee for Preferred Housing Compounds (NCPHC), with planning and licensing residential compounds.[53] But with planning at the government level so clearly fragmented and complex, can it adequately address the challenges?

This question is reinforced by examination of the local planning system. Regional planning and building committees, comprising mainly government clerks, translate national planning principles into detailed[54] regional plans, the purpose of which is "the determination of the details necessary for the implementation of the national outline plans in the district."[55] Elected members of city and municipal councils serve on local committees responsible for producing the local plans.[56] These plans implement the national and regional planning principles while tailoring them to the interests of local residents. Likewise, they must designate specific tracts of lands for specific purposes, on the basis of general national and regional frameworks.[57] Issuing building and usage permits according to plans is usually the task of the local levels.

## Inefficiency and Bureaucratic Problems

The mechanisms for producing plans suffer from various problems that degrade their efficiency. They are extremely slow and plagued with bureaucratic issues. The planning institutions involve convoluted components that often further hamper the composition of a desired policy. Planning that operates at the local level often creates a divide between the national plans themselves and their execution. Not only do local governments encounter difficulties in the implementation of planning principles established at the national level, but they sometimes deliberately confound the implementation of the national policy.[58]

The tension between the desire to make the governmental system more efficient and the fear of corruption and infringement on general public interests is fundamental to the ongoing political debate over the degree of authority that should be granted to local government.⁵⁹ Planning institutions have suffered from principal-agent problems with elected officials over the past few years, as well as from corruption. The most famous case of such corruption is that of former prime minister Ehud Olmert, who was convicted of accepting bribes in the "Holyland" construction saga, which took place while he served as mayor of Jerusalem.⁶⁰

As if it were not enough for planning to have to bridge the gap between central government and local authorities, it must now bridge various governmental institutions. The interests of these bodies may well clash with one another. For example, protecting agricultural land does not necessarily go hand in hand with developing residential compounds, on the one hand, or with protecting open territories and biological diversity, on the other. The National Council and the government attempt to settle conflicting interests but must ultimately choose one policy direction over another. Since Israel's founding, there have been constant changes in the planning system's general preferences. In the early days of the state, protecting security interests and agricultural lands was the top priority. Over time, the authorities gave more weight to the protection of open and green territories. In the past few years, the planning system has delved hastily into developing infrastructure and catching up with urgent housing needs. These changes are evident both in the special institutions established for the specific purpose of advancing the government's preferred policy and in the structure of the planning bodies.⁶¹

Such problems result in plans that do not respond quickly enough to challenges, as evidenced in Israel's inability to supply the ever-increasing demand for housing. Apartment "production chains," the average amount of time needed to plan and build an apartment in Israel, used to be somewhere between twelve and fifteen years. A survey of plans approved in Israel since 1990 for the construction of over fifty housing units each has estimated on average six years to draw up the plans, five years to approve them, and two to three years to finish the building itself. The time it takes to draw up the plans has now been cut, to three years on average since 2015.⁶² The extended period between planning and operation makes it hard to address updated market needs properly and requires planning based on projections. From 2000 to 2010, plans for an average of twenty-six thousand housing units were approved per year, whereas if the market had kept up with population growth, it should have hit forty-five thousand. Actual construction during those years, including the execution of older plans, did not meet market demands, reaching only thirty-two thousand units. This resulted in a cumulative shortage of eighty thousand units,[63] which led to a string of price hikes at high rates. In 2009, the price of apartments went up by 19 percent, and from 2001 to 2017, by 80 percent (a 5% average annual increase).[64]

We have seen that the structure of the planning systems created an inherent difficulty in executing Israel's planning principles. Hence, the inordinate power of the bureaucracy formed another challenge that had to be met. Bearing this obstacle in mind, we will now turn to the products of the national planning institution and examine its principles, as reflected in National Outline Plans, to ascertain to what degree they met the challenges described above.

## Responding to Challenges: Planning Principles

### NATIONAL PLANS: GENERAL OUTLINE

National planning in Israel addresses three major issues: infrastructure, zoning at the national level, and the setting of general guidelines for urban construction. National planning with respect to these topics is quite concentrated; the local government has only enough maneuvering space to implement the national planning guidelines. The centralization of the system is due to Israel's small size and limited land resources.

Approximately thirty National Outline Plans (NOPs) are currently in place in Israel, and a few others are in preparatory stages. Most of these plans deal with infrastructure: roads, railroads, airports and seaports, water, electricity, communications, quarry excavation, natural gas plants, sanitation plants, gas stations, cemeteries, prisons, hotels, heritage sites, and hospitals (in preparatory stages).[65] The NCPB prepared an NOP meant to consolidate all infrastructure-related instructions in a single plan, which finally came into force in February 2020.[66] The National Infrastructure Committee (NIC) has created nearly 244 highly targeted national infrastructure plans, with emphasis on transportation and energy.[67] In the following subsections we will briefly review the solutions that these various national programs have offered for Israel's planning challenges.

### INFRASTRUCTURE

The government of Israel has attempted to make outlying areas more attractive and accessible, upgrading and expanding train networks and highways as well as initiating major transportation projects in the metropolitan areas of Jerusalem, Tel Aviv, and Haifa. The majority of national infrastructure plans thus far have focused on these projects.[68] Former Prime Minister Benjamin Netanyahu has repeatedly stated that "we are bringing the periphery closer to the center."[69]

In addition, government planning has promoted Israel's energy independence and met international standards in this field. On a national scale, the focus is on the establishment of power stations for various types of energy: cogeneration, hydroelectric, pumped storage hydroelectric, thermosolar, photovoltaic, and wind turbine. Special planning efforts have likewise been made to develop natural gas power stations and mains.[70]

Finally, many efforts, like the establishment of water desalination plants and mains, have been invested in coping with the unique problems posed by Israel's geography and climate.[71] Special plans have been put in force to protect the Dead Sea from rising levels due to the industrial production of minerals at its southern end.[72]

#### OPEN SPACES AND URBAN SPRAWL

National planning also deals with protecting open spaces. Most relevant is the National Outline Plan for Construction, Development and Conservation (NOP 35).[73] This plan delineates land designations for construction and development and outlines the principles that guide the preservation of open spaces from the threat of urban sprawl. The plan entered into force in 2005 and was updated in 2015 and 2016. It is currently Israel's most important NOP.[74]

The main goal of NOP 35 is zoning at the national level. It tries to preserve lands for future generations and protect valuable natural resources, agriculture, landscape and heritage sites, and the rural character of agricultural settlements. It must also consider security needs and differentiate between regions suited for development and those suited for preservation. Most development efforts are directed toward building up the four metropolitan regions and holding back suburban development to preserve a stretch of uninterrupted open territory.[75]

Before the NOP came into force, the government had pushed an aggressive policy of population dispersion, and to that end it had established hundreds of settlements, both rural and urban. The goal was to absorb immigrants on an enormous scale and to demonstrate in peripheral regions sovereignty over absentee properties.[76] These considerations became less pressing at the turn of the millennium as the security situation improved and the immigration rate slowed down. The policy of population dispersion exacted a heavy price: because of the distance from the periphery to the center, residents faced social and economic discrimination. With the growing awareness of the need to preserve open territories in light of increasing urban sprawl, NOP 35 led to a novel change in orientation.[77]

By consolidating the centers through high-rise growth, urban renewal, and improved public transport, NOP 35 has attempted to curb urban expansion. Its main operative instructions are to stop local and regional planning authorities from approving construction that is not "wall-adjacent" (i.e., that does not border extant developed territory)[78] and from approving additional construction when urban renewal and saturation of existing structures meet the needs.[79] NOP 35 has instituted net minimal density requirements as a condition for approving any new plans for residential construction by regional and local planning authorities;[80] it has set limits for construction in rural settlements;[81] limited the procedures for establishing new settlements and fixed guidelines for determining possible locations within areas suited for development;[82] and set guidelines for improving infrastructure systems and public transportation to accommodate higher population density.[83]

Another goal of NOP 35 is to bridge the divide between the center of Israel and the periphery,[84] with preference given to the development of Jerusalem, the Galilee, and the Negev.[85] The guidelines that increase density caps and prohibit expansion are stricter in central areas and laxer in the periphery.[86] Likewise, since 2014, the NCPHC has been advancing plans for thousands of residential units. It has located a substantial portion of these units in urban swaths of peripheral areas, where the state has greater land reserves. Construction is also underway on the purlieus but not centers of areas that are highly in demand.[87]

National planning efforts have likewise undertaken the transfer of army camps and security compounds from Israel's center to the periphery. The aim of this move is twofold: to increase land reserves in central areas and to fortify the periphery.[88] Another direction for planning efforts over the past several years has been the development of urban renewal plans. The government's national housing plan aimed at accelerating urban renewal from 12 percent (in 2005) to 45 percent by 2036–40.[89] The National Economic Council holds that the average demand for housing from 2017 to 2040 will reach sixty thousand units per year, which translates to a total increase of 1.5 million units, or 60 percent of the current housing inventory in Israel today.[90] The council's experts predict that unless urban renewal is sped up, Israel will face a total "planning catastrophe."[91]

#### PRESERVING THE NATURAL ENVIRONMENT

National planning also deals with operative plans for preserving the natural environment. A small albeit significant portion of the NOPs is directly involved with national parks, nature reserves, landscape preservation, and forestation.[92] Various laws and NOPs limit activity and construction in and around beaches, especially within one hundred meters of the coastline.[93] NOP 35 also ascribes great importance to preventing plan-related damage to the environment.[94] The main directive of the new NOP 1 is to preserve territories for infrastructure and at the same time to preserve open territories and prevent environmental damage.[95]

As the pressure for urban development increases and land reserves in the central strip of the country decrease, it becomes far more difficult to protect the natural environment. For example, a bill to loosen the restrictions on beachfront construction of hotels was put forward, but it was ultimately rejected.[96] There is an ongoing debate, both public and academic, between those who believe that the planning authorities' current measures for protecting the environment are inadequate and those who claim that environmental regulations unjustifiably suppress development options in so small a country. Nevertheless, there has been an increase in environmental awareness over the years.[97]

#### PREPARING FOR AN EARTHQUAKE

Another prominent issue in national planning is the urgent need to reinforce building structures in the expectation of earthquakes. As noted above, there is no question that a massive earthquake will hit Israel at some point, so construction must be strong enough to resist it. In 1975, the Standards Institution of Israel (SII) formulated a standard for structural wherewithal in the face of earthquakes, which was then amended several times before finally meeting international standards in 1995. Today, all new construction in Israel must meet these standards.[98] To this end, NOP 38, for the reinforcement of existing structures in the face of earthquakes, in force since 2005, provides economic incentives for homeowners in older condominiums to reinforce their buildings. The incentives include the provision of tax-exempt building rights for reinforcement and additional construction to cover costs. The four standard situations in which rights are given refer to the reinforcement and expansion of existing apartments, the reinforcement and construction of new apartments, the demolition and reconstruction of reinforced buildings, and reinforcement with additional building rights in an adjacent location.[99] Most requests submitted under the umbrella of these incentives are for the reinforcement of existing structures, while only a third are for demolition and reconstructing.[100] However, since 2015 about 50 percent of the final approved requests are for demolition and reconstructing.[101]

NOP 38 suffers from a number of weaknesses, the worst of them being its failure to incentivize structural reinforcement in peripheral areas. NOP 38 is most in demand in the Tel Aviv region, and to some extent in the central and Haifa regions. However, it has had little effect in the seismically active peripheral regions of the North and South, where a particularly high number of buildings stand in need of reinforcement to bear the brunt of a major earthquake.[102] While the nature of the incentives is identical across the country, their value depends on geographic differences in property value. In peripheral areas property values are not high enough to incentivize such an undertaking. This has been a point of sharp public criticism. Detractors claim that the plan all but neglects the periphery and grants disproportionate benefits to economically well-established regions.[103]

Another major weakness of NOP 38 is the difficulty in coordinating between all condominium owners in a given building that holds reinforcement agreements. In response to this problem, the Knesset enacted a law to approve reinforcement on the basis of majority rather than unanimous agreement.[104] The courts have dealt with numerous cases of homeowner opposition to majority-based decisions, generally upholding the decisions' legality even though, at times, they infringe on private property rights.[105]

NOP 38 has not succeeded in overcoming the challenge of seismic hazards. From 2005 through 2016, planning authorities approved reinforcement for 27,400 housing units, of which 14,700 are new units authorized by the plan.[106] Since only a tiny percentage (approximately 2.7%) of the more than a million housing units that require it have been reinforced,[107] the NCPB decided that NOP 38 will end on October 1, 2022.[108] However, the new government established in 2021 has stated that the NOP38 would remain in effect but will be amended by changing tax incentives and integrating reinforcement of individual constructions into a more comprehensive framework of urban renewal plans. These changes are intended to address criticism from local mayors that tax exemptions provided by NOP 38 reduced the resources that are needed to enable the municipal infrastructure to carry out the additional constructions that NOP 38 encourages.[109]

#### SUMMARY OF CURRENT PLANNING RESPONSES TO CHALLENGES

Planning in Israel must bridge conflicting interests between center and periphery. Although there has been momentum in the development of transportation infrastructure linking the two, it has strengthened the center rather than the periphery. Another difficulty lies in trying to narrow the gap between the rise in housing needs and the principle of preserving open spaces. The emphasis on safeguarding open spaces slows the process of meeting housing needs in the densely populated central areas, and it has led to a potential "catastrophe," according to the government's definition of the word. With respect to energy and water, planning has apparently been successful in tracking needs, yet land reserves diminish nonetheless. Israel's response to planning challenges remains somewhat conservative. The answers it has provided do not meet future exigencies. Adequate solutions will only be reached through a more creative and innovative approach, as we shall see in the following paragraphs.

## Creativity and Innovation: New Frontiers

### *In Search of New Spaces*

The limited land reserves in core regions of Israel, coupled with growing needs, have led the government to designate the development of two new expanses: underground and maritime space. These spaces are plentifully available beneath and adjacent to the dense urban regions at the center of the country. Their exploitation has thus far been minor in proportion to ground-level continental land territory. Former Supreme Court chief justice Aharon Barak termed the underground space "the *Terra-Nullius* of the age of progress."[110] It is an accurate declaration regarding the sea as well.

### *Utilizing the Underground Space*

#### THE VISION OF UNDERGROUND UTILIZATION

Back in 1999, the government decided to prepare for "more efficient land usage, including underground space and the integration and implementation of various infrastructures therein."¹¹¹ The past few years have seen Israel in a major sweep of transportation projects, including the Carmel tunnel and road tunnels in the approach to Jerusalem, the Tel Aviv light rail, and a cross-country highway.¹¹² The introduction of minimum standards for parking spaces has led to extended construction of underground parking garages.¹¹³ The space shortage has even inspired plans for multilevel cemeteries.¹¹⁴

The underground expanse is uniquely important from both a military and a political standpoint. In recent years, Israel has had to deal with high-trajectory fire and threats of underground terror attacks from Gaza and Lebanon. The underground is a strategic defense component against such threats.¹¹⁵ Moreover, politicians have proposed separating the ground-level expanse and the underground expanse as a solution to the division of sovereignty between Israel and the Palestinian Authority.¹¹⁶ The rich history of Israel and the countless antiquities it holds demand the separation of ancient strata, considered antiquities and therefore belonging to the state, and ground-level space, privately owned at times and used for current needs. Prime examples of this are the remains of the invaluable Crusader Knights' palaces located under private homes in the Old City of Acre.¹¹⁷

The State of Israel has recently begun developing regulatory, professional, and technological infrastructure meant to integrate the government's goal of multilevel land usage. Israel seems to be at the forefront of global innovation in some of these domains. Let us outline some of them.

#### PLANNING AND SURVEYING UNDERGROUND SPACE

Planning authorities in Israel are creating professional standards for multilevel, three-dimensional planning. The guidelines for three-dimensional outline plans show that multilevel planning must take into account the minimum distance required between levels to ensure adequate safety and engineering integrity for the intended usage of each level ("distance range"), as well as the required easements or usage rights for passage between levels, infrastructure laying, and parking lots, among other things.¹¹⁸

Likewise, since 2007, planning authorities have developed a draft NOP for the underground expanse (NOP 40) recommending that multilevel planning should place special emphasis on the full exploitation of the underground level. It proposes the establishment of priorities for developing different land levels based on a "duration of stay" index, according to which land usage that does not require extended human presence should be located underground. It further proposes designating the highest underground level for human activity that requires relatively short-term stay, such as shopping centers, performance and conference halls, sports arenas, museums, theaters, and other cultural venues; the next level down would include transportation centers and systems such as roads and railroads, and parking and storage space. The deepest level would be used for city infrastructure networks.[119]

Preparatory work on this plan had reached advanced stages by 2011, but the rate of progress has since slowed.[120] In March 2012, the government decided to consolidate all NOPs dealing with infrastructure as a single, uniform plan (NOP 1).[121] The draft of NOP 1 does not even mention most of the ideas expressed in the NOP 40 draft. It deals only with a single aspect of underground space usage: the preservation of groundwater and runoff water.[122] The media's central assumption was that the shelving of the plan, or at least the public censure of its further development, was due to possible security and military concerns.[123] However, in May 2019, the government announced its intention to establish a professional team to prepare an updated version of NOP 40 by 2020. The team will also formulate planning and legal recommendations for the implementation of the plan, as well as supplementary measures to permit economic incentives for entrepreneurs to carry out projects at the underground level.[124] Updated versions of NOP40 were presented to planning authorities in March 2021.[125]

Israel acknowledged preparing the legal and cadastral surveying aspects of multilevel land development. One aim of the Survey of Israel was to construct a three-dimensional cadastre at a leading global standard.[126] To that end, it created a national three-dimensional geodetic oversight network and regulated survey methodology.[127]

### CHANGING THE LEGAL PERCEPTION OF UNDERGROUND SPACE

At the legal level, the government published a new bill recognizing 3D land parcels as separate and independent property units.[128] The Knesset has now voted in favor of the new bill and the law came into force on December 12, 2019.[129] This changes the legal doctrine in effect today, *Cujus est solum, ejus est usque ad coelum ed ad inferos*, according to which land ownership extends, like a cone, from the ground down toward the center of the earth and up toward the sky.[130] Current law already allows the registration of units in condominiums as independent property units.[131] The Supreme Court has likewise established, in the Akunas case (2000), that the state can expropriate ownership of three-dimensional spaces to construct tunnels.[132] At this time the land registry unit in the Ministry of Justice is taking steps toward registration of three-dimensional land parcels beneath or above ground level.[133]

But the question of the ownership of underground levels beneath three-dimensional properties has yet to be decided. The draft of NOP 40 suggests that ownership of all land at a certain depth should remain public.[134] Former Supreme Court chief justice Barak expressed positive support of this in an obiter dictum he made in Akunas, saying that "we must rethink the extension of ownership underground so that the law may suit modern life."[135] This statement fits in with Barak's distributive approach, which views expropriation of the underground expanse as an actualization of private property owners' social responsibility. Such responsibility justifies the infringement of private property rights for public purpose when it causes minimal damage to property owners and is randomly and equally distributed among them.[136] Another former Supreme Court chief justice, Miriam Naor, expressed a different attitude in the Akunas case, stating that "no expropriation, even downwards, [should be permitted] beyond what is necessary."[137]

The governmental appraiser has developed an equation for calculating damages to be paid to an owner whose underground land has been expropriated, according to which said owner will receive payment even for expropriations that cause "no physical or planning damage" and even "in cases wherein the underground usage was not felt at all." This privilege, however, is limited to expropriations up to thirty meters below ground.[138]

In summary, land shortage has led Israel to become a world leader in the legal regulation of underground space. This is an expression of the Israeli spirit of creativity and innovation stemming from a crucial shortage of land reserves in its core urban areas. In the spirit of Jules Verne's writings, one could say that Israel is "truly about to take our first step into the Interior of the Earth, never before visited by man since the first creation of the world."[139]

## Utilizing Maritime Space

### THE AREA OF MARITIME SPACE

Another area that has aroused great interest in Israel in recent years is the Mediterranean Sea. Israel's coastline extends along 195 kilometers west of the densely populated central strip, and its maritime space is greater than the total area of the State of Israel, encompassing 26,000 square kilometers.[140] Though the entirety of this is public territory, it consists of several units with different statuses. Beaches and seaports are scattered along the coast, and their ownership is vested in the state, the Ports Authority, or the municipalities.[141] The strip of territorial waters, which is twelve nautical miles wide (approximately twenty-two kilometers from the coast), is spread across a total area of 4,000 square kilometers and is under complete state sovereignty and ownership.[142] To the west of Israel's territorial waters, the strip of the "adjacent area" extends for a distance of another twelve nautical miles, in which the state does not have full sovereignty but is allowed to exert some customs, immigration, sanitation, and archeological authority.[143]

The EEZ may principally extend up to 200 nautical miles (approximately 370 kilometers) from the coast according to the sea treaty,[144] but practically it reaches only 110 nautical miles south of the Mediterranean coastline and around 70 nautical miles north of it, with a total area of 22,000 square kilometers (approximately the total land size of the country).[145] It extends to the midpoint between Israel and Cyprus, as agreed upon by the two countries.[146] There are no agreements or treaties on maritime borders with Lebanon, the Palestinian Authority, or Egypt.[147] The dispute over the EEZ border with Lebanon was intensified when the Lebanese government publicized a tender to grant offshore licenses in maritime areas.[148] Israel has not signed the maritime treaty but has accepted its customary instructions, including those relating to maritime territory. However, the passage of legislation to officially establish the status of maritime space, especially that of the EEZ, has been delayed for many years, mainly because of concerns about the implications of such rules for Israel's relations with its neighbors.[149]

### THE USE OF MARITIME SPACE

The use of maritime space in Israel has increased in recent years, with the search for natural gas and fuel, resulting in the discovery of natural gas reserves at a great depth below the sea, and a further need to create production plants and main lines.[150] The maritime space has long been used by fuel and coal terminals, as well as for pumping and releasing cooling water from power plants located near the shore.[151] Maritime transportation has grown more common, and the plans to expand the seaports are becoming a reality.[152] Desalination plants have been erected on the shore.[153] The need for underwater communication infrastructure has grown.[154] There are plans to expand aquaculture and fishing cages[155] and even to create artificial islands.[156] These innovations join the traditional uses of this space, including fishing and recreation.

Awareness of the ecological and environmental importance of the coastlines and their waters has also increased. In 2004, a law was passed for the protection of "the coastal environment," meaning "an area extending 300 meters inland, measured from the Mediterranean coastline ... as well as the area measured from the Mediterranean coastline ... seaward to the limit of the territorial waters."[157] The law is meant to protect and preserve the coastal environment and the natural treasures and heritage sites within it, for the utility and benefit of the public and for future generations, according to the principles and limitations of its management, development, and sustainable use.[158] Israel signed the Barcelona Convention for the Protection of the Mediterranean Sea together with twenty-one other countries.[159] The importance of nature reserves has garnered greater recognition, and the Mediterranean Sea currently has nine official marine reserves.[160] Awareness of risks, like tsunamis caused by earthquakes, to residents of densely populated coastal areas has also increased.[161]

#### INNOVATIVE MARITIME PLANNING INITIATIVES

The increasing attraction to maritime space has led to innovative planning and survey initiatives aimed at facilitating more efficient, intensive uses. Primarily, the Israel Survey and the Ministry of Justice have commenced the project of mapping and registering the state's maritime space rights.[162] Many nautical blocks in the Mediterranean Sea, from the north to the south, have already been surveyed, mapped, and registered.[163]

Likewise, government ministries have begun compiling a maritime strategy and thinking in terms of maritime space planning. Within this planning process, Israelis work together with the European Union's Integrated Maritime Policy in the Mediterranean (IMP-MED) project, which supports dialogue regarding maritime policy among nine countries with Mediterranean borders: Algeria, Egypt, Israel, Jordan, Lebanon, Libya, Morocco, Tunisia, and the Palestinian Authority.[164] Policy principles for the future have yet to be articulated and published at the governmental level, although current policy reports show three main planning avenues: traditional uses (security, shipping, recreation, and fishing); new developments (marine and coastal structures, aquaculture, hydrocarbon production); and environmental planning (preservation and prevention of pollution).[165]

A team of researchers from the Technion, the Israel Institute of Technology, published ideas for an Israel Maritime Plan[166] as part of a wide international cooperative effort for the encouragement of marine spatial planning, with the aim of achieving sustainable use and biodiversity conservation in coastal areas.[167] The plan's vision clearly defines the purpose of maritime space in future national planning: "The marine area will be an integral part of the Israeli space and an essential component of its future economic well-being, environmental resilience and social and cultural development for the benefit of its residents, guests and future generations."[168] In accordance with this vision, the plan suggests more focused, though still quite general, guidelines for implementation. As one of the plan's integrated team members wrote, the very idea of planning maritime space "breaks new ground both in the planning and in the public policy fields."[169]

The Technion's plan recommends twelve policy measures for maritime space. Most of them relate to an additional, innovative development of fields already in play, including the protection of the maritime environment, energy source development, shipping and ports development, and aquaculture and coastal development.[170] Likewise, the plan proposes zoning the maritime space by dividing it into marine areas differentiated by their intended purposes.[171]

The most innovative recommendation is the use of "the marine space as an alternative for land uses," which at this stage is still limited, for environmental and engineering reasons, to the development of "small facilities that do not require a fixed connection to the shore . . . and that could be placed on foundation piles or developed as floating and anchored facilities."[172] The plan advises against using maritime space for urban development in the short term. Researchers believe that the engineering feasibility and the economic ratability of such a course of action are dubious at present, and they worry that "artificial offshore urban development might divert investment and focus from the country's main urban goals for the next few decades—urban regeneration and the development of the Negev and the Galilee."[173] They recommend leaving the possibility of urban development adjacent to the coastline to "generations to come."[174] The government team that is formulating a planning strategy for the maritime space has not yet suggested the construction of specific artificial islands for residential and other urban uses. Yet it proposed organizing the marine space in a way that would allow for the future establishment of such islands, as far as the need for their establishment will be decided and as far as technology will allow.[175]

Once again we see that land shortage has led Israel to seek innovative and creative solutions. There are countries with stronger connections to their maritime space and naval powers with a glorious marine tradition. It is precisely in Israel, whose maritime space is not particularly large and has no developed marine tradition, that we find extraordinary planning initiatives to exploit the maritime space. Here again "vulnerability is the birthplace of... creativity."[176]

## Concluding Remarks

This chapter has reviewed the unique challenges posed by Israel's geography and demography and analyzed the ways in which its land planning system attempts to address them. The analysis reveals how the planning system generates an abundance of initiatives and innovations and tries to turn disadvantages into advantages. The State of Israel is in the midst of a wave of land development and planning in a wide range of areas, particularly transportation, energy, and water. Technological and planning innovations aim at the efficient development and use of subterranean and marine space. There are original initiatives for the exploitation of natural resources and for dealing with natural disasters (most prominently, earthquakes). On the other hand, the attempts to deal with various challenges do not always end successfully. The system is vexed with problems involving coordination and bureaucracy as well as natural barriers. Israel's genuine planning problems are expected to worsen in the future, and government officials even warn of a "planning catastrophe."[177]

The Israeli Ministry of Foreign Affairs has dedicated several pages on their website to describe Israel as "the world's innovation nation." The website designers wonder to what extent this title coincides with the notion of being such a small country:

> Indeed, Israel's self-proclaimed "Startup Nation" title often comes as a surprise due to the country's small size, relatively young economy and culturally diverse population. Yet anyone who knows a thing or two about Israel knows that the country itself is a kind of "startup" endeavor that takes risks, constantly seeks improvement and knows that innovation and creativity will pave the way forward.... Still, in order to maintain its "Innovation Nation" title, Israel must not rest on its laurels... Israel must also continue to engage all of the components of its society to ensure that innovation remains a key national industry.[178]

While being innovative reflects a general vision of Israel and is rooted deep in Israel's identity, the notion of being small in size has even deeper roots in Israeli identity. As we have seen in this chapter, both are reflected in the land planning system of Israel. If Israel really wishes to overcome its natural limitations, it must continue to pursue creativity and innovation in the area of land planning.

## Notes

1. Meir Goldberg, "A Little Country with a Moustache" (song) (Hebrew) (1989).

2. Dan Breznitz, *Innovation and the State* (New Haven, CT: Yale University Press, 2007), 41–44; Morris Teubal, "The Innovation System of Israel: Description, Performance and Outstanding Issues," in *National Innovation Systems: A Comparative Analysis*, ed. Richard R. Nelson (Oxford: Oxford University Press, 1993), 476, 476–80; Michael Raska, *Military Innovation in Small States: Creating a Reverse Asymmetry* (Abingdon: Routledge, 2016), 60.

3. Israel Central Bureau of Statistics, *Israel Statistic Year Book 2019* (2019), 7 (Hebrew), https://www.cbs.gov.il/he/publications/DocLib/2019/Shnaton70_mun.pdf.

4. "Data: Land Area (sq. km.)," World Bank, accessed June 10, 2020, https://data.worldbank.org/indicator/AG.LND.TOTL.K2; World Bank, *World Development Report 2009: Reshaping Economic Geography* (Washington, DC, 2009), 332–34, http://documents.worldbank.org/curated/en/730971468139804495/pdf/437380REVISED01BLIC1097808213760720.pdf.

5. *Statistic Year Book* 2019, supra note 3, at 21–22.

6. *Statistic Year Book* 2019, supra note 3, at 11.

7. Aharon Kellerman, *Society and Settlement: Jewish Land of Israel in the Twentieth Century* (New York: SUNY Press, 1993), 196–204.

8. "Data: Population Growth (% annual)," World Bank, accessed December 3, 2017, https://data.worldbank.org/indicator/SP.POP.GROW?name_desc=true.

9. "Data: Population Growth."

10. "Data: Population Density," World Bank, accessed December 3, 2017, https://data.worldbank.org/indicator/EN.POP.DNST.

11. Israel Central Bureau of Statistics (ICBS), *Long-Range Population Projections for Israel: 2009–2059* (2012) (Hebrew), 5, 46–47, https://www.cbs.gov.il/he/publications/DocLib/tec/tec27/tec27.pdf.

12. ICBS, *Long-Range Population Projections*, 47; S. Ilan Troen, *Imagining Zion: Dreams, Designs, and Realities in a Century of Jewish Settlement* (New Haven, CT: Yale University Press, 2003), 285 (Earlier forecasts).

13. *World Development Report 2009*, supra note 4, at 56–58.

14. *World Development Report 2009*, supra note 4, at 336; ICBS, *Long-Range Population Projections*, supra note 11, at 425; Rachelle Alterman, "The Land of Leaseholds: Israel's Extensive Public Land Ownership in an Era of Privatization," in *Leasing Public Lands: Policy Debates and International Experiences*, ed. Steven C. Bourassa and Yu-Hung Hong (Cambridge, MA: Lincoln Institute of Land Policy, 2002), 115, 116–17.

15. *World Development Report 2009*, supra note 4, at 335–37, (table A2).

16. Moti Kaplan et al., *Patterns of Use of Built-Up Areas in Israel* (Jerusalem: Jerusalem Institute for Israel Studies, 2007) (Hebrew), 19.

17. Shlomo Angel et al., *The Dynamics of Global Urban Expansion* (Washington, DC: World Bank, 2005), 57–58, http://documents.worldbank.org/curated/en/138671468161635731/pdf/355630Globalurbanosept200501PUBLIC1.pdf.

18. Israel Central Bureau of Statistics, "Table 2.24, Population and Density per sq. km. in Localities with 5000 Residents and More on 31.12.2018," *Statistical Abstract of Israel*, 2019, https://www.cbs.gov.il/he/publications/doclib/2019/2.shnatonpopulation/st02_24.pdf; Israel Central Bureau of Statistics, "Table 2.25, Localities, Population and Density per sq. km. by Metropolitan Area and Selected Localities on 31.12.2018," *Statistical Abstract of Israel*, September 26, 2019, https://www.cbs.gov.il/he/publications/doclib/2019/2.shnatonpopulation/st02_25.pdf.

19. Amir Eidelman and Yael Yavin, "Built Areas and Open Spaces in Israel," in *Israel Sustainability Project 2030: Indices—Sustainability Yesterday, Today and Tomorrow* (Jerusalem: Israeli Ministry of the Environment and Jerusalem Institute for Policy Research, 2011) (Hebrew), 3, https://jerusaleminstitute.org.il/wp-content/uploads/2019/11/indicators_main_messages_outlook2030.pdf; Kaplan et al., *Patterns of Use*, supra note 16, at 89.

20. Eidelman and Yavin, "Built Areas," supra note 19, at 4; Kaplan et al., *Patterns of Use*, supra note 16, at 157–58.

21. Marjo Kasanko et al., "Are European Cities Becoming Dispersed?: A Comparative Analysis of 15 European Urban Areas," 77 *Landscape and Urban Planning* (2006): 111, 117; Kaplan et al., *Patterns of Use*, supra note 16, at 48.

22. Angel et al., *Dynamics*, supra note 17, at 183.

23. Angel et al., *Dynamics*, supra note 17, at 56–57.

24. Eidelman and Yavin, "Built Areas," supra note 19, at 5; Kaplan et al., *Patterns of Use*, supra note 16, at 93.

25. Amiram Oren, "Shadow Lands: The Use of Land Resources for Security Needs in Israel," 12 *Israel Studies* (2007): 149, 157; Israel State Comptroller, *Annual Report No. 55A* (2004) (Hebrew), 78, http://www.mevaker.gov.il/he/Reports/Report_576/ec73fobd-cc0f-42e0-82a5-db3780ec3d4c/2004-55a-220-Tipul.pdf.

26. *Statistic Year Book* 2019, supra note 3, at 9.

27. Nurit Alfasi and Roy Fabian, "Preserving Urban Heritage: From Old Jaffa to Modern Tel-Aviv," 14 *Israel Studies* (2009): 137, 146; Michael Dumper and Craig Larkin, "The Politics of Heritage and the Limitations of International Agency in Contested Cities: A Study of the Role of UNESCO in Jerusalem's Old City," 38 *Review of International Studies* (2012): 25, 52; "Information to the Public," Israel Antiquities Authority, accessed June 6, 2020 (Hebrew), http://www.antiquities.org.il/bestsitesmap_heb.asp; Troen, *Imagining Zion*, supra note 12, at 170–71.

28. Noam Shoval, "Transformation of the Urban Morphology of Jerusalem: Present Trends and Future Scenarios," in *Jerusalem in the Future: The Challenge of Transition*, ed. Shlomo Hasson (Jerusalem: Floersheimer Institute for Policy Studies, 2007), 90, 96–97.

29. "Press Release: 8% of ILA Land Available for Planning," Israel Lands Authority, last modified December 7, 2004 (Hebrew), http://land.gov.il/PR_MSG/Pages/Karkaot_07122004.aspx.

30. Ofer Raz-Dror and Noam Kost, *The Strategic Plan for Housing for the Years 2017–2040* (Jerusalem: National Economic Council, Prime Minister's Office, 2017) (Hebrew), 23, http://economy.pmo.gov.il/councilactivity/housing/documents/strategy050717.pdf.

31. Author translation. Raz-Dror and Kost, *Strategic Plan*, supra note 30, at 24.

32. Alon Tal, *The Land Is Full: Addressing Overpopulation in Israel* (New Haven, CT: Yale University Press, 2016), 188.

33. Israel Central Bureau of Statistics, "Table 1.1, Area of Districts, Sub-districts, Natural Regions and Lakes," *Statistical Abstract of Israel*, 2019, https://www.cbs.gov.il/he/publications/doclib/2019/1.shnatongeography/st01_01.pdf; "Dead Sea Works Ltd," Israel

Ministry of Environmental Protection, accessed June 10, 2020 (Hebrew), http://www.sviva.gov.il/subjectsEnv/BusinessLicensingIndustry/IndustryEnvironmentExb2013/Pages/DeadSeaIndChil.aspx.

34. "Potential and Use of Natural Resources," Geological Survey of Israel, accessed June 10, 2020, https://www.gov.il/en/Departments/General/potential-of-natural-resources; Amit Segev and Moshe Shirav, "Natural Treasures in Negev Craters—Minerals" (Report GSI/22/94, Submitted to the Executive Committee of Israeli Government Ministries, Jerusalem, 1994) (Hebrew).

35. Israel Ministry of Environmental Protection et al., *Policy Document—The Dead Sea Basin: Assessment of Current Situation and Prospects for the Future under Continued Dead Sea Water-Level Decline* (2006) (Hebrew), https://icl-group-sustainability.com/wp-content/uploads/2020/08/%d7%9e%d7%a1%d7%9e%d7%9a-%d7%9e%d7%93%d7%99%d7%a0%d7%99%d7%95%d7%aa-%d7%90%d7%92%d7%9f-%d7%99%d7%9d-%d7%94%d7%9e%d7%9c%d7%97-%d7%a9%d7%9c%d7%9d.pdf; Nir Hasson, "The Dead Sea: A Dramatic Look at Israel's Endangered Natural Wonder," *Haaretz*, March 1, 2016, https://www.haaretz.com/st/c/prod/global/deadsea/eng/5/; Zafrir Rinat, "Are Things Finally Looking Up for the Dead Sea?," *Haaretz*, February 25, 2017, https://www.haaretz.com/israel-news/science/.premium-1.773631.

36. Jonathan M. Samet, *Human Health Considerations Related to the Siting and Operation of an Open-Pit Phosphate Mine at Sdeh Barrir* (Report submitted to Israel Ministry of Health, March 31, 2014), https://www.health.gov.il/PublicationsFiles/Barir-Report.pdf; HCJ 4189/18 Local Council Turaan v. Government of Israel (February 27, 2019) (Pending injunction against the respondent to state why it would not draw the National Outline Plan for Mining and Quarrying for the reason that this plan did not establish a methodology for examining health effects derived from it) (Hebrew).

37. Brenda Shaffer, "Israel—New Natural Gas Producer in the Mediterranean," 39 *Energy Policy* (2011): 5379, 5380–81; Haim Srebro, "Implementation of Marine Cadastre in Israel," *International Federation of Surveyors—Monthly Articles* (September 2015): 3, http://fig.net/resources/monthly_articles/2015/srebro_september_2015.asp; "Oil & Gas Exploration in Israel—History," Israel Ministry of Energy, accessed June 10, 2020, https://www.gov.il/en/departments/general/gas_oil_history; "Geoscience Data Sources," Israel Ministry of Energy, accessed June 10, 2020, http://www.energy-sea.gov.il/English-Site/Pages/Data%20and%20maps/Data-sources.aspx.

38. David Broday et al., "Emissions from Gas Processing Platforms to the Atmosphere: Case Studies versus Benchmarks," 80 *Environmental Impact Assessment Review* (2019), 106313:1-9; Sue Surkes, "Scientists: Noble Energy 'Grossly Underestimates' Gas Pollution Threat to Israel," *Times of Israel*, October 22, 2019, https://www.timesofisrael.com/noble-energy-grossly-underestimating-leviathan-gas-rig-pollution-scientists/.

39. "Renewable Energies," Israel Ministry of Energy, accessed June 10, 2020, https://www.gov.il/en/departments/general/renewable_energy; Itay Fischhendler et al., "Marketing Renewable Energy through Geopolitics: Solar Farms in Israel," 15 *Global Environmental Politics* (2015): 98, 103–4.

40. Israel Water Authority, "Water Sector in Israel: Zoom on Desalination," *7th World Water Forum* 9 (2015), https://www.gov.il/BlobFolder/reports/water-authority-data-english/he/05-Water%20Sector%20in%20Israel%20-%20Zoom%20on%20Desalination.pdf; Nir Becker et al., "Desalination and Alternative Water-Shortage Mitigation Options in Israel: A Comparative Cost Analysis," 2 *Journal of Water Resource and Protection* (2010): 1042, 1042–46.

41. JPost.com Staff, "Full text of Netanyahu's Speech to 71st UN General Assembly," *Jerusalem Post*, September 23, 2016, http://www.jpost.com/Israel-News/Benjamin-Netanyahu/READ-Full-text-of-Netanyahus-speech-to-UN-General-Assembly-468500.

42. Ehud Segal et al., "Devising 'Policy Packages' for Seismic Retrofitting of Residences," 89 *Natural Hazards* (2017): 497, 505–6.

43. Brené Brown, *Dearing Greatly* (New York: Gotham Books, 2012), 34.

44. Town Planning Ordinance 1921, Vol. 2 of *The Laws of Palestine*, ed. Robert Harry Drayton (London: Waterlow and Sons on behalf of the Government of Palestine, 1934), 1437; Town Planning Ordinance 1936, *Official Gazette*, suppl. 1, 157; Frederic Goadby and Moses Doukhan, *The Land Law of Palestine* (Tel Aviv: Shoshany's, 1935), 332–43.; Rachelle Alterman, "Israel," in *Takings International: A Comparative Perspective on Land Use Regulations and Compensation Rights*, ed. Rachelle Alterman (Chicago: American Bar Association Publishing, 2010), 313–14.

45. 19 LSI 330 (Original text), available at https://knesset.gov.il/review/data/eng/law/kns5_planning_eng.pdf; The most updated version is available only in Hebrew. In the absence of an updated translation, I refer the reader to the combined Hebrew version published by Nevo.

46. §49–54 Planning and Building Law; Rachelle Alterman, "Land Use Law in the Face of a Rapid-Growth Crisis: The Case of Mass-Immigration to Israel in the 1990s," 3 *Washington University Journal of Law & Policy* (2000): 773, 784–87.

47. §2 Planning and Building Law.

48. §2 Planning and Building Law. These include the Association of Engineers and Architects, women's organizations, academic institutions, Zionist settlement institutions, sociologists, environmental preservation NGOs, social and welfare issue NGOs, and a representative of the young generation.

49. Suppl. 1, Planning and Building Law.

50. Suppl. 2, Planning and Building Law.

51. Suppl. 1, Planning and Building Law as amended by §139 Planning and Building Law (43rd Amendment), 5751–1995, *Sefer Ha-Hukim* 450 (Hebrew).

52. §6a Planning and Building Law as amended by §18 The Economic Arrangements Law (Legislative Amendments to Achieve the Budget and Economic Policy Goals for the 2002 Fiscal Year) 5762–2002, *Sefer Ha-Hukim* 146 (Hebrew).

53. Promotion of Construction in Preferred Housing Compounds (Temporary Order) Law, 5714–2014, *Sefer Ha-Hukim* 750 (Hebrew) (Preferred Housing Law); Nir Mualam, "Playing with Supertankers: Centralization in Land Use Planning in Israel—A National Experiment Underway," 75 *Land Use Policy* (2018): 269, 269–70.

54. §7 Planning and Building Law.

55. §55 Planning and Building Law.

56. §18–19 Planning and Building Law.

57. §61 Planning and Building Law.

58. Rachelle Alterman, "Decision-Making in Urban Plan Implementation: Does the Dog Wage the Tail, or the Tail Wag the Dog?," 3 *Urban Law and Policy* (1980): 41, 53–54.

59. Ernest R. Alexander et al., "Evaluating Plan Implementation: The National Statutory Planning System in Israel," 20 *Progress in Planning* (1983): 101, 156–58; Alterman, "Land Use Law," supra note 46, at 792–93; Ernest R. Alexander, "Governance and Transaction Costs in Planning Systems: A Conceptual Framework for Institutional Analysis of Land-Use Planning and Development Control—The Case of Israel," 28 *Environment and Planning B: Urban Analytics and City Science* (2001): 755, 768; Ravit Hananel, "Planning Discourse versus Land

Discourse: The 2009–12 Reforms in Land-Use Planning Policy and Land Policy in Israel," 37 *International Journal of Urban and Regional Research* (2013): 1611, 1617–18, 1620.

60. Crim. App. 5720/14 Olmert v. State of Israel (2015) (Hebrew); Revital Hovel, "Former Prime Minister Ehud Olmert Convicted of Accepting Bribes in Holyland Case," *Haaretz*, March 31, 2014, https://www.haaretz.com/israel-news/1.582901.

61. Alterman, "Land Use Law," supra note 46, at 810–13; Mualam, "Playing with Supertankers," supra note 53, at 270, 274.

62. Raz-Dror and Kost, *Strategic Plan*, supra note 30, at 7–8.

63. Raz-Dror and Kost, *Strategic Plan*, supra note 30, at 19.

64. Israel Central Bureau of Statistics, "Table 6.1, House Prices Index," *Price Statistics Monthly* 10/2017 (Hebrew); "Israel House Price Index 1994–2020," *Trading Economics*, accessed June 10, 2020, https://tradingeconomics.com/israel/housing-index; Mualam "Playing with Supertankers," supra note 53, at 274.

65. "List of National Outline Plans," Israel Ministry of Finance, Planning Administration (PA), accessed June 10, 2020 (Hebrew), http://mavat.moin.gov.il/MavatPS/Forms/SV9.aspx?tid=91&esid=10; "National Outline Plans," Israel Land Authority, accessed June 10, 2020 (Hebrew), http://land.gov.il/Planning/Pages/toch_MitarArzi.aspx.

66. "Planning Entity Details—NOP 1," Israel Ministry of Finance, Planning Administration, last modified February 19, 2020 (Hebrew), http://mavat.moin.gov.il/MavatPS/Forms/SV4.aspx?tid=4&mp_id=6vCdEltSxBV3f6xS%2Fm9dDQrYmiuv1fx5hQCXY%2FocjCZxgIfPTm75lgirO4br%2BTJrfiO4V1MYHNLKVXrcKCobcoBVxNZHLUeEDvHBdXoaTAw%3D&et=1.

67. "List of National Infrastructure Plans (NIP)," Israel Ministry of Finance, Planning Administration, accessed June 10, 2020 (Hebrew), http://mavat.moin.gov.il/MavatPS/Forms/SV3.aspx?tid=31&bid=30.

68. "List of National Infrastructure Plans," supra note 67; Government of Israel, *Infrastructure for Growth* 2017–2021 (April 2017) (Hebrew), 23–29, https://www.gov.il/BlobFolder/news/spoketashtit310817/he/%D7%AA%D7%A9%D7%AA%D7%99%D7%95%D7%AA%20%D7%A6%D7%9E%D7%99%D7%97%D7%94%202017.pdf.

69. "PM Netanyahu's Speech at the Opening of the 18th Section of the Cross-Israel Highway," Prime Minister's Office, last modified July 20, 2009, https://www.gov.il/en/departments/news/speechkvish200709; Itamar Eichner and Asaf Zagrizak, "Gov't Unveils Infrastructure Investment Super-program," *YNetNews*, September 3, 2017, https://www.ynetnews.com/articles/0,7340,L-5011351,00.html.

70. National Infrastructure Plans (NIP) 11, 20, 23, 29, 34, 41, 42, 47, 50, 51, 54, 55, 57, 58, 59, 61–63, 76–78, 82, 85, 91, "List of National Infrastructure Plans," supra note 67; *Infrastructure for Growth* 2017–2021, supra note 68, at 8, 14; Israel Ministry of Energy, "Renewable Energies," supra note 39.

71. National Infrastructure Plans (NIP) 24, 36, "List of National Infrastructure Plans," supra note 67.

72. National Infrastructure Plans (NIP) 35, "List of National Infrastructure Plans," supra note 67.

73. National Outline Plan for Construction, Development and Conservation No. 35 (NOP 35) (November 11, 2005) (Hebrew), https://www.gov.il/BlobFolder/generalpage/tama_35_docs/he/Water_Energy_Communication_tama_35_1.pdf.

74. OECD, *National Urban Policy in OECD Countries* (2017), 75–76, https://www.oecd.org/governance/the-state-of-national-urban-policy-in-oecd-countries-9789264271906

-en.htm; Shamay Assif, "Principles of Israel's Comprehensive National Outline Plan for Construction, Development and Conservation (NOP 35) (2009)," Israel Ministry of Interior, accessed December 11, 2017, http://archive.moin.gov.il/SubjectDocuments/Tma35 _PrinciplesDocument.pdf.

75. §3 NOP 35.
76. Troen, *Imagining Zion*, supra note 12, at 185–95.
77. Amnon Frenkel and Daniel E. Orenstein, "Can Urban Growth Management Work in an Era of Political and Economic Change? International Lessons from Israel," 78 *Journal of the American Planning Association* (2012): 16, 17–21; Arie Hershkowitz, "Ideological Shifts and Doctrine Changes in National Level Planning in Israel," 81 *Town Planning Review* (2010): 261, 267–69, 272–73.
78. §6.1 NOP 35.
79. §6.5 NOP 35.
80. §6.3, 12.2 NOP 35.
81. §8 NOP 35.
82. §13 NOP 35.
83. §3, 6.4, 12 NOP 35.
84. §3(e) NOP 35.
85. §3(c) NOP 35.
86. §7.1(2), 8.1.4, 12.2 NOP 35.
87. Preferred Housing Law, supra note 53; Mualam, "Playing with Supertankers," supra note 53, at 277–78; "List of Preferred Housing Plans," Planning Administration, National Committee for Planning and Construction of Preferred Housing Areas, accessed June 10, 2020 (Hebrew), http://mavat.moin.gov.il/MavatPS/Forms/SV3.aspx?tid=96&bid=150; "List of Preferred Areas," Planning Administration, National Committee for Planning and Construction of Preferred Housing Compounds, last modified March 4, 2020 (Hebrew), https://www.gov.il/BlobFolder/generalpage/areas_declared/he/National_planning _institutions_compounds_declared.pdf.
88. Israel Ministry of Defense, Relocation Administration, *Test Case City of Training Bases* (November 2016), 8–9, 25, http://www.negev.mod.gov.il/Documents/2441%20EN.pdf; Niv Elis, "Cabinet Approves Relocating IDF Bases, Clearing Land for Real Estate," *Jerusalem Post*, January 4, 2015, https://www.jpost.com/israel-news/cabinet-approves-relocating -idf-bases-clearing-land-for-real-estate-386644; Anna Ahronheim, "Defense Ministry Presents Plans for Two Additional IDF Bases in the Negev," *Jerusalem Post*, November 13, 2017, http://www.jpost.com/Israel-News/Defense-Ministry-presents-plans-for-two -additional-IDF-bases-in-the-Negev-514126; Ori Chudy, "3,000 Homes Approved for Tzrifin Base," *Globes*, December 4, 2017, http://www.globes.co.il/en/article-3000-homes-approved -on-former-tzrifin-base-1001214373.
89. Decision No. 2457 of the Thirty-Fourth Government of Israel, "Strategic Housing Plan," March 2, 2017 (Hebrew), https://www.gov.il/he/departments/policies/2017_dec2457; Raz-Dror and Kost, *Strategic Plan*, supra note 30, at 24.
90. Raz-Dror and Kost, *Strategic Plan*, supra note 30, at 11.
91. Raz-Dror and Kost, *Strategic Plan*, supra note 30, at 24.
92. NOP 8 National Parks, Nature Reserves and Landscape Reserves (June 21, 1981) (Hebrew), NOP 22 Forest and Forestry (January 1, 1995) (Hebrew).
93. §12(4) NOP 13 (Partial) Mediterranean Coastline (July 31, 1983) (Hebrew); Protection of the Coastal Environment Law, 5764-2004 *Sefer Ha-Hukim* 540 (Hebrew), English version:

http://www.sviva.gov.il/English/Legislation/Documents/Seas%20and%20Coasts%20 Laws%20and%20Regulations/ProtectionOfCoastalEnvironmentLaw2004.pdf; §156 (b) and the Second Supplement Planning and Building Law, 5725–1965.

94. §3(f), 3(h) NOP 35.

95. NOP 1, supra note 66, at part 1.

96. Minutes of Session No. 153 of the Twentieth Knesset 198–236 (August 1, 2016) (Hebrew); Sharon Udasin, "Plans to Build 27,000 Hotel Rooms Receive Knesset Approval," *Jerusalem Post*, August 2, 2016, http://www.jpost.com/Israel-News/Plans-to-build-27000 -hotel-rooms-likely-to-receive-Knesset-approval-462991.

97. Deborah F. Shmueli et al., "Scale and Scope of Environmental Planning Transformations: The Israeli Case," 16 *Planning Theory & Practice* (2015): 336, 356–57; Eran Feitelson, "Muddling toward Sustainability: The Transformation of Environmental Planning in Israel," 49 *Progress in Planning* (1998): 39, 41–42; Deborah F. Shmueli, "Housing and Highway Planning in Israel: An Environmental Debate," 35 *Urban Studies* (1998): 2131, 2134.

98. Standards Institution of Israel, *Standard 413: Design Provisions for Earthquake Resistance of Structures* (June 1, 1995) (Hebrew).

99. National Outline Plan for Strengthening Existing Buildings against Earthquakes (Integrated version December 2016) (NOP 38) (Hebrew), https://www.gov.il/BlobFolder /generalpage/tama_38/he/National_planning_institutions_tama38_2016.pdf.

100. Israel Ministry of Finance, Planning Administration, *NOP 38 Implementation Report for 2015* (2016) (Hebrew), 8, https://www.gov.il/BlobFolder/generalpage/tama_38_4/he /National_planning_institutions_UsageReporNOP38_2015.pdf.

101. Government Authority for Urban Renewal, Urban Renewal Report for 2020 (2021) (Hebrew), 31, https://www.gov.il/BlobFolder/reports/urban_renewal_report_2020/he /hithadshut_ironit_documents_urban_renewal_report_2020.pdf.

102. *NOP 38 Implementation Report for* 2015, supra note 100, at 3, 9, 10; Segal et al., "Devising 'Policy Packages,'" supra note 42, at 506–7.

103. BIMKOM—Planners for Planning Rights, *National Outline Plan 38 for the Seismic Strengthening of Existing Buildings: A Genuine Answer or a Fabricated Solution?* (2011) (Hebrew), 43–51, http://bimkom.org/wp-content/uploads/%D7%AA%D7%9E%D7%90-38 .pdf, English executive summary: http://bimkom.org/eng/wp-content/uploads/Tama-38 -English.pdf.

104. The Land (Reinforcement of Condominiums against Earthquakes) Law, 5768–2008, *Sefer Ha-Hukim* 154 (Hebrew).

105. PCA 1002/14 Shomroni v. Kofman (Nevo, July 9, 2014) (Hebrew); APA 7381/15 S. Dorfberger Ltd v. Oded (Nevo, October 30, 2016) (Hebrew).

106. *NOP 38 Implementation Report for* 2015, supra note 100, at 3, 14.

107. Segal et al., "Devising 'Policy Packages,'" supra note 42, at 506.

108. Gili Melnitcki, "Israel's Quake-Proofing Program Now Slated to End in 2022," *Haaretz* November 7, 2019, https://www.haaretz.com/israel-news/.premium-israel-s-quake-proofing -program-now-slated-to-end-in-2022-1.8091901; Gili Melnitcki, "Ending Earthquake Proofing Program Leaves 1 Million Israeli Homes at Risk," *Haaretz*, July 7, 2019, https://www .haaretz.com/israel-news/business/ending-earthquake-proofing-program-leaves-1-million -israeli-homes-at-risk-1.7453984.

109. Zev, Stub, "As Israel Looks to Solve Housing Crisis, Future of Tama 38 in Question," *Jerusalem Post*, July 12, 2021, https://www.jpost.com/israel-news/as-israel-looks-to-solve -housing-crisis-future-of-tama-38-in-question-673607.

110. CA 119/01 Akunas v. State of Israel (2003), PD 57(1): 817, 862 (Hebrew); Haim Sandberg, "Three-Dimensional Partition and Registration of Subsurface Space," 37 *Israel Law Review* (2004): 119, 123.

111. Sandberg, "Three-Dimensional Partition," supra note 110, at 122.

112. Sandberg, "Three-Dimensional Partition," supra note 110, at 121, 127; Nati Yefet, "Tel Aviv Light Rail Tunneling Begins," *Globes*, February 15, 2017, http://www.globes.co.il/en/article-red-line-tunneling-begins-1001177146; Abigail Klein Leichman, "High-Speed Tel Aviv–Jerusalem Rail Coming Down the Track," *Israel 21C*, March 22, 2017, https://www.israel21c.org/high-speed-tel-aviv-jerusalem-rail-coming-down-the-track/; TOI Staff, "Jerusalem–Tel Aviv Highway Reopens with New Tunnels, Bridge," *Times of Israel*, January 20, 2017, https://www.timesofisrael.com/jerusalem-tel-aviv-highway-reopens-with-new-tunnels-bridge/; Shmueli, "Housing and Highway Planning," supra note 97, at 2138–40.

113. Planning and Building Regulations (Installation of Parking Spaces), 5743–1983, *Kovetz Hatakanot* (Regulations) 1737 (Hebrew).

114. Renee Ghert-Zand, "Underground Cemetery Project Looks to the Past for the Graveyard of the Future," *Times of Israel*, November 14, 2017, https://www.timesofisrael.com/underground-cemetery-project-looks-to-the-past-for-the-graveyard-of-the-future/.

115. IDF Chief of Staff's Office, *IDF Strategy*, August 2015 (Hebrew), 28, https://www.idf.il/media/5679/%D7%90%D7%A1%D7%98%D7%A8%D7%98%D7%92%D7%99%D7%99%D7%AA-%D7%A6%D7%94%D7%9C.pdf; Belfer Center for Science and International Affairs, *Deterring Terror: English Translation of the Official Strategy of the Israel Defense Forces*, trans. Susan Rosenberg (Cambridge, MA: Harvard Kennedy School, August 2016), 39, https://www.belfercenter.org/sites/default/files/legacy/files/IDFDoctrineTranslation.pdf; IDF Chief of Staff's Office, *IDF Strategy*, April 2018 (Hebrew), 37, https://www.idf.il/media/34416/strategy.pdf; Ron Ben-Yishay, "The 'Lab' Uncovering Cross-border Tunnels from Gaza," *Ynet*, December 12, 2017, https://www.ynetnews.com/articles/0,7340,L-5055087,00.html; Anton Berkowski and Arnon Sofer, *Sub-ground: A Geo-Strategic Perspective* (Haifa: National Security College and Haifa University, 2014) (Hebrew), 12–13.

116. Sandberg, "Three-Dimensional Partition," supra note 110, at 122; Menachem Klein, "Negotiating Jerusalem: Detailed Summary of Ideas Raised in Track Two," in *Track Two Diplomacy and Jerusalem: The Jerusalem Old City Initiative*, ed. Tom Najem et al. (Abingdon: Routledge, 2017), 112, 125; White House, *Peace to Prosperity: A Vision to Improve the Lives of the Palestinian and Israeli People* (Washington, DC: January 2020), 16, 18, https://trumpwhitehouse.archives.gov/wp-content/uploads/2020/01/Peace-to-Prosperity-0120.pdf.

117. §2 The Antiquities Law, 5738–1978, *Sefer Ha-Hukim* 76 (Hebrew); Israel Ministry of Foreign Affairs, "The Antiquities Law—1978" (Summary), December 24, 1988, http://mfa.gov.il/MFA/PressRoom/1998/Pages/Antiquities%20Law-%201978.aspx; Uri Shoshani et al., "A Multi Layers 3D Cadastre in Israel: A Research and Development Project Recommendations," FIG Working Week (Cairo, 2005): 3, http://www.gdmc.nl/3DCadastres/literature/3Dcad_2005_04.pdf.

118. Planning Administration, "Guidelines for Preparing Three-Dimensional Plans," *Procedure for Uniform Structure of Plan* (2020) (Hebrew), 94–95, https://www.gov.il/BlobFolder/policy/mavat_2009/he/mavat_mavat_guidelines2020.pdf.

119. NOP 40 National Outline Plan for the Protection and Development of Subterranean Land—Policy Document (Final edition to be presented to the National Council) (June 29, 2011) (Hebrew) (Copy reserved by the author).

120. NOP 40 National Outline Plan for the Protection and Development of Subterranean Land—Protocols of Planning Institutions 2007–2011 (Hebrew), http://mavat.moin.gov.il/MavatPS/Forms/SV4.aspx?tid=4.

121. Decision No. 4434 of the Thirty-Second Government "Land and Planning—Updating the National Planning Concept," March 18, 2012 (Hebrew), https://www.gov.il/he/departments/policies/2012_des4434.

122. NOP 1, supra note 66, at 25, 73, 92; Yael Darel, "The Defense Plan Promised by the Ministry of Interior Has Been Stuck for Two Years," *Calcalist*, July 15, 2014 (Hebrew), https://www.calcalist.co.il/real_estate/articles/0,7340,L-3636080,00.html.

123. Eli Eshed, "The Solution to the Housing Crisis: Living under the Ground," *Makor Rishon*, March 13, 2015 (Hebrew), http://www.nrg.co.il/online/55/ART2/683/343.html; Walter Pincus, "U.S. Overseeing Mysterious Construction Project in Israel," *Washington Post*, November 28, 2012, https://www.washingtonpost.com/world/national-security/us-overseeing-mysterious-construction-project-in-israel/2012/11/28/e5682d8e-38b6-11e2-a263-foebffed2f15_story.html?utm_term=.ccf37bfde9d0.

124. "NOP 40/1," Planning Administration, accessed October 3, 2019 (Hebrew), https://www.gov.il/he/departments/general/tama_40_a; Adi Cohen, "Shopping Malls and Underground Streets: The Plan to Solve the Problem of Overcrowding," *TheMarker*, May 2, 2019 (Hebrew), https://www.themarker.com/realestate/.premium-1.7189228; Adi Cohen, "As Israel Grows More Crowded, State Plans Incentives for More Underground Building," *Haaretz*, May 2, 2019, https://www.haaretz.com/israel-news/.premium-as-israel-grows-more-crowded-state-plans-incentives-for-more-underground-building-1.7189758.

125. Adi Cohen, "Israel's Novel Solution to Housing Shortage: Build Underground," *Haaretz*, March 17, 2021, https://www.haaretz.com/israel-news/business/.premium-israel-s-novel-solution-to-housing-shortage-build-underground-1.9624899.

126. Peter Van Oosterom, *Survey of Israel Three-Dimensional Cadastre and the ISO 19152: The Land Administration Domain Model—Report* (Tel-Aviv: Israel Survey of Israel and TU Delft, 2014), 2, http://mapi.gov.il/ProfessionalInfo/MapiPublications/3D%20Cadastre%20SOI_Report2_v2final.pdf.

127. Survey Regulations (Surveying and Mapping), 5776–2016, *Kovetz Hatakanot* (Regulations) 1344 (Hebrew).

128. "Memorandum of the Land Law (Amendment), 5778–2017," Ministry of Justice, last modified October 16, 2017 (Hebrew), https://www.justice.gov.il/Pubilcations/NewsOld/Documents/AttachFile.docx.

129. Land Law (Amendment No. 33), 5779–2018, *Sefer Ha-Hukim* 80 (Hebrew).

130. §11 Land Law 5729–1969, *Sefer Ha-Hukim* 259 (Hebrew), English version: 5 *Isr. L. Rev.* (1970): 292, 319; Sandberg, "Three-Dimensional Partition," supra note 110, at 123–24; Bava Bathra 63B.

131. §54 Land Law 5729–1969.

132. Akunas case, supra note 110, at 854, 860.

133. Ministry of Justice, Planning and Policy Department, *Final Report: Registration and Land Settlement Department* (January 2017) (Hebrew), 22, http://regulation.gov.il/uploads/reports/7/%D7%93%D7%95%D7%97%20%D7%9E%D7%A1%D7%9B%D7%9D%20%D7%90%D7%92%D7%A3%20%D7%A8%D7%99%D7%A9%D7%95%D7%9D%20%D7%95%D7%94%D7%A1%D7%93%D7%A8%20%D7%9E%D7%A7%D7%A8%D7%A7%D7%A2%D7%99%D7%9F%20%D7%99%D7%A0%D7%95%D7%90%D7%A8%202017%20cleaned.pdf.

134. NOP 40, supra note 119, at 37.
135. Akunas case, supra note 110, at 863.
136. Akunas case, supra note 110, at 863; CA 3901/96 The Local Planning and Building Committee, Raanana v. Horowitz (2002), PD 56(4): 913, 942–44 (Hebrew); Rachelle Alterman, "When the Right to Compensation for Regulatory Takings Goes to the Extreme: The Case of Israel," 6 *Wash. U. Global Stud. L. Rev.* (2007): 121, 151.
137. Author translation. Akunas case, supra note 110, at 844.
138. Author translation. Ministry of Justice, Land Appraisal Department, *Guidelines: Compensation Appraisal for Public Use of the Deep Layers of the Subsoil* (2010) (Hebrew), 3–4, http://www.justice.gov.il/Units/ShomatMekrkein/ProfessionalInfo/Kavim/Kavim/kavim19.pdf.
139. Jules Verne, *A Journey to the Center of the Earth* (New York: Scribner, Armstrong, 1874; first published 1864, Paris), 97.
140. Technion—Israel Institute of Technology, *Israel Marine Plan* (Haifa: Technion—Israel Institute of Technology, 2015), 7, http://msp-israel.net.technion.ac.il/files/2015/12/MSP_plan.compressed.pdf.
141. Land Law 1969, §107, 154.
142. Land Law 1969, §8; Interpretation Law, 5741–1981, §3 as amended by Territorial Waters (Amendment) Law, 5750–1990, *Sefer Ha-Hukim* 90 (Hebrew), English version: http://www.un.org/depts/los/LEGISLATIONANDTREATIES/PDFFILES/ISR_1990_AmendmentLaw.pdf; Technion, *Israel Marine Plan*, supra note 140, at 6.
143. Technion, *Israel Marine Plan*, supra note 140, at 6.
144. §56–58 United Nations Convention on the Law of the Sea, 21 *ILM* (1982): 1261.
145. Technion, *Israel Marine Plan*, supra note 140, at 7.
146. Technion, *Israel Marine Plan*, supra note 137, at 6; Michelle E. Portman, "Marine Spatial Planning in the Middle East: Crossing the Policy-Planning Divide," 61 *Marine Policy* (2015): 8, 10; Agreement between the Government of the State of Israel and the Government of the Republic of Cyprus on the Delimitation of the Exclusive Economic Zone, 59 *Kitvei Amana* (Treaties) 1 (1566) (Signed December 27, 2010, ratified and entered into force February 25, 2011); 2740 *Treaty Series UN* (2011): 55, https://treaties.un.org/doc/Publication/UNTS/Volume%202740/v2740.pdf.
147. Technion, *Israel Marine Plan*, supra note 140, at 6; Portman, "Marine Spatial Planning," supra note 146, at 10; Srebro, "Implementation of Marine Cadastre," supra note 37, at 12–13; Yael Teff-Seker et al. "Israel Turns to the Sea," 72 *Middle East Journal* (2018): 610, 621–24.
148. Communication from the Permanent Mission of Israel to the United Nations Secretary-General, February 2, 2017, http://www.un.org/depts/los/LEGISLATIONANDTREATIES/PDFFILES/communications/isr_nv_02022017.pdf; Communication from the Permanent Mission of Lebanon to the United Nations Secretary-General, March 20, 2017, http://www.un.org/depts/los/LEGISLATIONANDTREATIES/PDFFILES/communications/2017_03_20_lbn.pdf; §14 UN Security Council, *Report of the Secretary-General: Implementation of Security Council Resolution 1701 (2006)—Reporting Period from March 1, 2018 to June 20, 2018 (S/2018/703)*, July 13, 2018, https://undocs.org/S/2018/703.
149. Bill of Marine Areas Law, 5778–2017, *Hatzaot-Hok* 48 (Hebrew); Sharon Udasin, "Israel Set to Regulate Sea's Legal Status," *Jerusalem Post*, August 7, 2017, http://www.jpost.com/Israel-News/Israel-set-to-regulate-its-seas-501825; Former Energy Minister Moshe Shahal

in the Debate on the Bill, Minutes of the 779th Meeting of the Economic Committee of the Twentieth Knesset 9–10 (June 12, 2018) (Hebrew).

150. Planning Administration, Ministry of the Interior, *Policy Paper for the Israeli-Mediterranean Sea Area: Phase I Report* (November 2015) (Hebrew), 121–34, https://www.gov.il/BlobFolder/guide/current_situation_policy/he/Report_1.pdf; see references supra note 37.

151. Planning Administration, *Policy Paper*, supra note 150, at 136, 38.

152. Planning Administration, *Policy Paper*, supra note 150, at 135, 143–144; Rickey Ben-David, "Israel Inaugurates Chinese-Run Haifa Port Terminal, in Likely Boost for Economy," *Times of Israel*, September 2, 2021, https://www.timesofisrael.com/israel-inaugurates-new-haifa-port-terminal-in-expected-boost-for-economy/.

153. Planning Administration, *Policy Paper*, supra note 150, at 138.

154. Planning Administration, *Policy Paper*, supra note 150, at 138–39.

155. Planning Administration, *Policy Paper*, supra note 150, at 140.

156. Planning Administration, *Policy Paper*, supra note 150, at 333.

157. §2 Protection of the Coastal Environment Law, supra note 93.

158. §1 Protection of the Coastal Environment Law, supra note 93.

159. Amendments to the Convention for the Protection of the Mediterranean Sea Area against Pollution (Barcelona Convention) 56 *Kitvei Amana* (Treaties) 1 (Ratified September 9, 2005, in force October 10, 2005).

160. Technion, *Israel Marine Plan*, supra note 140, at 7; §15 NOP 13, supra note 93; Ruth Yahel and Nir Engert, *Conservation Policy in the Mediterranean* (Israel Nature and Parks Authority, 2012) (Hebrew), 6, https://static.parks.org.il/wp-content/uploads/2018/01/2-mediniyutYamTichon.pdf.

161. Planning Administration, *Policy Paper*, supra note 150, at 302–4.

162. Srebro, "Implementation of Marine Cadastre," supra note 37, at 6–19.

163. Israeli Government Map Site, accessed June 11, 2020 (Hebrew), https://www.govmap.gov.il/ (Mark as *"Shhavot"* (Layers) *"Gushim"* (Blocks), and *"Helkot"* (Parcels) and zoom in on the Mediterranean area); Copy of registration of block 60036, parcel 1 from the Haifa Land Registry, August 19, 2014 (The owner: the State of Israel; the Land Registrar's comments: "Ownership—public lands, sub-marine land").

164. Planning Administration, *Policy Paper*, supra note 150, at 19.

165. Planning Administration, *Israel Maritime Policy Document: Mediterranean; Phase II Report—Maritime Space Policy* (November 2019) (Hebrew), 49–134, https://www.gov.il/BlobFolder/guide/policy_suggest/he/Report_4.pdf.

166. Technion, *Israel Marine Plan*, supra note 140; Technion—Israel Institute of Technology, *Israel Marine Plan: Implementation and Monitoring Report* (Haifa: Technion—Israel Institute of Technology, 2016) (Hebrew), http://msp-israel.net.technion.ac.il/files/2017/06/%D7%93%D7%95%D7%97-%D7%94%D7%98%D7%9E%D7%A2%D7%94.pdf.

167. "Marine Spatial Planning Program: Israel," UNESCO & Intergovernmental Oceanographic Commission (IOC), accessed June 11, 2020, http://msp.ioc-unesco.org/world-applications/middle-east/israel/.

168. Technion, *Israel Marine Plan*, supra note 140, at 22.

169. Portman, "Marine Spatial Planning," supra note 146, at 14.

170. Technion, *Israel Marine Plan*, supra note 140, at 22.

171. Technion, *Israel Marine Plan*, supra note 140, at 45–54.

172. Technion, *Israel Marine Plan*, supra note 140, at 37.

173. Technion, *Israel Marine Plan*, supra note 140, at 38.

174. Technion, *Israel Marine Plan*, supra note 140, at 38.
175. Planning Administration, *Israel Maritime Policy Document*, supra note 165, at 88.
176. Brené Brown, *Dearing Greatly*, supra note 43.
177. Supra note 31.
178. "Israel—The World's Innovation Nation," Israel Ministry of Foreign Affairs, accessed June 11, 2020, https://mfa.gov.il/MFA/InnovativeIsrael/ScienceTech/Pages/Israel-World-Innovation-Nation.aspx.

# 5

## JEWISH AND DEMOCRATIC

*Land Policy and the Arab Minority*

> We . . . hereby declare the establishment of a Jewish state. . . . The State . . . will foster the development of the country for the benefit of all its inhabitants . . . it will ensure complete equality of social and political rights to all its inhabitants.
>
> Israel's Proclamation of Independence, *Megilat Ha-Atzmaut*

A DECISIVE IDENTITY ISSUE FACING THE STATE OF Israel has been the aspiration to act as the nation-state of the Jewish people and at the same time as a state that advocates full social and political equality for all citizens. This dual promise is enshrined in the Proclamation of Independence signed in 1948 and in the Basic Law: Human Dignity and Liberty of 1992, the purpose of which is "to stipulate the values of the State of Israel as a Jewish and democratic state."[1] In fact, this dual promise had been made decades before the establishment of the State of Israel, under Section 2 of the Mandate of the League of Nations from 1922, which subjected the British Mandate to a "dual obligation": to "secure the establishment of the Jewish national home," and to safeguard "the civil and religious rights of all the inhabitants of Palestine, irrespective of race and religion."[2] Then as today, such a pledge raised multiple practical difficulties, and it remains a major concern for Israel.

In view of the complex relationship between Israel's Jewish majority and Arab minority, the double promise necessitates the bridging of two essentially conflicting nationalist aspirations. This poses an existential paradox with practical implications for nearly every aspect of life in Israel. Israel's land policy is one of the key areas in which the paradox of the dual promise finds real expression. In the present chapter we shall consider the background of Israel's problematic Jewish-Democratic dual identity and examine two important and controversial aspects of its land policy as it relates to the Arab minority: the land and property outcome of the War of Independence, and the allocation of land resources to Israel's Arab minority. Finally, we shall analyze the relevant data and the degree of inequality in Israel's land policy toward its Arab minority.

## The Dual Jewish-Democratic Identity of the State of Israel

### The National Identity of the Arab Minority

Israel has a large minority of Arab citizens who today constitute about 21 percent of its population (1.88 million people). In 1951 this figure was just 11 percent, and it has been rising ever since.[3] In 2012, the proportion of Arab citizens was predicted to reach 20 percent to 27 percent by 2034 and to level off at 15 percent to 34 percent by 2059.[4] Official forecasts in 2019 predicted a proportion of 18.4 percent to 20.2 percent by 2065.[5] The gap between these forecasts stems from the uncertain rate of decline in fertility among the Arab and ultra-Orthodox Jewish populations. The assumption here is that there will be no significant migration processes or transition between populations.[6] Today, by way of comparison, the proportion of Arabs in Israel's population is greater than that of Hispanics/Latinos (18.3%) or African Americans (13.4%) in the population of the United States.[7]

Members of the Arab minority in Israel share various group characteristics. Their language (Arabic) is different from the language of the majority (Hebrew). Religiously, Israeli Arabs are a heterogeneous group: most are Muslim (about 85%), and a minority are Druze[8] (about 8%) or Christian (about 7%).[9] Religious differences account for a surprisingly negligible rate of intermarriage and conversion between the Jewish majority and the Arab minority in Israel.[10]

Another key characteristic of the Arab minority is their nationalist dispositions. Most members of this minority view themselves as belonging to the Arab nation and the Arab-Palestinian people. In a 2015 representative survey of the Arab public in Israel, comprising seven hundred interviewees, 63 percent defined their identity as "only" (31%) or "mainly"(32%) "Palestinian-Arab," 15.8 percent viewed themselves as "Equally Palestinian-Arab and Israeli-Arab," and only 20.1 percent defined themselves as "only" (8.5%) or "mainly"(11.6%) "Israeli-Arab." Just 5.9 percent defined themselves as "Israeli."[11] Most of the interviewees ascribed little weight to their Israeli citizenship (13.4%) as compared to the religious (46.5%) and national-Palestinian (39.5%) components of their identity.[12] A study conducted a decade earlier revealed that Arab citizens self-identified according to a number of criteria, but for Muslims and Christians, their Arab or Palestinian identities were the most salient.[13] The low relative weight given by Arab citizens of Israel to the Israeli component of their identity as opposed to their Arab, Palestinian, or religious identities remains consistent, despite certain changes that have occurred over the years in the degree of their identification as Israelis. Polls published in 2017 indicate the same.[14] *The Future Vision*, drafted by Arab minority leaders in 2006, defined its collective identity as follows: "We, the Palestinian Arabs in Israel, are indigenous peoples, residents of the State of Israel, and an integral part of the Palestinian, Arab, Muslim and human nation."[15]

The strength of the Arab minority's national identity in comparison to their identity as citizens of Israel stems from their complex positions vis-à-vis the existence of the State of Israel and its Jewish character. Although most Arab citizens accept Israel as a Jewish state, only a few accept its Jewish-Zionist nature as a democratic state inhabited by a Jewish majority that asserts the Jewish people's right to exercise self-determination.[16] There are two main reasons for this.

First, the Palestinian national movement has from the outset viewed the territory of the Land of Israel (*Eretz-Israel*; in their eyes, Palestine) as the space in which the rights to self-determination of the land's residents must be realized. It did not recognize a similar right for Jews. Therefore, the movement opposed the Balfour Declaration and the British Mandate, which promised a Jewish homeland for the Jewish people.[17] Even during and after the Holocaust, it opposed Jewish immigration, as well as the establishment of the State of Israel. This opposition to any expression of Jewish national independence has been consistent and violent,[18] and it carries through to this day in various ways. Leaders of the Palestinian Authority still do not recognize Israel's right to exist as a Jewish state,[19] nor do the Islamic factions within the Palestinian nationalist movement, and particularly Hamas, which rules Gaza.[20] The overwhelming majority of Israel's Arab citizens do not participate actively in the violent aspects of the Palestinian resistance, although some still support it.[21] For Israeli citizens who view their Arab-Palestinian identity as a central component of their identity, it is difficult to disengage from the nationalist sentiments of their compatriots.

Their de facto acceptance of minority status in a Jewish-majority state is overshadowed by the perception that they are not a minority in the territory they inhabit and thus have natural rights of primary ownership.[22]

Secondly, and in continuation of the first reason above, Israel's Arab citizens find it difficult to accept the geographical and demographical transformation wrought by Israel's War of Independence. In the wake of this war, most of Palestine's Arab-Palestinian residents found themselves refugees beyond its borders, and their holdings became the property of the State of Israel. Even some of those who had remained within the state's borders became "present absentees" vis-à-vis their properties, to which they were not allowed to return.[23] The transformation became known in Arab culture as the *Nakba*, meaning "catastrophe" or "Holocaust," a word intended to emphasize the scope of the upheaval wrought from the Arab perspective.[24] Israel's Arab citizens view the *Nakba* as an intolerable national disaster and an injustice for which the State of Israel and its Jewish majority bear full responsibility.[25] The primary concern of Israeli-Arab leaders and their public is the rectification of this injustice. Their vision statement includes the demand that "the State should acknowledge responsibility for the Palestinian Nakba and its disastrous consequences for the Palestinians in general and for Palestinian Arab citizens of Israel in particular."[26] Holding the State of Israel accountable for the *Nakba* and demanding that their pre-1948 status be restored accords with the original Palestinian-Arab objection to the establishment of the State of Israel. The complexities described above have resulted in the view of some Palestinian Arabs that their lives as a national minority within a Jewish-Zionist state are inherently disadvantaged and rooted in historical injustice. This feeling creates a fundamental mistrust of Israel's aspiration to function as both a Jewish-Zionist state and a democracy.[27]

## *The Zionist Perception: Jewish Nationality and Democratic State*

The attitude of the Jewish majority toward its Arab minority is similarly complex. The Zionist movement has from its inception aimed to create a Jewish homeland and nation-state in the Land of Israel. As we already elaborated in chapter 2, the demand to realize the Jewish people's right to self-definition specifically in the Land of Israel (*Eretz Israel*) is based on the long history of the Jewish people in this territory and the experience of the Diaspora, culminating in the horrors of the Holocaust. The establishment of Israel as a Jewish state is the realization of this demand.[28] Clearly, in light of the sacrifices and the blood that was shed to achieve the national goals of Zionism, foremost among them the establishment of a Jewish state, Israel's majority have no intention of relinquishing the achievement of their goals and endangering their existence. Many Jews fear the minority will harm the state and its Jewish character. Indeed, the level of mistrust between the two populations is high.[29]

The bitter experiences of the ongoing struggle between the two peoples naturally affect the willingness, and sometimes the ability, of the state to keep its two pledges. The State of Israel's formal legal system adheres to the double promise and the ability to fulfill it. It does not view the two as contradictory, and its leaders have stated this explicitly more than once. In his ruling on the Ka'adan case, former Supreme Court chief justice Aharon Barak wrote: "There is, therefore, no contradiction between the values of the State of Israel as a Jewish and democratic state and between the absolute equality of all of its citizens. The opposite is true: equality of rights for all people in Israel, be their religion whatever it may be and be their nationality whatever it may be, is derived from the values of the State of Israel as a Jewish and democratic state."[30]

Former attorney general Elyakim Rubinstein was of a similar opinion, saying: "We are committed to equal rights for all citizens. I have already stated in the past that, just as we must fight with all our might to preserve Israel as a Jewish and a democratic state, so we must fight for equality for Arabs . . . we fight in court . . . against discrimination, overt or covert, towards Arabs; but our duty towards the Jewish People and towards the Zionist vision is not overlooked and is never forgotten, even for a moment."[31]

Despite the State of Israel's official adherence to the double promise, its two components are often difficult to reconcile. The state cannot afford to act in a manner that compromises its Jewish-Zionist character or its actual existence. It also cannot deny the legitimacy of settling Jews in particular regions of the state or of taking actions to strengthen Israeli sovereignty in regions close to hostile borders. As noted by Justice Barak, a Jewish state is a "state whose primary concern is the settlement of Jews on open land, in cities and in villages."[32]

Increasingly, Israel's Jewish public contends that the "Jewish and democratic" combination downplays the state's Jewish character in favor of its democratic values, transmuting it from a national Jewish state into a "state of all citizens." The new Basic Law: Israel the Nation-State of the Jewish

People (hereafter: Nation-State Basic Law) clearly expresses this position.[33] Its aim is to emphasize and legislate the Jewish nature of the state.[34] Section 1 of the law, titled "The State of Israel," declares that "Israel is the historic homeland of the Jewish people in which the State of Israel was established," that "the State of Israel is the nation-state of the Jewish people, in which it fulfills its natural, religious, and historic right to self-determination," and, moreover, that "the fulfillment of the right of national self-determination in the State of Israel is *unique* to the Jewish people" (emphasis added). The draft proposal of the law also alludes to the second, democratic aspect of the double promise, proposing in Section 2 that it aims "to codify in a basic law the values of Israel as a Jewish *democratic* state in the spirit of the principles of its Declaration of Independence" (emphasis added). The final legislation does not include these words. The drafts of the law provoked a spirited public debate in Israel before its legislation,[35] and the law itself met with fierce public criticism and protest after its enactment.[36]

Some critics claim that the law favors the Jewish-national character of the state over the principles of democracy and equality.[37] Supporters argue that the law does not touch the democratic component of the double promise but only reinforces the status of the Jewish-national component.[38] As Prime Minister Benjamin Netanyahu stated in the Knesset shortly after the enactment of the National Law, "Israel is the nation state of the Jewish people, a nation state that respects the individual rights of all its citizens."[39] A variety of opponents, including Druze citizens, Bedouin, and members of opposition parties, filed petitions against the law to the Supreme Court.[40] Former minister of justice Ayelet Shaked has warned that if the court annuls the law it will set off a "war of authorities."[41] The hearing of the case was broadcast live from the courtroom, and this was one of the first cases in which the court allowed it.[42] A majority of ten judges dismissed the petitions and ratified the constitutionality of the law. The majority clarified, in the spirit of the court's traditional approach, that there is no contradiction between the Jewish national character of the state and either its democratic nature or the principle of equality and that it would be correct and possible to interpret the law in this way in the future.[43] The minority judge, George Karra, a Christian Arab, believed that the law should be rejected because "Despite the rhetoric . . . the [nation state] law creates a preference for the values of the state as a Jewish state over its values as a democratic state."[44] The enactment of this law, as well as the opposition to its enactment, shows yet again how deeply the paradox of the double promise is rooted in the identity of the State of Israel and its inhabitants.

The complex relationship between the Jewish majority and the Arab minority in Israel thus poses a significant challenge to the realization of the double promise in various realms of government policy. We shall now examine two central challenges that this double promise poses to Israel's land policy: the consequences of the War of Independence on the land ownership of Arab citizens and the equitable allocation of land resources to the Arab minority.

## Handling of the Consequences of the War of Independence

### Israel's Policy toward the Property of Palestinian Refugees

As noted in chapter 1, following the War of Independence, lands owned by Palestinian refugees were transferred to public ownership, and today they fall under the administration of the Israel Lands Authority. On some, though not all, of these lands, the state established new settlements. Israel's consistent position internationally has been that refugees shall not return to Israel and that their property shall not be restored to the original owners. There are two rationales for this position. First, the State of Israel does not take responsibility for the refugee problem, regarding it rather as a consequence of the War of Independence, a war of survival and self-defense against Arab aggression. Second, there is general agreement in Israel that in practice the right of return would controvert the Jewish character of Israel and end its existence as a Jewish state as such—or a state of any kind, for that matter. Moreover, the implementation of the right of return could lead to displacement of Israeli citizens en masse from their current residences. Hence, Israel prefers the idea of resettling the refugees beyond its borders.[45]

As for compensating the refugees, Israel does not rule it out but raises counterclaims for the compensation of Jewish refugees from Arab states. Israel's position is that return and compensation are diplomatic issues to be resolved through international negotiations.[46] Israel's internal laws do not recognize the rights of Palestinian refugees who are not citizens or residents of the state to sue for compensation for loss of property.[47] "External refugees"—that is, those who are located mainly in Arab countries or within the West Bank and Gaza—would not sue for compensation in any event and insist on the right of return.[48] All the same, as noted in chapter 1, most of the property left by refugees remains under separate formal ownership and administration of the Development Authority, and incomes derived from it, are formally marked as loans to the state treasury.[49] An outside observer might interpret this policy as a sign of willingness to negotiate over refugee compensation or as a long-standing practice no one would wish to challenge for fear of invoking restitution or return.

### Israel's Policy toward the "Present Absentees"

Israel's policy is somewhat different with regard to "present absentees," those Palestinian refugees who remained within its borders as citizens when the state was established (but prior to 1967). These citizens too were defined as "absentees" if they left their "ordinary place of residence in Palestine . . . for a place in Palestine held at the time by forces which sought to prevent the establishment of the State of Israel or which fought against it after its establishment."[50] Thus, residents who left their homes for regions captured by the Israel Defense Forces (IDF) became citizens of Israel, but the property they left behind in their place of origin was considered an absentee asset that was transferred to the government administration. These assets constitute about 325 square kilometers of mainly agricultural land and, to a lesser extent, urban properties lying within the precincts of former villages or towns abandoned during the war. They constitute 28.3 square kilometers of Jewish-owned property, about 239 square kilometers of privately owned Arab property, about 66 square kilometers of properties belonging to Islamic trusts, and 0.101 square kilometers of church properties, all of which have been expropriated under Israeli law.[51] Added to the overall reasoning against the return of assets at the basis of this policy is the fear that it could become a precedent for the general recognition of claims to the right of return.[52]

Nevertheless, the state's position regarding these assets is more moderate. First, Israel did not rule out restoration categorically. The government decided in the early 1950s to release all urban property that was not vacant and earmarked for development to absentees residing in Israel legally.[53] It established a special commission to recommend the release of absentee properties and issued about 5,200 release certificates by 1966/67, and about 8,600 by 1976.[54] Second, regardless of its position on refugees outside of Israel, the state granted all present absentees the right to receive compensation for the land they had lost as the result of the War of Independence. This was one of the main goals of the Land Acquisition Law (Validation of Acts and Compensation), 5713–1953 (hereafter: LAA).[55]

In the debates leading up to the passing of this law, the chairman of the Knesset Constitution, Law and Justice Committee presented its goals thus: "There was a need for a special law aimed at . . . establishing a legal foundation for the acquisition of these lands, but at the same time also appropriately providing their owners with the right to compensation. Obviously, it is impossible ever to achieve total justice, yet it is imperative that we rectify what was done perforce when the state was established and the developments that ensued."[56]

Over and beyond the normal laws governing expropriated lands, the LAA provided two extraordinary benefits to those affected. First, it allowed for payment in the form of alternate land in addition to monetary compensation. This possibility was limited to property that had been used for agricultural purposes by the previous owners and that had served as their primary source of livelihood. By the end of 2005, the LAA had awarded a total of 71.7 square kilometers of land as compensation (about 22% of all the land expropriated).[57] Second, the monetary compensation was determined, not according to the value of the property at the time of its abandonment during the war, but according to a later and higher value (January 1, 1950). An annual interest of 3 percent beginning on January 1, 1950, was supposed to protect this value.[58] However, rampant inflation in the years that followed caused severe devaluation of the currency. Consequently, regulations regarding compensation payments were periodically adjusted upward. Not all those who were eligible claimed compensation, but it would appear that most claimants realized their rights soon after the enactment of the law.[59] By the end of 2005, compensation was paid out, in money and in land, for 206 square kilometers of property (about 63% of all expropriated land).[60]

As we see, the state implements the double promise in terms of the consequences of the War of Independence in the following way: as a Jewish state, it cannot restore the original situation in kind; as a democratic state, it is obligated to compensate its citizens for damages incurred.

## Internal Claims for Restitution of Refugee Assets

The traditional position of the Arab states and members of the Palestinian national movement is the reverse: it demands a full and implementable right of return for the refugees and allocates sole responsibility for the *Nakba* to the State of Israel.[61] The majority of the Arab public in Israel support this demand and agree with it.[62] Moreover, the leadership of the Arab public in Israel has never acquiesced to the position precluding the return of refugee assets, at least those of present absentees. The Arab leadership expressed its objections when the LAA was enacted for the right to restitution, not just compensation.[63] The Israeli Arab Vision from 2006 includes the demand for a guarantee of "their right of return" to "present absentees."[64] At the same time, the Vision also expresses a more moderate position emphasizing compensation over return.[65] Adalah, the Legal Center for Arab Minority Rights in Israel, an NGO that plays an active and central role in defending the rights of Israel's Arab minority, views "blocking Palestinian restitution claims" as one of the key expressions of the unequal treatment of the Arab minority.[66] Adalah's website displays an interactive map of the "State of Israel's Expropriation of Land from the Palestinian People," in which the results of the *Nakba* do not exist. In this map, all the villages that ceased to exist after the War of Independence are still there, while Jewish settlements established after the war do not appear. The borders and districts of the land are those drawn by the government of the British Mandate.[67] The Islamic Movement in Israel likewise fosters the notion of restitution, looks after abandoned Muslim properties (cemeteries and mosques), and submits injunctions against their use.[68]

Most Jewish citizens of Israel, however, deny responsibility for the consequences of the War of Independence in terms of Arab property because the implications of the issue threaten the very existence of the state and its Jewish character.[69] Nevertheless, public opinion surveys reveal that 11 percent to 15 percent of Jews in Israel believe that the state bears responsibility for the *Nakba*.[70] Jewish Israeli scholars even support restitution of internal refugee property in some cases, particularly when it is not being used for other purposes.[71] The nonprofit organization *Zochrot* (Remembering) came into being in 2002 with European funding. The vision of this organization is the "return of the Palestinian refugees to their country," and its overarching goal is "to promote Israeli Jewish society's acknowledgement of and accountability for the ongoing injustices of the Nakba."[72] Israeli universities hold symposia and conferences about the *Nakba* and its consequences.[73]

Academic literature in Israel and abroad tends to condemn the consequences of the *Nakba*. For example, many publications claim that most of the land owned by the State of Israel (93%) was expropriated from Arab ownership and control as a result of the establishment of the State of Israel.[74] According to this argument, Israel expropriated Negev land that had been entirely under Arab control, while in fact most of it (ten to twelve thousand square kilometers of land) was never under Arab ownership or control.[75] The estimate is based on an indiscriminate calculation of all refugee assets (three to five thousand square kilometers) plus "present absentee" lands (about three hundred square kilometers) and the appropriations carried out during the decades after the establishment of the state (a few tens of square kilometers). The exaggeration and reasoning behind this argument create a false impression that the State of Israel has obtained most of its land by dispossessing its citizens. This impression undercuts the justification for the existence of the State of Israel and upholds the notion of return and restitution.[76]

## Claims for Restitution in the Supreme Court

The demand for restitution of "present absentee" properties has reached the legal arena in recent years. Although the Supreme Court expressed support in principle for the notion that expropriated land should be returned to owners if it is no longer needed for public use, it decreed that the law is not applicable to demands for the return of present absentees' assets.[77] In 2010, the Knesset limited that judgment with new legislation determining that this basic principle cannot be applied retroactively. The court approved the legality of this limit, with full knowledge of its implications for claims of restitution by present absentees.[78]

To date, Israeli courts have not granted claims for restitution. Their reasoning is usually legal, but it also reveals the more fundamental political issue that prevents the return. Thus, for example, Justice Dalia Dorner explained the rejection of the claim for restitution by landowners in the village of Iqrit as follows: "In this time, when the Palestinian demand for the right of return has come up again, the precedent of returning the dispossessed can harm important interests of the State. This position is related to affairs of the state, where the government has broad consideration, and the leeway for reasonableness it is afforded is very wide."[79]

In the Jabareen case, initiated by the aforementioned *Zochrot* organization, absentees from the abandoned village of *al-Lajjun* petitioned to overturn the expropriation of a plot of land now located within the boundaries of Kibbutz *Megiddo* that is mostly forested and used in part as the site of a water facility. The court denied the request on the mundane grounds that the forest serves a vital public need and is therefore inseparable from the plot of land under claim.[80] Justice Rubinstein added that "the issue of forestation in an area that is unsettled or was abandoned earlier, has assumed a central place in the ethos under which the State of Israel was established, as development of the country and making the wilderness bloom."[81]

In the case of the Museum of Tolerance, the Islamic Movement in Israel objected to the construction of the Center for Human Dignity planned by the Simon Wiesenthal Center on land in central (west) Jerusalem. The plot previously served as a public parking lot, but in earlier times it had been part of a Muslim cemetery. The Islamic Movement argued that the land belonged to a Muslim charitable trust and that the dead were being desecrated. The Supreme Court rejected the claim for restitution and determined that the Supreme Muslim Council, which had owned the land and was headed during the British Mandate period by Amin al-Husseini, was "absentee" since its members had left the country when the state was established, or even earlier (al-Husseini had worked with Nazi Germany). Nevertheless, to avoid desecrating the remains of the dead, the court ordered their proper reburial, despite testimony that the Supreme Muslim Council had not objected to the construction of a hotel on this land during the British Mandate period.[82]

Indeed, the law is extremely restrictive when it comes to restitution. Section 3 of the Basic Law: Human Dignity and Liberty, which was enacted in 1992 and was considered to have supreme constitutional legal status, determines that "there shall be no violation of the property of a person," albeit Section 10 further stipulates that this Basic Law shall "not affect the validity of any law in force prior to its commencement."[83] Notwithstanding, the court has expressed its uneasiness about this situation on a number of occasions.

In the Dinar case, former Supreme Court president Justice Dorit Beinisch explained the historical reasoning behind the LAA legislation, as well as its inherent difficulties: "The severe nature of the provisions of the Acquisition Law . . . can only be understood through the lens of the unique historical circumstances of the State's early years; against the background of that period's needs and at a time when lands were abandoned by their owners as a result of the war. These historical circumstances led to the enactment of the Acquisition Law, whose provisions seriously infringe upon property rights, and there is no doubt that such legislation today would not stand up to the test of constitutionality."[84]

Justice Esther Hayut gave a similar explanation in the Al-Uqbi case, when she rejected a petition by Bedouin citizens to overturn the expropriations of land in the northern Negev:

> There is no opening whatsoever in the Acquisition Law allowing the return of the expropriated land to its original owners, even if the owners returned thereto. There is no denying that the Acquisition Law severely infringes the right to property that was recognized as a constitutional right.... However, it is an old law that is at issue, and the preservation of laws section... does not allow harming its validity, despite the constitutional difficulty it raises. Additionally, it had been ruled that in light of the Acquisition Law's special nature and the unique historical circumstances that led to its legislation, it is inappropriate at the present time to appeal the constitutionality of the expropriations that were affected by virtue thereof.[85]

In the Shawahna case, present absentees sued for the return of land they had worked after it was appropriated. Here, too, the court rejected their suit because of a fifty-year delay in its submission and because the circumstances regarding the time of the expropriation remained "shrouded in mist." At the same time, the court added that "it should be admitted that the conclusion we have arrived at is not easy" and therefore recommended that the state again consider "the petitioners' compensation arrangements, including the option of leaving in their possession plots of land that do not fill essential public needs."[86]

Israel's Supreme Court positions clearly reflect the tensions between the two components of the double promise. The court is bound by legal restrictions set by the legislature in the interest of preventing a reversal of the outcome of the War of Independence and maintaining the character of the Jewish state. At the same time, notwithstanding historical circumstances, the court is uncomfortable about such undemocratic infringements on the property of Israel's citizenry.

The issue of refugee property and particularly the assets of present absentees has remained on Israel's legal agenda since the establishment of the state. The existing situation clearly prioritizes the outcomes of the War of Independence and rules out the restoration of the past disposition of lands. Meanwhile, academic and civil attempts to alter the balance intensify, in part through legal actions. The Supreme Court continues to support the traditional political position of the state, but the texts of its judgments reveal its discomfort with it. The concern over increasing legal support for restitution claims may be one explanation for the current Knesset majority's reaffirmation of the Jewish character of the state in the new Nation-State Basic Law.

## The Claim to Indigenousness

A relatively new legal assertion of defiance against the Jewish character of the state and the demand to turn back the wheels of history is expressed in Arab and Bedouin citizens' petitions to be recognized as indigenous people. This demand exists in public discourse in relation to all Arabs in Israel,[87] but it has reached the Supreme Court through a small group of Bedouin Arabs,[88] accompanied by their demand for autonomy.[89]

The argument that Arabs or Bedouin are indigenous people derives primarily from a conceptual framework that refers to colonial conquests by foreign societies with no prior affinity to the conquered territory. The recognition of indigenous rights is the continuation of the process of decolonization.[90] The employment of this terminology in relation to Arab-Jewish relations in Israel equates the status of the Jews with that of the majority in any country that has undergone colonial conquest. It implies that the Jews are a group of outsiders, "settlers" in a foreign land inhabited and ruled by an indigenous people.[91] This approach ignores the link between Jews and the land, as well as the extraordinary circumstances of their migration and settlement in Israel.[92] It does not simply critique the actions of the state toward the minority and seek redress. It undermines the legitimacy of Jewish control over the territory and the idea of the State of Israel as a Jewish nation-state in which the Jewish people have realized their right to self-determination.

As expressed in Israel's Declaration of Independence, the state views Jews as the original indigenous people of the land. It points to the existence of a spiritual link between the Jewish People and the Land of Israel, similar to the link an indigenous group is required to have in order to establish its rights in its territory: "The Land of Israel was the birthplace of the Jewish people. Here their spiritual, religious and political identity was shaped. Here they first attained to statehood, created cultural values of national and universal significance and gave to the world the eternal Book of Books. After being forcibly exiled from their land, the people kept faith with it throughout their Dispersion and never ceased to pray and hope for their return to it and for the restoration in it of their political freedom."[93]

Section 1 of Nation-State Basic Law recently reaffirmed this notion.[94] Arab claims of indigenousness ignore the indigenous Jewish affinity to the same territory. This omission is particularly glaring in light of the relatively weak claim Bedouin make for affinity with the Negev areas in which they demand autonomy. The duration of their inhabitancy in the region is relatively brief, they have no particular spiritual affinity with that part of the country, and they have never had political independence. The claim for indigenous rights is aimed specifically at the sovereignty of the State of Israel in the Negev and has not to date been raised by Bedouin residing in other Middle Eastern states.[95] It is a claim that only emerged in the 1990s.[96]

The State of Israel, thus, cannot recognize claims that its Arab or Bedouin citizens are an indigenous group, because that would undermine its Jewish national character. Indeed, Israel has never signed international treaties recognizing the rights of indigenous people. The Supreme Court rejected the claim that Bedouin have indigenous rights as put forward in the Al-Uqbi case. The court determined that prior to the establishment of the state, Bedouin did not enjoy autonomy, that they were never recognized as indigenous, and that no norm of international law obligates the State of Israel to recognize them as indigenous.[97]

The aim of the refusal to recognize claims to indigeneity is consistent with protecting the Jewish component of the double promise rather than with its democratic component, which requires some sort of recognition of the Bedouin and their rights. The court gave expression to this by clarifying, alongside its rejection of the claim to indigenous rights, that "It is undisputed that the matter of the Bedouin tribes' rights in and to the Negev lands is a weighty matter for which a solution must be found, to the satisfaction of all of the parties, and the sooner that happens, the better."[98]

In a third discussion of the same case, Supreme Court president Justice Miriam Naor repeated this call: "The question of formalizing the rights of Bedouin tribes to Negev lands is a complicated, complex and sensitive social-legal-political issue that has yet to be fully resolved . . . it is appropriate that a solution be found to this question, which is acceptable to all sides and which is based on a broad perspective and mutual respect, and the sooner the better."[99] Another Supreme Court justice, Elyakim Rubinstein, outlined a practical way to resolve the problem: to establish new towns for the resettlement of the Bedouin community.[100]

In other words, the court rejects claims that undermine the independence, sovereignty, and Jewish character of the State of Israel, thereby fulfilling the Jewish component of its double promise. Its admonishments that the plight of the Bedouin be addressed are aimed at encouraging the realization of the democratic component of that promise, by providing an appropriate response to Bedouin settlement needs.

## The Allocation of Land Resources

### Separation or Integration? The Debate

#### THE DIFFERENT MODELS

A further challenge, perhaps the greatest, to the realization of the double promise is the call to forge an equitable policy for the allocation of land resources to the Arab minority. There are two possible and contradictory models for this. One, which we shall call the "separation model," assumes that the majority and minority populations do not assimilate with one another and do not aspire to. According to this model, the government would allocate land resources to settlements or neighborhoods with distinct ethnonational affiliations. Indeed, according to the separation model, it is neither possible nor desirable for the two populations to integrate, and therefore they must continue to live separately, side by side. In contrast, according to another model, which we shall call the "integration model," it is both possible and appropriate to integrate the two population groups into mixed communities, neighborhoods, or settlements. Each model strives to achieve equality in a different way. The separation model tends to allocate land resources to population groups, whereas the integration model provides individuals of all population groups with equal opportunities to participate in all types of common land use.

Choosing between the two models is difficult both for policy makers and for citizens. Both the Arab and the Jewish public are divided in their actual willingness to live in mixed settlements.[101] Arab leadership tends to prefer collective and separate allocation. The vision statement of Israel's Arabs calls for *"special collectively-based* allocation in the distribution of physical public resources in the state."[102] The English translation of the document omits the demand for "collectively-based" allocation of land and makes do instead with the call for "equal distribution of resources, such as budget, land and housing."[103] Some advocates of the collective allocation of land resources hold this position as a protest against the Jewish-Zionist character of the state. They rule out the integration option because they view it as acceptance of the State of Israel in its existing form.[104] The integration model is also criticized for the opposite reason: the fear that the intermingling of populations would weaken the Jewish character of Jewish population centers and thereby undermine the Jewish nature of the state.[105] Both the majority and the minority, thus, are unwilling or at least not eager to integrate with one another.

### THE POSITION OF THE SUPREME COURT

Rulings of the Supreme Court show no clear preference for one model over the other. The precedent-setting ruling of the Supreme Court in the Ka'adan case promoted the integration model.[106] The court's president, Justice Aharon Barak, ruled, "Dissimilar treatment on the basis of religion or nationality is 'suspect' treatment and is therefore prima facie discriminatory treatment."[107] Influenced by *Brown v. Board of Education*,[108] he ruled that "a 'separate but equal' policy is 'inherently unequal.' At the core of this approach is the notion that separation conveys an affront to a minority group that is excluded, sharpens the difference between it and others, and cements feelings of social inferiority."[109] Accordingly, he determined that when land resources are allocated to a settlement without unique community characteristics, "every person in Israel, regardless of nationality, would have been eligible to compete for the right to build a house in it."[110]

Barak's approach perceives Arab citizens as equal citizens, following the integration model, but it does not totally rule out the possibility of a separate allocation for Arabs on a national basis. Thus, for example, he rules that "occasionally, separate treatment may be considered equal, or in the alternative, that separate treatment may be justified, despite the violation of equality. This is especially so, inter alia, when it is the minority group itself that initiates the separate but equal treatment, seeking to preserve its culture and lifestyle and hoping to prevent 'forced assimilation.'"[111] Accordingly, Barak did not rule out the establishment of communities for Arabs or Jews exclusively but noted that "in point of fact, there has been no request for the establishment of an exclusively Arab communal settlement. In actuality, the State of Israel only allocates land for Jewish communal settlements. The result ('the effect') of the separation policy, as practiced today, is discriminatory."[112]

Barak's overall approach supports the integration model, particularly as it pertains to Arab populations in new settlements or existing Jewish settlements. Barak does not rule out the establishment of separate Jewish settlements, if Arab settlements are established as well, but Israel's land policy would clearly be hard pressed to maintain the principle of equality if it were required to allocate land resources for the establishment of separate settlements for the two groups. Such a double land policy would require greater land reserves than the state has to offer.[113] Thus, the default option he arrives at is apparently the equitable allocation of resources on an individual basis in mixed settlements and neighborhoods. For this reason, Barak's judgment was vociferously critiqued—from the right by those who believe that integration would undermine the Jewish component, and from the left by those who believe that integration would strengthen that component too much.[114]

The court expressed a somewhat different position in the Harel case.[115] This case entailed a debate over the constitutionality of a law allowing the government to grant a certain amount of authority in the area of rural settlement to the Settlement Division of the World Zionist Organization. The plaintiffs argued that the Settlement Division might discriminate against the Arab population, since its primary mission is to deal with Jewish settlements.[116] The state argued in response that the division is committed to the principle of equality and that it deals with the settlements of all sectors, including Arab settlements,[117] and thus expressed adherence to the collective "separated" model in the rural context. Justice Rubinstein accepted the state's position that the inequitable policy has yet to be proven, although he shared the fear that granting authority could undermine equality.[118] He endorsed the Ka'adan ruling but at the same time supported the collective interpretation offered by the state:

> The petitions before us do not refer to a violation of a concrete right of one specific person or another, and rather, deal with claims pertaining to the right of the Arab public as a whole. I am of the opinion, that in the areas of activity that the Division is charged with . . . the right to equality applies also in the realm of the Arab public's collective rights . . . the Arab population—and not only specific Arab citizens or residents—are entitled to an equitable distribution of state resources, including the allocation of land. . . . The important interest—the Zionist and national-state—of promoting Jewish settlement in various areas of the country should not detract from sincere parallel concern about promoting and developing settlements in other sectors of Israeli society. . . . This is not about "communicating vessels" and a zero-sum game, whereby greater development and thriving among Jewish settlements will accordingly reduce the promotion of rural and agriculture settlement in other sectors of Israeli society. . . . For me, they are linked . . . indeed, such an enterprise, if managed fairly and properly, could be an example of prosperity for all, including the non-Jewish sectors.[119]

Rubinstein's approach, then, supports a policy of promoting collective-based equality in the rural sector, separate but equal.

### THE DEBATE WITHIN THE NATION-STATE LAW

The dry text of the new Nation-State Basic Law apparently decided the issue of the proper land allocation standard favoring the separation model. Early drafts of this law proposed formulas that were closer to Barak's attitude in the Ka'adan case and supported the possibility of an integration model. An early draft by MK Ayelet Shaked, who was later to become minister of justice, suggested adopting a formula whereby the "*individual* rights of all its citizens," rather than their collective rights, should be reserved.[120] Another draft of this law was vaguer, since it proposed to codify "the values of Israel as a Jewish state in the spirit of the principles of its Declaration of Independence."[121] The declaration did not assert an explicit position on the issue of separation or integration, and thus, each side may interpret it as it wills. A later draft included support for a limited general arrangement for separation: "The State may permit a community, including the members of a single religion or the members of a single nationality, to establish separate community settlements."[122] The final, enacted version firmly supported the separation model. Section 7, titled "Jewish Settlement," stated that "the state views Jewish settlement as a national value and will labor to encourage and promote its establishment and development."[123] Apparently, this formulation deals only with separate settlements for Jews and not with the other side of the equation—namely, Israel's obligation toward minority settlements, either separate or integrated. However, the law does not negate this obligation, which, as mentioned above, the Supreme Court recognized. Since the law does not define the term *Jewish Settlement*, it does not negate the possibility of using the integration model within settlements that have no special Jewish community characteristics. Such an interpretation could reconcile, albeit narrowly, the law with the approach expressed in the Ka'adan case. Indeed, reaffirming the constitutionality of the Nation-State law, the Supreme Court fully accepted the government's interpretation to Section 7 of this Law according to which this section "does not include in its contents a permit for the establishment of separate settlements for Jews, which will not allow the acceptance of non-Jews, in the name of recognizing Jewish settlement as a national value. Also, and without exhausting the examples, section 7 does not give the state authorities the power to grant incentives only to Jewish citizens . . . without granting these incentives to non-Jewish citizens."[124]

## Integration or Separation in Practice

### AREAS OF INTEGRATION

In practice, government policy combines the two models but tends primarily toward the collective model of separation. The integration model guides the government in the allocation of land when establishing urban settlements or new neighborhoods in existing urban settlements not of a special community and having no special social characteristics. However, this mode of action is quite limited, since in recent decades the government has established very few new settlements; it is relevant primarily to the establishment of neighborhoods in existing urban settlements, cities or towns. Here another element comes into play, which, though gradually diminishing, is the overwhelming tendency of both populations to avoid integration and prefer living in cities or neighborhoods with homogeneous populations.[125] Therefore, the realization of the integration model during the stage of the initial allocation of resources for urban settlement is relevant only to those areas where a heterogeneous demand for government allocation of lands has emerged. The government likewise expressed its commitment to full individual equality in these areas in relation to the secondary leasing market—that is, the government's acquiescence to the transfer of leases from Jews to Arabs or the transfer of ownership through Israel lands to Arab lessees in urban settlements.[126] The effect of the government second leasing market is thus more significant in settlements established on Israel lands, settlements that tend to be newer, located in the periphery, and of less importance in established older urban settlements where there is a high percentage of privately owned land.

The key factor advancing the process of integration in urban settlements is not the hand of the government but, first and foremost, the hidden hand of market forces, and also to some extent, history and geography. About a quarter of the Arab population has been living for many years in eight mixed cities with an Arab minority of more than 10 percent of the overall population. Seven of these cities have always had an Arab population core (Jerusalem, Tel Aviv-Jaffa, Haifa, Acre, Ramla, Lod, and Ma'alot-Tarshiha).[127] Within these cities, the populations tend to segregate into distinct separate neighborhoods, but in some neighborhoods in these mixed cities, there is a process of integration. The result of this process is the creation of new mixed neighborhoods and, sometimes, their abandonment by the former population.[128] In recent years, the migration of Arab populations to cities previously settled by Jewish populations has increased. One such city, Nazareth Illit (now called Nof HaGalil, "Galilee View"), has long since become a mixed city according to the definitions of the Central Bureau of Statistics, since its Arab population has surpassed 20 percent and there are predictions that it will no longer have a Jewish majority by 2030. Between 1 percent and 1.5 percent of the country's Arab population have moved into twenty additional cities. In some of these cities, the proportion of Arab residents is extremely small, but the overall trend is of growth. Reasons for migration are primarily economic and include housing shortages in the place of origin or employment and social considerations.[129]

Resistance from the Jewish public often accompanies the process of integration. This resistance has on occasion required legal intervention.[130] Thus, for example, when Arab citizens won a tender for self-building in a new neighborhood in Afula, the losing Jewish bidders petitioned the Supreme Court with the argument that the winners' success was the result of unfair collusion on the price. The Supreme Court examined the claims and rejected most of them. It also remarked that, although no concrete evidence has been found to that effect, "the suspicion arises that the background to the petition might have been the desire to prevent Arabs from settling in Afula."[131]

### AREAS OF SEPARATION

The government manages a clear policy that apparently enables nationality-based collective segregation concerning two types of settlements. The first type includes settlements with special character, such as collective farming settlements (*kibbutzim* and *moshavim*) or community settlements under four hundred households. The former were mostly established as Jewish collective communities prior to the establishment of the state or in its early years and were inhabited exclusively by a Jewish population. The latter were established mainly over the past few decades. Penetrating the veteran collective settlements, as well as similar small community settlements being established today, will in most cases entail passing an internal review or "admissions committee." Although this mechanism does not permit discrimination on the basis of nationality, it does permit objections based on ethnicity to be masked as considerations of unsuitability to the community's social and cultural fabric and lifestyle. The requirement of an interview and entry test creates a social barrier to the unhindered integration of minority groups into such settlements.[132] Even today, the population of these settlements is primarily Jewish, and Arab candidates find it extremely difficult to navigate their admissions committee,[133] though there are some successful exceptions.[134] This barrier makes it similarly difficult for members of other communities in Israeli society to join these settlements.[135]

In the Sabach case, the Supreme Court rejected, by a majority of five to four, a petition against the constitutionality of the admissions committee mechanism in community settlements. It believed that insufficient evidence of the mechanism's inequitable function had accumulated.[136] Data submitted to a Knesset subcommittee in 2017 revealed that the rate of those rejected had decreased threefold since the process was regulated through legislation and currently stood at about 2.5 percent (out of 3,120 applicants).[137] One of the justices in the minority in the Sabah case, Justice Salim Joubran, who is himself a Christian Arab, held that the law was unconstitutional and that the reason for the legislation was "the majority's desire that the minority should *not integrate* into it."[138]

The debate over the legitimacy of the admissions committee mechanism in small community settlements thus reflects, overtly or as a subtext, the deliberations in Israeli society between the model of collective separation and the model of individual integration. A 2019 report revealed that such communities continue to use the practice of the admissions committee even when their population exceeds the quota of four hundred households. It is not clear to what extent the government was aware of this, and in any case, it has done nothing to prevent it so far.[139] Private bills either to formally rehabilitate this practice with communities of more than seven hundred households or to completely abolish it are pending in the Knesset.[140]

The second type of settlement for which the land allocation policy is collective and ethnicity based includes more than 129 settlements, urban and rural, in which the majority of Israel's Arab population reside.[141] Most of these settlements existed prior to the establishment of the state, and only a few, primarily in the Bedouin sector, were founded later. The Jewish population shows no interest in living in these settlements. The integration of Jews in non-Jewish urban settlements is rare and, indeed, finds no expression in official statistics.[142] The allocation of resources to these settlements by the state is intended solely for the needs of the Arab population. The government's strategic housing plan for 2017–40 establishes "exclusive goals for homogeneous Arab settlements."[143] As part of the concentrated government effort to resolve the housing crisis in the Arab sector, the housing cabinet defined favored zones for housing in Arab settlements.[144] Following a government decision from 2008, a special national outline plan was prepared for the establishment of a new urban settlement in the Galilee "for the entire minority population of the entire Galilee region of Israel."[145] The plan has yet to be finally approved and implemented, and it appears to have opponents in the Arab public as well.[146]

The government applies a similar policy toward the Bedouin population, a seminomadic Muslim ethnic minority group that constitutes about 16 percent of Israel's Arab population and about 3.5 percent of the entire population and that is undergoing a process of permanent settlement.[147] The government seeks to settle most of the Bedouin in urban settlements established specifically in accordance with their needs.[148] The Supreme Court endorsed this separate policy while remarking that it is a "transition period policy, until Bedouin are *assimilated* into Israeli society, as they see fit."[149] It should be mentioned that since the 1990s the government has also established separate settlements and neighborhoods for the Haredi-Jewish population, whose orthodox lifestyle makes its integration into heterogeneous urban environments difficult.[150]

### *Separate or Integrated? Concluding Remarks*

In conclusion, real estate in Israel is largely "separate but equal." Among the various communities, complex differences, both historical and cultural, and mutual mistrust support separation. The government likewise appears to accept this reality, and to a certain extent, so does the judicial authority. However, against all odds, a slow but accelerating process of integration does exist. The primary responsibility for this process of integration lies with the invisible hand of the free market, but some also lies with the Supreme Court's messages in support of integration, which have removed some of the barriers that might otherwise hinder progress. Although on the face of it the new Nation-State Basic Law strengthens the practical trend of separation, it leaves ample room for interpretation to permit the moderate integration currently prevailing.

## Claims of Inequality: Where and to What Extent?

### *Different Criteria for the Evaluation of Inequality*

How successful has the State of Israel been in meeting the democratic challenge of equality in the allocation of land resources? The coexistence of two conflicting models for a shared existence, the separation model and the integration model, has a large bearing on the matter. For example, where populations live separately in territorial blocks of a homogeneous ethnic identity, it is possible to compare general characteristics of these blocks, such as rates of land ownership and expropriations, municipal status, planning, and investment. When the populations are intermixed, it becomes more difficult to compare such parameters. Another method of comparing minority and majority groups is to break down the statistics of their socio-economic status—by income and education level, for example. This method provides a population overview of both mixed and separate settlements. Supporters of the separation model point to inequality in parameters of the first type since remedying inequality in this case entails separate collective allocation of resources. Reliance on parameters of the latter kind may indicate support for the integration model, especially if it turns out that integration improves socioeconomic status.

In the following paragraphs, we shall examine some common assertions concerning inequality of the first type and analyze claims of discrimination against Arab settlements in the following areas of land policy: distribution of private property rights in real estate, land expropriation, allocation of public land in the planning and development of settlements, the number of new settlements established, and the distribution of municipal space. We will conclude with a note on socioeconomic inequality.

## Distribution of Private Property Rights in Real Estate

One common claim concerning inequality in the treatment of Israel's Arab minority is that the proportion of land they own privately (3.5%, about 700 square kilometers) is considerably smaller than their percentage in the population (over 20%).[151] In fact, the private ownership of land in Israel overall is only 7 percent (about 1500 square kilometers). Thus, the share of land privately owned by Israeli Arabs is in fact larger than their population proportion (almost 50%). All the same, this quantitative advantage in terms of private land holdings is not the result of a deliberate and generous policy of land allocation by the State of Israel, but rather of historical circumstances.[152]

The argument that the remaining 93 percent of Israeli land is allocated to Jews is unfounded as well. Most of the Israel lands are open terrain not allocated to anyone.[153] Urban Israel lands total just 251 square kilometers,[154] which are leased and sold to the Arab population as well, both in separate settlements and mixed ones, and so far there is no accurate data on the ethnic distribution of this resource. Residential built-up coverage of

Arab settlements in proportion to total residential built-up coverage (18%) is higher than their percentage in the population as a whole (14%, excluding mixed cities).[155]

In sum, the Arab minority in Israel has a slight advantage over the Jewish majority in terms of private land holdings in Arab settlements, as well as in residential built-up coverage of the land. This data does not evidence equality in the allocation of other land resources, but it certainly indicates that the picture of inequality is neither simple nor one-dimensional.

## Land Expropriation

Another area that raises common claims of inequality is land expropriation. One such claim is that Israel has expropriated more land from its Arab citizenry than from its Jewish citizens and even that this is the reason for Arab ownership of only 3.5 percent of all private land in Israel.[156] This claim is certainly true with respect to the property of present absentees, whose various petitions for restitution were discussed above. However, this was a one-time act of seizure under extraordinary wartime circumstance. It is not an expression of consistent and ongoing discriminatory land policy by the state. The lands of the present absentees mentioned above are not considered part of the existing Arab settlements in Israel.

If we were to focus only on the expropriations that have taken place in these settlements since the War of Independence in the context of "business as usual," the picture of inequality would appear quite different. The extent of lands the State of Israel expropriated from all its citizens between the years of 1948 and 1998 only amounts to between 75 and 125 square kilometers. Although there is no precise data about their ethnic distribution through the years, up until 1964, only 15 percent of the expropriations were from settlements with Arab populations (about 19 square kilometers) and an additional 15 percent were from mixed cities.[157] Only a few notable examples of land expropriation have drawn the attention and criticism of academic literature: lands for the establishment of Nazareth Illit (about 1.2 square kilometers); lands near the village of Makr for the establishment of a new city in the Galilee (about 5.5 square kilometers); and Galilee lands expropriated in the 1970s (about 6.3 square kilometers), which led to the civil revolt known as Land Day.[158] In absolute numbers, these expropriations deducted from the land inventory of private Arab owners are minimal.

Israel did indeed use these expropriations for the establishment of cities for the settlement of the Jewish population, which was growing very fast at the time, but as already noted, the cities established during that period are today migration destinations for the Arab population of nearby settlements.[159] Nevertheless, for the past forty years, the Arab public has marked these expropriations with an annual memorial protest. More than just a protest against the relatively minor injustice entailed in the expropriations, the event is primarily a collective display of Arab nationalist devotion to the land, entailing a general protest against the Jewish nature of the state.[160]

A further criticism with regard to some of the land expropriations focuses on the decades-long delay in realizing their stated purposes, a possible indication that they were unnecessary to begin with. This was not a widespread phenomenon, but there are sporadic examples, most striking among them the expropriation of lands around the village of Makr in 1976 for establishing an Arab city. The city has yet to be founded, but in 1988 and again in 2009, the Supreme Court repeatedly rejected the Arab landowners' petitions, which were based on the long delay in realizing the plan. The court did indeed determine that "30 years of delay are a fairly long period of time. In the terms of a private individual this is a period that is almost inconceivable," but it expressed its trust in the state's promise that "there are signs of progress in actions towards beginning to realize the goals of the expropriation."[161] The court even suggested that the state should consider compensating the owners with alternative lands and perhaps integrate them into the urban area to be established, but the owners refused the compensation "because of their deep connection to their own land."[162] Not until 2014 did the state complete an advanced version of National Outline Plan 44 for the establishment of an "urban tier for the Arab population" on these lands. This new urban space will cover 2.7 contiguous square kilometers of state land and offer housing solutions for a population of forty thousand residents.[163] Yet the plan has yet to receive final approval, and its implementation continues to move forward slowly.[164]

The slow progress in planning and development does not reflect well on the policy. It also reveals the difficulties faced by the government in implementing the separation model. All the same, there are similar examples of delays in realizing the purposes of expropriation in Jewish cities, and the bureaucratic reasons behind these delays are not necessarily reflective of a discriminatory policy.[165]

## Allocation of Public Land to Existing Arab Settlements

Some raise the claim that the state is not enthusiastic enough about developing existing Arab settlements or neighborhoods. This claim actually reflects, in part if not in full, differences of opinion as to the optimal way of utilizing private land in Arab settlements. The high proportion of private land holdings in these settlements is not necessarily a blessing. Land ownership in Arab villages is the result of land distribution among families and clans (*hamullot* or *hama'il*). Owners view land as family property passed from one generation to another, with very few transfers between families. The land is viewed as promised to the next generation and as insurance against troubles. As a result, there is almost no modern real estate market in most of the Arab cities and villages. Long-term family ownership results in the fragmentation of properties through inheritance and creates serious obstacles to cooperation. Land development is thus far from optimal, and building rates are usually lower than those typical in Jewish urban settlements.[166] That is why the average population density in Arab settlements is lower than in Jewish urban settlements.[167] There are not enough properties on the market, and the price of the few that are there is extremely high.[168] There is not enough land available for infrastructure and other public needs in core areas. Property owners do not willingly contribute land for public usage, and local authorities are hesitant to expropriate private land for such purposes. That is why there are also fewer independent planning initiatives in Arab settlements.[169] The lack of planning leads to the widespread phenomenon of unplanned construction, which is illegal in Israel.[170] All these internal problems create obstacles to the development of private land in Arab settlements and contribute to a shortage of land for expansion and development.

The situation described here has given rise to a debate over the appropriate way to solve the acute shortage of land in Arab settlements. One proposed solution is to allocate additional state lands for the development of these settlements. This solution lies in the hands of the state, which must allocate the additional lands and provide development plans for areas generally concentrated on the periphery of existing settlements rather than at their center because that is where the public land reserves are found.[171] The solution would accept the existing distribution of private holdings and assign the primary responsibility for resolving the shortage to the state. Another solution, usually endorsed by the state, seeks a more efficient use of private land reserves and their incorporation into the real estate market to fulfill the state's desire to halt illegal construction and to move toward a regime of construction according to outline planning.

A good example of the conflicts between these two approaches is the Arara case, at the center of which was a plan prepared by the local council of an Arab settlement that included post facto approval of illegal construction, expansion of the settlement's borders, and allocation of additional state lands for development. Various state appeals committees rejected this plan, with the argument that there are ample reserves of private land in the town, of which only 50 percent have been utilized according to existing plans. Both the District Court and the Supreme Court instructed the state to reconsider the plan while giving weight to the unique characteristics of Arab settlements.[172] In the Mahul case, mentioned above, the Supreme Court refused to annul an expropriation of lands for establishing an Arab city with the argument that "in Arab settlements throughout the country and in the Galilee in particular, there exists a problem of incomplete utilization of building rights on privately owned land."[173]

In recent years, the government has made efforts to promote planning in Arab settlements. The National Committee for Planning and Construction of Preferred Housing Areas has declared development zones in Arab settlements, and plans for some are already prepared.[174] The deputy attorney general also approved plans that include recognition of illegal construction, so long as this is not their primary purpose and the local authority commits to a strict enforcement of planning laws in the future.[175]

The tension between different approaches to developing Arab settlements is yet another expression of the dilemma surrounding the equality model. The demand for merging privately held land inventories into the real estate market clearly adopts the integration model, while the demand for special consideration of the unique characteristics of these land inventories acquiesces to the separation model.

### Establishment of New Arab Settlements

Another commonly raised claim about discrimination is that, in contrast to hundreds of new settlements for Jews, the State of Israel has established no new Arab settlements.[176] The demand for equality in the number of new settlements, as noted, supports the separation approach. However, the claimed numerical inequality merits a more precise and in-depth discussion. First, as noted, several Bedouin settlements have been established, as have new neighborhoods in towns with Arab populations. Second, the unequal number of newly established settlements does not necessarily reflect inequality in the number of localities available to the minority group for separate living. Thus, for example, according to data from 2003, the number of Arab settlements within each urban settlement cluster with a population ranging between two thousand and one hundred thousand matches the relative proportion of the Arab population within the overall population living in similarly sized settlements, as detailed in table 5.1.[177]

Most of the Arab population is concentrated in midsize urban settlements. In 2015, Arabs constituted 14 percent of the urban population in Israel, 58 percent of the population of local councils, and 8.5 percent of the population in regional councils. Table 5.2 shows that in each of the municipal administration categories there is a correlation between the number of Arab local authorities and the Arab population proportion for each category.[178]

The most significant numerical difference between Arab and Jewish settlements exists in the number of rural settlements. In 2015[179] there were over one thousand small settlements in Israel with populations of less than nine thousand. Of these roughly 673 were kibbutzim and moshavim, and only 47 were Arab settlements (4.5%), whose overall population comprises 8.5 percent of the total population of small settlements in regional authorities.[180] This minor representation of the Arab population in the rural sphere does not diverge significantly from the proportion of Arabs within the overall population in this sector, which, by its nature, represents only a small fraction of the total population (10%).[181]

All the same, the rural areas predominantly consist of a small scattered Jewish population. Furthermore, most of these settlements fall under the jurisdiction of Jewish regional councils, while most of the land under the jurisdiction of these regional councils is open and uninhabited, or sparsely populated land in the Negev, Arava, Golan, Jerusalem corridor, and other areas. Yet the total area under the municipal jurisdiction of non-Jewish settlements comes to just 3 percent of the total area of the country (about 687 square kilometers).[182] In terms of land allocation, this is certainly the most explicit manifestation of the preference given to the Jewish side of the double promise. The purpose of maintaining control of the rural areas through municipal administration of regional and local councils is to ensure the sovereignty of the State of Israel over this space, particularly in the periphery. The demand that this space be distributed collectively to Arabs

Table 5.1. Arab and Jewish Settlements: Number of Settlements and Population (2003).

| Settlement Size | Number of Settlements (percent) | | Population (percent) | |
|---|---|---|---|---|
| | Jewish | Arab | Jewish & Mixed | Arab |
| 50,000–100,000 | 7 (88%) | 1 (12%) | 537,078 (90%) | 62,706 (10%) |
| 20,000–50,000 | 34 (85%) | 6 (15%) | 1,188,318 (86%) | 185,173 (14%) |
| 10,000–20,000 | 14 (39%) | 22 (61%) | 217,570 (29%) | 535,340 (71%) |
| 2,000–10,000 | 41 (45%) | 51 (55%) | 249,531 (46%) | 291,833 (54%) |

Table 5.2. Arab and Jewish Settlements, by Municipal Administration Categories: Number of Settlements and Population (2015).

| Municipal Administration | Number of Authorities (percent) | | Population in All Settlements (percent) | |
|---|---|---|---|---|
| | Jewish & Mixed | Arab | Jewish & Others | Arab |
| Municipality | 65 (85.5%) | 11 (14.5%) | 85.9% | 14.1% |
| Local Authority | 58 (46.4%) | 67 (53.6%) | 41.5% | 58.5% |
| Regional Authority | 51 (94.4%) | 3 (5.6%) | 91.5% | 8.5% |

as well is viewed as an attempt to undermine this sovereignty.[183] The democratic part of the double promise obligates the expansion of opportunities for individual participation and the integration of Arab minority members in this space. As noted above, the Ka'adan case sought to meet this obligation under the model of individual integration, with limited success. It is unclear how many Arabs wish to integrate into existing rural Jewish settlements such as kibbutzim.[184] All the same, as noted above, there are still major obstacles to their integration into most rural settlements. Although this applies only to a small proportion of the populace, here the Jewish dimension of the double promise clearly trumps the democratic dimension.

## Socioeconomic Inequality

Finally, there are many arguments pertaining to the socioeconomic inequality between Arab and Jewish settlements. The inequality is not necessarily the result of discrimination in terms of land resource allocations, but rather it derives from other areas of governmental policy, as well as from internal blocks within the Arab settlements and Arab society. A discussion of these is beyond the scope of this book. In any case, Arab settlements figure primarily in the lower ranks of the combined socioeconomic index published by the Central Bureau of Statistics. The index examines a number of variables related to demography, education, employment, and standard of living. Mixed cities are placed higher on this index.[185] The Arab population migrating to cities that have become mixed only in recent years is more established socioeconomically.[186] These findings certainly indicate that the democratic promise to the Arab minority of Israel has yet to be realized but, at the same time, they also reveal that, at the moment, integration may promote equality more significantly than separation.

## Concluding Remarks

One of the central and most fundamental identity issues in the State of Israel is its aspiration to be the nation-state of the Jewish people, on the one hand, and a state that maintains complete equality for all its citizens, on the other. The realization of this double promise is a significant challenge in light of the complex relationship between the Arab minority and the Jewish majority. The realization of the promise must bridge two conflicting national aspirations, and it reflects the existential paradox at the root of the State of Israel's identity, as well as that of each of its citizens. This dual identity problem finds expression in central and controversial areas of Israel's land policy toward its Arab minority.

The first such expression concerns the policy related to the outcomes of the War of Independence. As the Jewish homeland, Israel cannot return to its prewar circumstances for fear that restitution might affect its Jewish character. As a democratic state, it is obligated to compensate citizens whose property was expropriated. The majority of the Arab public in Israel and its leadership, as well as a minority of the Jewish public, support restitution, at least for the present absentees. Generally, if not universally, endorsement of this solution is also an expression of resistance to the Jewish nature of the state. The policy of not returning expropriated lands is enshrined in law and immune to judicial statutory criticism. The Supreme Court supports this policy, even while expressing its unhappiness with the damage it has done in terms of the property rights of Arab citizens.

The second expression of the problems with the dual promise is related to the policy of land resource allocation in Israel. The state authorities and its citizens are conflicted over two contradictory models to guide this policy: a separation model, according to which the majority and minority groups continue to reside in separate settlements, or an integration model, according to which the two population groups live together in mixed communities, neighborhoods, and settlements. Public opinion regarding a practical willingness to live in mixed settlements is split in both Jewish and Arab populations. Neither the majority nor the minority shows an eagerness to integrate, and it is doubtful whether they would be prepared to do so. In reality, land allocation in Israel is primarily separate but equal. The historical and cultural differences of the two populations and the complexities of their mutual mistrust all support the separation model. It would appear that the government accepts and sometime even supports this trend, and so, to some extent, does the judicial authority. Nonetheless, and against all odds, a slow but accelerating process of integration does exist. The primary reason for this is the hidden force of the free market, combined with messages issued by the Supreme Court regarding integration and the removal of some of the obstacles to its operation.

How successful has the State of Israel been in meeting the challenges of an equitable allocation of its land resources? The Arab minority holds about 50 percent of private lands, and its holding of land allocated for residential purposes does not fall short of its percentage in the population. The expropriations carried out by the state soon after its establishment, beyond the refugee villages, have had a relatively small impact on the reserves of privately owned Arab land. However, Arab settlements do suffer from a shortage of land and appropriate plans. Progress is very slow, and that has resulted in problems within Arab society that make further development more difficult and place a greater burden on the state to live up to its responsibilities. State authorities have made efforts to do so, however inadequately, but have stipulated that the allocation of additional space for the development of Arab settlements is contingent upon a more efficient utilization of private lands.

Since the establishment of the State of Israel, very few new Arab settlements have been established (and these, mainly for Bedouin), but the proportional number of Arab settlements in the midsize urban localities, where most of the Arab population is concentrated, correlates with the overall proportion of Arabs within the general population of settlements of this size. There is also a correlation in each of the municipal administration categories, between the proportion of the Arab population and the proportion of Arab municipal authorities. The rural sector is predominantly inhabited by Jewish rural settlements, and furthermore, most of it is under the jurisdiction of Jewish regional councils. This, indeed, is the most blatant expression of the preference for the Jewish aspect of the double promise in terms of land policy.

Another prominent expression is the low socioeconomic ranking of Arab settlements according to a combination of demographic, educational, employment, and living standard variables. The Arab population of mixed cities and of cities that have only recently become mixed have fared better. It would appear that integration advances socioeconomic equality.

In sum, these different fields of land policy reflect the problem of Jewish-democratic identity with regard to the status of the Arab minority in Israel. The problem continues to haunt the State of Israel today, more than seventy years after its establishment, and will apparently continue to do so for many years to come.

## Notes

1. Basic Law: Human Dignity and Liberty, 5752–1992, *Sefer Ha-Hukim* 150, §1 (Hebrew), unofficial English translation, The Israeli Ministry of Foreign Affairs, https://www.mfa.gov.il/mfa/mfa-archive/1992/pages/basic%20law-%20human%20dignity%20and%20liberty-.aspx.
2. §2 The Mandate for Palestine (July 24, 1922), Israeli Foreign Ministry, http://www.mfa.gov.il/mfa/foreignpolicy/peace/guide/pages/the%20mandate%20for%20palestine.aspx.
3. Israel Central Bureau of Statistics, "Table 2.1, Population by Population Group," 70 *Statistical Abstract of Israel 2019* (September 26, 2019), https://www.cbs.gov.il/he/publications/doclib/2019/2.shnatonpopulation/st02_01.pdf.
4. Israel Central Bureau of Statistics, *Long-Range Population Projections for Israel: 2009–2059* (2012), 7 (Hebrew), https://www.cbs.gov.il/he/publications/DocLib/tec/tec27/tec27.pdf.
5. Israel Central Bureau of Statistics, "Table 2.10, Projection of Population in Israel for 2020–2065, by Population Group, Sex and Age," 70 *Statistical Abstract of Israel 2019* (September 26, 2019), https://www.cbs.gov.il/he/publications/doclib/2019/2.shnatonpopulation/st02_10.pdf.
6. *Long-Range Population Projections*, supra note 4, at 7–9.
7. "Population Estimates July 1, 2019," United States Census Bureau, accessed June 12, 2020, https://www.census.gov/quickfacts/fact/table/US/PST045216.
8. The relationships between the Druze and the State of Israel are special. For this reason, many Druze do not strongly identify themselves as Arabs. This chapter will not discuss the complicated aspect of Druze identity in Israel. For further discussion, see Rabah Halabi, "Invention of a Nation: The Druze in Israel," 49 *Journal of Asian & African Studies* (2014): 267, 272–74; Mordechai Nisan, "The Druze in Israel: Questions of Identity, Citizenship, and

Patriotism," 64 *Middle East Journal* (2010): 575, 575–77, 582–83; Muhammad Amara and Izhak Schnell, "Identity Repertoires among Arabs in Israel," 30 *Journal of Ethnic and Migration Studies* (2004): 175, 183.

9. Israel Central Bureau of Statistics, "Table 2.19, Population, by Population Group, Religion, Age and Sex, District and Sub-district," 70 *Statistical Abstract of Israel 2019* (September 26, 2019), https://www.cbs.gov.il/he/publications/doclib/2019/2.shnatonpopulation/st02_19x.pdf.

10. *Long-Range Population Projections*, supra note 4, at 19; Matthijs Kalmijn and Frank Van Tubergen, "A Comparative Perspective on Intermarriage: Explaining Differences among National-Origin Groups in the United States," 47 *Demography* (2010): 459, 468–69 (Intermarriage rates in the United States).

11. Sammy Smooha, *Still Playing by the Rules: Index of Arab-Jewish Relations in Israel 2015* (Haifa: Pardes, 2017), 13, 49–50 (Hereafter: Index 2015).

12. Smooha, Index 2015, supra note 11, at 48; Raphael Cohen-Almagor, "Israeli Democracy and Rights of Its Palestinian Citizens," 45 *Ragion Pratica* (2015): 351, 362.

13. Amara and Schnell, "Identity Repertoires," supra note 8, at 183.

14. Tamar Hermann et al., *A Conditional Partnership: Jews and Arabs, Israel 2017* (Jerusalem: Israel Democracy Institute, 2017) (Hebrew), 29.

15. National Committee for the Heads of the Arab Local Authorities in Israel, *The Future Vision of the Palestinian Arabs in Israel* (Nazareth: National Committee for the Heads of the Arab Local Authorities in Israel, 2006), 5.

16. Smooha, Index 2015, supra note 11, at 37–39; Ahiya Raved, "Poll: 51% of Israeli Arabs Refuse to Recognize Israel as Jewish State," *Ynet-News*, July 3, 2018, https://www.ynetnews.com/articles/0,7340,L-5148927,00.html.

17. Wedi' Faris Boustany, *The Palestine Mandate: Invalid and Impracticable* (Beirut: American Press, 1936), 196–201.

18. Yehoshua Porat, *The Palestinian-Arab National Movement*, vol. 2: *From Riots to Rebellion 1929–1939* (London: Frank Cass, 1977), 127–30, 274–77; Nathan Feinberg, *The Arab-Israeli Conflict in International Law* (Jerusalem: Hebrew University Press, 1970), 21, 44, 50–51; Alexander Yakobson and Amnon Rubinstein, *Israel and the Family of Nations: The Jewish Nation-State and Human Rights*, trans. Ruth Morris and Ruchie Avital (Abingdon: Routledge, 2009; first published 2003, Tel Aviv), 25–26, 28.

19. Khalid Abu Toameh, "Abbas: Palestinians Won't Accept Jewish State," *Jerusalem Post*, March 4, 2015, http://www.jpost.com/Middle-East/Abbas-Palestinians-wont-accept-Jewish-state-Islamization-of-struggle-in-Mideast-392910.

20. "Hamas Covenant 1988: The Covenant of the Islamic Resistance Movement," Avalon Project, Yale Law School, August 18, 1988, §28, http://avalon.law.yale.edu/20th_century/hamas.asp; MEE Staff, "Hamas in 2017: The Document in Full," *Middle East Eye*, May 2, 2017, http://www.middleeasteye.net/news/hamas-charter-1637794876; Mordechai Kedar, "The Future Vision of the Islamic Movement," in *Muslim Minorities in Non-Muslim Majority Countries: The Test Case of the Islamic Movement in Israel*, ed. Elie Rekhess and Arik Rudnitzky (Tel Aviv: Tel Aviv University, 2011) (Hebrew), 117, 119–21.

21. Smooha, Index 2015, supra note 11, at 58–59, 69, 74, 78; Itamar Radai et al., "The Arab Citizens in Israel: Current Trends According to Recent Opinion Polls," 18 *Strategic Assessment* (2015): 101, 104–5.

22. Smooha, Index 2015, supra note 11, at 34–35.

23. See chap. 2.

24. Esther Webman, "The Evolution of a Founding Myth: The Nakba and Its Fluctuating Meaning," in *Palestinian Collective Memory and National Identity*, ed. Meir Litvak (New York: Palgrave Macmillan, 2009), 27, 34–35.

25. Smooha, Index 2015, supra note 11, at 49, 104.

26. *Future Vision of the Palestinian Arabs in Israel*, supra note 15, at 10.

27. Smooha, Index 2015, supra note 11, at 28, 30, 39, 62.

28. Chaim Gans, *A Just Zionism: On the Morality of the Jewish State* (Oxford: Oxford University Press, 2008), 25–51; Walter Laqueur, *A History of Zionism* (New York: Schocken Books, 2003; first published 1972, Weidenfeld and Nicolson, London), 599.

29. Smooha, Index 2015, supra note 11, at 33–34.

30. HCJ 6698/95 Ka'adan v. Israel Land Administration (2000), PD 54(1): 258, 282 (Hebrew), formal English translation, Barak J. Par. 31: https://supremedecisions.court.gov.il/Home/Download?path=EnglishVerdicts\95\980\066\a14&fileName=95066980_a14.txt&type=5 (Hereafter: Ka'adan case); VERSA: Opinions of the Supreme Court of Israel, Translated Opinions, http://versa.cardozo.yu.edu/opinions/ka%E2%80%99adan-v-israel-land-administration.

31. Author translation. Elyakim Rubinstein, "Israel Lands—A Legal Perspective: Long Term Revival or a Long-Term Catastrophe," 52 *Karka (Land)—Journal of the JNF Land Policy and Land Use Research Institute* (2001) (Hebrew): 21, 29; Elyakim Rubinstein, "The Attorney-General in Israel: A Delicate Balance of Power and Responsibilities in a Jewish and Democratic State," in *Israeli Institutions in the Crossroads*, ed. Raphael Cohen-Almagor (Abingdon: Routledge 2005), 143, 151.

32. Aharon Barak, *Interpretation in Law*, vol. III: *Constitutional Interpretation* (Srigim: Nevo, 1995) (Hebrew), 332.

33. *Sefer Ha-Hukim* 5768–2018 898 (July 28, 2018) (Hebrew), informal English translations: JPost.com Staff, "Read the Full Jewish Nation-State Law," *Jerusalem Post*, July 19, 2018, https://www.jpost.com/Israel-News/Read-the-full-Jewish-Nation-State-Law-562923; Simon Rabinovitch (ed.), *Defining Israel: The Jewish State, Democracy, and the Law* (Cincinnati: Hebrew Union College Press, 2018), 121; Unofficial translation by Dr. Susan Hattis Rolef, Knesset, https://main.knesset.gov.il/EN/activity/Documents/BasicLawsPDF/BasicLawNationState.pdf.

34. Proposed Bill and Explanatory Notes, Basic Law: Israel as the Nation-State of the Jewish People, *Hatzaot-Hok* 134 (2018) (Hebrew); Chagai Vinizky and Shaul Sharf, *Basic Law Proposal: Israel as the Nation State of the Jewish People* (Jerusalem: Bursi Publishers and Menachem Begin Heritage Center, 2017) (Hebrew), 1–2, 5–7; Simon Rabinovitch, "Jewish and Democratic According to the Law," in *Defining Israel*, supra note 33, at 1, 6, 16.

35. "Basic Law: Israel the Nation State of the Jewish People," Knesset National Legislation Database, last modified July 26, 2018 (Hebrew), http://main.knesset.gov.il/Activity/Legislation/Laws/Pages/LawBill.aspx?t=lawsuggestionssearch&lawitemid=565913; Rabinovitch, "Jewish and Democratic," supra note 34, at 5–18; Jonathan Lis, "Israel's Governing Coalition to Advance Nation-State Bill That Subordinates Democracy to Judaism," *Haaretz*, December 18, 2017, https://www.haaretz.com/israel-news/.premium-coalition-to-advance-nation-state-bill-that-subordinates-democracy-to-judaism-1.5628953.

36. Rabinovitch, "Jewish and Democratic," supra note 34, at 18–25; Tamar Zieve, "Tens of Thousands Attend Druze-Led Protest against Nation-State Law," *Jerusalem Post*, August 4, 2018, https://www.jpost.com/Israel-News/Tens-of-thousands-attend-Druze-protest-against-Nation-State-Law-564130.

37. Yousef T. Jabareen, "Enshrining Exclusion: The Nation-State Law and the Arab Palestinians in Israel," in *Defining Israel*, supra note 33, at 249, 251–53; Michael Bachner, "Retired High Court Judge Urges Ex-colleagues to Overrule Nation-State Law," *Times of Israel*, July 31, 2018, https://www.timesofisrael.com/retired-high-court-judge-urges-ex-colleagues-to-overrule-nation-state-law/.

38. Sara Greenberg, "Netanyahu's Adviser to 'Post': Nation-State Law Critics are Misinformed," *Jerusalem Post*, August 6, 2018, https://www.jpost.com/Opinion/PMs-adviser-to-Post-Jewish-Nation-State-law-critics-are-misinformed-564267; Ruth Gavison, "Reflections on the Nation-State Law Debate," in *Defining Israel*, supra note 33, at 337, 340–42.

39. Minutes of Session No. 359 of the Twentieth Knesset 1274 (July 17, 2018) (Hebrew).

40. Tamar Ben-Ozer, "Bedouin Join Druze in High Court Petitions against Nation-State Law," *Jerusalem Post*, August 5, 2018, https://www.jpost.com/Israel-News/Bedouins-join-Druze-in-High-Court-petitions-against-Nation-State-Law-564193.

41. Revital Hovel and Noa Shpigel, "Israel's Justice Minister Warns of 'An Earthquake' If Top Court Kills Nation-State Law," *Haaretz*, August 5, 2018, https://www.haaretz.com/israel-news/.premium-justice-minister-warns-of-earthquake-if-court-kills-nation-state-law-1.6343122.

42. Israeli Public Broadcasting Corporation (Kan 11), "The High Court Hears Petitions against the Nation State Law" *Kan11 New*, December 22, 2020, https://www.youtube.com/watch?v=RFozxsh5uLE.

43. HCJ 5555/18 Hasson v. Knesset, C.J. Hayut, at par. 41 (Nevo, July 8, 2021)(Hebrew); Amy Spiro, "High Court Rejects Petitions Seeking to Strike Down Nation-State Law," *Times of Israel*, July 8, 2021, https://www.timesofisrael.com/high-court-rejects-petitions-seeking-to-strike-down-nation-state-law/.

44. Hasson case, supra note 43, J. Karra at par. 22.

45. See chap. 1, text under title "Transferring Palestinian Refugee Lands to the Public Administration."

46. Yaffa Zilbershats and Nimra Goren-Amitai, *Position Paper: Return of Palestinian Refugees to the State of Israel*, ed. Ruth Gavison (Jerusalem: Metzilah Center for Zionist, Jewish, Liberal and Humanist Thought, 2011), 22, 31–33, 42, http://din-online.info/pdf/mz7.pdf; Joel Singer, "Point/Counterpoint: No Palestinian 'Return' to Israel," 8 *Human Rights Brief*, no. 2 (Winter 2001): 5–8.

47. §3–4 Trading with the Enemy Ordinance, 1939, *Official Gazette*, supp. 1 (September 5, 1939), 95; §2 Absentees' Property Law (Compensation), 5733–1973, *Sefer Hukim* 164 (Hebrew); 27 LSI 176.

48. Haim Sandberg, "The Politics of 'Over-victimization': Palestinian Proprietary Claims in the Service of Political Goals," 19 *Israel Affairs* (2013): 488, 496–500.

49. See chap. 1, note 58 and text.

50. §1(b)(1)(iii)(b) Absentees' Property Law, 5710–1950, 4 LSI 68.

51. Haim Sandberg, *The Lands of Israel: Zionism and Post-Zionism* (Jerusalem: Sacher Institute, Hebrew University, 2007) (Hebrew), 78–80; Israel Lands Administration, *Report on Activities for the 1964–1965 Budget Year* (1965) (Hebrew), 165–66; Joseph Weitz, *Summary of Activities for the Implementation of the Land Acquisition (Validation of Acts and Compensation) Law, 5713–1953* (April 12, 1954), Central Zionist Archive (CZA), Section 246A, File 275.

52. Sandberg, *Zionism and Post-Zionism*, supra note 51, at 80–82; Hillel Cohen, "The Internal Refugees in the State of Israel: Israeli Citizens, Palestinian Refugees," 9 *Palestine-

*Israel Journal*, no. 2 (June 2002): 43, 44–45; Hillel Cohen, *The Present Absentees: The Palestinian Refugees in Israel since 1948* (Jerusalem: Van Leer Jerusalem Institute, 2000) (Hebrew), 7.

53. Minister of Finance Eliezer Kaplan to the Knesset, *Divrei Ha-Knesset*, vol. 12, col. 2209 (June 3, 1952) (Hebrew); Letter from the Minister of Foreign Affairs to the Custodian of Absentees' Property Dated June 20, 1951, Israel State Archive (ISA), 74th Division, Box 5746/c, File 5 (Hebrew); Summary of the meeting held at the office of the Director General of the Ministry of Finance on June 26, 1951, regarding the determination of prices for land in transfers from the Custodian of Absentees' Property to the Development Authority, ISA, 74th Division, Box 5741/C, File 14 (Hebrew).

54. Israel Lands Administration, *Report on the Activities for 1966–1967 Budget Year* (1967) (Hebrew), 73; Israel Lands Administration, *Report on the Activities for the 1975–1976 Budget Year* (1976) (Hebrew), 203; Hillel Cohen, *Present Absentees*, supra note 52, at 70.

55. §2, *Sefer Ha-Hukim* 58 (Hebrew); 7 LSI 43.

56. Author translation. MK Moshe Unna to the Knesset, *Divrei Ha-Knesset*, vol. 13, col. 856 (March 4, 1953) (Hebrew); see also Minister of Finance Eliezer Kaplan to the Knesset, *Divrei Ha-Knesset*, vol. 12, col. 202 (June 3, 1951) (Hebrew).

57. §3(b) LAA; Israel Lands Administration, *Report on the Activities for the 2005 Budget Year* (2006) (Hebrew), 128.

58. §5 LLA; MK Moshe Unna to the Knesset, *Divrei Ha-Knesset*, vol. 13, col. 857 (March 4, 1953) (Hebrew).

59. Weitz, *Summary of Activities*, supra note 51; ILA, 1964–65 Report, supra note 51, at 167; Israel Lands Administration, *Report on the Activities for the 2000 Budget Year* (2001), 100; Hillel Cohen, *Present Absentees*, supra note 52, at 83, 86, 91, 94.

60. ILA, 2005 Report, supra note 57, at 128; Ministry of Finance, Assets Division, "Payment of Compensation" (A file with reports of the Bureau for the Implementation of the Acquisition of Land Law in Haifa from the early 1960s), ISA, 99th Division, Box 3131/C, File 1.

61. Zilbershats and Goren-Amitai, *Position Paper*, supra note 46, at 9–10, 50, 62–64, 76; Sandberg, "'Over-victimization,'" supra note 48, at 496–500.

62. Smooha, Index 2015, supra note 11, at 104, 111.

63. MK Tawfik Toubi to the Knesset, *Divrei Ha-Knesset*, vol. 13, col. 858 (March 4, 1953) (Hebrew).

64. *Future Vision of the Palestinian Arabs in Israel*, supra note 15, at 15.

65. *Future Vision of the Palestinian Arabs in Israel*, supra note 15, at 10.

66. Adalah, *Inequality Report: The Palestinian Arab Minority in Israel* (Haifa: Adalah—The Legal Center for Arab Minority Rights in Israel, 2011), 4–5, 23–24, https://www.adalah.org/uploads/oldfiles/upfiles/Christian%20Aid%20Report%20December%202010%20FINAL(1).pdf.

67. "Interactive Map and Database on the History of the State of Israel's Expropriation of Land from the Palestinian People," Adalah—The Legal Center for Arab Minority Rights in Israel, accessed June 12, 2020, https://www.adalah.org/uploads/oldfiles/features/land/flash/.

68. Elie Rekhess, "The Arab Minority in Israel: Reconsidering the '1948 Paradigm,'" 19 *Israel Studies* (2014): 187, 200; HCJ 10163/09 Moasesset Al-Aqsa Ltd. v. The Municipality of Rehovot (December 13, 2012); HCJ 5703/12 Moasesset Al-Aqsa Ltd. v. Tel Aviv University (August 13, 2012); HCJ 3112/10 Moasesset Al-Aqsa Ltd. v. Municipality of Tel Aviv-Jaffa (May 4, 2010); HCJ 3280/10 Moasesset Al-Aqsa Ltd. v. Israel National Roads Company Ltd. (May

4, 2010); HCJ 4199/06 Al-Aqsa Company for the Development of Islamic Waqf Assets Ltd. v. Moshav Habonim (July 9, 2009); HCJ 516/08 Al-Aqsa Al-Mobarak Company Ltd. v. Moshav Ahihud (June 18, 2009); HCJ 8497/04 Al-Aqsa Company for the Development of Hekdesh Properties v. Moshav Kerem Maharal (June 17, 2009); HCJ 4734/08 Al-Aqsa Al-Mobarak Company Ltd. v. Mekorot—The National Water Company (January 18, 2009); HCJ 3172/08 Al-Aqsa Al-Mobarak Company Ltd. v. The Municipality of Yehud (June 23, 2008). All resources in this note are written in Hebrew.

69. Smooha, Index 2015, supra note 11, at 63, 64, 129, 131.
70. Smooha, Index 2015, supra note 11, at 63.
71. Hillel Cohen, *Present Absentees*, supra note 52, at 7–8; Eyal Benvenisti and Eyal Zamir, "Private Claims to Property Rights in the Future Israeli-Palestinian Settlement," 89 *Am. J. Int'l L.* (1995): 295, 300–301.
72. "Our Vision," Zochrot, accessed June 5, 2020, http://zochrot.org/en/content/17; Yifaat Gutman, *Memory Activism: Reimagining the Past for the Future in Israel-Palestine* (Nashville: Vanderbilt University Press, 2017), 112–42; Gerald M. Steinberg, "Europeans Fund Anti-Israel Libels," 22 *Middle East Quarterly*, no. 1 (Winter 2015): 1–15.
73. Bashir Bashir and Amos Goldberg, *The Holocaust and the Nakba: Memory, National Identity and Jewish-Arab Partnership* (Jerusalem: Van Leer Jerusalem Institute and Hakibbutz Hameuchad, 2015) (Hebrew); Ephraim Lavie and Amal Jamal (eds.), *The Nakba in the National Memory of Israel* (Tel Aviv University—Tami Steinmetz Center and Walter-Libach Institute for Jewish-Arab Coexistence, 2015) (Hebrew); Minerva Humanities Center, Tel Aviv University, *Annual Academic Report 2014–2015* (October 2015), 30–31 (Reporting "Conference: Zionist Resistance to the 1948 Expulsions, June 2015"), https://humanities.tau.ac.il/sites/humanities.tau.ac.il/files/MinervaAnnual-2014-2015-Web-Version_0.pdf.
74. Alexandre Kedar, "The Legal Transformation of Ethnic Geography: Israeli Law and the Palestinian Landholder 1948–1967," 33 *NYU J. Int'l L. & Pol.* (2001): 923, 947; Alexandre (Sandy) Kedar and Oren Yiftachel, "Land Regime and Social Relations in Israel," in *Swiss Human Rights Book*, ed. Hernando de Soto and Francis Cheneval (Zurich: Ruffer & Rub, 2006), 1: 127, 136–37.
75. Government of Palestine, *Survey of Palestine—Prepared in December 1945 and January 1946 for the Information of the Anglo-American Committee of Inquiry* (Palestine: Government Printer, 1946), 1:257–58.
76. Haim Sandberg, "Land Expropriations of Private Arab Land in Israel: An Empirical Analysis of the Regular Course of Business," 43 *Israel Law Review* (2010): 590–91; Sandberg, *Zionism and Post-Zionism*, supra note 51, at 18, 38–41.
77. HCJ 2390/96 Karsik v. State of Israel (2001), PD 55(2): 625 (Hebrew), English translation: https://supremedecisions.court.gov.il/Home/Download?path=EnglishVerdicts\96\900\023\g10&fileName=96023900_g10.txt&type=4; HCJ 840/97 Sabith v. Government of Israel (2003), PD 57(4): 803, 815 (Hebrew) (Hereafter: Sabith case).
78. HCJ 2254/13 Samuel v. Minister of Finance (Nevo, May 15, 2014) (Hebrew); Haim Sandberg, "Strategic Considerations behind Normative Explanations: Lessons From Israel's Supreme Court Takings Case," 11 *International Journal of Constitutional Law* (2013): 751, 765.
79. Sabith case, supra note 77, at 814.
80. CA 4067/07 Jabareen v. State of Israel, J. Danziger at par. 36 (Nevo, January 3, 2010) (Hebrew).
81. CA 4067/07 Jabareen v. State of Israel, J. Rubinstein at par. b.

82. HCJ 52/06 Al-Aqsa for the Development of Islamic Waqf Assets in Palestine Ltd. v. Simon Wiesenthal Center Museum Corp., J. Procaccia par. 12, 38, 60, 62, 120–22, 257 (Nevo, October 29, 2008) (Hebrew).
83. Basic Law: Human Dignity and Liberty, supra note 1, §3, 10.
84. CA 3535/04 Dinar v. State of Israel—Minister of Finance, J. Beinisch, par. 6–7 (Nevo, April 27, 2006) (Hebrew).
85. CA 4220/12 Al-Uqbi v. State of Israel, J. Hayut, par. 29 (Nevo, May 14, 2012) (Hereafter: Al-Uqbi case), official English translation: https://supremedecisions.court.gov.il/Home/Download?path=EnglishVerdicts\12\200\042\v29&fileName=12042200.V29&type=5.
86. HCJ 9804/09 Shawahna v. State of Israel—Development Authority, J. Barak-Erez pars. 2, 19 (Nevo, May 19, 2014) (Hebrew).
87. *Future Vision of the Palestinian Arabs in Israel*, supra note 15, at 5.
88. Al-Uqbi case, supra note 85, J. Hayut pars. 8, 18.
89. Al-Uqbi case, supra note 85, J. Hayut pars. 3, 5, 12, 33–43.
90. Sigfried Weissner, "Indigenous Self-Determination, Culture and Land: A Reassessment in Light of the 2007 UN Declaration on the Rights of Indigenous Peoples," in *Indigenous Rights in the Age of the UN Declaration*, ed. Elvira Pulitano (Cambridge: Cambridge University Press, 2012), 31, 37–38.
91. Kedar and Yiftachel, "Land Regime and Social Relations," supra note 74, at 133, 136–37.
92. Ran Aaronsohn, "Settlement in Eretz Israel—A Colonialist Enterprise? 'Critical' Scholarship and Historical Geography," 1 *Israel Studies* (1996): 214, 224–26; Yoav Gelber, "Is Zionism Colonialism?," in *The British Mandate in Palestine: A Centenary Volume, 1920-2020*, ed. Michael Cohen (Abingdon: Routledge 2020), 221, 228–32.
93. Provisional Government of Israel, The Declaration of the Establishment of the State of Israel, 1 *Official Gazette* 1 (May 14, 1948) (Hebrew), English translation Knesset, https://www.knesset.gov.il/docs/eng/megilat_eng.htm.
94. Supra note 33–35 and text.
95. Havatzelet Yahel et al., "Are the Negev Bedouin an Indigenous People? Fabricating Palestinian History," 19 *Middle East Quarterly* (2012): 3, 9–13; Seth J. Frantzman, "The Politization of History and the Negev Bedouin Land Claims: A Review Essay on Indigenous (In)justice," 19 *Israel Studies* (2014): 48, 51; Majd Al Naber and Francois Molle, "The Politics of Accessing Desert Land in Jordan," 59 *Land Use Policy* (2016): 492, 493–94.
96. Seth J. Frantzman et al., "Contested Indigeneity: The Development of an Indigenous Discourse on the Bedouin of the Negev, Israel," 17 *Israel Studies* (2012): 78–104.
97. Al-Uqbi case, supra note 85, J. Hayut par. 43, 81.
98. Al-Uqbi case, supra note 85, J. Hayut par. 82.
99. FD 3751/15 Al-Uqbi v. State of Israel, C.J. Naor, par. 7 (July 19, 2015).
100. Al-Uqbi case, supra note 85, J. Rubinstein par. b; Havatzelet Yahel, "Land Disputes between the Negev Bedouin and Israel," 11 *Israel Studies* (2006): 1, 5, 13; Arnon Medzini, "Bedouin Settlement Policy in Israel: Success or Failure?," 79 *Themes in Israeli Geography* (2012): 37–48.
101. Smooha, Index 2015, supra note 11, at 21–22; Sammy Smooha, *Still Playing by the Rules: Index of Arab-Jewish Relations in Israel 2013* (Haifa: Israel Democracy Institute & Haifa University, 2013) (Hebrew), 35–36.
102. Emphasis added. *Future Vision of the Palestinian Arabs in Israel*, supra note 15, at 14.
103. *Future Vision of the Palestinian Arabs in Israel*, supra note 15, at 15.
104. Hassan Jabareen, "The Future of Arab Citizenship in Israel: Jewish-Zionist Time in a Place with no Palestinian Memory," in *Challenging Ethnic Citizenship: German and Israeli*

*Perspectives on Immigration*, ed. Daniel Levy and Yifaat Weiss (New York: Bergham Books, 2002), 196, 201–11.

105. Ruth Gavison, "Zionism in Israel? A Note on Qaadan," 6 *Mishpat Umimshal* (Law and Government)—*Haifa University Law Review* (2001) (Hebrew): 25, 28–29, 40–41; Yaffa Zilbershats, "The Right of the Majority to Choose Residence," 6 *Mishpat Umimshal* (Law and Government)—*Haifa University Law Review* (2001) (Hebrew): 87, 103–6; Gerald M. Steinberg, "'The Poor in Your Own City Shall Have Precedence': A Critique of the Katzir-Qaadan Case and Opinion," 16 *Israel Studies Bulletin*, no. 1 (Fall 2000): 12–18.

106. Ka'adan case, supra note 30; S. Ilan Troen, *Imagining Zion: Dreams, Designs, and Realities in a Century of Jewish Settlement* (New Haven, CT: Yale University Press, 2003), 289–90.

107. Ka'adan case, supra note 30, C. J. Barak at par. 24.

108. Brown v. Board of Education of Topeka, 347 US 483 (1954).

109. Ka'adan case, supra note 30, C. J. Barak at par. 30.

110. Ka'adan case, supra note 30, C. J. Barak at par. 33.

111. Ka'adan case, supra note 30, C. J. Barak at par. 30.

112. Ka'adan case, supra note 30, C. J. Barak at par. 30.

113. See chap. 4.

114. Supra note 105.

115. HCJ 9518/16 Harel v. Knesset of Israel (Nevo, September 5, 2017) (Hebrew) (Hereafter: Harel case).

116. Harel case, supra note 113, J. Rubinstein at par. 12.

117. Harel case, supra note 113, J. Rubinstein at par. 18.

118. Harel case, supra note 113, J. Rubinstein at pars. 59–60.

119. Harel case, supra note 113, J. Rubinstein at par. 61–62.

120. Emphasis added. §3(b) Proposed Bill and Explanatory Notes, Basic Law: Israel as the Nation-State of the Jewish People (July 22, 2013) (Initiatives: MKs Ayelet Shaked, Yariv Levin, Robert Ilatov) (Hebrew); Rabinovitch, *Defining Israel*, supra note 33, at 83; Herb Keinon and Lahav Harkov, "PM to Push Basic Law That Will Define Israel as 'Jewish State,'" *Jerusalem Post*, May 1, 2014, http://www.jpost.com/Diplomacy-and-Politics/PM-to-push-Basic-Law-that-will-define-Israel-as-Jewish-state-351057.

121. § II Proposed Basic Law: Israel as the Nation-State of the Jewish People (June 8, 2015), Knesset National Legislation Database, supra note 35.

122. §IX(2) Proposed Basic Law: Israel as the Nation-State of the Jewish People (July 29, 2015), Knesset National Legislation Database, supra note 35; Rabinovitch, *Defining Israel*, supra note 33, at 105.

123. Supra note 33.

124. Hasson case, supra note 43, C.J. Hayut at par. 89.

125. Smooha, Index 2015, supra note 11, at 21; Ran Goldblat and Itzhak Omer, "The Association between Land-Use Distribution and Residential Patterns: The Case of Mixed Arab-Jewish Cities in Israel," 6 *Journal of Urban and Regional Analysis* (2014): 15, 19.

126. HCJ 7452/04 Abu-Raya v. Israel Land Administration (Nevo, September 28, 2008) (Hebrew).

127. Israel Central Bureau of Statistics (ICBS), "The Arab Population in Israel," 27 *Statistilite* (2002): 1, 3; Amnon Beeri-Sulitzeanu and Uri Gopher, *Mixed Cities and Regions: The Future Face of Israel* (Jerusalem: Abraham Fund Initiatives, 2009), 6, 8; Nicola Yozgof-Auerbach and Arnon Soffer, *Between Judaization and Lost Galilee: The Case of Upper Nazareth in the Years 1956–2016* (Haifa: Chaikin Chair for Geostrategy, University of Haifa, 2016) (Hebrew), 19.

128. Ran Goldblat and Omer, Mixed Cities, supra note 125, at 5, 30–31; Haim Yacobi, "Planning Control and Spatial Protest: The Case of the Jewish-Arab Town of Lydd/Lod," in *Mixed Towns, Trapped Communities*, ed. Daniel Monterescu and Dan Rabinowitz (Abingdon: Routledge 2016), 135, 140; Auerbach and Soffer, *Upper Nazareth*, supra note 127, at 18; Yitzhak Schnell, "New Concepts in the Study of Mixed Cities: The Israeli Case," in *Together but Apart: Mixed Cities in Israel*, ed. Elie Rekhess (Tel Aviv: Moshe Dayan Center for Middle Eastern and African Studies, 2007) (Hebrew), 19, 24–26; Regev Nathansohn, "Living in a Mixing Neighborhood: Reflexive Coexistence and the Discourse of Separation" (PhD diss., University of Michigan, 2017), 11, 132–86.

129. Auerbach and Soffer, *Upper Nazareth*, supra note 127, at 19–22, 43; Beeri-Sulitzeanu and Gopher, *Mixed Cities*, supra note 127, at 7–9; Dana Shevah, "Social Dynamics, Urban Civility and Spatial Capacity in a Newly-Mixed Town: The Case of Karmiel" (PhD diss., Technion—Israel Institute of Technology, 2017) (Hebrew), 53–54, 116; Israel Central Bureau of Statistics, "Settlements in Israel and Their Population 2018" (2019) (Hebrew), https://www.cbs.gov.il/he/publications/doclib/2019/ishuvim/bycode2018.xlsx.

130. Auerbach and Soffer, *Upper Nazareth*, supra note 127, at 19–22; Shevah, "Social Dynamics," supra note 129.

131. APA 4282/16 Saig v. David, J. Baron par. 14 (Nevo, August 7, 2017) (Hebrew); Yonah Jeremy Bob, "ACRI: Ruling by Top Court Might Be Insufficient for Mixed-Housing," *Jerusalem Post*, August 16, 2017, http://www.jpost.com/Israel-News/ACRI-Ruling-by-top-court-might-be-insufficient-for-mixed-housing-502540.

132. §6 of the Cooperative Societies Ordinance, as amended in the Amendment to the Cooperative Societies Ordinance (No. 8) Law, 5771–2011, *Sefer Ha-Hukim* 683 (Hebrew); §1, 5 Decision 1504 of the Israel Land Council "Residential Construction in Agricultural Settlements Which Are Workers' Moshav, Cooperative Village, Cooperative Moshav, Kibbutz or Agricultural Cooperative Society" (January 16, 2017) (Hebrew); Amnon Lehavi, "Residential Communities in a Heterogeneous Society: The Case of Israel," in *Private Communities and Urban Governance: Theoretical and Comparative Perspectives*, ed. Amnon Lehavi (Springer International, 2016), 95, 109–11; Michael Tamir, "The Freedom to Exclude: The Case of Israeli Society," 49 *Israel Law Review* (2016): 237, 252–54.

133. HCJ 2311/11 Sabach v. the Knesset, J. Joubran pars. 46–48, 51 (Nevo, September 17, 2014) (Hebrew) (Hereafter: Sabach case); Neta Ziv and Chen Tirosh, "The Legal Struggle against the Classification of Candidates for Community Settlements: A Catch in a Drowning and Boring Network," in *Gated Communities*, ed. Amnon Lehavi (Tel Aviv: Buchman Faculty Law Series, Tel Aviv University, 2010) (Hebrew), 311, 329–30, 335, 341–47.

134. Ben Sales, "First Arab Muslim Accepted as Kibbutz Member," *Jerusalem Post*, June 12, 2008, https://www.jpost.com/israel/first-arab-muslim-accepted-as-kibbutz-member; Yoav Itiel and Eli Ashkenazi, "The New Member of Kibbutz Sdot Yam: Muhammad from Kafr Qara," *Walla-New*, June 22, 2021 (Hebrew).

135. Sabach case, supra note 133, J. Joubran pars. 49–50; Ziv and Tirosh, "Legal Struggle," supra note 134, at 330, 338–41, 343–45.

136. Sabach case, supra note 133, Justices Grunis, Naor, Rubinstein, Hayut, and Meltzer v. Justices Joubran, Arbel, Danziger, and Hendel.

137. Minutes of Session No. 8 of the Special Committee for Distributive Justice and Social Equality of the Twentieth Knesset 9, 15 (January 30, 2017) (Hebrew).

138. Emphasis added. Sabach case, supra note 133, J. Joubran par. 58.

139. Matan Shahar, *Admissions Committees in Communities in the Negev and the Galilee* Knesset Research and Information Center, May 2, 2019 (Hebrew), https://fs.knesset.gov.il/globaldocs/MMM/8076aeaa-ce01-e911-80e1-00155d0a98a9/2_8076aeaa-ce01-e911-80e1-00155d0a98a9_11_12403.pdf.

140. Proposed Amendment to the Cooperative Societies Ordinance (Number of Houses in a Community Settlement), 5701–2018 (November 19, 2018); Proposed Amendment to the Cooperative Societies Ordinance (Cancellation of Amendment No. 8), 5766–2016 (March 30, 2016).

141. ICBS, "Arab Population," supra note 127, at 3; Israel Central Bureau of Statistics, "The Arab Population in Israel," 102 *Statistilite* 8 (2008), https://old.cbs.gov.il/www/statistical/arab_popo8e.pdf.

142. ICBS, "Arab Population," supra note 127, at 3; ICBS, "Settlements in Israel" 2018, supra note 129.

143. Ofer Raz-Dror and Noam Kost, *The Strategic Plan for Housing for the Years 2017–2040* (Jerusalem: National Economic Council, Prime Minister's Office, 2017) (Hebrew), 4, 21–22, http://economy.pmo.gov.il/councilactivity/housing/documents/strategy050717.pdf.

144. National Committee for Planning and Construction of Preferred Housing Areas (NCPCPHA), *Annual Report 2017* (2018) (Hebrew), 19–20, https://www.gov.il/BlobFolder/reports/vatmal_2017/he/National_planning_institutions_vatmal_2017.pdf; National Committee for Planning and Construction of Preferred Housing Areas (NCPCPHA), *Annual Report 2018* (2019) (Hebrew), 21–22, https://www.gov.il/BlobFolder/reports/vatmal_2018/he/vatmal_2018.pdf.

145. National Outline Plan 44 (NOP 44) A New Urban Area for the Non-Jewish Population in Northern Israel (July 3, 2015) (Hebrew), http://mavat.moin.gov.il/MavatPS/Forms/SV4.aspx?tid=4.

146. Jack Khoury, "Israel Promised to Build Its First Modern Arab City since 1948. Here's What Came of It," *Haaretz*, October 17, 2017, https://www.haaretz.com/israel-news/.premium.MAGAZINE-israel-vowed-to-build-its-first-modern-arab-city-since-48-then-nothing-1.5457042.

147. Arik Rudnitzky, "The Bedouin Population in the Negev: Social, Demographic and Economic Factors," in *The Bedouin Population in the Negev* (Jerusalem: Abraham Fund Initiatives, 2012), 1, 7.

148. Havatzelet Yahel, "The Policy of the Israeli Government and State Authorities regarding the Negev Bedouin: 1947–1989" (PhD diss., Hebrew University of Jerusalem, 2015) (Hebrew), 101–9, 119–24; Shaul Krakover, "Urban Settlement Program and Land Dispute Resolution: The State of Israel versus the Negev Bedouin," 47 *GeoJournal* (1999): 551–61.

149. Emphasis added. HCJ 528/88 Avitan v. Israel Land Administration (1989), PD 43(4): 297, 306 (Hebrew).

150. NCPCPHA, *Annual Report 2017*, supra note 144, at 19; NCPCPHA, *Annual Report 2018*, supra note 144, at 25; Yosseph Shilhav, "The Emergence of Ultra-Orthodox Neighborhoods in Israeli Urban Centers," in *Local Communities and the Israeli Polity: Conflict of Values and Interests*, ed. Efraim Ben-Zadok (New York: SUNY Press 1993), 157–88; Lee Cahaner, "The Development of the Spatial and Hierarchic Structure of the Ultra-Orthodox Jewish Population in Israel" (PhD diss., University of Haifa, 2009) (Hebrew), 160–87.

151. Kedar and Yiftachel, "Land Regime and Social Relations," supra note 74, at 139.

152. See chap. 1, table 1.

153. Text referring to notes 74–76 above.
154. HCJ 729/10 Tnua'at Dror Israel v. State of Israel, J. Beinisch par. 18 (Nevo, May 24, 2012).
155. Moti Kaplan et al., *Patterns of Use of Built-Up Areas in Israel* (Jerusalem: Jerusalem Institute for Israel Studies, 2007) (Hebrew), 19.
156. Kedar and Yiftachel, "Land Regime and Social Relations," supra note 74, at 135.
157. Sandberg, "Land Expropriations," supra note 76, at 596–603; Sandberg, *Zionism and Post-Zionism*, supra note 51, at 87–98.
158. David Kretzmer, *The Legal Status of the Arabs in Israel* (Abingdon: Routledge, 2019; first published 1990, Westview, Boulder), 52; Eli Rekhess, *Israeli Arabs and the Expropriation of Lands in the Galilee: Background, Events and Implications 1975–1977* (Tel Aviv: Shiloah Research Center, Tel Aviv University, 1977) (Hebrew), 46.
159. Sandberg, "Land Expropriations," supra note 76, at 98–100; see also the references supra note 129.
160. Adam Rasgon and Udi Shaham, "Arabs on Land Day: We Won't Move; Israeli Arabs Set for General Strike, Protests on 40th Annual Land Day," *Jerusalem Post*, March 31, 2017, http://www.jpost.com/Arab-Israeli-Conflict/Arabs-on-Land-Day-We-wont-move-485730; Efraim Karsh, "Israel's Arabs: Deprived or Radicalized?," 19 *Israel Affairs* (2013): 2, 12; Elie Rekhess, "The Evolvement of an Arab-Palestinian National Minority in Israel," 12 *Israel Studies* (2007): 1, 9.
161. HCJ 3421/05 Mahul v. Finance Minister, J. Arbel par. 33 (Nevo, June 18, 2009) (Hebrew) (Hereafter: Mahul case).
162. Mahul case, supra note 161, at par. 37.
163. NOP 44, supra note 145.
164. Supra note 146.
165. HCJ 10784/02 Keren Kayemeth LeIsrael v. Atarim on the Tel Aviv Coast Tourism Development Corporation Tel Aviv Jaffa (2004), PD 58(3): 757.
166. Rassem Khamaisi, "Housing Transformation within Urbanized Communities: The Arab Palestinians in Israel," 33 *Geography Research Forum* (2013): 184, 190–200; Said Sliman, "The Structure of Housing Decision Making in Arab Towns in Israel" (PhD diss., Tel Aviv University, 2011) (Hebrew), 22–28, 125–26; Rassem Khamaisi, "Land Ownership as a Determinant in the Formation of Residential Areas in Arab Localities," 26 *Geoforum* (1995): 211, 215–16.
167. Kaplan et al., *Patterns of Use*, supra note 155, at 19; Israel Central Bureau of Statistics, "Table 2.24, Population and Density per sq. km. in Localities Numbering 5000 Residents and More on 31.12.2018," 70 *Statistical Abstract of Israel* (2019), https://www.cbs.gov.il/he/publications/doclib/2019/2.shnatonpopulation/st02_24.pdf; Israel Central Bureau of Statistics, "Table 2.25, Localities Population and Density per sq. km. by Metropolitan Area and Selected Localities on 31.12.2018," 70 *Statistical Abstract of Israel* (2019), https://www.cbs.gov.il/he/publications/doclib/2019/2.shnatonpopulation/st02_25.pdf.
168. Nasr Kheir and Boris A. Portnov, "Economic, Demographic and Environmental Factors Affecting Urban Land Prices in the Arab Sector in Israel," 50 *Land Use Policy* (2016): 518, 520–21, 525.
169. Nurit Alfasi, "Doomed to Informality: Familial versus Modern Planning in Arab Towns in Israel," 15 *Planning Theory & Practice* (2014): 170, 175–77.
170. Ministry of Justice, *Report of the Team for Dealing with the Illegal Construction Phenomenon* (Jerusalem, January 2016) (Hebrew), 13–17, 40–42, https://www.gov.il

/BlobFolder/reports/deal_with_the_construction_phenomenon/he/The_team_to_deal_with_the_construction_phenomenon_Kaminitz_report.pdf; Udi Shaham, "New Law Stiffens Punishment for Construction Violations," *Jerusalem Post*, April 6, 2017, https://www.jpost.com/Israel-News/Politics-And-Diplomacy/New-law-stiffens-punishment-for-construction-violations-486234; Jonathan Lis, "Israel Passes Law Meant to Crack Down on Illegal Building in Arab Communities," *Haaretz*, April 5, 2017, https://www.haaretz.com/israel-news/.premium-israel-passes-law-cracking-down-on-illegal-building-in-arab-communities-1.5457966; The Planning and Building Law (Amendment No. 116), 5767–2017, *Sefer Ha-Hukim* 884 (Hebrew).

171. Rassem Khamaisi, *Between Customs and Laws: Planning and Managing Land in Arab Localities in Israel* (Jerusalem: Floersheimer Institute for Policy Studies, 2007) (Hebrew), 31.

172. APA 3542/11 Sub-committee for Appellants of the National Council for Planning and Construction v. The Arara Local Council (Nevo, April 24, 2012) (Hebrew); Administrative Petition (Haifa Dist. C.) 29869-01-10 The Arara Local Council v. The Appeals Sub-committee of the National Council for Planning and Building (Nevo, March 28, 2011) (Hebrew).

173. Author translation. Mahul case, supra note 161, J. Arbel par. 28.

174. NCPCPHA, Annual Reports, supra note 144.

175. Amitai Gazit, "Rehabilitation after Decades: The Legal Advisor Approves Illegal Construction in Arab Communities," *Calcalist*, July 4, 2017 (Hebrew), https://www.calcalist.co.il/real_estate/articles/0,7340,L-3716424,00.html; Ori Chudy, "Israeli Arabs Do Not Cooperate with Lotteries for Residential Flats ('*Mehir Lamishtaken*')," *Globes*, September 25, 2017 (Hebrew), https://www.globes.co.il/news/article.aspx?did=1001205920.

176. Kedar and Yiftachel, "Land Regime and Social Relations," supra note 74, at 142; Ka'adan case, supra note 30, C. J. Barak, at par. 30.

177. Based on data published in Kaplan et al., *Patterns of Use*, supra note 155, at 133.

178. Based on data published in "Local Authorities in Israel 2015," Israel Central Bureau of Statistics (Hebrew), https://www.cbs.gov.il/he/publications/Pages/2017/%D7%94%D7%A8%D7%A9%D7%95%D7%99%D7%95%D7%AA-%D7%94%D7%9E%D7%A7%D7%95%D7%9E%D7%99%D7%95%D7%AA-%D7%91%D7%99%D7%A9%D7%A8%D7%90%D7%9C-2015.aspx; "National Profile 2015," https://www.cbs.gov.il/he/publications/doclib/2017/local_authorities15_1683/04_05.pdf; "Profile of Municipalities—Total 2015" (Hebrew), https://www.cbs.gov.il/he/publications/doclib/2017/local_authorities15_1683/06_07.pdf; "Profile of Local Councils-Total 2015" (Hebrew), https://www.cbs.gov.il/he/publications/doclib/2017/local_authorities15_1683/08_09.pdf; "Profile of Regional Councils—Total 2015" (Hebrew), https://www.cbs.gov.il/he/publications/doclib/2017/local_authorities15_1683/10_12.pdf. All links were accessed on September 9, 2021.

179. There was no significant change in the data published by ICBS for the year 2017. "Local Authorities in Israel 2017: Profile of Regional Councils—Total," ICBS, accessed June 12, 2020 (Hebrew), https://www.cbs.gov.il/he/publications/doclib/2019/local_authorities17_1759/14_16.pdf.

180. ICBS, "Profile of Regional Councils—Total (2015)," supra note 178.

181. "National Profile," supra note 178.

182. "Local Authorities Excel File 2017," Israel Central Bureau of Statistics, accessed June 11, 2020, https://www.cbs.gov.il/he/publications/doclib/2017/local_authorities15_1683/p_libud.xls.

183. Arnon Soffer, "Territorialism, Nation and State," 21 *Iyuney-Mishpat—Tel-Aviv University Law Review* (1998) (Hebrew): 747, 757–65.

184. See supra note 133–34 and text.

185. Israel Central Bureau of Statistics, *Characterization and Classification of Geographical Units by the Socio-Economic Level of the Population 2013: Introduction—List of Variables* (November 30, 2017), 19–21, https://www.cbs.gov.il/he/publications/doclib/2017/socio_eco13 _1694/intro_e.pdf; Israel Central Bureau of Statistics, "Table 1, Socio Economic Index 2015 of Local Authorities in Ascending Order of Index Values: Index Value, Rank and Cluster," *Characterization and Classification of Statistical Areas within Municipalities and Local Councils by the Socio-Economic Level of the Population 2015* (August 15, 2019), https://www .cbs.gov.il/he/mediarelease/doclib/2018/351/24_18_351t1.pdf.

186. Beeri-Sulitzeanu and Gopher, *Mixed Cities*, supra note 127, at 11–12.

# 6

## CREATIVE JUDICIARY

*Equitable and Constitutional Safeguards to Property Rights*

> Locally made (*Tozeret Ha-Aretz*) equitable property rights must be allowed to develop as independent Israeli law.
>
> Justice Aharon Barak

SINCE THE FOUNDING OF THE STATE, ONE OF Israel's distinguishing features has been its development of a strongly independent and innovative judiciary.[1] Judicial activism—that is, the tendency of the judiciary not merely to implement the law but also to create it—is a controversial aspect of this independence.

The status and independence of the judicial authority are key features of democratic states. A strong and independent judiciary is necessary to guarantee the rights of every individual, yet the level of judicial activism adopted by the court is open to debate. The independence of Israel's judicial system, its creativity, and the judicial review against the actions of other government authorities has increased considerably over recent decades. Various authors deem it as activist in the extreme,[2] and since the turn of the millennium, the limits of its authority have been heatedly debated, not only by jurists but at every level of society. This has been a central issue in recent election campaigns.[3]

In this chapter we shall focus on two prominent expressions of Israeli judicial activism in the field of land law: the original protection of equitable rights to land and the constitutional protection of property rights. Against the general background of activism in these two legal channels, we shall proceed to analyze the original judicial developments of each and conclude with a few remarks about the way these developments reflect the controversy over the judicial branch's role in designing Israel's land law and its democratic identity.

## The Development of Judicial Activism in Israel: A Short Background

### Disassembling the Chains of the Past

The creativity of Israel's judicial system reflects the growing power and independence that gradually developed along two different channels. The first and earlier of the two followed the disengagement of Israel's judiciary from the British Mandate legal system. Article 46 of the Palestine Order in Council 1922, which was a sort of constitution introduced into Palestine by the British prior to the establishment of the State of Israel, stipulated that local courts should interpret laws or fill lacunae "in conformity with the substance of the common law, and the doctrines of equity in force in England."[4] The State of Israel did not repeal this provision upon its establishment, and therefore, during Israel's early years, the precedents developed by English courts were legally binding, subject to the process of their "absorption" by the local courts.[5]

Starting from its second decade, the State of Israel began a process of disengagement from English law. In contemporary terms, the severance of this connection was a sort of exit from the influence of the English legal system, similar to Brexit, the British legal system's departure from European Union law.[6] Israel's process of legal exit, initiated by the Israeli legislature with the goal of demonstrating the political independence of the state, unfolded gradually. It began in the 1960s and 1970s with the enactment of a series of laws in an effort to shape private/civil law. Some of the laws included an explicit provision regarding the "independence of the law," stipulating that English law would no longer have any binding force in areas dealt with by each of the new laws.[7] The enactment of the Foundations of Law Act, 5740–1980 completed the transformation and finally and definitively voided the authority of references to English law, decreeing that thereafter the court would fill lacunae in the law "in the light of the principles of freedom, justice, equity and peace of Israel's heritage."[8]

Nonetheless, the gradual abolition of the requirement to rely on English case law did not eliminate the natural tendency of some judges to rely on foreign sources for inspiration. Reliance on American sources, in particular, increased with time. The Israeli Supreme Court, likewise, did not rush to implement the principles of either Jewish law or Jewish heritage in its rulings. All the same, the judicial process gradually became more independent, and the tendency to rely on foreign sources declined significantly. The local courts began to develop an autonomous normative law, independent of foreign legal systems.[9] As we shall see below, Israel land laws hold a place of honor in this process.

## *The Intensification of Judicial Review*

The second channel through which the Israeli judicial system has accumulated a great deal of independent power is that of internal relations vis-à-vis the other two branches of government: the legislative and the executive branches. Israel is a democratic state in which the principle of separation of powers applies, and the relationship between government branches is based on checks and balances. US Supreme Court justice Felix Frankfurter once wrote (relying on Hamilton's Federalist) that the court's authority is "neither the purse nor the sword" but rather the "sustained public confidence in its moral sanction" and "the Court's complete detachment... from political entanglements."[10] In this spirit, the rulings of the courts during the first decades of Israel's existence tended to be conservative and were not often characterized by judicial activism or legal creativity. Justices were also careful not to become involved in controversial political issues. In more recent decades, however, this situation has changed.[11]

During this time, three parallel processes increased the power of the Supreme Court in relation to the other two branches of government. First, the Supreme Court gradually abandoned the conservative approach that had characterized its rulings in the past. The Supreme Court increasingly expanded the scope of its judicial discretion by means of very broad and creative interpretations of various legislative concepts, such as good faith, negligence, or reasonableness. It thus tended more and more to base its rulings on values and normative considerations rather than solely on doctrines and formalist interpretations of legislation. The court's creative approach commonly veered away from adherence to the letter of laws and contracts and inclined more toward "judicial legislation" based on an independent and creative interpretation of the legislator's original intent. Since the 1980s, such "judicial legislation" has characterized the Supreme Court's rulings in almost all branches of law, including private law, administrative law, and constitutional law.[12]

Second, in 1992, the Knesset enacted the Basic Law: Human Dignity and Liberty (hereafter in this chapter: the Basic Law).[13] The Basic Law, which is envisioned as part of the future constitution of the State of Israel, prohibits the violation of various human rights, including the rights to life, body, dignity (article 2), and property (article 3). Article 8 of the law, which over the years has come to be referred to as the "limitation clause," established cumulative conditions under which violation of these rights is permitted. The violation must be anchored in legislation or under explicit authorization in legislation. The violation should serve an "appropriate purpose," and it should not be excessive ("proportionality") but should match the values of the State of Israel as a "Jewish and democratic state." In a precedential judgment, the Supreme Court ruled that this (and other) Basic Laws have constitutional status and that the court is empowered to invalidate laws or decisions made in accordance with those laws if, according to the court's interpretation, they do not meet the provisions of the Basic Law.[14] Israel's Supreme Court has, through this ruling, executed a move similar to the one made by the US Supreme Court in the Marbury v. Madison case.[15] It granted constitutional status to a Basic Law that superseded Knesset legislation and granted itself the ultimate authority to exercise the supremacy of constitutional law by disqualifying ordinary laws that it deems contradictory to the Basic Law or by giving an activist interpretation to laws in the spirit of the Basic Law.[16] The enactment of the Basic Law and the higher constitutional status granted to it by the court were viewed in Israel as a "constitutional revolution."[17] The move greatly strengthened the status of the judiciary and made it, in addition to its traditional roles, a kind of constitutional court, similar to the US Supreme Court or to constitutional courts in Europe.[18]

The third process that has increased the power of Israel's Supreme Court of Justice, as well as its activism, is the weakening of other governmental systems. The fracturing of the Israeli political system into small parties beginning in the 1980s greatly weakened the power of the executive and legislative branches, leading to what many experts call a "problem of governmentality." The Supreme Court considered itself to be, and was often perceived by the public and by politicians as, an island of stability and a last resort (perhaps even preferred) when other authorities were unable to help.[19]

One of the leading instigators of this change was Justice Aharon Barak, who later became chief justice of the Supreme Court. The judicial activism of Barak's rulings reflect his academic background as a law professor, his professional background as a former attorney general, his favorable impression of the US legal system, and his experience as a child survivor of the Holocaust who recognized the importance of an independent judiciary to protect democracy.[20] Upon his retirement, he set forth his worldview in a special issue of the *Harvard Law Review*.[21] Barak was a mentor to many Israeli jurists; indeed, Prof. Oz Almog likened him to a Hassidic rabbi in secular society.[22] Barak became the very model of judicial activism and, as a result, a prime target for harsh criticism by opponents.[23]

## The Public Debate over the Judicial Role

The three processes outlined above have increased the relative power of the Supreme Court vis-à-vis the other authorities to such an extent that it has provoked exacting criticism of the court. Academic critics have argued that the Supreme Court has assumed powers that exceed the accepted and proper role of the courts and that might ultimately even damage the court itself.[24] Prof. Menachem Mautner attributed this change to an attempt by the social stratum to which the Supreme Court justices belong to maintain power and liberal values.[25] In chapter 2 we analyzed the expression of this theory in the context of the court's judgments concerning the administration and privatization of public land.[26] The increasing number of rulings on politically controversial issues has led to growing criticism of the court on the part of politicians.[27]

In recent years, the status of the Supreme Court has been the focus of constant political pressure aimed at reducing the court's activism. Two of Israel's minsters of justice in recent decades have been fervent critics of judicial activism: Prof. Daniel Friedmann, who served as minister of justice in 2007–9, summarized his critical approach in his book *The Purse and the Sword*.[28] Former minister of justice Ayelet Shaked, who was in office in 2015–19, took concrete steps to weaken judicial activism, including substantially and successfully supporting the appointment of "conservative" justices[29] and introducing a Basic Law that will allow the Knesset to pass laws that override Supreme Court rulings.[30] While the increase in judicial activism or its criticism led to a certain gradual decline in public confidence in the Supreme Court, public opinion polls since 2009 indicate a consistently moderate trend toward a return to the level of public trust it had prior to the constitutional revolution.[31]

Judicial creativity, then, is a central albeit controversial characteristic of Israel's judiciary system. This phenomenon has been at the center of public discourse for years, and, recently at least, it has been an integral feature of Israeli identity. Like several other marked features of the State of Israel, judicial creativity is clearly manifest in land laws, as I shall attempt to show in my analysis of two areas that reflect the increasing power of Israel's judiciary: the independent development of equitable rights and the evolution of the court's rulings in the field of constitutional protection of private property. The first is an expression of the desire to disengage from Britain's legal heritage and develop an original Israeli law. The second example is an expression of the court's growing power vis-à-vis other government authorities but also an expression of the relative restraint of the court in the area of constitutional protection for private property.

## Developing Equitable Property Rights

### The British Heritage of Equitable Doctrines

English equity law and common law had binding legal status in Mandatory Palestine. As already noted, this was rooted in the Mandatory Constitution, which remained in force even after the establishment of the State of Israel. During that period, English law served as the normative source for various doctrines in the field of land law, particularly of rights developed in the courts of equity.[32] Thus, for example, Israeli courts ruled, in accordance with precedents imported from English law, that a person holding a contract to acquire rights in land has an equitable right of ownership in that property, even though the transferor remains the owner by law. The main significance of this rule is that the equitable right to property supersedes the rights of any of the transferor's creditors, with the exception of creditors who have completed the purchase of the asset in value and without notice. This ruling was based on the assumption by the courts of equity that a relationship of constructive trust exists between the legal owner and the equitable owner and that, therefore, the creditors of the trustee (the transferor) cannot collect debts from the assets that he or she holds in trust for the beneficiary (the transferee).[33] Another doctrine adopted was that of equitable interests by virtue of estoppel. Israeli courts have ruled in accordance with this doctrine that the legal owner of property cannot claim rights from someone who mistakenly held, used, and invested in the property over time without express permission, but only with the knowledge of and in the absence of an objection from that legal owner.[34]

### Should Original "Made in Israel" Doctrines Replace British Doctrines?

The Land Law, 5729–1969, which to date has constituted the primary legislation defining real estate law in Israel, came into effect in 1970.[35] One of its aims was to ground Israeli land law in independent Israeli legislation and to eliminate the complex old and foreign historical layers of land law left over from Ottoman and English legislation. Article 161 of the Land Law, entitled "No Equitable Rights," gave prominent expression to this aim: "From the coming into force of this Law, there shall be no rights in immovable property save under an enacted Law." Israeli jurists all agreed that the aim of this article was to discontinue, from that point onward, the conventional obligatory reference to English rulings in order to adopt equitable doctrines. All the same, article 161 elicited a fierce legal debate about whether it was meant to annul doctrines that had already been introduced and thus bring about a substantive change in law or, alternatively, it merely sought to change the normative way of establishing them.

In 1971, shortly after the enactment of the Land Law, the Supreme Court decided in the Boker ruling that the intention of article 161 was not only declaratory but substantive, meaning that the Israeli law would no longer recognize equitable rights in land. Thereafter, anyone who had rights in land under a contract but had not yet registered them in the land registry would no longer have an advantage over other creditors of the registered owner. The purpose of this ruling was to encourage the complete registration of transactions.[36] Supreme Court Justice Moshe Landau, who composed the main opinion in this precedent-setting ruling, was the former head of the committee that had drafted the Land Law, so his ruling reflected the legislative intent in real terms.[37] It also expressed his conservative and nonactivist approach regarding the role of a judge. Many years later, when he retired, Judge Landau became one of the most outspoken public critics of the judicial activism developed by the Supreme Court after his retirement.[38] The first signs of this position became evident in his ruling that revoked equitable rights.

Israeli legal scholars, led by Prof. Joshua Weisman, one of Israel's preeminent experts in property law, rigorously criticized Landau's conservative approach in the Boker case. He argued that the severance of Israeli law from its sources in English law of equity did not require a change in the substantive law but only a change of its normative source. He claimed that the same equitable rights imported from England should and could be transformed into local "made in Israel" (*Tozeret Ha-Aretz*) equitable rights, hereinafter based on Israeli legislation.[39] The difficulty in implementing this approach was that the court could not always find an original and explicit Israeli legal provision on which to base laws similar to those established by English equity laws.

### *The Creation of "Made in Israel" Equitable Rights (The Aharonov Case)*

For thirty years after the Boker case, the Supreme Court was unwilling to create original Israeli rights of equity in land laws. The courts were gradually gaining power at the time, but it was not until 1999 that the court felt strong enough to develop local "made in Israel" rights stemming from equity. A secondary partner in the new Supreme Court project was Mazal Aharonov. She had divorced her husband in 1990, and in accordance with the divorce agreement, her husband had undertaken an effort to transfer the ownership of a plot of land to her. However, before she was able to register the transaction in the land registry, her former husband's creditors sued for the foreclosure of his registered rights to the land. In accordance with the Boker ruling, which eliminated equitable rights, she could not prevail in the case, but her legal counsels would not back down; they tried to convince the courts that their client had acquired the equity rights. This argument obliged the courts not only to deviate from its previous precedents but to create original "made in Israel" equitable rights. This time, in contrast to failed attempts in the past, the court was persuaded to cross the Rubicon.

The court now ruled[40] that a person holding a contract to acquire rights in a real estate property has equitable rights that trump those of the transferor's creditors, with the exception of a third party who has purchased the property in value and without notice.[41] The court did not base this right on the English equity laws but rather on a creative and activist interpretation of Israeli legal provisions. Although no Israeli statutory provision explicitly grants priority to the purchaser of immovable property over the transferor's creditors, the court concluded that such priority exists by analogy from another legal provision. While this provision does not deal directly with the issue, it grants priority to an agreement for the purchase of real estate property over a later transaction made for the same asset.[42] Thus, the court ruled that the preference for the first agreement in one case attests to the privileged status of that right in other cases as well. Thirty years earlier, the Supreme Court had rejected this analogy on the grounds that such a legal provision indicated a preference in an unusual case constituting an exception to the rule.[43] However, by now the climate was changing, activism had replaced conservatism, and Chief Justice Barak and his colleagues were willing to take that step forward and establish "made in Israel" equitable rights on the basis of a creative interpretation that their predecessors had not dared to adopt.[44]

The court did not limit itself to interpreting this particular article of the law but gave a moral justification for preferring equitable rights to the rights of competing creditors. According to this moral explanation, the owner of an equitable right is seeking rights for a specific asset and relying on the contract for that particular asset, whereas a typical creditor did not rely on a particular asset at the time the debt was created and therefore received no guarantee from the owner regarding the specific asset that the creditor wishes to foreclose. The creditors assumed the risk that the debtor would not have the assets by the time they sought to recover the debt. The court therefore held that a creditor whose claim derives from reliance on a particular asset takes precedence over a creditor whose claim does not derive from such reliance.[45] This is a logical, reasonable, and perhaps even justifiable rule, but it has no explicit basis in any Israeli legislation.

In order to create original and independent equitable rights, the court had to overcome several obstacles. The first was the thirty-year-old precedent whereby Israel had no equitable rights. The justices, of course, believed that this precedent was inherently wrong. Chief Justice Barak explained his deviation from the precedent by claiming that previous rulings did not recognize the legislator's underlying intent.[46] Justice Strasberg-Cohen supported changing the law in order to realize "legal harmony between various arrangements relating to the same issue."[47] Nonetheless, if the precedent was inherently wrong, why had the court waited nearly three decades to revise the ruling? Justice Strasberg-Cohen cited various reasons: the age of the old ruling; the need to adapt it to "changing realities"; the growing number of relevant cases; substantial criticism of the old ruling; and new "developments in the law which has come a long way from formalism to substance."[48] This final reason appears to encapsulate the entire list: the power of the court and its overall tendency toward judicial activism had finally reached, at the dawn of the third millennium, the realm of real estate law.

Another obstacle faced by the court was the need to find a normative Israeli source for the independent creation rights stemming from equity. The court, as noted, had overcome this obstacle by creatively interpreting an article in Israeli law and by repeatedly emphasizing that it was an original Israeli creation that must be developed in an original way.[49] The court was careful not to base equitable rights on the legal doctrine of "constructive trust," which was founded in the English and American equity laws. This doctrine assigns to the transferor and the transferee a relationship of trust by force (constructive) and, hence, infers a preference for the transferee, as the beneficiary, over the transferor's creditors. The Israeli Supreme Court sought to avoid basing its ruling on this doctrine, preferring to demonstrate its reliance on the provisions of Israeli law.[50]

However, Israeli equitable rights were, ultimately, similar—almost identical—to the rights created by English laws of equity. Even the court's moral explanations served to explicate the logic of the English law while it was in force.[51] In fact, the Supreme Court's action in 1999 was the very same judicial move made by the courts of equity hundreds of years earlier. The Aharonov ruling is more of an English-style judicial legislation than a conservative application of explicit legislation. Just as the English law developed step by step with each ruling, so did the Israeli courts, at all levels, continue to develop equitable rights through a series of rulings. They ruled that equitable rights are relevant to transactions other than the sale of ownership (such as mortgage or trust)[52]; that they take precedence over the transferor's creditors in insolvency proceedings[53]; and that they exist, albeit in a weaker sense, even when the transaction is a gift.[54] Ultimately, the court ruled, without relying directly on English law but in a similar vein, that there is a constructivist relationship of trust between the transferor and the transferee and that a claim for equity rights expires in the same way as a beneficiary's claim against a trust.[55] The development of rights stemming from equity has become part of Israel's original common law. The increasing power and intellectual and interpretive independence of Israel's Supreme Court is clearly in evidence, yet with respect to judicial activism it is not much different from powerful courts of other legal systems. The task of judging is ultimately a universal one, even when a judge attempts to show originality.[56]

### "Made in Israel" Proprietary Estoppel (The Ganz Case)

Just four years after the development of original equitable rights to land, the Supreme Court independently developed yet another doctrine well known from English equity laws: the doctrine of estoppel.[57] Here, too, the court overturned a decades-old ruling and relied instead on an original, creative, moral, and activist interpretation of Israeli law. Here, too, Chief Justice Aharon Barak led the move.

In the Ganz case,[58] a landowner undertook to transfer his rights to one person (Mr. Ganz) and seventeen years later undertook to transfer the same rights to a second buyer (Afek Ltd.). Neither of the buyers completed the transaction in the land registry, but the later buyer received the property in good faith, without notice, and in value. According to the explicit instruction of article 9 of the Israeli Land Law, in such a case, the right of the first transaction overrides the latter, since the latter did not succeed in registering the transaction in the land registry in good faith. Although the first purchaser could have prevented the creation of the later transaction by registering a warning caveat, Israeli law did not oblige a purchaser to register a caveat, nor did it state that failure to register it should prejudice the preference of the earlier purchaser over the later.[59] The later, second, purchaser in this case (Afek) argued that, despite these explicit provisions of the law, he should be preferred over the first purchaser because of the negligence of the former, who had refrained for a very long time (seventeen years) from recording a caveat notice in the land registry. As a result of this failure, damage was incurred by the second purchaser: he did not know about the existence of the first and therefore had entered into a contract to buy the property and even paid consideration and received possession.[60]

When the court encountered similar issues prior to the enactment of the Land Law, it could resolve them by integrating the doctrine of estoppel from English law.[61] The enactment of the Land Law blocked this path, since the legislation established explicitly that there are no rights stemming from equity and that any resolution should be based on original Israeli legislation. During the thirty years that had passed between the enactment of the Land Law and the Ganz case, the Supreme Court consistently refused to add to the Israeli legislation any conditions that had not been written in it. The court refused to rule that there is an obligation to register a warning caveat and refused to determine that misconduct of the first transaction bears any significance in the competition with later conflicting transactions. It insisted on this point even when adamant academic criticism provided a compelling substantive reason for changing the rule. Critics' main argument was that posing an obligation on a prior transaction to register a warning caveat is necessary to prevent damage to others and to impose responsibility for the consequences of the misconduct inherent in the failure to register a caveat. When an earlier transaction did not record a caveat and this omission led to the engagement in good faith and in value of a later transaction, the negligent party responsible for the failure should not prevail.[62] For many years, the court, including Justice Barak, refused to accept the recommendations of its critics, despite explicit identification with their rationales. The main reason for this refusal lay in the explicit provisions of the law: the law does not impose any express obligation on the first purchaser.[63] This was a clear example of judicial conservatism.

The Supreme Court's conservatism ended with the Ganz case. The court's first task was to find in original Israeli law an article on which to base the overruling of Ganz's priority (Ganz was the earlier purchaser, whose years long failure caused damage to Afek). Although the court had argued for years that there was no such clause, it now found it easily. With the support of some but not all of his fellow justices, Justice Barak ruled that the obligation to prevent damage, including the obligation to register a warning caveat, stems from a general principle that applies in Israeli law: the principle of good faith.

Barak presented this principle at the beginning of his ruling in the Ganz case: "The general doctrines of the law apply to all parts of the law. Specific legislation does not stand in isolation.... One of those general doctrines that apply in all areas of law is the principle of good faith.... Good faith sets an objective criterion of fair conduct by a right holder who seeks to realize their self-interest, against the background of the overall social interest and taking into consideration the interests of others.... The principle of good faith also applies within the framework of the laws of property."[64]

Of course, Barak did not "discover" this principle when he came to the Ganz case. It is a general principle in various Israeli legislations,[65] and over the decades preceding the Ganz case, many scholarly articles analyzed it, some of which even suggested using it as a platform for establishing a doctrine of estoppel, as in English law.[66] Barak himself had mentioned and developed this principle in previous rulings.[67] He even defined the way in which previous rulings had dealt with it as "salutary."[68] The good faith doctrine is a convenient and flexible platform for interpretive creativity in the court's rulings. However, it was adopted only in the Ganz case, after thirty years, to bring about the change in immovable property laws that Barak himself had hesitated to implement in the past.

Once the suitable doctrine was identified, Barak was left with the task of imbuing it with substance. Barak adopted academic scholars' critical arguments as to why a purchaser of real estate must be charged with registering a caveat: neglecting to record the caveat causes a "legal accident" for the later purchaser, and therefore it is the duty of the first purchaser to prevent that mishap.[69]

All that remained, then, was for Barak to formulate the obligation by means of judicial legislation of his own device: "The principle of good faith requires that the owner of the first transaction act fairly, taking into consideration the reasonable expectation of the owner of the second transaction. From this principle of good faith is derived the obligation, in principle, of the first transaction owner to do his best to record a caveat so as to prevent the owner of the second transaction from entering into contract with the seller."[70]

As a judicial legislator, Barak was not satisfied with merely determining the rule, and he continued to set exceptions, some of which were obiter dicta that had nothing to do with the facts of the case at hand. One was so general that it allowed the court, in future, to disqualify the rule no less freely than it was set. Thus, Barak ruled that refraining from recording a caveat would not be considered a failure "if under the circumstances there are weighty considerations of a legal policy that justify the absence of a caveat."[71] He also provided an example of such a consideration: one spouse's failure to register a caveat regarding rights in the property of the other spouse "for reasons of family unity."[72] Barak's ruling in the Ganz case was, thus, a masterpiece of judicial legislation. By interpreting a general principle anchored in Israeli legislation, Barak enacted both a general obligation and a set of reservations, about which there is no explicit mention in the legislation and which for years the court, including Barak himself, had argued could not be based on Israeli legislation. This is a clear expression of Barak's power, as well as the power of the Supreme Court at the time of the judgment in the Ganz case.

Some of Barak's colleagues on the bench in the Ganz case expressed reservations about the breadth of the obligation he created. All agreed that, in this specific case, Ganz should pay for his misconduct and that the decision could be based on the Israeli principle of good faith. However, most tended to restrict the rule to the special circumstances of the Ganz affair: the long duration of the failure of the first right holder to register a caveat (seventeen years) and the later purchaser's extended and significant reliance on this delay, which had caused harm.[73] These circumstances are very similar to the conditions of the English equitable doctrine of estoppel: the estopping of a claimant's right because of a long-term failure and an ongoing long-term reliance that causes damage to another person.[74] The Ganz case thus symbolized the birth of an independent Israeli twin to the English doctrine of equitable estoppel: the Israeli doctrine of estoppel. Although, as noted, the justices based the doctrine on the Israeli principle of good faith, they often used the term *estoppel*, derived from English equity laws.[75] Justice Barak had no reservations about basing his rulings on the principle of estoppel.[76] Thus, the Ganz ruling set another independent foundation for the Israeli laws of equity: the "estopping" of a right holder whose misconduct caused significant harm to others.

## The New Israeli Canon of Equity

The Ganz ruling, like the Aharonov ruling before it, opened the door to further development of Israel's laws of equity. It also created uncertainty and left open questions: Should we prefer a broad or narrow interpretation of the principle of good faith? How should one rule on a less severe misrepresentation than in Ganz's case? The courts in Israel have since been actively engaged in implementing and developing the Ganz ruling. For example, conditions were set for its application or its inapplicability in cases where the misrepresentations that caused the damage were of shorter duration or less severe.[77] Rules were set regarding failures caused by trust relations between neighbors or distant family members in a traditional Arab village.[78] The court even applied the ruling to registration failures other than failure to register a caveat, such as refraining from registering an agreement between common owners.[79] The new doctrine of estoppel was also applied to misrepresentations, written or oral, that do not concern registration.[80]

The court also clarified the relationship between the Ganz and Aharonov rulings. Ostensibly, these were contradictory rulings, since the Aharonov ruling established that an equity right supersedes the rights of the transferor's creditors even without a recorded caveat, whereas the Ganz ruling determined that a person who did not record such a caveat is liable to lose priority. Justice Barak, who played a part in both rulings, clarified that while the Aharonov ruling was intended to provide priority over creditors who did not rely on the disputed property, the subsequent (Ganz) case involved the determination of priority in a competition between two transactions that, in turn, both relied on the property. In the first case, failure to register a caveat in favor of the first transaction did not harm the creditor, who had no interest in the property at all. In the second case, failure to register a caveat in favor of the first owner misled the subsequent owner and caused him damages.[81]

The Ganz and Aharonov rulings, along with subsequent judicial developments, became an important component of Israel's independent equity laws. Though these laws are similar to English equity law, they are the product of an original Israeli development. Why did the Israeli judiciary invest so much energy in this independent creation if it ultimately led to a result that could have been imported? The answer to this question lies in the deep connection between the manner in which the ruling was made and the identity of the state. The independent development of "made in Israel" judicial doctrines is evidence of the success of Israeli law in freeing itself from the bounds of British law, but also of the emerging power of the judiciary vis-à-vis the legislature and the willingness of the former to fill the many lacunae the latter was not eager to fulfill.

## Judicial Involvement in the Constitutional Safeguards for Property

### The "Constitutional Revolution": Expectations

Another manifestation of the independence and growing power of Israel's judicial system in recent decades has been its ability to conduct constitutional reviews of legislation. This ability has also found expression in the field of constitutional protection of private property. Land expropriations or planning injuries are the most prominent examples of such harm to private property, and it might therefore be expected that the power of the Israeli judicial system would be particularly apparent in this area. As will be explained below, it is precisely in this area that the Supreme Court did not exhibit its full power but chose to exercise relative judicial restraint. One of the reasons for this is apparently the distributive approach of some of the justices.

Even before the aforementioned constitutional revolution, courts in Israel recognized the important status of private property rights and the obligation to compensate for expropriation of land.[82] Furthermore, key legislations in Israel dealing with expropriations have always established the right to compensation, even if partial and incomplete, for expropriations and for planning injuries.[83] The enactment of article 3 of the Basic Law: Human Dignity and Liberty in 1992, whereby "a person's property is not to be infringed [on]" except by law, apparently reinforced this recognition.[84]

Indeed, article 10 of the Basic Law, "preservation of laws," according to which the law shall not apply to legislation enacted prior to its entry into force, limited the courts' jurisdiction to carry out constitutional reviews of expropriations and planning injuries. This restriction precluded the court's authority to revoke earlier legislation that infringes on private property. However, the Supreme Court adopted the approach whereby it is authorized to interpret previous legislation differently in light of the Basic Law. In accordance with this approach, the court does have the authority to carry out judicial review of actions that rely on old legislation, while interpreting this legislation in a manner that legitimates only actions that are consistent with the tenets of the Basic Law.[85]

Thus, despite the "preservation of laws" clause, the enactment of the Basic Law created among both jurists and landowners far-reaching expectations for a "revolution" that would strengthen the protections of private property in real estate in comparison to the protections that existed before the Basic Law was enacted.[86] The courts themselves defined the interpretive transformation as "revolutionary" in their rhetoric.[87] However, in practice, the court's willingness to effect a change in the laws of land expropriation and planning injuries was limited. We shall demonstrate this below through two main infringements on real estate: the actual authority to carry out expropriation of land and the obligation to provide just compensation for land expropriations and injuries.

### Judicial Restraint in Reviewing the Authority to Expropriate Land

One might expect to find expanded judicial review of the expropriation laws in the framework of the authority to expropriate. The two central laws dealing with expropriation in Israel, the Lands (Expropriation) Ordinance of 1943 and the Planning and Building Law of 1965, define the purpose of permitting expropriation under the broad term "public need."[88] The US Constitution uses the similar term "public use."[89] This term can be interpreted narrowly, to include only the use by the public, as well as broadly, to indicate any public purpose. The narrow interpretation does not allow the expropriation of lands for the purpose of transferring them to private entities or individuals, while the broader interpretation allows expropriation for the purpose of transferring lands to private entities or individuals so long as the transfer fulfills its public purpose. The US Supreme Court has debated these two possible interpretations, and the majority has favored the broad interpretation.[90] This is also the perspective of the Israeli Supreme Court. Much of the land expropriation in Israel was undertaken for the purpose of constructing residential neighborhoods, which were ultimately given to individuals. The public reasoning for the expropriation was usually that the land was distributed among multiple private owners, creating coordination problems that prevented development and thus required expropriation.[91]

Following the enactment of the Basic Law: Human Dignity and Liberty, petitioners in the Nusseibeh case attempted to challenge the broader interpretation. They argued that, following the enactment of the Basic Law and the tests set forth therein, there were no longer grounds to expropriate land for a public purpose that the petitioners could carry out on their own.[92] A minority of the Supreme Court justices held that in light of the Basic Law there was indeed no longer a justification for expropriating land for such a purpose and that market forces alone should resolve the problem of coordination.[93] The majority opinion, on the other hand, permitted such expropriations and held that the market failure inherent in the problem of coordination between multiple owners would lead to an intolerable delay in carrying out the public purpose of the expropriation.[94]

The court adhered to this position even when the owners of the land who wanted to realize the commercial purpose of the expropriation themselves were not Palestinian residents of East Jerusalem, as in the Nusseibeh case, but an Israeli businessman and the Jewish National Fund. The court did not accept the declaration of the owners' desire to realize a commercial public project themselves as a good enough reason to find that the expropriation of their land in the heart of Tel Aviv was ultra vires.[95] Moreover, the courts refused to invalidate expropriations for public purposes even when the realization of that public purpose was delayed for decades after the expropriation. Such a delay ostensibly indicates that the expropriation was no better a solution than waiting for market forces. The constitutional protection of private property in the Basic Law: Human Dignity and Liberty did not convince the court to declare such old expropriations ultra vires.[96] What ultimately brought about a change in this area was legislation that in

2010 enacted the obligation to specify a date for the execution of an expropriation and furthermore established a right to recover land in the event that the purpose of an expropriation was not realized within the period specified.[97] However, this legislative amendment was not applied retroactively, nor does it apply to expropriations under the Planning and Building Law, which is the main law that currently deals with expropriations in Israel. Thus, the relevance of the amendment at present is very minor.

Yet another far-reaching transformation that could be achieved through the interpretation of expropriation laws involved cases in which the public need for expropriation had expired or been realized and so the land was no longer required for said public need. In the Karsik case, the court supposedly created a revolution when it ruled that, in principle, the state must return land to its original owners when the purpose of its expropriation expires. The court based this ruling on a creative interpretation of the authority to expropriate for "public needs," whereby this ongoing authority expires when the public need for the expropriated land expires.[98]

However, this activist interpretation remained a matter of principle only. The court was not prepared to rule accordingly in practice and to return expropriated land to its owners. Instead, it instructed the legislature to work out the details of the arrangement. The legislature consequently labored on a proposed legislation that overrode the court's ruling in principle almost entirely. It determined that the right of restitution shall not apply to expropriations that were carried out in the past but only to expropriations to be executed in the future, and when applicable, it will only give the original owner priority to purchase the land at market value.[99] The Supreme Court did not at any point insist on the principle that it had defined, and it even approved the constitutionality of the law that overrode it.[100]

It appears, therefore, that in the context of the constitutional revolution, the Israeli Supreme Court was extremely cautious, if not conservative, in its review of the state's authority to execute expropriations.

### Moderate Judicial Activism toward Widening the Right for Compensation

In contrast, the court demonstrated greater judicial activism in its constitutional review of the extent of compensation that should be paid for expropriation of or damage to land. As noted, the two main laws that permit the state and local authorities to carry out expropriations of land determined even prior to the enactment of the Basic Law that expropriations must be compensated for. The Planning and Building Law also granted the right to sue for injuries to real estate as the result of local outline plans.[101] However, these laws included various sections that exempted the authorities from paying full compensation for the expropriation and obliged them to pay only partial compensation. The scope of the exemption from compensation ranged from 25 percent at the national level to 40 percent at the local level.[102] The exemption for planning injuries applies to any damage that "does not exceed the reasonable."[103] In the past, the Supreme Court interpreted these exemptions as a kind of tax imposed on landowners. Therefore, it ruled that within those exemptions authorities could expropriate land without paying compensation even when the expropriation does not improve the balance of the land remaining in the hands of the owners and even if the land is expropriated in full, without leaving the owner any land whatsoever.[104] With the enactment of the Basic Law, the court changed its interpretation of this legislation. This was the most far-reaching amendment in the area of expropriations, even though it too was more moderate than might have been expected from a "constitutional revolution."

In the Holzman case, the Supreme Court ruled that if a plot of land is expropriated in its entirety, the owner should be fully compensated and not burdened with taxes embedded in the statutory exemption of the compensation.[105] The court was less clear as regards the exemption where authorities expropriate only some of the land and the expropriation does not improve the land remaining in the owner's hands. While Justice Dorner supported eliminating the exemption from compensation in such cases, Chief Justice Barak did not concur on this point. He proposed that, notwithstanding the protection of private property, the landowner had a "social responsibility" that exemption from compensation might be seen to express. In his typical manner, Barak left the determination of such cases to the future discretion of the courts.[106] A few years later, following Barak's retirement, the Supreme Court ruled in the Rotman case that owners should be fully compensated for an expropriation of even a part of their plot if the expropriation does not improve the part remaining with the owner.[107] Furthermore, the legislature had canceled the exemption for expropriations carried out on a national level but not those on the local level.[108] Yet there is no empirical evidence that the new compensation requirements decreased the extent of expropriation.[109]

The justices of the Supreme Court were similarly divided over the interpretation of the article in the law exempting the authorities from the compensation requirement for planning injuries that "do not exceed the limits of reasonableness."[110] In the Horowitz case, some of the judges held that in light of the constitutional protection of property, local authorities should compensate for any damage suffered beyond *de minimis*.[111] Here, too, Chief Justice Barak proposed a broader interpretation of the exemption from compensation, based on the idea that private property owners should be charged with "social responsibility."[112] He proposed evaluating the question of compensation in accordance with the scope of the damage, the importance of its public purpose, and the extent to which the damage is distributed. The greater the damage, the less important the public goal, and the less evenly distributed, the greater the requirement to compensate. On the other hand, the smaller the damage, the more important its public purpose becomes, and the more equally and randomly the damage is distributed among the entire population, the smaller the requirement to compensate.[113]

The Supreme Court ordered another hearing in the case, and this time a panel of seven justices did not produce a binding decision, which created even more uncertainty among those involved and increased the dependence on judicial discretion.[114] This aptly demonstrates the ideological differences between the justices. Opposing Chief Justice Barak's distributive approach, which supported the imposition of social responsibility on property owners, was his deputy, Justice Mishael Cheshin. Cheshin, who consistently upheld the defense of private property in his rulings, objected to the imposition of social responsibility. The following socioeconomic worldview is the foundation for his position on the issue: "Today's real-estate owners—including the respondent—are not necessarily more well-to-do economically and financially than others in their community. And for some of them, the land infringed upon is their only property. Indeed, today's feudal lords are capitalist feudalists. They are no longer the feudal lords of days past. It behooves us therefore to be more careful with those whose property, possibly their only property, is harmed by planning programs. . . . This is also how to uphold the justice of equality, which is so vital to the existence of a healthy community."[115]

We see that the judicial activism of the court regarding the constitutional protection of property was more significant vis-à-vis the owner's right to compensation for expropriation than the authority's right to expropriate. The court changed the law that preceded the Basic Law through an authority it took upon itself, the authority to interpret previous legislation. But it was not conservatism so much as ideological differences that forestalled far-reaching precedents in the field of constitutional protection of property in real estate.

## Concluding Remarks

In this chapter, we have seen how Israel land law reflects the independence and legal creativity of Israel's judiciary. In the area of private law, Israeli jurisprudence has been quite creative in the innovation of local doctrines similar to those developed by English courts of equity hundreds of years ago. The Supreme Court devised local "made in Israel" (*Tozeret Ha-Aretz*) rights of equity and rights of estoppel to demonstrate the independence of Israel's legal system from foreign doctrines. In the first chapter, we analyzed a similar process in the liberation of Israeli law from the Ottoman heritage, but the independent canon of Israeli equitable doctrines also demonstrates the judiciary's activist approach to the interpretation of legislation.

Judicial activism is also expressed, albeit more limitedly, in the way the Supreme Court changed the laws of expropriation and planning injuries to land after the enactment of the Basic Law: Human Dignity and Liberty, by assuming the authority to interpret the laws in the spirit of the Basic Law even though the Basic Law does not explicitly apply to them. The court's creative and activist interpretation of these laws led to a significant reduction in the number of cases in which it is permissible to expropriate land without compensation. On the other hand, the court's judicial review of the very authority to expropriate led only to minor changes. The main reason for this was not the court's conservative approach to its judicial role but the ideological disagreements within the court. These coincided with the gradual shift in the economic identity of Israel discussed in the previous chapters. The relatively moderate intervention of the court in defense of private property attests to the dispute between judges with leftist economic views, who were concerned with protecting the expropriation powers of the state, and judges with more right-wing views, who favored private property rights. Hence, the study of the increased activism of the judiciary in the field of land expropriations is also indicative of transitions in Israel's economic identity.

However, the Supreme Court's decisions in defending private property rights to land illustrates a further crisis of identity that has swept over Israel in recent years: the widening rift between the ideal of a healthy democracy based on respect for an independent judiciary and the ideal of limited judicial power. Israel boasts a creative, strong, and independent legal system, as reflected in these rulings, but fears it may have gone too far. The overall picture of the case law in this chapter indicates a powerful though restrained judiciary.

## Notes

1. Shimon Shetreet, "The Critical Challenge of Judicial Independence in Israel," in *Judicial Independence in the Age of Democracy: Critical Perspectives from around the World*, ed. Peter H. Russell and David M. O'Brien (Charlottesville: University Press of Virginia, 2001), 233, 233–35.

2. Eli Salzberger, "Judicial Activism in Israel," in *Judicial Activism in Common Law Supreme Courts*, ed. Brice Dikson (Oxford: Oxford University Press, 2008), 217; Yoav Dotan, "Judicial Accountability in Israel: The High Court of Justice and the Phenomena of Judicial Hyperactivism," 8 *Israeli Affairs* (2002): 87–106.

3. Yuval Shany, "Judicial Activism? It Depends Who You Ask," *Jerusalem Post*, June 26, 2019, https://www.jpost.com/Opinion/Judicial-activism-It-depends-who-you-ask-593196.

4. *Official Gazette*, September 1, 1922, 1.

5. Uri Yadin, "Reception and Rejection of English Law in Israel," 11 *International and Comparative Law Quarterly* (1962): 59, 59–61, 72; Daniel Friedmann, "Infusion of the Common Law into the Legal System of Israel," 10 *Israel Law Review* (1975): 324, 350, 359–60.

6. Maimon Schwarzschild, "Complicated—but Not Too Complicated: The Sunset of EU Law in the UK after Brexit," 39 *Cardozo Law Review* (2018): 905, 908; Graham Gee and Alison L. Young, "Regaining Sovereignty: Brexit, the UK Parliament and the Common Law," 22 *European Public Law* (2016): 131, 146–47.

7. Daniel Friedmann, "Independent Development of Israeli Law," 10 *Israel Law Review* (1975): 515, 536–37.

8. Foundations of Law, 5740—1980, *Sefer Ha-Hukim* 163, 34 LSI 181; Menachem Elon, "The Legal System of Jewish Law," 17 *NYU J. Int'l L. & Pol.* (1985): 221, 239–41; Aharon Barak, "The Civil Code Interpretation in Israel," in *Israel among the Nations*, ed. Alfred E. Kellermann et al. (The Hague: Kluwer Law International, 1998), 1, 8.

9. Yoram Shachar et al., "Citation Practices of the Supreme Court, Quantitative Analysis," 27 *Mishpatim—The Hebrew University Law Review* (1996) (Hebrew): 119, 151–60; Yoram Shachar, "The Reference Area of the Supreme Court 1950–2004," 50 *Hapraklit—The Israel Bar Law Journal* (2008) (Hebrew): 29, 41–52.

10. Baker v. Carr 369 US 186, 267 (1962); Alexander Hamilton, "The Federalist 78," in *The Federalist Papers* (New York: Dover, 2014; first printed 1788), 380.

11. Daniel Friedmann, *The Purse and the Sword: The Trials of Israel's Legal Revolution*, trans. Haim Watzman (Oxford: Oxford University Press, 2016), 15–28; Oren Soffer, "Judicial Review of Legislation in Israel: Problems and Implications of Possible Reform," 12 *Israel Affairs* (2006): 307, 311–14.

12. Friedmann, *Purse and the Sword*, supra note 11, at 51–56, 183–88; Menachem Mautner, *Law & the Culture of Israel* (Oxford: Oxford University Press, 2011), 91–96; Gary J. Jacobsohn, "Judicial Activism in Israel," in *Judicial Activism in Comparative Perspective*, ed. Kenneth M. Holland (New York: St. Martin's, 1991), 90–116.

13. Basic Law: Human Dignity and Liberty, 5752–1992, *Sefer Ha-Hukim* 150, §1 (Hebrew), unofficial English translation by Dr. Susan Hattis Rolef, Policing Law, https://www.policinglaw.info/assets/downloads/1992_Basic_Law_of_Israel_Human_Dignity_and_Liberty.pdf.

14. CA 6821/93 United Mizrahi Bank Ltd. v. Migdal Cooperative Village (1995), PD 49(4): 221 (Hebrew), official English translation, https://supremedecisions.court.gov.il/Home/Download?path=EnglishVerdicts\93\210\068\z01&fileName=93068210_z01.txt&type=4; VERSA: Opinions of the Supreme Court of Israel, Translated Opinions, http://versa.cardozo.yu.edu/opinions/united-mizrahi-bank-v-migdal-cooperative-village.

15. Marbury v. Madison 5 US 137 (1803); Yoram Rabin and Arnon Gutfeld, "Marbury v. Madison and Its Impact on Israeli Constitutional Law," 15 *U. Miami Int'l & Comp. L. Rev.* (2007): 303, 318–20.

16. Suzie Navot, *Constitution Law of Israel*, 2nd ed. (The Hague: Kluwer Law International, 2016), 42–50; Daphna Barak-Erez, "Broadening the Scope of Judicial Review in Israel: Between Activism and Restraint," 3 *Ind. J. Const. L.* (2009): 119, 121.

17. Navot, *Constitution Law*, supra note 16, at 42–43; Miguel Deutch, "Protection of Obligatory Rights as Property within the Framework of the Constitutional Revolution in Israel," 15 *Tel Aviv U. Stud. L.* (2000): 147, 150; Ran Hirschl, "The 'Constitutional Revolution' and the Emergence of a New Economic Order in Israel," 2 *Israel Studies* (1997): 136, 137–38.

18. Soffer, "Judicial Review," supra note 11, at 308, 319.

19. David Nachmias and Itai Sened, "Governance and Public Policy," 7 *Israel Affairs* (2001): 3–20; Assaf Meydani, *The Israeli Supreme Court and the Human Rights Revolution: Courts as Agenda Setters* (Oxford: Oxford University Press, 2011), 116–20, 152–56; Soffer, "Judicial Review," supra note 11, at 312.

20. Nomi Levitsky, *The Supremes* (Tel Aviv: Hakibbutz Hameuchad, 2006) (Hebrew), 307–8; Pnina Lahav, "American Moment[s]: When, How, and Why Did Israeli Law Faculties Come to Resemble Elite U.S. Law Schools?," 10 *Theoretical Inquiries in Law* (2009): 653, 657–58; Nir Kedar, "A Scholar, Teacher, Judge, and Jurist in a Mixed Jurisdiction: The Case of Aharon Barak," 62 *Loy. L. Rev.* (2016): 659, 677–86.

21. Aharon Barak, "A Judge on Judging: The Role of a Supreme Court in a Democracy," 116 *Harv. L. Rev.* (2002): 16, 33–36.

22. Oz Almog, "Shifting the Centre from Nation to Individual and Universe: The New 'Democratic Faith' of Israel," 8 *Israel Affairs* (2001): 31, 35–36.

23. As'ad Ghanem, *Ethnic Politics in Israel: The Margins and the Ashkenazi Centre* (Abingdon: Routledge, 2010), 117; Richard A. Posner, "Enlightened Despot," *New Republic*, April 23, 2007, https://newrepublic.com/article/60919/enlightened-despot; Leslie Susser and Elie Rekhess, "Israel," 23 *Middle East Contemporary Survey* (1999): 295, 307.

24. Friedmann, *Purse and the Sword*, supra note 11, at 342–43; Ruth Gavison, "The Role of Courts in Rifted Democracies," 33 *Israel Law Review* (1999): 216, 233–34; Yoav Dotan, "Judicial Review and Political Accountability: The Case of the High Court of Justice in Israel," 32 *Israel Law Review* (1998): 448, 468–73; Yoav Dotan, "Judicial Accountability in Israel: The High Court of Justice and the Phenomenon of Judicial Hyperactivism," 8 *Israel Affairs* (2002): 87, 99–102.

25. Mautner, *Law & the Culture of Israel*, supra note 12, at 90–103.

26. Chap. 2, §3.3.

27. TOI Staff and Jacob Magid, "MKs Push Ahead with Bill Curbing High Court in West Bank Land Disputes," *Times of Israel*, May 28, 2018, https://www.timesofisrael.com/mks-push

-ahead-with-bill-curbing-high-court-in-west-bank-land-disputes/; Lahav Harkov, "The Fiercest Warrior against Judicial Activism," *Jerusalem Post*, November 29, 2017, https://www.jpost.com/Diplomatic-Conference/The-fiercest-warrior-against-judicial-activism-515595; Lahav Harkov, "Bayit Yehudi's Yogev in Hot Water over High Court Bulldozer Comments," *Jerusalem Post*, July 29, 2015, https://www.jpost.com/Israel-News/Politics-And-Diplomacy/Left-calls-Right-wing-criticism-of-High-Court-criminal-410485;

28. Friedmann, *Purse and the Sword*, supra note 11.

29. Yonah Jeremy Bob, "Supreme Court Gets More Conservative with Appointment of Two New Justices," *Jerusalem Post*, February 22, 2018, https://www.jpost.com/israel-news/supreme-court-gets-more-conservative-with-appointment-of-two-new-justices-543418.

30. Proposed Basic Law: Human Dignity and Liberty (Amendment—Clause of Overcoming) (March 12, 2018), Knesset, http://fs.knesset.gov.il//20/law/20_lst_491213.docx; Shahar Hay, "Knesset Committee Approves Override Power Over High Court," *Ynet-News*, June 5, 2018, https://www.ynetnews.com/articles/0,7340,L-5252771,00.html; Raoul Wootliff, "Chief Justice to PM: Bill for 61 MKs to Overturn Rulings 'a Danger to Democracy,'" *Times of Israel*, April 29, 2018, https://www.timesofisrael.com/pm-chief-justice-end-meeting-without-agreement-on-bid-to-limit-supreme-court/; Lahav Harkov, "Netanyahu, Levin Push for Dramatic Judiciary Restructuring," *Jerusalem Post*, April 15, 2018, https://www.jpost.com/Israel-News/Top-Likud-minister-Well-even-go-to-election-to-limit-Supreme-Court-549850.

31. Eran Vigoda-Gadot et al., *Israeli Public Sector Performance: Citizens' Attitudes Analysis and National Assessment* (Haifa: Haifa University and Ben-Gurion University of the Negev, 2016) (Hebrew), 29; Soffer, "Judicial Review," supra note 11, at 323–25; Haim Sandberg, "Strategic Considerations behind Normative Explanations: Lessons from Israel's Supreme Court Expropriations Case," 11 *Int'l J. Cont. L.* (2013): 751, 767–68.

32. Joshua Weisman, "The Land Law, 1969: A Critical Analysis," 5 *Israel Law Review* (1970): 379, 382–84; Friedmann, "Infusion of Common Law," supra note 5, at 350.

33. Leah Doukhan-Landau, *Equitable Rights to Land and the Remedy of Specific Performance of Contracts of Sale of Land* (Jerusalem: Institute for Legislative Research and Comparative Law, 1968), 37–41; A. M. Apelbom, "Book [Review]: *Equitable Rights to Land and the Remedy of Specific Performance of Contracts of Sale of Land*," 4 *Israel Law Review* (1969): 165, 166–67; David Kretzmer, "The Acquiring of Equitable Title," 4 *Israel Law Review* (1969): 452–58; Friedmann, "Infusion of Common Law," supra note 5, at 350, 375–76; Hanoch Dagan, "Codification, Coherence, and Priority Conflicts," in *The Draft Civil Code for Israel in Comparative Perspective*, ed. Kurt Siehr and Reinhard Zimmermann (Tübingen: Mohr Siebeck, 2008), 149, 166.

34. Weisman, "Land Law, 1969," supra note 32, at 383; Willmott v. Barber (1880), 15 Ch D 96: 105; CA 74/53 Razabi v. Razabi (1955), PD 9: 520, 526–28 (Hebrew).

35. "Land Law 5729–1969," §153, 5 *Israel Law Review* (1970) (Hereafter: Land Law 1969): 292, 319.

36. PCA 178/71 Boker v. Anglo-Israeli Co. Ltd. (1971), PD 25(2): 121; Friedmann, "Independent Development," supra note 7, at 552.

37. Moshe Landau, "General Remarks on the Land Law and Servitudes under the Land Law," 1 *Tel Aviv U. Stud. L.* (1975): 110, 110–11; Letter from Moshe Landau to Minister of Justice with the Final Report of the Land Law Amendment Committee (January 25, 1950) (Hebrew) (A copy with the author).

38. Moshe Landau, "Judicial Activism," 7 *Hamishpat Law Review* (2002) (Hebrew): 535, 536–37; Friedmann, *Purse and the Sword*, supra note 11, at 303; Tomer Zarchin, "Eichmann

Trial Judge, Moshe Landau, Dies at 99," *Haaretz*, May 2, 2011, https://www.haaretz.com/1.5006533.

39. Weisman, "Land Law, 1969," supra note 32, at 386–88; Friedmann, "Independent Development," supra note 7, at 552–54.

40. CA 189/95 Bank Otzar Ha-Hayal v. Aharonov (1999), PD 53(4): 199, 251 (Hebrew) (Hereafter: Aharonov case).

41. Aharonov case, supra note 40, at 241–42.

42. Land Law 1969, §9.

43. Boker case, supra note 36, at 134 (J. Landau).

44. Aharonov case, supra note 40, at 244–45, 249.

45. Aharonov case, supra note 40, at 232–35, 246–47; CA 790/97 United Mizrahi Bank Ltd. v. Gadi (2004), PD 59(3): 697, 707–10 (Hebrew) (Hereafter: Gadi case); Dagan, "Codification," supra note 33, at 169, 176–77.

46. Aharonov case, supra note 40, at 249.

47. Author's translation. Aharonov case, supra note 40, at 231.

48. Aharonov case, supra note 40, at 226.

49. Aharonov case, supra note 40, at 248, 251.

50. Aharonov case, supra note 40, at 227–30, 253–54.

51. FD 30/67 Stern v. Stern (1968), PD 22(2): 36, 49 (Hebrew).

52. CA 5955/09 The Receiver v. Tauber (Nevo, July 19, 2011) (Hebrew); George Rosenberg and Niv Goldstein, "Bank Leumi Le'Israel Ltd v Tauber—Israel Supreme Court Judgment on Trust Law," 10 *Trust Quarterly Review*, no. 2 (June 2012): 9, 10–12; Insolvency case (Jerusalem District Court) 5250/08 Frenkel v. Kastenbaum (Nevo, April 3, 2011) (Hebrew).

53. CA 3911/01 Caspi v. Nes (2002), PD 56(6): 752, 760–61.

54. CA 11502/05 Lanyado v. Holland Israel Ltd. (Nevo, February 24, 2008) (Hebrew).

55. CA 1559/99 Tzimbler v. Turgeman (2003), PD 57(5): 49, 63–67 (Hebrew); Nili Cohen, "Distributive Justice in the Enforcement of Contracts," in *Festschrift für Gunther Kuhne zum 70. Geburtstag*, ed. H. Erausgcgcben et al. (Frankfurt: Recht und Wirtschaft, 2009), 971, 1002.

56. Ralph A. Newman, "The Principles of Equity as a Source of World Law," 1 *Israel Law Review* (1966): 616–31.

57. John McGee (ed.), *Snell's Equity*, 32nd ed. (London: Sweet and Maxwell, 2010), 387.

58. CA 2643/97 Ganz v. British & Colonial (2003), PD 57(2): 385 (Hereafter: Ganz case).

59. Land Law 1969, §9, 126, 127.

60. Ganz case, supra note 58, at 391–92.

61. Supra note 34.

62. Dagan, "Codification," supra note 33, at 161–62, 172; Menachem Mautner, "The Eternal Triangle of the Law: Toward a Theory of Priorities in Conflicts Involving Remote Parties," 90 *Mich. L. Rev.* (1991): 95, 117; Nili Cohen, "A Minor's Contract to Acquire an Interest in Land, as against the Vendor's Creditor," 41 *Hapraklit—The Israel Bar Law Journal* (1993) (Hebrew): 161–94; Menachem Mautner, "Conflicting Transactions and the Negligence of a Purchaser Who Does Not Register a Caveat," 40 *Hapraklit—The Israel Bar Law Journal* (1992) (Hebrew): 525, 521; Miguel Deutch, *Property* (Tel Aviv: Bursi, 1997) (Hebrew), 1:174.

63. FD 21/80 Wertheimer v. Harari (1981), PD 35(3): 253, 263–67 (Hebrew); CA 839/90 Raz Construction Company Ltd. v. Irenstein (1991), PD 45(5): 739, 748 (Hebrew); CA 1235/90 Herbst v. M. Arian Electrical Works Contractor Ltd. (1992), PD 46(4): 661, 672 (Hebrew); Dagan, "Codification," supra note 33, at 172.

64. Ganz case, supra note 58, at 400–401.

65. The Contracts (General Part) Law, 5733-1973, §39, 61(b), *Sefer Ha-Hukim* 118 (Hebrew), 27 LSI 117; The Land Law 1969, §14.
66. Wladimir Zeev Zeltner, "Reflections of the Contracts Law (General Part), 5733-1973," 1 *Tel Aviv U. Stud. L.* (1975): 153, 162; Aharon Barak, "Codification of Civil Law and the Law of Torts," 24 *Israel Law Review* (1990): 628, 632-38.
67. CA 4628/93 State of Israel v. Apropim (1995), PD 49(2): 265, 305-6 (Hebrew); VERSA: Opinions of the Supreme Court of Israel, Translated Opinions, J. Barak, par. 9-10, http://versa.cardozo.yu.edu/opinions/state-israel-v-apropim; PCA 6339/97 Roker v. Salomon (1999), PD 55(1): 199, 275-78.
68. Barak, "Codification," supra note 66, at 638.
69. Ganz case, supra note 58, at 404.
70. Ganz case, supra note 58.
71. Ganz case, supra note 58, at 406.
72. Ganz case, supra note 58.
73. Ganz case, supra note 58, J. Shtrasberg-Cohen, at 416, J. Levin, at 418, J. Matza, at 426, J. Rivlin, at 431.
74. McGee, *Snell's Equity*, supra note 57.
75. Ganz case, supra note 58, J. Levin, at 418, J. Rivlin, at 431.
76. Ganz case, supra note 58, at 407.
77. CA 9245/99 Weinberg v. Arian (2004), PD 58(4): 769, 804-6 (Hebrew); CA 8881/07 Lev v. Tubi, J. Melcer, par. 24-25, J. Rivlin, par. 3-4 (Nevo, August 27, 2012) (Hebrew).
78. Lev case, supra note 77, J. Melcer, par. 26-27; CA1217/03 Awnallah Group for Initiating and Investments Ltd. v. Khazen (2003), PD 58(1): 224, 236-40; CA 4836/06 Hamoud v. Harb, J. Rubinstein, par. 36 (Nevo, July 13, 2008).
79. CA 48/16 Dahan v. Simhon, J. Barak-Erez, par. 45 (Nevo, August 9, 2017).
80. CA 580/10 Nir Cooperative—National Cooperative Society for Settlement Workers v. Hod Hasharon Municipality, J. Melcer, pars. 24-26 (Nevo, July 25, 2013); CA 136/14 Dan Op Ltd. v. Cornucopia Equities Ltd., J. Melcer, pars. 62-63 (Nevo, September 6, 2017).
81. Gadi case, supra note 45, at 707-8; Dagan, "Codification," supra note 33, at 176-77.
82. CA 216/66 City of Tel Aviv v. Abu Daia (1966), PD 20(4): 522, 546 (Hebrew); CA 695/76 Rosen v. City of Haifa (1978), PD 33(1): 175, 188; Rachelle Alterman, "Israel," in *Takings International: A Comparative Perspective on Land Use Regulations and Compensation Rights*, ed. Rachelle Alterman (Chicago: American Bar Association Publishing, 2010), 313, 315.
83. Lands (Expropriation) Ordinance, 1943, *Palestine Gazette* [*Official Gazette* during the Mandatory Government], supp. I 32 (1943) §4, 20; Planning and Building Law 5725-1965, §190, 197, 200, 19 LSI 330 (Original text), unofficial consolidated translation by the Israel Ministry of Environmental Protection, 2008, https://www.gov.il/blobFolder/legalinfo/rules_and_regulations_contaminated_land/en/laws_and_regulations_planning_and_building_law_1965_unofficial_translation.pdf. Consolidated binding most updated version is available only in Hebrew. In the absence of an updated translation, I shall refer to the combined updated Hebrew version published by Nevo.
84. Alterman, *Takings International*, supra note 82, at 316-17
85. FD 2316/95 Ganimat v. The State of Israel (1995), PD 49(4): 589, 652-54; FD 4466/94 Nusseibeh v. Minister of Finance (1995), PD 43(4): 68, 85-89 (Hebrew) (Hereafter: Nusseibeh case).
86. Yifaat Holzman-Gazit, *Land Expropriation in Israel: Law, Culture and Society* (Aldershot: Ashgate, 2007), 167-68.

87. Alterman, *Takings International*, supra note 82, at 316.
88. Supra note 83.
89. US Const. Art. 5.
90. Kelo v. City of New London, 545 US 469, 485 (2005).
91. Holzman-Gazit, *Land Expropriation*, supra note 86, at 44–51; Haim Sandberg, "Land Expropriations of Private Arab Land in Israel: An Empirical Analysis of the Regular Course of Business," 43 *Israel Law Review* (2010): 590, 605; Haim Sandberg, "Land Title Settlement in Jerusalem: Legal Aspects," 23 *Journal of Israeli History* (2004): 216, 222–25.
92. Nusseibeh case, supra note 85, at 76.
93. Nusseibeh case, supra note 85, J. Dorner, at 90–91, J. Matza, at 93, J. Levin, at 93.
94. Nusseibeh case, supra note 85, J. Goldberg, at 81–83, J. Or, at 93.
95. HCJ 10784/02 Keren Kayemeth LeIsrael v. Atarim on the Tel Aviv Coast Tourism Development Company in Tel Aviv Jaffa (2004), PD 58(3): 757, 767–68 (Hebrew) (Hereafter: Atarim case); Admin. App. 7859/11 Rabbi HaLevi Krakovsky v. Local Planning and Building Committee Tel Aviv-Jaffa (Nevo, July 22, 2013) (Hebrew).
96. Atarim case, supra note 95, at 765–766; Nusseibeh case, supra note 85, at 79; HCJ 3421/05 Mahul v. Finance Minister, J. Arbel, par. 33 (June 18, 2009). See also chap. 5 at note 162 and text.
97. Amendment of Land (Expropriation) Ordinance (No. 3) Law 2010–5770, *Sefer Ha-Hukim* 346 (Hereafter: 2010 Amending Law).
98. HCJ 2390/96 Karsik v. State of Israel (2001), PD 55(2): 625 (Hebrew), English translation, J. Barak, at par. 9: https://supremedecisions.court.gov.il/Home/Download?path =HebrewVerdicts\96\900\023\n45&fileName=96023900_n45.txt&type=5; VERSA: Opinions of the Supreme Court of Israel, Translated Opinions, J. Cheshin, at par. 31 (Hereafter: Karsik case), http://versa.cardozo.yu.edu/opinions/karsik-v-state-israel; Holzman-Gazit, *Land Expropriation*, supra note 86, at 168; Danielle Marx, "Takings and the Requirement of Ongoing Public Purpose: The Effect of the Constitutionalization of the Right to Property on the Law of Takings (Karsik v. the State of Israel, Israel Land Authority, 55(II) PD, 625)—Case Note," 36 *Israel Law Review*, no. 2 (Summer 2002): 149–58.
99. Karsik case, supra note 98, J. Cheshin, at par. 91; 2010 Amending Law, supra note 97; Sandberg, "Strategic Considerations," supra note 31, at 753.
100. HCJ 2254/13 Samuel v. Minister of Finance (Nevo, May 15, 2014) (Hebrew).
101. Supra note 83; Alterman, *Takings International*, supra note 82, at 318, 325–30.
102. Lands (Expropriation) Ordinance, 1943, §20; Planning and Building Law 5725–1965, §190.
103. Planning and Building Law 5725–1965, §200; Alterman, *Takings International*, supra note 82, at 332–33.
104. CA 377/79 Faiser v. Local Construction and Planning Committee Ramat Gan (1981), PD 35(3): 645.
105. CA 5546/97 Kiryat Ata Planning and Building Commission v. Holzman (2001), PD 55(4): 629 (Hebrew) (Hereafter: Holzman case), official English translation: https://supreme .court.gov.il/sites/en/Pages/SearchJudgments.aspx?&OpenYearDate=1997&CaseNumber=55 46&DateType=1&SearchPeriod=8&COpenDate=null&CEndDate=null&freeText=null&Imp ortance=null; VERSA: Opinions of the Supreme Court of Israel, Translated Opinions, http:// versa.cardozo.yu.edu/opinions/local-building-v-holzman.
106. Holzman case, supra note 105, J. Barak, at pars. 7–8, J. Dorner, at par. 9.
107. CA 8622/07 Rotman v. The Israel National Roads Company Ltd., J. Fogelman, par 110 (Nevo, May 14, 2012).

108. 2010 Amending Law, supra note 97, §23(5).

109. Ronit Levine-Schnur and Gideon Parchomovsky, "Is the Government Fiscally Blind? An Empirical Examination of the Effect of the Compensation Requirement on Eminent-Domain Exercises," 45 *Journal of Legal Studies* (2016): 439, 458–63.

110. Supra note 103.

111. CA 3901/96 Ra'Anana Local Planning Committee v. Horowitz (2002), PD 56(4): 913, 928–30 (Hebrew).

112. Ra'Anana case 2002, supra note 111, at 937–39.

113. Ra'Anana case 2002, supra note 111, at 942–44.

114. FD 1333/02 Ra'Anana Local Planning Committee v. Horowitz (2004), PD 58(6): 289 (Hebrew) (Hereafter: FD Horowitz); Alterman, *Takings International*, supra note 82, at 335.

115. FD Horowitz, supra note 114, at 315–16.

# EPILOGUE

## *Identity in Flux*

> Things of this world are in so constant a flux that
> nothing remains long in the same state.
>
> John Locke

THE STATE OF ISRAEL HAS A COMPLEX IDENTITY. A multitude of different processes, worldviews, and internal conflicts seethe within it. This book attempts to trace the imprint of these characteristics in the realm of Israel's land laws and its public land policy. It focuses on the state's ongoing efforts to cope with its past; the gradual shift from a centralized leftist-socialist worldview to a right-wing capitalist worldview; the tension between the sense of restrictiveness that comes from being a small country and the striving for innovation and creativity; the aspiration to serve as the nation-state of the Jewish people while upholding the complete equality of all its citizens; and the notion of a healthy democracy with an independent judiciary in conflict over the limits of judicial power.

Identity is abstract, while land law and land policy are concrete. This book seeks to explore the expression of the above characteristics of Israel's abstract identity within the concrete subdisciplines of its land policy: the composition of public land inventory, the management of the public inventory, the privatization of public land, the land planning system, the land policy toward minorities, and the role of the judiciary in the development of land law. The book demonstrates the ways in which these fields reflect broader attributes of state and society, leading to better understanding of the state's identity. In the following paragraphs, I will analyze the main insights gleaned from this analysis and what it teaches us about the identity of the State of Israel.

## Struggling with the Past

The first chapter demonstrates how the composition of Israel's land inventory reflected Israeli's consistent struggle to overcome its past and how the long reach of legal history continues to disrupt the Israeli land market of the twenty-first century. While Israel abolished the legal heritage of the Ottoman and Mandatory governments, denied the restitution of the Palestinian refugees' land to their original owners, and took over the management of the JNF's assets, these old issues have not yet been removed from the national agenda and have left their indelible fingerprints on the structure of the land inventory.

Ottoman land laws may no longer apply, but thanks to them, most of the territory of Israel today is state owned. Likewise, most private landowners in Israel should be grateful to the Ottomans for authorizing private land ownership and to the British for creating a mechanism for its registration. Yet the question "How long will the Ottoman land laws govern us?"[1] still hangs over the management of Israel's land inventory, and nobody knows when Ottoman influence will finally fade. In effect, however, the Ottoman heritage has turned out to be very helpful since it is responsible for the private inventory in core areas of Israel.

In the same way, although control over lands belonging to Palestinian refugees transferred to the State of Israel in the 1950s, about 2,500 square kilometers of lands formerly owned by refugees are still registered in the name of the Development Authority. This formal, fictitious body is no longer active, yet no one has asked to take away its formal ownership, and it still lends the state billions of shekels in income derived from the lands. Does such a distinction indicate an intention to return the assets or their income to refugees or their representatives? This question will likely continue to hover over the structure of Israel's land inventory until a comprehensive political solution to the problem of the Palestinian refugees is found.

The management of 2,500 square kilometers of JNF lands has been in the hands of state authorities in Israel since the 1960s, while the incomes derived from the lands are transferred back to the JNF. The architect of this arrangements, Levi Eshkol, predicted that it would last for "10, maybe 20 generations."[2] Yet both the state and the JNF have repeatedly questioned their commitment to this arrangement. While the state casts doubt on the necessity for the JNF, the latter casts doubt on the extent of the state's commitment to JNF interests and occasionally considers the possibility of returning the lands to its control.

All these fingerprints in the composition of Israel's land inventory indicate that the past, at least in part, remains embedded in the identity of the state and cannot as yet be removed.

## The Transition from Socialism to Capitalism

The second and third chapters clarify how the management of the public land inventory and the process of privatizing parts of it reflect the changes that have taken place over time in the economic identity of Israel. While a centralized leftist-socialist worldview held sway on the eve of the state's establishment and during its first decades, from the late 1970s on, Israel gradually moved away from its socialist underpinnings. Its leadership and economy began to march at an accelerating pace to the tune of a more capitalist instrument that encouraged a free market, increased competition, and privatization. The tension between these extremes and the process of economic transformation are clearly reflected in Israel's management of public land.

Thus, chapter 2 demonstrates how a socialist frame of reference shaped and continues to affect the overarching administrative framework of public land in the State of Israel. In accordance with this socialist perspective, the government retains ownership of most of its public land. This principle is set forth in a Basic Law of constitutional status that shapes the rules for administering the public inventory of land. From its earliest days, values such as equality and distributive justice have underpinned the state's public land policy, and even today, land legislation and court rulings are grounded in these principles. The socialist worldview also has a Zionist-nationalist component, which finds expression in the Zionist-Jewish historical backdrop of the state's control over most of its lands.

All the same, Israel in the third millennium is more of a capitalist state, oriented toward a free market. Since the 1980s, this orientation has led to the privatization of small but crucial portions of its land inventory. Chapter 2 focuses on the political and ideological aspects of this process and shows how the balancing point of governmental land administration in Israel has gradually shifted away from the socialist end of the political-ideological scale toward its more capitalist extremity and privatization. Chapter 3 focuses on the practical dimension of public land privatization and reveals that this process was not a single, immediate move but an ongoing process that is still evolving. Privatization usually starts slowly with small transfers of government-owned economic resources to individuals. Informal steps occur many years prior to the enactment of a formal policy of privatization. While the urban public lands have already reached the formal stage of privatization, privatization of public agricultural lands are still in the initial, informal stages.

The process of land privatization manifests the internal dilemmas and conflicts that accompany the transition from centralized control. Privatization does not involve a mere change in ideology. It is a slow development in which the legal and administrative frameworks confront a changing reality. The pioneers and dreamers, with their ideals of equality, were gradually replaced by bureaucrats negotiating to improve efficiency. Looking deep into this process teaches us lessons on the maturation of Israel's economic identity.

## Being Small and Innovative

Chapter 4 clarifies how Israel's land planning policy and laws reflect the tension between two inherent and contrasting aspects of identity: feelings of constriction stemming from Israel's geography and demography alongside the nation's pride in being a powerhouse of entrepreneurship and innovation.

Israel's small size and elongated shape, combined with the demographic growth of its population, pose enormous challenges to its land planning system. The amount of land for urban development in core areas of Israel continues to decrease. The gap between center and periphery increases. Other difficult planning challenges are the need to preserve the environment and nature and deal with its curses and blessings. Israel must confront a growing threat of earthquakes and water shortages, on the one hand, and utilize its unique resources, such as minerals, natural gas, and solar energy, on the other.

In turn, these challenges stimulate more creative and innovative solutions for the shortage of space. The State of Israel is undergoing a wave of land infrastructure development in many areas, particularly transportation, energy, and water. Innovative technological developments have proceeded in the planning and efficient use of subterranean and marine space.

The attempts to deal with various challenges do not always end successfully. The system suffers from problems caused by flawed administrative structures and a cumbersome bureaucracy, in addition to factors of nature. Israel's genuine planning problems are expected to worsen in the future. Is Israel on the way to a "planning catastrophe," as an official forecast warns,[3] or will it overcome the challenges with the help of technology and innovation? An abundance of creativity will be needed to face the challenges. Does Israel possess such a degree of creativity? The analysis of its current land planning system indicates that efforts to cope with these problems will persist for decades to come.

## A Jewish and Democratic State

Israel's land policies toward the Arab minority reflect a central and fundamental identity issue: the aspiration to act both as the nation-state of the Jewish people and as a state that affords equal treatment to all citizens. The realization of this "double promise" poses a considerable challenge in light of the complex relationship between the country's majority and minority, as well as the need to bridge two conflicting national aspirations. This existential paradox exists at the core of Israel's unique collective identity and the identity of each of its citizens.

Chapter 5 demonstrates how Israel's problem of dual identity, Jewish and democratic, finds prominent and controversial expressions in the state's land policies as they pertain to the Palestinian-Arab minority. The first expression has to do with the policy regarding the outcomes of Israel's War of Independence. As a Jewish state, Israel has no interest in returning lands to the people who owned them prior to the war, both because the state fears that restitution will lead to return and affect the Jewish character of the state and because Israel does not see itself as responsible for the outcome of the war. As a democratic state, Israel is obligated to compensate citizens whose property is expropriated. The policy of non-restitution is accompanied by a policy of monetary compensation. It is enshrined in law and impervious to judicial constitutional review.

The problem of dual identity finds its second expression in Israel's policy regarding allocation of land resources. Both the state authorities and its citizens are conflicted over which of two contradictory models should govern this policy: a "separation" model, according to which the majority and minority groups will continue to live in separate settlements, as they see fit, or an "integration" model that will encourage the merging of the two population groups in mixed communities, neighborhoods, and settlements. The willingness to actually reside in mixed settlements is questioned by Jewish and Arab sectors alike. Neither is enthusiastic about the prospect of assimilation. In terms of real estate, the historical backdrop, cultural differences, and the complex relationship between the two groups all point to separation. Likewise, the government appears to support this policy, as does, to a certain extent, the judicial authority.

Did the State of Israel successfully meet the challenge of equality in the allocation of land resources to the Arab minority? Though there is always room for improvement, the image of inequality is in reality more complex than usually thought. In terms of the extent of privately owned land, as well as land used for residence, the Arab minority has an advantage over the Jewish majority. The state-executed expropriations that followed the establishment of Israel, with the exception of refugee villages, have had a very small impact on the inventory of privately owned land in the Arab sector. However, rural spaces are occupied almost exclusively by Jewish settlements, and rural lands are primarily located in the jurisdiction of Jewish regional councils. The development of Arab settlements is slow and hindered by a shortage of lands and urban planning. Additional internal problems in Arab society make development difficult. Arab settlements are ranked very low on a socioeconomic index that considers a range of variables, including demographics, education, employment, and standards of living. The situation places an extra burden on the state as it seeks to fulfill its responsibility to develop Arab villages and towns, and it is working actively, though not actively enough, in this arena.

Yet, despite all of the above, and against all odds, a slow but accelerating process of integration is taking place. This can be ascribed primarily to the invisible hand of the free market, as well as to certain messages from the Supreme Court that removed some of the potential barriers to integration. Will trends of integration expand in the future, or will the trend of separation deepen? The study of Israel's land policy toward the Arab minority reveals that the state is still debating which way it will go. In the realm of land policy, the tension between "Jewish" and "democratic" is not merely theoretical. It affects the daily life of millions of citizens, Jews and Arabs alike. It will most likely continue to haunt both land policy and Israel's identity for many years to come.

## Judicial Activism and Its Limits

The State of Israel is blessed with an independent and creative judiciary, and its justices are well respected abroad. One of the more controversial aspects of this independence is the phenomenon of judicial activism—that is, the tendency of the judiciary not merely to implement the law but also to create it. Since the turn of the millennium, the judiciary has been at the center of a heated public debate over the limits to its activism. The debate has engaged not only jurists but members of every level of society. The status and independence of the judicial authority are key features of every democratic state and are highly significant to Israeli society. The rulings of the Supreme Court in the realm of land law perfectly reflect the dilemmas concerning judicial power.

Chapter 6 analyzes two prominent examples of the Israeli Supreme Court's rulings in the domain of land laws and the ways in which they reflect the independence and creativity of the judicial system. In the field of private land law, Israeli jurisprudence has established creative and independent local doctrines of equity similar to those developed centuries ago by British courts of equity. In the areas of constitutional law, the Supreme Court has led an activist change of laws pertaining to expropriation and to planning damage to real estate. In both cases the court, under the leadership of Justice Aharon Barak, used a highly innovative and activist interpretation of laws that led to the creation of significant "judicial legislation." The court's decisions illustrate the conflict that has swept over Israel in recent years between the nation's identity as a healthy democracy that respects an independent judiciary and one that limits its judicial powers. Israel boasts a strong and independent judicial system, as reflected in these rulings, but worries that it may have gone too far. The overall picture of case law in the sphere of land law indicates a powerful albeit restrained judiciary.

## Identity in Flux

In my analysis of Israel's land policy and land laws in this book, I have attempted to identify the characteristics of the state on a Freudian couch, as it were. The underlying theme of this analysis is that Israel is in a constant state of flux, looking to the future while remaining haunted by the past. It is a state that aspires to capitalism but retains certain socialist modes. Israel is quite conscious of the limitations imposed by its size and strives to become an innovative technological superpower, yet it is forced to contend with the limitations of geography and demography, as well as with the indomitable powers of bureaucracy. It seeks to be Jewish and democratic, but the enduring aftereffects of the War of Independence still cloud the relationship between the Jewish majority and the Arab minority. So do quandaries concerning their integration and the allocation of separate but equal resources. Israel boasts a creative, strong, independent legal system but fears it may have gone too far.

The Freudian analyst would probably conclude that the imaginary patient is a conflicted soul fraught with dilemmas and uncertainty. Perhaps he would explain that these are signs of maturation in a country that has passed the age of seventy. Following his examination, the analyst would probably draw the patient's attention to the ways in which these conflicts influence daily life. This book is an attempt to do the same. Though I do not draw conclusions from the analyst's couch, I have shown how the very soul of the State of Israel is embedded in the practical rules of its land policy and land laws.

Where do these rules lead? It seems to me that in all the areas surveyed, the State of Israel is at a crossroads. The dilemmas will not become easier in the future. It is possible that they will continue in perpetuity. This possibility accords with Theodore Herzl's vision: "I once called Zionism an infinite ideal . . . as it will not cease to be an ideal even after we attain our land, the land of Israel. For Zionism . . . encompasses not only the hope of a legally secured homeland for our people . . . but also the aspiration to reach moral and spiritual perfection."[4]

Though much has been achieved, there is still much to hope for.

## Notes

1. Joshua Weisman, "How Long Will the Ottoman Land Laws Govern Us?," 12 *Mishpatim—The Hebrew University of Jerusalem Law Review* (1982) (Hebrew): 3–17.

2. Minutes of the Committee for Clarifying the Problem of the Jewish National Fund 14–15 (October 23, 1957), CZA Section 246A, File 107.

3. Chap. 4, at note 32–33.

4. English text quoted from an exhibit in the Ben-Gurion Airport exit gates 2018. See the same text in Arieh Saposnik, "Zionism in the Twenty-First Century?," in *Understanding Israel: Political, Societal and Security Challenges*, ed. Joel Peters and Rob Geist Pinfold (Abingdon: Routledge, 2018), 10. For the Hebrew translation that is the source of this quotation, see Theodore Herzl, *Bifnei Am VeOlam—Zionist Speeches and Articles*, vol. 1 (Jerusalem: Zionist Library Press of the Zionist Organization, 1976) (Hebrew), 285. The text originally appeared in German within an issue of the youth journal *Unsere Hoffnung* dedicated to Herzl (Vienna, August 1904).

# BIBLIOGRAPHY

*General Note: Website contents and personal communications are cited in endnotes and are not included in the bibliography.*

## Primary Sources

### Legislation and Legislation Proceedings (Listed Chronologically)

#### ISRAELI LAWS, REGULATIONS, AND ORDERS

*Explanatory Note.* Official Hebrew texts of Israeli Laws and Bills of Legislation are published in official *Sefer Ha-Hukim* (The Book of Laws) and *Hatzaot-Hok* (Bills of Laws), respectively. Official texts of British Mandate Palestine legislation were published both in English and in Hebrew, in the Palestine government's *Official Gazette*. Official revised new Israeli versions of British Mandate legislation that is still in force are published in *Diney Meinat Israel-Nosah Hadash* (New Version). Subsidiary legislation (regulations, orders, plans) is officially published in *Kovetz Hatakanot* (Regulations) and *Yalkut Ha-Pirsumim* (Collections of Publications of Official Orders). Each item can be identified in the relevant publication by the year of legislation and page on which the item commences. The Hebrew original version and updated amended versions of all kinds of legislation are available electronically on the Nevo Publishing Group website (www.nevo.co.il). Official English translations of some of the Israeli laws were published till the 1990s in The Laws of the State of Israel (LSI) and are also available on the Nevo Publishing Group website (www.nevo.co.il). Some laws were translated in *Israel Law Review* (e.g., 5 Israel Law Review 292 [1970]) and other sporadic forums referred to in the footnotes.

\* \* \*

The Ottoman Land Code 1858
Land (Mewat) Ordinance 1921
Town Planning Ordinance 1921
The Mandate for Palestine 1922
Palestine Order in Council 1922
Land (Settlement of Title) Ordinance 1928
Town Planning Ordinance 1936
Trading with the Enemy Ordinance 1939
Lands (Expropriation) Ordinance 1943
The Declaration of the Establishment of the State of Israel (*Megilat Ha-Atzmaut*) 1948
Law and Administration Ordinance (No. 1) 1948
Absentees' Property Law 1950
Development Authority (Transfer of Property) Law 1950
State Property Law 1951
Land Acquisition (Validation of Acts and Compensation) Law 1953

Prescription Law 1958
Basic Law: Israel Lands 1960
Israel Lands Administration/Authority Law 1960
Israel Lands Law 1960
The Planning and Building Law 1965
Agricultural Settlement (Restrictions on the Use of Agricultural Land and Water) Law 1967
Jerusalem Declaration (Expansion of the Municipal Area) 1967
Law and Administration Order (No. 1) 1967
Land (Settlement of Title) Ordinance (New Version) 1969
Land Law 1969
Absentees' Property Law (Compensation) 1973
The Contracts (General Part) Law 1973
The Antiquities Law 1978
Basic Law: Jerusalem, Capital of Israel 1980
Foundations of Law 1980
The Golan Heights Law 1981
Interpretation Law 1981
Public Land (Removal of Invaders/Land Evacuation) Law 1981
Land Settlement Order 1983
Planning and Building Regulations (Installation of Parking Spaces) 1983
Territorial Waters (Amendment) Law 1990
Basic Law: Human Dignity and Liberty 1992
Israel Lands Administration (Amendment) Law 1995
Planning and Building Law (43rd Amendment) 1995
Basic Law: Jerusalem, Capital of Israel (Amendment) 2000
The Economic Arrangements Law (Legislative Amendments to Achieve the Budget and Economic Policy Goals for the 2002 Fiscal Year) 2002
Protection of the Coastal Environment Law 2004
Public Land Law (Removal of Invaders) (Amendment) 2005
The Arrangements in the State Economy (Legislative Amendments for Achieving Budget and Economic Policy Goals for the 2006 Fiscal Year) Law 2006
The Land (Reinforcement of Condominiums against Earthquakes) Law 2008
The Economic Efficiency (Legislative Amendments for Implementing the Economic Plan for 2009 and 2010) Law 2009
Israel Lands Administration (Amendment No. 7) 2009
Amendment of Land (Expropriation) Ordinance (No. 3) Law 2010
Amendment to the Cooperative Societies Ordinance (No. 8) Law 2011
The Israel Lands Law (Amendment No. 3) 2011
Promotion of Constructions in Preferred Housing Compounds (Temporary Order) Law 2014
Promotion of Construction in Preferred Housing Compounds (Temporary Order) (Amendment No. 3) 2016
Survey Regulations (Surveying and Mapping) 2016
The Planning and Building Law (Amendment No. 116) 2017
Promotion of Constructions in Preferred Housing Compounds (Temporary Order) (Amendment No. 4) 2017
Basic Law: Israel the Nation State of the Jewish People 2018
Land Law (Amendment No. 33) 2018

## RECORDS OF KNESSET LEGISLATION PROCEEDINGS

*Explanatory Note.* Protocols of Knesset Plenary Sessions are officially published in *Divrei Ha-Knesset* ("Minutes of the Knesset," DK) and are identified by the year of the session, volume number, and column or page number. Since 1992 (the Thirteenth Knesset) the protocols of the Plenary Sessions are identified online in the Knesset website (https://main.knesset.gov.il/Activity/plenum/pages/sessions.aspx) by the number of the Knesset, number of the session, and date. The PDF copies of the official publications of prior Plenary Sessions of Knesset First through Twelfth in *Divrei Ha-Knesset* can be identified online in the same way.

The protocols of the Sessions of all Knesset Committees are identified online on the Knesset website (https://main.knesset.gov.il/Activity/committees/pages/allcommitteeprotocols.aspx) by the number of the Knesset, title of the Committee, number of the session, and date.

\* \* \*

*Plenary Sessions*

DK Vol. 3 (1949)
DK Vol. 6 (1950)
DK Vol. 7 (1951)
DK Vol. 8 (1951)
DK Vol. 12 (1951–52)
DK Vol. 13 (1953)
DK Vol. 28 (1960)
DK Vol. 29 (1960)
DK Vol. 47 (1967)
DK Vol. 90 (1981)
Minutes of Session No. 142 of the Eighteenth Knesset (June 9, 2010)
Minutes of Session No. 205 of the Eighteenth Knesset (January 18, 2011)
Minutes of Session No. 153 of the Twentieth Knesset (August 1, 2016)
Minutes of Session No. 359 of the Twentieth Knesset 1274 (July 17, 2018)

*Knesset Committee Sessions*

Minutes of Session No. 22 of the Constitution, Law and Justice Committee of the Fourth Knesset (March 21, 1960)
Minutes of Session No. 25 of the Constitution, Law and Justice Committee of the Fourth Knesset (March 30, 1960)
Minutes of Session No. 240 of the Sixteenth Knesset (March 29, 2005)
Minutes of Session No. 19 of the Economics Committee of the Eighteenth Knesset (June 3, 2009)
Minutes of Session No. 36 of the Economics Committee of the Eighteenth Knesset (June 23, 2009)
Minutes of Session No. 367 of the Constitution, Law and Justice Committee of the Eighteenth Knesset (March 16, 2011)
Minutes of Session No. 9 of the Economics Committee of the Nineteenth Knesset (May 8, 2013)

Minutes of Session No. 268 of the Internal Affairs and Environment Committee of the Nineteenth Knesset (April 29, 2014)

Minutes of Session No. 8 of the Special Committee for Distributive Justice and Social Equality of the Twentieth Knesset (January 30, 2017)

Minutes of the 779th Meeting of the Economic Committee of the Twentieth Knesset 9–10 (June 12, 2018)

## Judgments (Listed Chronologically)

*Explanatory Note.* Decisions of the Israel Supreme Court (ISC) are identified by their case number, which is assigned as soon as the petition is received and begins afresh each calendar year. Decisions of Israeli district courts are identified by their case number and the name of the district. The date of final judgment in each case is mentioned in parentheses. Each case is categorized according to its procedural nature: HCJ (High Court of Justice); Civ. App. (civil appeal); Admin. App. (administrative appeal); FD (further discussion of an extended panel of judges); PCA (permission to file a civil appeal); APA (administrative petition appeal).

Decisions of the Supreme Court are officially published in *Piskey Din* ("Judgments," PD) and are identified by the year of the decision, volume number, and page on which the judgment commences. These are published by the Nevo Publishing Group both in hard copy and on the internet (https://www.nevo.co.il). Judgments of district courts are published on this website too.

Since PD usually appears a few years after the judgment itself, more recent judgments have to be found on the ISC's website (https://supreme.court.gov.il/Pages/fullsearch.aspx), where they can be located by their original case number. This website also includes translations to English of some of the judgments of the ISC. Translations of some ISC judgments also appear in the VERSA: Israel Supreme Court Project (ISCP), launched by the Benjamin N. Cardozo School of Law of Yeshiva University (https://versa.cardozo.yu.edu/opinions). Judgments of district courts have no English translation.

### ISRAELI SUPREME COURT JUDGMENTS

CA 74/53 Razabi v. Razabi (1955), PD 9: 520.
CA 216/66 City of Tel Aviv v. Abu Daia (1966), PD 20(4): 522.
FD 30/67 Stern v. Stern (1968), PD 22(2): 36.
PCA 178/71 Boker v. Anglo-Israeli Co. Ltd. (1971), PD 25(2): 121.
CA 630/70 Tamrin v. State of Israel (1972), PD 26(1): 197.
CA 695/76 Rosen v. City of Haifa (1978), PD 33(1): 175.
FD 21/80 Wertheimer v. Harari (1981), PD 35(3): 253.
CA 377/79 Faiser v. Local Construction and Planning Committee Ramat Gan (1981), PD 35(3): 645.
HCJ 528/88 Avitan v. Israel Land Administration (1989), PD 43(4): 297.
CA 839/90 Raz Construction Company Ltd. v. Irenstein (1991), PD 45(5): 739.
CA 1235/90 Herbst v. M. Arian Electrical Works Contractor Ltd. (1992), PD 46(4): 661.
HCJ 4713/93 Golan v. Special Committee under Section 29 of the Absentees' Property Law (1994), PD 48(2): 638.
FD 4466/94 Nusseibeh v. Minister of Finance (1995), PD 43(4): 68.
CA 4628/93 State of Israel v. Apropim (1995), PD 49(2): 265.

CA 6821/93 United Mizrahi Bank Ltd. v. Migdal Cooperative Village (1995), PD 49(4): 221.
FD 2316/95 Ganimat v. the State of Israel (1995), PD 49(4): 589.
CA 189/95 Bank Otzar Ha-Hayal v. Aharonov (1999), PD 53(4): 199.
PCA 6339/97 Roker v. Salomon (1999), PD 55(1): 199.
HCJ 6698/95 Ka'adan v. Israel Lands Administration (2000), PD 54(1): 258.
HCJ 2390/96 Karsik v. State of Israel (2001), PD 55(2): 625.
CA 5546/97 Kiryat Ata Planning and Building Commission v. Holzman (2001), PD 55(4): 629.
CA 3901/96 The Local Planning and Building Committee, Raanana v. Horowitz (2002), PD 56(4): 913.
HCJ 244/00 The New Discourse Organization for a Democratic Discourse in Israel v. the Minister of National Infrastructures (2002), PD 56(6): 25.
CA 3911/01 Caspi v. Nes (2002), PD 56(6): 752.
CA 119/01 Akunas v. State of Israel (2003), PD 57(1): 817.
CA 2643/97 Ganz v. British & Colonial (2003), PD 57(2): 385.
HCJ 840/97 Sabith v. Government of Israel (2003), PD 57(4): 803.
CA 1257/01 Avi-ezer v. State of Israel (2003), PD 57(5): 625.
HCJ 840/97 Sbeit v. Government of Israel (2003), PD 57(4): 803.
CA 1559/99 Tzimbler v. Turgeman (2003), PD 57(5): 49.
CA 1217/03 Awnallah Group for Initiating and Investments Ltd. v. Khazen (2003), PD 58(1): 224.
HCJ 10784/02 Keren Kayemeth LeIsrael v. Atarim on the Tel Aviv Coast Tourism Development Corporation Tel Aviv Jaffa (2004), PD 58(3): 757.
CA 9245/99 Weinberg v. Arian (2004), PD 58(4): 769.
CA 790/97 United Mizrahi Bank Ltd. v. Gadi (2004), PD 59(3): 697.
FD 1333/02 Ra'Anana Local Planning Committee v. Horowitz (2004), PD 58(6): 289.
CA 3535/04 Dinar v. State of Israel—Minister of Finance (2006).
HCJ 7452/04 Abu-Raya v. Israel Land Administration (2008).
HCJ 9205/04 Adalah—the Legal Center for Arab Minority Rights in Israel v. Israel Lands Administration (2008).
HCJ 52/06 Al-Aqsa for the Development of Islamic Waqf Assets in Palestine Ltd. v. Simon Wiesenthal Center Museum Corp. (2008).
CA 11502/05 Lanyado v. Holland Israel Ltd. (2008).
CA 4836/06 Hamoud v. Harb (2008).
HCJ 3172/08 Al-Aqsa Al-Mobarak Company Ltd. v. the Municipality of Yehud (2008).
HCJ 3421/05 Mahul v. Finance Minister (2009).
PCA 6382/09 Keren Kayemeth Le Israel (JNF) v. Diamant (2009).
HCJ 4734/08 Al-Aqsa Al-Mobarak Company Ltd. v. Mekorot—the National Water Company (2009).
HCJ 8497/04 Al-Aqsa Company for the Development of Hekdesh Properties v. Moshav Kerem Maharal (2009).
HCJ 516/08 Al-Aqsa Al-Mobarak Company Ltd. v. Moshav Ahihud (2009).
HCJ 4199/06 Al-Aqsa Company for the Development of Islamic Waqf Assets Ltd. v. Moshav Habonim (2009).
CA 4067/07 Jabareenn v. State (2010).
HCJ 3112/10 Moasesset Al-Aqsa Ltd. v. Municipality of Tel Aviv-Jaffa (2010).
HCJ 3280/10 Moasesset Al-Aqsa Ltd. v. Israel National Roads Company Ltd. (2010).
HCJ 1027/04 Independent Cities Forum v. Israel Lands Council (2011).

CA 5955/09 The Receiver v. Tauber (2011).
APA 3542/11 Subcommittee for Appellants of the National Council for Planning and Construction v. the Arara Local Council (2012).
HCJ 729/10 Tnua'at Dror Israel v. State of Israel (2012).
HCJ 5703/12 Moasesset Al-Aqsa Ltd. v. Tel Aviv University (2012).
HCJ 10163/09 Moasesset Al-Aqsa Ltd. v. the Municipality of Rehovot (2012).
HCJ 11087/05 General Cooperative Workers Company in Palestine Ltd. v. State of Israel (2012).
CA 8622/07 Rotman v. the Israel National Roads Company Ltd. (2012).
CA 8881/07 Lev v. Tubi (2012).
CA 4220/12 Al-Uqbi v. State of Israel (2012).
CA 8573/08 Ornan v. Ministry of Interior (2013).
CA 580/10 Nir Cooperative—National Cooperative Society for Settlement Workers v. Hod Hasharon Municipality (2013).
Admin. App. 7859/11 Rabbi HaLevi Krakovsky v. Local Planning and Building Committee Tel Aviv—Jaffa (2013).
HCJ 9804/09 Shawahna v. State of Israel—Development Authority (2014).
HCJ 2311/11 Sabach v. the Knesset, J. Joubran (2014).
CA 8325/12 State of Israel Lands Administration v. Mehadrin Ltd. (2014).
HCJ 2254/13 Samuel v. Minister of Finance (2014).
PCA 1002/14 Shomroni v. Kofman (2014).
PCA 3094/11 Al-Qi'an v. State of Israel (2015).
CA 4220/12 Al-Uqbi v. State of Israel (2015).
FD 3751/15 Al-Uqbi v. State of Israel (2015).
FD 3751/15 Al-Uqbi v. State of Israel (2015).
HCJ 5931/06 Hussein v. Cohen (2015).
CA 7340/13 State of Israel v. Al-Sha'ar (2015).
HCJ 9205/04 Adalah—the Legal Center for Arab Minority Rights in Israel v. Israel Lands Administration (2016).
APA 7381/15 S. Dorfberger Ltd. v. Oded (2016).
APA 4282/16 Saig v. David (2017).
HCJ 9518/16 Harel v. Knesset of Israel (2017).
CA 136/14 Dan Op Ltd. v. Cornucopia Equities Ltd. (2017).
CA 48/16 Dahan v. Simhon (2017).
HCJ 6411/16 The National Committee for the Heads of the Arab Local Authorities in Israel v. Knesset Israel (2018).
HCJ 4189/18 Local Council Turaan v. Government of Israel (2019).
HCJ 5555/18 Hasson v. Knesset (2021).

### ISRAELI DISTRICT COURT JUDGMENTS

Criminal Case (Tel Aviv Magistrate Court) 8438/03 State of Israel v. Oded (2008).
Insolvency Case (Jerusalem District Court) 5250/08 Frenkel v. Kastenbaum (2011).
Criminal Case (Tel Aviv District Court) 23843-06-10 State of Israel v. Ida (2011).
Administrative Petition (Haifa District Court) 29869-01-10 The Arara Local Council v. the Appeals Subcommittee of the National Council for Planning and Building (2011).
Civil Case (Tel Aviv District Court) 1523/07 Mehadrin Ltd. v. Israel Lands Administration (2012).

Originating Motion (Jerusalem District Court) 8304/09 Viderman v. Keren Kayemeth LeIsrael (2013).
Criminal Case (Tel Aviv District Court) 10291–01-12 State of Israel v. Cherney (2014).
Crim. App. 5720/14 Olmert v. State of Israel (2015).

## Other Official Documents

### ISRAELI GOVERNMENT DECISIONS (HEBREW) (LISTED CHRONOLOGICALLY)

*Explanatory Note.* Decisions of Israeli governments are identified by the chronological number of the government (Provisional, 1–35), the serial number of the decision, the date, and the title of the decision. Since the Twenty-Ninth Government, they may be searched and retrieved, only in Hebrew, within the website of the Government Secretariat of the Prime Minster Office (https://www.gov.il/he/Departments/policies?OfficeId=e744bba9-d17e-429f-abc3-50f7a8a55667&policyType=30280ed5-306f-4f0b-a11d-cacf05d36648&limit=10).

\* \* \*

Decision No. 4434 of the Thirty-Second Government "Land and Planning—Updating the National Planning Concept," March 18, 2012.
Decision No. 2047 of the Thirty-Third Government "Regulation of the Budget Transferred to the Jewish National Fund for Development and Housing," October 7, 2014.
Decision No. 563 of the Thirty-Fourth Government of Israel "An Outline of an Arrangement with the Jewish National Fund," October 11, 2015.
Decision No. 2457 of the Thirty-Fourth Government of Israel "Strategic Housing Plan," March 2, 2017.

### DECISIONS OF ISRAEL LAND COUNCIL (HEBREW) (LISTED CHRONOLOGICALLY)

*Explanatory Note.* Decisions of the Israel Land Council are identified by their serial number. An official text of each decision is available on the Israel Land Authority's website (https://land.gov.il/Land_Policy/LandCouncil/Pages/hahlatot_moaza.aspx). Since April 4, 2019, all of these decisions have been codified in "Decisions of Israel Lands Council (Consolidated)," which is available at https://apps.land.gov.il/CouncilDecisions/#/main.

\* \* \*

Decision 1 "Land Policy in Israel," May 17, 1965.
Decision 130 "Changes in the Conditions of Leasing Land to Saturated Public Housing," September 10, 1973.
Decision 146 "Jubilee Lease—Rules for Extending the Lease Contract—Land for Urban Housing," February 3, 1975.
Decision 166 "Jubilee Lease—Rules for Extending the Land Lease Contract for Urban Housing and Businesses, Workshops and Municipal Industrial Enterprises," February 23, 1976.
Decision 259 "Granting Land Rights to Foreigners," June 29, 1982.
Decision 269 "Jubilee Lease—Rules for Extending the Lease Contract for Urban Land," August 22, 1983.

Decision 427 "Lease Fees for Agricultural Land under the Israel Lands Administration Law, 5719–1960," August 3, 1989.
Decision 717 "Long-Leasing of Land for Factories of Kibbutzim, Collective Moshavim, Moshavim and Cooperative Villages," June 20, 1995.
Decision 727 "Agricultural Land whose Purpose Was Changed under the Israel Lands Administration Law, 5720–1960," July 3, 1995.
Decision 737 "Expansion of Residential Units in Agricultural Settlements That Are Workers' Moshav, Cooperative Village, Cooperative Moshav, Kibbutz or Agricultural Cooperative Society," December 17, 1995.
Decision 1066 "Reforming the Land of Israel," January 11, 2006.
Decision 979 "Determination of Rights in the Residential Plot in Agricultural Settlements That Are Moshavim, Cooperative Village, Cooperative Moshav, Kibbutz or Agricultural Cooperative Association," March 27, 2007.
Decision 1144 "Allocation of Land Ownership for Industrial and Commercial Purposes," March 9, 2008.
Decision 1148 "Granting Land Rights to Foreigners and Those Entitled to Immigrate to Israel under the Law of Return, 5710–1950," March 9, 2008.
Decision 1185 "Reform in the Administration of Israel Lands," December 28, 2009.
Decision 1370 "Reform in the Administration of Israel Lands," June 22, 2014.
Decision 1504 "Residential Construction in Agricultural Settlements That Are Workers' Moshav, Cooperative Village, Cooperative Moshav, Kibbutz or Agricultural Cooperative Society," January 16, 2017.

### GOVERNMENTAL REPORTS (IN HEBREW, EXCEPT WHEN EXPLICITLY STATED)

Government Authority for Urban Renewal, *Urban Renewal Report for 2020* (2021).
Government of Israel, *Government Year Book* 5716 (1956).
———, *Infrastructure for Growth 2017–2021* (2017).
Government of Palestine, *Survey of Palestine—Prepared in December 1945 and January 1946 for the Information of the Anglo-American Committee of Inquiry*, vol. 1 (1946) (English).
———, *Village Statistics* (1945) (English).
IDF Chief of Staff's Office, *IDF Strategy* (2015).
———, *IDF Strategy* (2018).
Israel Central Bureau of Statistics, "The Arab Population in Israel," 27 *Statistilite* 1 (2002) (English).
———, "The Arab Population in Israel," 102 *Statistilite* 8 (2008).
———, *Characterization and Classification of Geographical Units by the Socio-Economic Level of the Population 2013: Introduction—List of Variables* (2017).
———, *Characterization and Classification of Statistical Areas within Municipalities and Local Councils by the Socio-Economic Level of the Population 2015* (2019).
———, *Israel in Figures: Selected Data from the Statistical Abstract of Israel* (2019) (English).
———, *Israel Statistic Year Book 2019* (2019).
———, *Long-Range Population Projections for Israel: 2009–2059* (2012).
———, *Price Statistics Monthly 10/2017* (2017).
———, *70 Statistical Abstract of Israel 2019* (2019).
Israel Lands Administration, *Report on Activities for the 1964–1965 Budget Year* (1965).
———, *Report on the Activities for the 1966–1967 Budget Year* 73 (1967).

———, *Report on the Activities of the Israel Lands Administration for the 1972/73 Budget Year* (1973).
———, *Report on the Activities for the 1975–1976 Budget Year* 203 (1976).
———, *Report on the Activities of the Israel Lands Administration for the 1989/90 Budget Year* (1990).
———, *Report on the Activities of the Israel Lands Administration for the 1992/93 Budget Year* (1994).
———, *Report on the Activities of the Israel Lands Administration for the 1999/2000 Budget Year* (2000).
———, *Report on the Activities for the 2000 Budget Year* 100 (2001).
———, *Report on the Activities for the 2005 Budget Year* (2006).
———, *Report on Activities for the 2011 Budget Year* (2012).
———, *Report on Activities for the 2012 Budget Year* (2013).
Israel Land Authority, *Report on Activities for the 2013 Budget Year* (2014).
———, *Report on Activities for the 2015 Budget Year* (2016).
———, *Report on Activities for the 2016 Budget Year* 57 (2017).
———, *Report on Activities for the 2017 Budget Year* (2018).
———, *Report on Activities for the 2018 Budget Year* (2019).
Israel Ministry of Defense, Relocation Administration, *Test Case City of Training Bases* (2016).
Israel Ministry of Environmental Protection et al., *Policy Document—The Dead Sea Basin: Assessment of Current Situation and Prospects for the Future under Continued Dead Sea Water-Level Decline* (2006).
Israel State Comptroller, *Annual Report No. 55A* (2004).
———, *Annual Report No. 64C* (2014).
Israel Water Authority, "Water Sector in Israel: Zoom on Desalination," *7th World Water Forum* (2015).
Ministry of Justice, Land Appraisal Division, *Guidelines: Compensation Appraisal for Public Use of the Deep Layers of the Subsoil* (2010).
———, *Guidelines: Preparation of Appraisals for the Calculation of Consent Fees in "Nahala" (Estate)* (2007).
———, *Guidelines: Special Issues in the Appraisals Carried Out for the Israel Lands Administration* (2011).
Ministry of Justice, Planning and Policy Department, *Final Report: Registration and Land Settlement Department* (2017).
Ministry of Justice, *Report of the Team for Dealing with the Illegal Construction Phenomenon* (2016).
National Committee for Planning and Construction of Preferred Housing Areas (NCPCPHA), *Annual Report 2017* (2018).
———, *Annual Report 2018* (2019).
Planning Administration, "Guidelines for Preparing Three-Dimensional Plans," *Procedure for Uniform Structure of Plan* (2020).
———, *Israel Maritime Policy Document: Mediterranean; Phase II Report—Maritime Space Policy* (2019).
———, *NOP 35 Follow-Up and Update: Phase III Report*, eds Ari Cohen et al. (2010).
———, *NOP 38 Implementation Report for 2015* (2016).
———, *Policy Paper for the Israeli-Mediterranean Sea Area: Phase I Report* (2015).

## PUBLIC COMMITTEES AND EXPERT REPORTS (HEBREW)
### (LISTED CHRONOLOGICALLY)

Land Law Amendment Committee, *Final Report* (1950).
The Goldenberg Committee, *Report of the Public Committee to Examine Land Policy Goals* (1986).
Amit Segev, Moshe Shirav, "Natural Treasures in Negev Craters—Minerals" (Report GSI/22/94, Submitted to the Executive Committee of Israeli Government Ministries, Jerusalem, 1994).
Tzaban Commission, *Report of the Committee to Examine New Urban Land Reorganization* (1995).
Ronen Committee, *Report of the Committee for Reform of the Israel Lands Policy* (1997).
Milgrom Committee, *Report of the Inter-ministerial Team to Examine All Aspects of Changing the Designation of Agricultural Land* (2000).
Gadish Committee, *Report of the Public Committee for Reform in the Israel Land Administration* (2005).
Haber Committee, *Report of the Committee to Examine the Rights in the Residential Area of the Agricultural Communities* (2005).
Ben-Eliyahu Committee, *The Committee for Examining the Separation of the Management of JNF Assets from the Administration of the Israel Land Administration* (2009).
Tamir Agmon, *The Rise of Housing Price in Israel: Implications and Ways of Coping* (Knesset Research and Information Center, 2009).
Amir Eidelman, Yael Yavin, "Built Areas and Open Spaces in Israel," in *Israel Sustainability Project 2030: Indices—Sustainability Yesterday, Today and Tomorrow* (Israeli Ministry of the Environment and Jerusalem Institute for Policy Research, 2011).
Ruth Yahel, Nir Engert, *Conservation Policy in the Mediterranean* (Israel Nature and Parks Authority, 2012).
Jonathan M. Samet, *Human Health Considerations Related to the Siting and Operation of an Open-Pit Phosphate Mine at Sdeh Barrir* (Report submitted to Israel Ministry of Health, 2014).
Ofer Raz-Dror, Noam Kost, *The Strategic Plan for Housing for the Years 2017–2040* (National Economic Council, Prime Minister's Office, 2017).
Matan Shahar, *Admissions Committees in Communities in the Negev and the Galilee* (Knesset Research and Information Center, 2019).

### ARCHIVES (LISTED CHRONOLOGICALLY)

*Explanatory Note.* Documents filed at the ISA (Israel's Archives) are identified by the subject division (22, Land Department of the British Mandate Government; 74, Israel Ministry of Justice; 99, Israel Land Administration) and the numbers of box and file. Documents filed at the CZA (Central Zionist Archive) are identified by the name of the archive and numbers of section and file.

\* \* \*

Decision of the Administrative Council of Jerusalem regarding the Improvement (or Revival) of the 'Mahlul' Sand Dunes by the Rishon-le-Zion People and an Official

Announcement by the High Commissioner of Palestine (1921), ISA 22nd Division, Box M/3497, File GP/2/35a.
Jaffa Land Dunes (1947), ISA 22nd Division, Box 3508, File SD 12(19).
Letter from the Minister of Foreign Affairs to the Custodian of Absentees' Property Dated June 20, 1951, ISA 74th Division, Box 5746/c, File 5 (Hebrew).
Summary of the Meeting Held at the Office of the Director General of the Ministry of Finance on June 26, 1951, regarding the Determination of Prices for Land in Transfers from the Custodian of Absentees' Property to the Development Authority, IAS, 74th Division, Box 5741/C, File 14 (Hebrew).
Valuation of Abandoned Arab Land in Israel ("Berncastle Report") (1951), CZA, Joseph Weitz Archive, Section 246A, File 199.
Agreement between the Custodian of Absentees' Property and the Development Authority, Appendixes A, B, C (A copy of an unsigned draft) (1953), CZA, Joseph Weitz Archive, Section 246A, File 275 (Hebrew).
Ministry of Finance, "Custodian of Absentees' Property, Report on the Use of Absentees' Lands in Completely Abandoned Villages by the End of 1952" (1953), CZA, Joseph Weitz Archive, Section 246A (Hebrew).
Joseph Weitz, *Summary of Activities for the Implementation of the Land Acquisition (Validation of Acts and Compensation) Law, 5713-1953* (April 12, 1954), CZA, Section 246A, File 275.
Minutes of the Committee for Clarifying the Problem of the Jewish National Fund ("Eshkol Committee") (1957), CZA Section 246A, File 107 )Hebrew).
"Proposal to End Land Settlement Operations (Surveying and Mapping) in the Entire Country," Appendix to Letter from Head of the Land Registration Division to State Comptroller (1960), ISA 74, 5733, File 3520/7 (Hebrew).
Ministry of Finance, Assets Division, "Payment of Compensation" (A file with reports of the Bureau for the Implementation of the Acquisition of Land Law in Haifa from the early 1960s), ISA, 99th Division, Box 3131/C, File 1.

## Comparative and International Primary Resources

### CONSTITUTIONS

Constitution of the Bolivarian Republic of Venezuela
Constitution of the People's Republic of China
Constitution of the Republic of Cuba
Constitution of the Russian Federation
Egypt Constitutional Declaration
Islamic Republic of Iran Constitution
United Nations Declaration on the Rights of Indigenous Peoples
US Constitution

### LEGISLATION

Crown Estate Act 1961, 10 Eliz 2, c.55 (English).
43 USC §1701 (1976).
43 USC §1712(c) (1976).

**JUDGMENTS (LISTED CHRONOLOGICALLY)**

Marbury v. Madison, 5 US 137 (1803).
Willmott v. Barber, 15 Ch D 96, 105 (1880).
Brown v. Board of Education of Topeka, 347 US 483 (1954).
Baker v. Carr, 369 US 186 (1962).
James v. United Kingdom, 96 Eur. Ct. HR Ser. A 67 (1986).
Kelo v. City of New London, 545 US 469 (2005).
Tsilhqot'in Nation v. British Columbia, BCJ No. 2465 (2007).

**REPORTS (LISTED CHRONOLOGICALLY)**

UN Conciliation Commission for Palestine, *15th Progress Report, Covering Period 1 Jan 1955–30 Sep. 1956, A/3199* (1956).
World Bank, *World Development Report 2009: Reshaping Economic Geography* (2009).
World Bank, *Global Monitoring Report 2012: Food Prices, Nutrition, and the Millennium Development Goals* (2012).
Organisation for Economic Co-operation and Development (OECD), *National Urban Policy in OECD Countries* (2017).
White House, *Peace to Prosperity: A Vision to Improve the Lives of the Palestinian and Israeli People* (2020).

# Secondary Sources

*Note on Translation.* Names of Hebrew resources were translated to English without transliterated text. After each such resource, the word *Hebrew* has been added in parentheses (Hebrew).

## Books and Articles

Aaronsohn, Ran. "Settlement in Eretz Israel—A Colonialist Enterprise? 'Critical' Scholarship and Historical Geography." 1 *Israel Studies* (1996): 214.
Abdelal, Rawi, et al. "Identity as a Variable." In *Measuring Identity: A Guide for Social Scientists*, edited by Rawi Abdelal et al., 17. Cambridge: Cambridge University Press, 2009.
Abu Hussein, Hussein, and Fiona McKay. *Access Denied: Palestinian Land Rights in Israel*. London: Zed Books, 2003.
Adalah. *Inequality Report: The Palestinian Arab Minority in Israel*. Haifa: Adalah—Legal Center for Arab Minority Rights in Israel, 2011.
Alexander, Ernest R. "Governance and Transaction Costs in Planning Systems: A Conceptual Framework for Institutional Analysis of Land-Use Planning and Development Control—The Case of Israel." 28 *Environment and Planning B: Urban Analytics and City Science* (2001): 755.
Alexander, Ernest R., et al. "Evaluating Plan Implementation: The National Statutory Planning System in Israel." 20 *Progress in Planning* (1983): 101.
Alexander, Gregory S. "Culture and Capitalism: A Comment on De Soto." In *Hernando De Soto and Property in a Market Economy*, edited by D. Benjamin Barros, 41. Abingdon: Routledge, 2010.

———. *Property and Human Flourishing.* Oxford: Oxford University Press, 2018.
Alexander, Gregory S., and Eduardo M. Peñalver. *An Introduction to Property Theory.* Oxford: Oxford University Press, 2010.
Alfasi, Nurit. "Doomed to Informality: Familial versus Modern Planning in Arab Towns in Israel." 15 *Planning Theory & Practice* (2014): 170.
Alfasi, Nurit, and Roy Fabian. "Preserving Urban Heritage: From Old Jaffa to Modern Tel-Aviv." 14 *Israel Studies* (2009): 137.
Almog, Oz. "Shifting the Centre from Nation to Individual and Universe: The New 'Democratic Faith' of Israel." 8 *Israel Affairs* (2001): 31.
Almog, Shmuel. "Redemption in Zionist Rhetoric." In *Redemption of the Land of Eretz-Israel: Ideology and Practice,* edited by Ruth Kark, 13. Jerusalem: Yad Ben-Zvi, 1990 (Hebrew).
Al Naber, Majd, and Francois Molle. "The Politics of Accessing Desert Land in Jordan." 59 *Land Use Policy* (2016): 492.
Alterman, Rachelle. "Decision-Making in Urban Plan Implementation: Does the Dog Wage the Tail, or the Tail Wag the Dog?" 3 *Urban Law and Policy* (1980): 41.
———. "Israel." In *Takings International: A Comparative Perspective on Land Use Regulations and Compensation Rights,* edited by Rachelle Alterman, 313. Chicago: American Bar Association Publishing, 2010.
———. "The Land of Leaseholds: Israel's Extensive Public Land Ownership in an Era of Privatization." In *Leasing Public Lands: Policy Debates and International Experiences,* edited by Steven C. Bourassa and Yu-Hung Hong, 115. Cambridge, MA: Lincoln Institute of Land Policy, 2002.
———. "Land Use Law in the Face of a Rapid-Growth Crisis: The Case of Mass-Immigration to Israel in the 1990s." 3 *Washington University Journal of Law & Policy* (2000): 773.
———. "National-Level Planning in Israel: Walking the Tightrope between Government Control and Privatization." In *National-Level Planning in Democratic Countries: An International Comparison of City and Regional Policy-Making,* edited by Rachelle Alterman, 257. Liverpool: Liverpool University Press, 2001.
———. *Planning in the Face of Crisis: Land Use, Housing and Mass Immigration in Israel.* Abingdon: Routledge, 2002.
———. "When the Right to Compensation for Regulatory Takings Goes to the Extreme: The Case of Israel." 6 *Wash. U. Global Stud. L. Rev.* (2007): 121.
———. "Who Can Retell the Exploits of the Israel Lands Authority? From the Aspects of Justifying the Continuation of Local Ownership of Land." 21 *Iyuney-Mishpat—Tel-Aviv University Law Review* (1998) (Hebrew): 535.
Amara, Muhammad, and Izhak Schnell. "Identity Repertoires among Arabs in Israel." 30 *Journal of Ethnic and Migration Studies* (2004): 175.
Anderson, Benedict. *Imagined Communities: Reflections on the Origin and Spread of Nationalism.* London: Verso, 2006.
Angel, Shlomo, et al. *The Dynamics of Global Urban Expansion.* Washington, DC: World Bank, 2005.
Antoun, Richard T. "Civil Society, Tribal Process, and Change in Jordan: An Anthropological View." 32 *Int. J. Middle East Stud.* (2000): 441.
Apelbom, A. M. "Book [Review]: *Equitable Rights to Land and the Remedy of Specific Performance of Contracts of Sale of Land.*" 4 *Israel Law Review* (1969): 165.
Ardrey, Robert. *The Territorial Imperative.* 1969 reprint. London: Collins, 1966.

Auster, Richard D., and Morris Silver. *The State as a Firm: Economic Forces in Political Development.* Boston: Martinus Nijhoff, 1979.

Avineri, Shlomo. *The Making of Modern Zionism: The Intellectual Origins of the Jewish State.* New York: Basic Books, 1981.

Aytekin, E. Attila. "Agrarian Relations, Property and Law: An Analysis of the Land Code of 1858 in the Ottoman Empire." 45 *Middle Eastern Studies* (2009): 935.

Barak, Aharon. "The Civil Code Interpretation in Israel." In *Israel among the Nations*, edited by Alfred E. Kellermann et al., 1. The Hague: Kluwer Law International, 1998.

———. "Codification of Civil Law and the Law of Torts." 24 *Israel Law Review* (1990): 628.

———. *Interpretation in Law.* Vol. 3: *Constitutional Interpretation.* Srigim: Nevo, 1995 (Hebrew): 332.

———. "A Judge on Judging: The Role of a Supreme Court in a Democracy." 116 *Harv. L. Rev.* (2002): 16.

Barak-Erez, Daphna. "An Acre Here, an Acre There: Israel Land Administration in the Vise of Interest Groups." 21 *Iyuney-Mishpat—Tel-Aviv University Law Review* (1998) (Hebrew): 613.

———. "The Administrative Process as a Domain of Conflicting Interests." 6 *Theoretical Inquiries in Law* (2005): 193.

———. "Broadening the Scope of Judicial Review in Israel: Between Activism and Restraint." 3 *Ind. J. Const. L.* (2009): 119.

Barak-Erez, Daphna, and Oren Perez. "Planning in State-Owned Land in Israel: Toward Sustainable Development." 7 *Mishpat Umimshal* (Law and Government)—*Haifa University Law Review* (2004) (Hebrew): 865.

Bar-Gal, Yoram. "The Blue Box and JNF Propaganda Maps 1930–1947." 8 *Israel Studies* (2003): 1.

———. *Propaganda and Zionist Education: The Jewish National Fund, 1924–1947.* Rochester, NY: University of Rochester & University of Haifa Press, 2003.

Bashir, Bashir, and Amos Goldberg. *The Holocaust and the Nakba: Memory, National Identity and Jewish-Arab Partnership.* Jerusalem: Van Leer Jerusalem Institute and Hakibbutz Hameuchad, 2015 (Hebrew).

Becker, Nir, et al. "Desalination and Alternative Water-Shortage Mitigation Options in Israel: A Comparative Cost Analysis." 2 *Journal of Water Resource and Protection* (2010): 1042.

Beeri-Sulitzeanu, Amnon, and Uri Gopher. *Mixed Cities and Regions: The Future Face of Israel.* Jerusalem: Abraham Fund Initiatives, 2009.

Belfer Center for Science and International Affairs. *Deterring Terror: English Translation of the Official Strategy of the Israel Defense Forces.* Translated by Susan Rosenberg. Cambridge, MA: Harvard Kennedy School, August 2016. https://www.belfercenter.org/sites/default/files/legacy/files/IDFDoctrineTranslation.pdf.

Bell, Abraham, and Eugene Kontorovich. "Palestine, *uti possidetis juris* and the Borders of Israel." 58 *Arizona Law Review* (2016): 633.

Benchetrit, Gilat, and Daniel Czamanski. "The Gradual Abolition of the Public Leasehold System in Israel and Canberra: What Lessons Can Be Learned?" 21 *Land Use Policy* (2004): 45.

Ben-Gurion, David. *Memories.* Vol. 1. Tel Aviv: Am Oved, 1971 (Hebrew).

Ben-Naftali, Orna, et al. *The ABC of the OPT: A legal Lexicon of the Israeli Control over the Occupied Palestinian Territory.* Cambridge: Cambridge University Press, 2018.

Ben-Porat, Guy. "Political Economy: Liberalization and Globalization." In *Israel since 1980*, edited by Guy Ben-Porat et al., 91. Cambridge: Cambridge University Press, 2008.
Ben Rafael, Eliezer. *Crisis and Transformation: The Kibbutz at Century's End*. New York: SUNY Press, 1997.
Benvenisti, Eyal, and Eyal Zamir. "Private Claims to Property Rights in the Future Israeli-Palestinian Settlement." 89 *Am. J. Int'l L.* (1995): 295.
Bergsma, John Sietze. *The Jubilee from Leviticus to Qumran: A History of Interpretation*. Leiden: Brill, 2007.
Berkowski, Anton, and Arnon Sofer. *Sub-ground: A Geo-strategic Perspective*. Haifa: National Security College and Haifa University, 2014 (Hebrew).
Boelens, Rutgerd, et al. "Contested Territories: Water Rights and the Struggles over Indigenous Livelihoods." 3 *International Indigenous Policy Journal*, no. 3, article 5 (January 2012): 1.
Boustany, Wedi' Faris. *The Palestine Mandate: Invalid and Impracticable*. Beirut: American Press, 1936.
Bowman, Glenn. "Christian Ideology and the Image of a Holy Land: The Place of Jerusalem Pilgrimage in the Various Christianities." In *Contesting the Sacred: The Anthropology of Christian Pilgrimage*, edited by John Eade and Michael J. Sallnow, 98. Urbana: University of Illinois Press, 2000.
Brewer-Carías, Allan R. "Guyana-Venezuela Border Dispute." In *Max Planck Encyclopedia of Public International Law*, edited by R. Wolfrum, online ed. Oxford: Oxford University Press, 2006.
Breznitz, Dan. *Innovation and the State*. New Haven, CT: Yale University Press, 2007.
Broday, David, et al. "Emissions from Gas Processing Platforms to the Atmosphere: Case Studies versus Benchmarks." 80 *Environmental Impact Assessment Review* (2019): 106313.
Brown, Brené. *Dearing Greatly*. New York: Gotham Books, 2012.
Brubaker, Rogers, and Frederick Cooper. "Beyond 'Identity.'" 29 *Theory and Society* (2000): 1.
Bulan, Ramy. "Indigenous Identity and the Law." 25 *Journal of Malaysian and Comparative Law* (1998): 127.
Cahaner, Lee. "The Development of the Spatial and Hierarchic Structure of the Ultra-Orthodox Jewish Population in Israel." PhD diss., University of Haifa, 2009 (Hebrew).
Chen, Lei, and Mark D. Kielsgard. "Evolving Property Rights in China: Patterns and Dynamics of Condominium Governance." 2 *Chinese Journal of Comparative Law* (2014): 21.
Chen, Ruoying. "Informal Sales of Rural Housing in China: Property, Privatization and Local Public Finance." Dr. Juris. diss., University of Chicago, 2010.
Cohen, Asher, and Bernard Susser. *Israel and the Politics of Jewish Identity: The Secular-Religious Impasse*. Baltimore: Johns Hopkins University Press, 2000.
Cohen, Beery, et al. *National Outline Plan 35: Follow-Up and Updating Guidance, Expansion to the Report Stage B; Texture Cards*. Israel Ministry of the Interior, Planning Administration, 2009 (Hebrew).
Cohen, Hillel. "The Internal Refugees in the State of Israel: Israeli Citizens, Palestinian Refugees." 9 *Palestine-Israel Journal*, no. 2 (June 2002): 43.
———. *The Present Absentees: The Palestinian Refugees in Israel Since 1948*. Jerusalem: Van Leer Jerusalem Institute, 2000 (Hebrew).

Cohen, Nili. "Distributive Justice in the Enforcement of Contracts." In *Festschrift filr Gunther Kuhne zum 70. Geburtstag*, edited by H. Erausgcgcben et al., 971. Frankfurt: Recht und Wirtschaft, 2009.

———. "A Minor's Contract to Acquire an Interest in Land, as against the Vendor's Creditor." 41 *Hapraklit—Israel Bar Law Journal* (1993) (Hebrew): 161.

Cohen-Almagor, Raphael. "Israeli Democracy and Rights of Its Palestinian Citizens." 45 *Ragion Pratica* (2015): 351.

Collins, Hugh. "European Private Law and the Cultural Identity of States." 3 *European Review of Private Law* (1995): 353.

Dagan, Hanoch. "Codification, Coherence, and Priority Conflicts." In *The Draft Civil Code for Israel in Comparative Perspective*, edited by Kurt Siehr and Reinhard Zimmermann, 149. Tübingen: Mohr Siebeck, 2008.

Dahan, Yossi. "Who Owns This Land? On the Rights and Concepts of Distributive Justice." 8 *Mishpat Umimshal* (Law and Government)—*Haifa University Law Review* (2005) (Hebrew): 223.

David, Ohad, and Daniel Bar-Tal. "A Sociopsychological Conception of Collective Identity: The Case of National Identity as an Example." 13 *Personality and Social Psychology Review* (2009): 354.

Davidson, Nestor M., and John J. Infranca. "The Sharing Economy as an Urban Phenomenon." 34 *Yale Law and Policy Review* (2016): 215.

Davis, Emily Jane, and Maureen G. Reed. "Governing Transformation and Resilience: The Role of Identity in Renegotiating Roles for Forest-Based Communities of British Columbia's Interior." In *Social Transformation in Rural Canada: Community, Cultures, and Collective Action*, edited by John R. Parkins and Maureen G. Reed, 249. Vancouver: University of British Columbia Press, 2013.

De Soto, Hernando. *The Mystery of Capital*. London: Black Swan, 2001.

Deutch, Miguel. *Property*. Vol. 1. Tel Aviv: Bursi, 1997 (Hebrew).

———. "Protection of Obligatory Rights as Property within the Framework of the Constitutional Revolution in Israel." 15 *Tel Aviv U. Stud. L.* (2000): 147.

Dorsett, Shaunnagh. "Since Time Immemorial: A Story of Common Law Jurisdiction, Native Title and the Case of Tanistry." 26 *Melb. U. L. Rev.* (2002): 32.

Dotan, Yoav. "Informal Privatization and Distributive Justice in Israeli Administrative Law." 36 *Hamline Law Review* (2014): 27.

———. "Judicial Accountability in Israel: The High Court of Justice and the Phenomena of Judicial Hyperactivism." 8 *Israeli Affairs* (2002): 87.

———. "Judicial Review and Political Accountability: The Case of the High Court of Justice in Israel." 32 *Israel Law Review* (1998): 448.

Doukhan-Landau, Leah. *Equitable Rights to Land and the Remedy of Specific Performance of Contracts of Sale of Land*. Jerusalem: Institute for Legislative Research and Comparative Law, 1968.

———. "The Land Law, 5729–1969 at First Sight." 26 *Hapraklit—Israel Bar Law Journal* (1971) (Hebrew): 101.

Dumper, Michael, and Craig Larkin. "The Politics of Heritage and the Limitations of International Agency in Contested Cities: A Study of the Role of UNESCO in Jerusalem's Old City." 38 *Review of International Studies* (2012): 25.

Efrat, Elisha. *The West Bank and Gaza Strip: A Geography of Occupation and Disengagement*. Abingdon: Routledge, 2006.

Elden, Stuart. "Land, Terrain, Territory." 34 *Prog. Hum. Geogr.* (2010): 799.
Elon, Menachem. *Jewish Law: History, Sources, Principles.* Vol 4. Translated by Bernard Auerbach and Melvin J. Sykes. Philadelphia: Jewish Publication Society, 1994.
———. "The Legal System of Jewish Law." 17 *NYU J. Int'l L. & Pol.* (1985): 221.
Fager, Jeffrey A. *Land Tenure and the Biblical Jubilee.* Sheffield: Sheffield Academic, 1993.
Fearon, James D. "What Is Identity (as We Now Use the Word)?" Unpublished manuscript, November 3, 1999, Stanford University, https://web.stanford.edu/group/fearon-research/cgi-bin/wordpress/wp-content/uploads/2013/10/What-is-Identity-as-we-now-use-the-word-.pdf.
Feinberg, Nathan. *The Arab-Israeli Conflict in International Law.* Jerusalem: Hebrew University Press, 1970.
Feitelson, Eran. "Muddling toward Sustainability: The Transformation of Environmental Planning in Israel." 49 *Progress in Planning* (1998): 39.
Felsenstein, Daniel, and Ziv Rubin. "Supply Side Constraints in the Israeli Housing Market: The Impact of State Owned Land." 65 *Land Use Policy* (2017): 266.
Fischbach, Michael R. *The Peace Process and Palestinian Refugee Claims: Addressing Claims for Property Compensation and Restitution.* Washington, DC: US Institute for Peace Press, 2006.
———. *Records of Dispossession: Palestinian Refugee Property and the Arab-Israeli Conflict.* New York: Columbia University Press, 2003.
Fischer, Stanley, et al. *Economics.* 2nd ed. New York: McGraw Hill, 1988.
Fischhendler, Itay, et al. "Marketing Renewable Energy through Geopolitics: Solar Farms in Israel." 15 *Global Environmental Politics* (2015): 98.
Fleischmann, Larisa, et al. *Changes in the Nature of Agriculture and the Farmland: Attitudes of Residents of the Rural Area in the Central Region.* Jerusalem: Jerusalem Institute for Policy Research, 2009 (Hebrew).
Forman, Geremy. "A Tale of Two Regions: Diffusion of the Israeli '50 Percent Rule' from the Galilee to the Occupied West Bank." 34 *Law and Social Inquiry* (2016): 671.
Frank, Rainer. "Privatization in Eastern Germany: A Comprehensive Study." 27 *Vand. J. Transnat'l L.* (1994): 809.
Frantzman, Seth J. "The Politization of History and the Negev Bedouin Land Claims: A Review Essay on Indigenous (In)justice." 19 *Israel Studies* (2014): 48.
Frantzman, Seth J., et al. "Contested Indigeneity: The Development of an Indigenous Discourse on the Bedouin of the Negev, Israel." 17 *Israel Studies* (2012): 78.
Frenkel, Amnon, and Daniel E. Orenstein. "Can Urban Growth Management Work in an Era of Political and Economic Change? International Lessons from Israel." 78 *Journal of the American Planning Association* (2012): 16.
Friedmann, Daniel. "Independent Development of Israeli Law." 10 *Israel Law Review* (1975): 515.
———. "Infusion of the Common Law into the Legal System of Israel." 10 *Israel Law Review* (1975): 324.
———. *The Purse and the Sword: The Trials of Israel's Legal Revolution.* Translated by Haim Watzman. Oxford: Oxford University Press, 2016.
Gal, Yoav, and Efrat Hadas. "Land Allocation: Agriculture vs. Urban Development in Israel." 31 *Land Use Policy* (2013): 498.
Gans, Chaim. *A Just Zionism: On the Morality of the Jewish State.* Oxford: Oxford University Press, 2008.

———. "The Palestinian Right of Return and the Justice of Zionism." 5 *Theoretical Inquiries in Law* (2004): 269.
Gavish, Dov. *A Survey of Palestine under the British Mandate, 1920–1948*. Abingdon: Routledge, 2005.
Gavison, Ruth. "Reflections on the Nation-State Law Debate." In *Defining Israel: The Jewish State, Democracy, and the Law*, edited by Simon Rabinovitch, 337. Cincinnati: Hebrew Union College Press, 2018.
———. "The Role of Courts in Rifted Democracies." 33 *Israel Law Review* (1999): 216.
———. "Zionism in Israel? A Note on Qaadan." 6 *Mishpat Umimshal* (Law and Government)—*Haifa University Law Review* (2001) (Hebrew): 25.
Gee, Graham, and Alison L. Young. "Regaining Sovereignty: Brexit, the UK Parliament and the Common Law." 22 *European Public Law* (2016): 131.
Gelber, Yoav. "Is Zionism Colonialism?" In *The British Mandate in Palestine: A Centenary Volume, 1920–2020*, edited by Michael Cohen, 221. Abingdon: Routledge, 2020.
Gerber, Haim. *The Social Origins of the Modern Middle East*. Boulder, CO: Lynne Reinner, 1987.
Ghanem, As'ad. *Ethnic Politics in Israel: The Margins and the Ashkenazi Centre*. Abingdon: Routledge, 2010.
Ghanim, Honaida. "Poetics of Disaster: Nationalism, Gender, and Social Change among Palestinian Poets in Israel after Nakba." 22 *International Journal of Politics, Culture, and Society* (2009): 23.
Gilbert, Jérémie. *Indigenous Peoples' Land Rights under International Law: From Victims to Actors*. Leiden: Brill Nijhoff, 2016.
Giuggioli, Luca, and V. M. Kenkre. "Consequences of Animal Interactions on Their Dynamics: Emergence of Home Ranges and Territoriality." 2 *Movement Ecology* (2014): 1.
Goadby, Frederic, and Moses Doukhan. *The Land Law of Palestine*. Tel Aviv: Shoshany's Printing, 1935.
Golan, Arnon. "Jewish Settlement of Former Arab Towns and Their Incorporation into the Israeli Urban System." In *The Israeli Palestinians: An Arab Minority in the Jewish State*, edited by Alexander Bligh, 149. London: Frank Cass, 2003.
———. *Wartime Spatial Changes: Former Arab Territories within the State of Israel, 1948–1950*. Sde Boker: Ben Gurion Heritage Center, Ben Gurion University of the Negev, 2001 (Hebrew).
Goldblat, Ran, and Itzhak Omer. "The Association between Land-Use Distribution and Residential Patterns: The Case of Mixed Arab-Jewish Cities in Israel." 6 *Journal of Urban and Regional Analysis* (2014): 15.
Gorman, Elizabeth R. "When the Poor Have Nothing Left to Eat: The United States' Obligation to Regulate American Investment in the African Land Grab." 75 *Ohio St. L. J.* (2014): 199.
Granovsky [Granot], Abraham. *The Battle for the Land*. Jerusalem: JNF Press, 1940 (Hebrew).
———. *Behitnahel Am (Settlement of a People)*. Jerusalem: JNF Press by Dvir Press, 1951 (Hebrew).
———. *Land Policy in Palestine*. New York: Bloch, 1940.
Gutman, Yifaat. *Memory Activism: Reimagining the Past for the Future in Israel-Palestine*. Nashville: Vanderbilt University Press, 2017.
Haila, Anne. "Real Estate in Global Cities: Singapore and Hong Kong as Property States." 37 *Urban Studies* (2000): 2241.

Halabi, Rabah. "Invention of a Nation: The Druze in Israel." 49 *Journal of Asian & African Studies* (2014): 267.
Hamilton, Alexander. "The Federalist 78." In *The Federalist Papers*, 380. New York: Dover, 2014; first printed 1788.
Hananel, Ravit. "The Land Narrative: Rethinking Israel's National Land Policy." 45 *Land Use Policy* (2015): 128.
———. "Planning Discourse versus Land Discourse: The 2009–12 Reforms in Land-Use Planning Policy and Land Policy in Israel." 37 *International Journal of Urban and Regional Research* (2013): 1611.
———. "Zionism and Agricultural Land: National Narratives, Environmental Objectives, and Land Policy in Israel." 27 *Land Use Policy* (2010): 1160.
Hannigan, A. St. J. J. "Native Custom, Its Similarity to English Conventional Custom and Its Mode of Proof." 2 *Journal of African Law* (1958): 101.
Henderson, Jane. "The Politics of the Emergence of Private Landholding in Russia." 7 *Journal of Comparative Law* (2012): 157.
Herb, Guntram H. "Identity and Territory." In *Nested Identities: Nationalism, Territory, and Scale*, edited by Guntram H. Herb and David H. Kaplan, 9. Oxford: Rowman & Littlefield, 1999.
Hermann, Tamar, et al. *A Conditional Partnership: Jews and Arabs, Israel 2017*. Jerusalem: Israel Democracy Institute, 2017 (Hebrew).
Hershkowitz, Arie. "Ideological Shifts and Doctrine Changes in National Level Planning in Israel." 81 *Town Planning Review* (2010): 261.
Herzl, Theodore. *Bifnei Am VeOlam*. Vol. 1: *Zionist Speeches and Articles*. Jerusalem: Zionist Library Press of the Zionist Organization, 1976 (Hebrew): 285.
———. *Old New Land: Altneuland*. Translated by David Simon Blondheim, 1916. Berlin: Contumax, 2015. First printed 1902, Leipzig.
Hidalgo, M. Carmen, and Bernardo Hernandez. "Place Attachment: Conceptual and Empirical Questions." 21 *Journal of Environmental Psychology* (2001): 273.
Hills, Gordon H. *Native Libraries: Cross-cultural Conditions in the Circumpolar Countries*. Lanham, MD: Scarecrow, 1997.
Hirschl, Ran. "The 'Constitutional Revolution' and the Emergence of a New Economic Order in Israel." 2 *Israel Studies* (1997): 136.
Holzman-Gazit, Yifat. *Land Expropriation in Israel: Law, Culture and Society*. Aldershot: Ashgate, 2007.
———. "Law as a Status Symbol: The Jewish National Fund Law of 1953 and the Struggle of the Fund to Maintain Its Status after Israel's Independence." 26 *Iyuney-Mishpat—Tel Aviv University Law Review*, no. 2 (2002) (Hebrew): 601.
Jabareen, Hassan. "The Future of Arab Citizenship in Israel: Jewish-Zionist Time in a Place with No Palestinian Memory." In *Challenging Ethnic Citizenship: German and Israeli Perspectives on Immigration*, edited by Daniel Levy and Yifaat Weiss, 196. New York: Bergham Books, 2002).
Jabareen, Yousef T. "Enshrining Exclusion: The Nation-State Law and the Arab Palestinians in Israel." In *Defining Israel: The Jewish State, Democracy, and the Law*, edited by Simon Rabinovitch, 249. Cincinnati: Hebrew Union College Press, 2018.
Jacobsohn, Gary J. "Judicial Activism in Israel." In *Judicial Activism in Comparative Perspective*, edited by Kenneth M. Holland, 90. New York: St. Martin's, 1991.

Jepsen, M. R., et al. "Transitions in European Land-Management Regimes between 1800 and 2010." 49 *Land Use Policy* (2015): 53.
Kabia, Fatmata S. "Behind the Mirage in the Desert: Customary Land Rights and the Legal Framework of Land Grabs." 47 *Cornell Int'l L. J.* (2014): 709.
Kahneman, Daniel, et al. "Anomalies: The Endowment Effect, Loss Aversion, and Status Quo Bias." 5 *Journal of Economic Perspectives* (1991): 193.
Kalmijn, Matthijs, and Frank Van Tubergen. "A Comparative Perspective on Intermarriage: Explaining Differences among National-Origin Groups in the United States." 47 *Demography* (2010): 459.
Kaminetzki, Amir. *Long-Term Lease*. Tel Aviv: Bursi, 2011 (Hebrew).
Kammen, Michael. "The Right of Property and Property in Rights: The Problematic Nature of Property in the Political Thought of the Founders and the Early Republic." In *Liberty, Property, and the Foundations of the American Constitution*, edited by Ellen Frankel Paul and Howard Dickman, 1. New York: SUNY Press, 1989.
Kaplan, Moti, et al. *Patterns of Use of Built-Up Areas in Israel*. Jerusalem: Jerusalem Institute for Israel Studies, 2007 (Hebrew).
Kark, Ruth. "Changing Patterns of Landownership in Nineteenth-Century Palestine: The European Influence." 10 *Journal of Historical Geography* (1984): 357.
———. "Consequences of the Ottoman Land Law: Agrarian and Privatization Processes in Palestine, 1858–1918." In *Societies, Social Inequalities and Marginalization*, edited by Raghubir Chand et al., 101. Cham, Switzerland: Springer International, 2017.
Kark, Ruth, and Dov Gavish. "The Cadastral Mapping of Palestine 1858–1928." 159 *Cartographic Journal* (1993): 70.
Kark, Ruth, and Haim Gerber. "Land Registry Maps in Palestine during the Ottoman Period." 21 *Cartographic Journal* (1984): 30.
Karsh, Efraim. "Israel's Arabs: Deprived or Radicalized?" 19 *Israel Affairs* (2013): 2.
Kasanko, Marjo, et al. "Are European Cities Becoming Dispersed? A Comparative Analysis of 15 European Urban Areas." 77 *Landscape and Urban Planning* (2006): 111.
Katz, Yossi. *The Battle for the Land*. Jerusalem: Hebrew University Press, 2005.
———. *The Land Shall Not Be Sold in Perpetuity: The Jewish National Fund and the History of State Ownership of Land in Israel*. Berlin: De Gruyter, 2016.
Kedar, Alexandre. "The Legal Transformation of Ethnic Geography: Israeli Law and the Palestinian Landholder 1948–1967." 33 *NYU J. Int'l L. & Pol.* (2001): 923.
Kedar, Alexandre, et al. *Emptied Lands: A Legal Geography of Bedouin Rights in the Negev*. Stanford, CA: Stanford University Press, 2018.
Kedar, Alexandre [Sandy], and Oren Yiftachel. "Land Regime and Social Relations in Israel." In *Swiss Human Rights Book*, vol. 1, edited by Hernando de Soto and Francis Cheneval, 127. Zurich: Ruffer & Rub, 2006.
Kedar, Mordechai. "The Future Vision of the Islamic Movement." In *Muslim Minorities in Non-Muslim Majority Countries: The Test Case of the Islamic Movement in Israel*, edited by Elie Rekhess and Arik Rudnitzky, 117. Tel Aviv: Tel Aviv University, 2011 (Hebrew).
Kedar, Nir. "A Scholar, Teacher, Judge, and Jurist in a Mixed Jurisdiction: The Case of Aharon Barak." 62 *Loy. L. Rev.* (2016): 659.
Kellerman, Aharon. *Society and Settlement: Jewish Land of Israel in the Twentieth Century*. New York: SUNY Press, 1993.

Kelly, Daniel G. "Indian Title: The Rights of American Natives in Lands They Have Occupied since Time Immemorial." 75 *Colum. L. Rev.* (1975): 655.
Kerr, Sandy, et al. "Planning at the Edge: Integrating across the Land Sea Divide." *47 Marine Policy* (2014): 118.
Khamaisi, Rassem. *Between Customs and Laws: Planning and Management of Land in Arab Localities in Israel*. Jerusalem: Floersheimer Institute for Policy Studies, 2007 (Hebrew).
———. "Centrifugal and Centripetal Factors' Influence on the Structure of the Arab Settlement." In *The Arab Community in Israel: Geographic Processes*, edited by David Grossman and Avinoam Meir, 114. Bar Ilan: Ben Gurion and Hebrew University Press, 1994 (Hebrew).
———. "Housing Transformation within Urbanized Communities: The Arab Palestinians in Israel." 33 *Geography Research Forum* (2013): 184.
———. "Land Ownership as a Determinant in the Formation of Residential Areas in Arab Localities." 26 *Geoforum* (1995): 211.
———. *Planning and Housing among Arabs in Israel*. Tel Aviv: International Center for Peace in the Middle East, 1990 (Hebrew).
Kheir, Nasr, and Boris A. Portnov. "Economic, Demographic and Environmental Factors Affecting Urban Land Prices in the Arab Sector in Israel." 50 *Land Use Policy* (2016): 518.
Kiely, Richard, et al. "The Markers and Rules of Scottish National Identity." 49 *Sociological Review* (2001): 33.
Klein, Menachem. "Negotiating Jerusalem: Detailed Summary of Ideas Raised in Track Two." In *Track Two Diplomacy and Jerusalem: The Jerusalem Old City Initiative*, edited by Tom Najem et al., 112. Abingdon: Routledge, 2017.
Knight, David B. "Identity and Territory: Geographical Perspectives on Nationalism and Regionalism." 72 *Annals of the Association of American Geographers* (1982): 514.
Krakover, Shaul. "Urban Settlement Program and Land Dispute Resolution: The State of Israel versus the Negev Bedouin." 47 *GeoJournal* (1999): 551.
Kram, Noa. "The Naqab Bedouins: Legal Struggles for Land Ownership Rights in Israel." In *Indigenous (In)justice: Human Rights Law and Bedouin Arabs in the Naqab/Negev*, edited by Ahmad Amara et al., 127. Cambridge, MA: Human Rights Program at Harvard Law School, 2012.
Kretzmer, David. "The Acquiring of Equitable Title." 4 *Israel Law Review* (1969): 452.
———. *The Legal Status of the Arabs in Israel*. Abingdon: Routledge, 2019. First published 1990, Westview, Boulder, CO.
Lahav, Pnina. "American Moment[s]: When, How, and Why Did Israeli Law Faculties Come to Resemble Elite U.S. Law Schools?" 10 *Theoretical Inquiries in Law* (2009): 653.
Landau, Moshe. "General Remarks on the Land Law and Servitudes under the Land Law." 1 *Tel Aviv U. Stud. L.* (1975): 110.
———. "Judicial Activism." 7 *Hamishpat Law Review* (2002) (Hebrew): 535.
Lapidoth, Ruth, and Moshe Hirsch, eds. *The Jerusalem Question and Its Resolution: Selected Documents*. Dordrecht: Martinus Nijhoff, 1994.
Laqueur, Walter. *A History of Zionism*. New York: Schocken Books, 2003. First published 1972, Weidenfeld and Nicolson, London.
Lassner, Jacob. *Medieval Jerusalem: Forging an Islamic City in Spaces Sacred to Christians and Jews*. Ann Arbor: University of Michigan Press, 2017.

Lavie, Ephrai, and Amal Jamal, eds. *The Nakba in the National Memory of Israel.* Tel Aviv University—Tami Steinmetz Center and Walter-Libach Institute for Jewish-Arab Coexistence, 2015 (Hebrew).

Lawson, Frederick H. *The Rational Strength of English Law.* London: Stevens & Sons, 1951.

Lee, Douglass B., Jr. "Land Use Planning as a Response to Market Failure." In *The Land Use Policy Debate in the United States*, edited by Judith Innes de Neufville, 149. New York: Plenum, 1981.

Lehavi, Amnon. "Land Law in the Age of Globalization and Land Grabbing." In *Comparative Property Law: Global Perspectives*, edited by Michele Graziadei and Lionel Smith, 290. Cheltenham, UK: Edward Elgar, 2017.

———. "Law, Collective Action and Culture: Condominium Governance in Comparative Perspective." 23 *Asia Pacific Law Review* (2015): 5.

———. "Residential Communities in a Heterogeneous Society: The Case of Israel." In *Private Communities and Urban Governance: Theoretical and Comparative Perspectives*, edited by Amnon Lehavi, 95. Springer International, 2016.

Lemieux, Victoria L. "Evaluating the Use of Blockchain in Land Transactions: An Archival Science Perspective." 6 *European Property Law Journal* (2017): 392.

Levine-Schnur, Ronit, and Gideon Parchomovsky. "Is the Government Fiscally Blind? An Empirical Examination of the Effect of the Compensation Requirement on Eminent-Domain Exercises." 45 *Journal of Legal Studies* (2016): 439.

Levitsky, Nomi. *The Supremes.* Tel Aviv: Hakibbutz Hameuchad, 2006 (Hebrew).

Lewis, Bernard. "Ottoman Land Tenure and Taxation in Syria." 50 *Studia Islamica* (1979): 109.

Low, Setha M., and Irwin Altman. "Place Attachment: A Conceptual Inquiry." In *Place Attachment*, edited by Irwin Altman and Setha M. Low, 1. New York: Plenum, 1992.

Lowry, William R. *Preserving Public Lands for the Future: The Politics of Intergenerational Goods.* Washington, DC: Georgetown University Press, 1998.

Mandelkern, Ronen, and Amir Paz-Fuchs. "Privatizing Israel: An Introduction." In *The Privatization of Israel: The Withdrawal of State Responsibility*, edited by Amir Paz-Fuchs et al., 1. New York: Palgrave Macmillan, 2018.

Mandelkern, Ronen, and Gideon Rahat. "Parties and Labour Federations in Israel." In *Left-of-Centre Parties and Trade Unions in the Twenty-First Century*, edited by Elin Haugsgjerd Allern and Tim Bale, 149. Oxford: Oxford University Press, 2017.

Marsh, A. H. *History of the Court of Chancery.* Toronto: Carswell, 1890.

Marx, Danielle. "Takings and the Requirement of Ongoing Public Purpose: The Effect of the Constitutionalization of the Right to Property on the Law of Takings (Karsik v. the State of Israel, Israel Land Authority, 55(II) PD, 625)—Case Note." 36 *Israel Law Review*, no. 2 (Summer 2002): 149.

Mautner, Menachem. "Conflicting Transactions and the Negligence of a Purchaser Who Does Not Register a Caveat." 40 *Hapraklit—Israel Bar Law Journal* (1992) (Hebrew): 525.

———. "The Eternal Triangle of the Law: Toward a Theory of Priorities in Conflicts Involving Remote Parties." 90 *Mich. L. Rev.* (1991): 95.

———. *Law and the Culture of Israel.* Oxford: Oxford University Press, 2011.

McGee, John, ed. *Snell's Equity.* 32nd ed. London: Sweet and Maxwell, 2010.

McIntyre, William David. *British Decolonization, 1946–1997.* London: Macmillan, 1998.

Medzini, Arnon. "Bedouin Settlement Policy in Israel: Success or Failure?" 79 *Themes in Israeli Geography* (2012): 37.
Meydani, Assaf. *The Israeli Supreme Court and the Human Rights Revolution: Courts as Agenda Setters*. Oxford: Oxford University Press, 2011.
Mickiewicz, Adam. *Pan Tadeusz: The Last Foray in Lithuania*. Translated by George Rapall Noyes. London: J. M. Dent & Sons, 1917. Reprint: Semicentennial Publications of the University of California, https://archive.org/stream/pantadeuszorlastoomickuoft/pantadeuszorlastoomickuoft_djvu.txt.
Middleton, Justice. "Sketch of the Ottoman Land Code for Cyprus." 2 *Journal of the Society of Comparative Legislation* (1900): 141.
Mirsky, Yehuda. "What Is a Nation State?" In *Defining Israel: The Jewish State, Democracy, and the Law*, edited by Simon Rabinovitch, 299. Cincinnati: Hebrew Union College Press, 2018.
Morris, Benny. *The Birth of the Palestinian Refugee Problem Revisited*. Cambridge: Cambridge University Press, 2004.
Mualam, Nir. "Playing with Supertankers: Centralization in Land Use Planning in Israel—A National Experiment Underway." 75 *Land Use Policy* (2018): 269.
Nachmias, David, and Itai Sened. "Governance and Public Policy." 7 *Israel Affairs* (2001): 3.
Naor, Arye. "The Political System: Government, Parliament and the Court." In *Israel since 1980*, edited by Guy Ben-Porat et al., 69. Cambridge: Cambridge University Press, 2008.
Nathansohn, Regev. "Living in a Mixing Neighborhood: Reflexive Coexistence and the Discourse of Separation." PhD Diss., University of Michigan, 2017.
National Committee for the Heads of the Arab Local Authorities in Israel. *The Future Vision of the Palestinian Arabs in Israel*. Nazareth: National Committee for the Heads of the Arab Local Authorities in Israel, 2006.
Navot, Suzie. *Constitution Law of Israel*. 2nd ed. The Hague: Kluwer Law International, 2016.
———. *The Constitution of Israel: A Contextual Analysis*. Oxford: Hart, 2014.
Near, Henry. "Redemption of the Soil and of Man: Pioneering in Labor Zionist Ideology, 1904–1935." In *Redemption of the land of Eretz-Israel: Ideology and Practice*, edited by Ruth Kark, 33. Jerusalem: Yad Ben-Zvi, 1990 (Hebrew).
Newman, Boaz. *Land and Desire in Early Zionism*. Translated by Haim Watzman. Waltham, MA: Brandeis University Press, 2011.
Newman, Ralph A. "The Principles of Equity as a Source of World Law." 1 *Israel Law Review* (1966): 616.
Nisan, Mordechai. "The Druze in Israel: Questions of Identity, Citizenship, and Patriotism." 64 *Middle East Journal* (2010): 575.
Noonan, Harold, and Ben Curtis. "Identity." In *The Stanford Encyclopedia of Philosophy*, edited by Edward N. Zalta. Stanford, CA: Metaphysics Research Lab Center for the Study of Language and Information, Stanford University, 2018. https://plato.stanford.edu/archives/sum2018/entries/identity.
Oded, Yitzhak. "Land Losses among Arab Villagers." 65 *New Outlook* (1964): 10.
Ongley, Frederick. *The Ottoman Land Code, Translated from the Turkish*. Revised by H. E. Miller. London: William Clowes and Sons, 1892.
Oren, Amiram. "Shadow Lands: The Use of Land Resources for Security Needs in Israel." 12 *Israel Studies* (2007): 149.
Oren, Amiram, and Rafi Regev. *Land in Uniform: Territory and Defence in Israel*. Haifa: Carmel, 2008 (Hebrew).

Oren-Nordheim, Michal. "And the Land Will Not Be Sold in Perpetuity." 16 *Studies in the Geography of the Land of Israel* (2003) (Hebrew): 146.
Ottolenghi, Emanuele. "A National Home." In *Modern Judaism: An Oxford Guide*, edited by Nicholas De Lange and Miri Freud-Kandel, 54. Oxford: Oxford University Press, 2005.
Paasi, Anssi. "The Institutionalization of Regions: A Theoretical Framework to Understanding the Emergence of Regions and the Constitution of Regional Identity." 164 *Fennia* (1986): 105.
Peiró, Nicolás Nogueroles, and Eduardo J. Martinez García. "Blockchain and Land Registration Systems." 6 *European Property Law Journal* (2017): 296.
Plato-Shinar, Ruth. "Israel: The Impact of the Anti-money Laundering Legislation on the Banking System." 7 *Journal of Money Laundering Control* (2004): 18.
Ploeger, Hendrik D., and Daniëlle A. Groetelaers. "The Importance of the Fundamental Right to Property for the Practice of Planning: An Introduction to the Case Law of the European Court of Human Rights on Article 1, Protocol 1." 15 *European Planning Studies* (2007): 1423.
Porat, Benjamin. "Social Justice as Embodied in the Law of the Jubilee Year." 13 *Akdamot* (2003) (Hebrew): 77.
Porat, Yehoshua. *The Palestinian-Arab National Movement*. Vol. 2: *From Riots to Rebellion 1929–1939*. London: Frank Cass, 1977.
Portman, Michelle E. "Marine Spatial Planning in the Middle East: Crossing the Policy-Planning Divide." 61 *Marine Policy* (2015): 8.
Posner, Richard A. "Enlightened Despot." *New Republic*, April 23, 2007, https://newrepublic.com/article/60919/enlightened-despot.
Prins, Herbert H. T., and Iain J. Gordon. "Testing Hypotheses about Biological Invasions and Charles Darwin's Two-Creators Rumination." In *Invasion Biology and Ecological Theory: Insights from a Continent in Transformation*, edited by Herbert H. T. Prins and Iain J. Gordon, 1. Oxford: Oxford University Press, 2014.
Rabin, Yoram, and Arnon Gutfeld. "Marbury v. Madison and Its Impact on Israeli Constitutional Law." 15 *U. Miami Int'l & Comp. L. Rev.* (2007): 303.
Rabinovitch, Simon. "Jewish and Democratic According to the Law." In *Defining Israel: The Jewish State, Democracy, and the Law*, edited by Simon Rabinovitch, 1. Cincinnati: Hebrew Union College Press, 2018.
Radai, Itamar, et al. "The Arab Citizens in Israel: Current Trends According to Recent Opinion Polls." 18 *Strategic Assessment* (2015): 101.
Radin, Margaret Jane. "Property and Personhood." 34 *Stanford Law Review* (1982): 957.
Raska, Michael. *Military Innovation in Small States: Creating a Reverse Asymmetry*. Abingdon: Routledge, 2016.
Rawls, John. *A Theory of Justice*. Cambridge, MA: Harvard University Press, 1971.
Raz, Joseph. "The Identity of Legal Systems." 59 *California Law Review* (1971): 795.
Rekhess, Eli. "The Arab Minority in Israel: Reconsidering the '1948 Paradigm.'" 19 *Israel Studies* (2014): 187.
——. "The Evolvement of an Arab-Palestinian National Minority in Israel." 12 *Israel Studies* (2007): 1.
——. *Israeli Arabs and the Expropriation of Lands in the Galilee: Background, Events and Implications 1975–1977*. Tel Aviv: Shiloah Research Center, Tel Aviv University, 1977 (Hebrew).

Rosenberg, George, and Niv Goldstein. "Bank Leumi Le'Israel Ltd v Tauber—Israel Supreme Court Judgment on Trust Law." 10 *Trust Quarterly Review*, no. 2 (June 2012): 9.

Rubinstein, Elyakim. "The Attorney-General in Israel: A Delicate Balance of Power and Responsibilities in a Jewish and Democratic State." In *Israeli Institutions in the Crossroads*, edited by Raphael Cohen-Almagor, 143. Abingdon: Routledge, 2005.

———. "Israel Lands—A Legal Perspective: Long Term Revival or a Long-Term Catastrophe." 52 *Karka (Land)—Journal of the JNF Land Policy and Land Use Research Institute* (2001) (Hebrew): 21.

Rudnitzky, Arik. "The Bedouin Population in the Negev: Social, Demographic and Economic Factors." In *The Bedouin Population in the Negev*, 1. Jerusalem: Abraham Fund Initiatives, 2012.

Salzberger, Eli. "Judicial Activism in Israel." In *Judicial Activism in Common Law Supreme Courts*, edited by Brice Dikson, 217. Oxford: Oxford University Press, 2008.

Sandberg, Haim. *Basic Law: Israel Lands—Commentary*. Commentary on the Basic Laws Series, edited by Izhak Zamir. Jerusalem: Sacher Institute, Hebrew University of Jerusalem, 2016 (Hebrew).

———. "Distributive Justice vs. the Denial of the Jewish Nation State." In *Land, Democracy and the Relations of the Majority-Minor*, edited by Yitzhak Schnell et al., 23. Tel Aviv: Walter Lebach Institute, Tel Aviv University, 2013 (Hebrew).

———. "From JNF to Viva Palestina—UK Policy towards Zionist and Palestinian Charities." 22 *Trust & Trustees* (2016): 195.

———. "Land Expropriations of Private Arab Land in Israel: An Empirical Analysis of the Regular Course of Business." 43 *Israel Law Review* (2010): 590.

———. *Land Title Settlement in Eretz-Israel and the State of Israel*. Jerusalem: JNF's Land Use Research Institute and Sacher Institute, Hebrew University of Jerusalem, 2001 (Hebrew).

———. "Land Title Settlement in Jerusalem—Legal Aspects." 23 *Journal of Israeli History* (2004): 216.

———. *The Lands of Israel: Zionism and Post-Zionism*. Jerusalem: Sacher Institute, Hebrew University of Jerusalem, 2007 (Hebrew).

———. "The Politics of 'Over-victimization': Palestinian Proprietary Claims in the Service of Political Goals." 19 *Israel Affairs* (2013): 488.

———. "Real Estate E-conveyancing: Vision and Risks." 19 *Information & Communications Technology Law* (2010): 101.

———. "Strategic Considerations behind Normative Explanations: Lessons from Israel's Supreme Court Takings Case." 11 *International Journal of Constitutional Law* (2013): 751.

———. "Three-Dimensional Partition and Registration of Subsurface Space." 37 *Israel Law Review* (2004): 119.

Sandberg, Haim, and Adam Hofri-Winogradow. "Arab Israeli Women's Renunciation of Their Inheritance Shares: A Challenge for Israel's Courts." 8 *International Journal of Law in Context*, no. 2 (June 2012): 253.

Saposnik, Arieh. "Zionism in the Twenty-First Century?" In *Understanding Israel: Political, Societal and Security Challenges*, edited by Joel Peters and Rob Geist Pinfold, 10. Abingdon: Routledge, 2018.

Sax, Joseph L. "The Legitimacy of Collective Values: The Case of the Public Lands." 56 *University of Colorado Law Review* (1985): 537.

Schaffer, Henry. *Hebrew Tribal Economy and the Jubilee.* Leipzig: J. C. Hinrichs'sche Buchhandlung, 1922.
Schenk, H. Jochen, et al. "Spatial Root Segregation: Are Plants Territorial?" 28 *Advances in Ecological Research* (1999): 145.
Schnell, Yitzhak. "New Concepts in the Study of Mixed Cities: The Israeli Case." In *Together but Apart: Mixed Cities in Israel,* edited by Elie Rekhess, 19. Tel Aviv: Moshe Dayan Center for Middle Eastern and African Studies, 2007 (Hebrew).
Schwarzschild, Maimon. "Complicated—but Not Too Complicated: The Sunset of EU Law in the UK after Brexit." 39 *Cardozo Law Review* (2018): 905.
Segal, Ehud, et al. "Devising 'Policy Packages' for Seismic Retrofitting of Residences." 89 *Natural Hazards* (2017): 497.
Shachar, Yoram. "The Reference Area of the Supreme Court 1950–2004." 50 *Hapraklit—Israel Bar Law Journal* (2008) (Hebrew): 29.
Shachar, Yoram, et al. "Citation Practices of the Supreme Court, Quantitative Analysis." 27 *Mishpatim—Hebrew University Law Review* (1996) (Hebrew): 119.
Shaffer, Brenda. "Israel—New Natural Gas Producer in the Mediterranean." 39 *Energy Policy* (2011): 5379.
Shapira, Anita. *Land and Power: The Zionist Resort to Force, 1881–1948.* Stanford, CA: Stanford University Press, 1999.
Sharp, Nonie. *Saltwater People: The Waves of Memory.* Toronto: University of Toronto Press, 2002.
Shetreet, Shimon. "The Critical Challenge of Judicial Independence in Israel." In *Judicial Independence in the Age of Democracy: Critical Perspectives from Around the World,* edited by Peter H. Russell and David M. O'Brien, 233. Charlottesville: University Press of Virginia, 2001.
Shevah, Dana. "Social Dynamics, Urban Civility and Spatial Capacity in a Newly-Mixed Town: The Case of Karmiel." PhD diss., Technion—Israel Institute of Technology, 2017 (Hebrew).
Shilhav, Yosseph. "The Emergence of Ultra-Orthodox Neighborhoods in Israeli Urban Centers." In *Local Communities and the Israeli Polity: Conflict of Values and Interests,* edited by Efraim Ben-Zadok, 157. New York: SUNY Press, 1993.
Shmueli, Deborah F. "Housing and Highway Planning in Israel: An Environmental Debate." 35 *Urban Studies* (1998): 2131.
Shmueli, Deborah F., et al. "Scale and Scope of Environmental Planning Transformations: The Israeli Case." 16 *Planning Theory & Practice* (2015): 336.
Shoshani, Uri, et al. "A Multi Layers 3D Cadastre in Israel: A Research and Development Project Recommendations." FIG Working Week, Cairo, 2005.
Shoval, Noam. "Transformation of the Urban Morphology of Jerusalem: Present Trends and Future Scenarios." In *Jerusalem in the Future: The Challenge of Transition,* edited by Shlomo Hasson, 90. Jerusalem: Floersheimer Institute for Policy Studies, 2007.
Singer, Joel. "Point/Counterpoint: No Palestinian 'Return' to Israel." 8 *Human Rights Brief,* no. 2 (Winter 2001): 5.
Sliman, Said. "The Structure of Housing Decision Making in Arab Towns in Israel." PhD diss., Tel Aviv University, 2011 (Hebrew).
Smith, Anthony. *National Identity.* Reno: University of Nevada Press, 1991.
Smooha, Sammy. *Still Playing by the Rules: Index of Arab-Jewish Relations in Israel 2013.* Haifa: Israel Democracy Institute & Haifa University, 2013 (Hebrew).

———. *Still Playing by the Rules: Index of Arab-Jewish Relations in Israel 2015*. Haifa: Pardes, 2017.
Soffer, Arnon. "Territorialism, Nation and State." 21 *Iyuney-Mishpat—Tel-Aviv University Law Review* (1998) (Hebrew): 747.
Soffer, Oren. "Judicial Review of Legislation in Israel: Problems and Implications of Possible Reform." 12 *Israel Affairs* (2006): 307.
Sprankling, John G. *The International Law of Property*. Oxford: Oxford University Press, 2014.
Srebro, Haim. "Implementation of Marine Cadastre in Israel." *International Federation of Surveyors—Monthly Articles* (September 2015). http://fig.net/resources/monthly _articles/2015/srebro_september_2015.asp.
Stack, Heather M. "The 'Colonization' of East Germany? A Comparative Analysis of German Privatization." 46 *Duke L. J.* (1997): 1211.
Steinberg, Gerald M. "Europeans Fund Anti-Israel Libels." 22 *Middle East Quarterly*, no. 1 (Winter 2015): 1–15.
———. "'The Poor in Your Own City Shall Have Precedence': A Critique of the Katzir-Qaadan Case and Opinion." 16 *Israel Studies Bulletin*, no. 1 (Fall 2000): 12.
Sternhell, Zeev. *The Founding Myths of Israel*. Translated by David Maisel. Princeton, NJ: Princeton University Press, 1998.
Stopler, Gila. "National Identity and Religion–State Relations: Israel in Comparative Perspective." In *Israeli Constitutional Law at a Crossroads*, edited by Gideon Sapir et al., 503. Oxford: Hart, 2013.
Strauss, Michael J. *The Leasing of Guantanamo Bay*. Westport, CT: Praeger Security International, 2009.
Susser, Leslie, and Elie Rekhess. "Israel." 23 *Middle East Contemporary Survey* (1999): 295.
Tal, Alon. *The Land Is Full: Addressing Overpopulation in Israel*. New Haven, CT: Yale University Press, 2016.
Tamir, Michael. "The Freedom to Exclude: The Case of Israeli Society." 49 *Israel Law Review* (2016): 237.
Technion—Israel Institute of Technology. *Israel Marine Plan*. Haifa: Technion—Israel Institute of Technology, 2015.
———. *Israel Marine Plan: Implementation and Monitoring Report*. Haifa: Technion—Israel Institute of Technology, 2016 (Hebrew).
Teff-Seker, Yael, et al. "Israel Turns to the Sea." 72 *Middle East Journal* (2018): 610.
Teubal, Morris. "The Innovation System of Israel: Description, Performance and Outstanding Issues." In *National Innovation Systems: A Comparative Analysis*, edited by Richard R. Nelson, 476. Oxford: Oxford University Press, 1993.
Tovy, Jacob. *Israel and the Palestinian Refugee Issue: The Formulation of Policy 1948–1956*. Abingdon: Routledge, 2014.
Troen, S. Ilan. *Imagining Zion: Dreams, Designs, and Realities in a Century of Jewish Settlement*. New Haven, CT: Yale University Press, 2003.
Tute, R. C. *The Ottoman Land Laws—with a Commentary on the Ottoman Land Code of 7th Ramadan 1274*. Jerusalem: Greek Conv. Press, 1927.
Van Oosterom, Peter. *Survey of Israel Three-Dimensional Cadastre and the ISO 19152: The Land Administration Domain Model—Report*. Tel Aviv: Israel Survey of Israel and TU Delft, 2014.
Verne, Jules. *A Journey to the Center of the Earth*. New York: Scribner, Armstrong, 1874. First published 1864, Paris.

Vigoda-Gadot, Eran, et al. *Israeli Public Sector Performance: Citizens' Attitudes Analysis and National Assessment*. Haifa: Haifa University and Ben-Gurion University of the Negev, 2016 (Hebrew).

Vinizky, Chagai, and Shaul Sharf. *Basic Law Proposal: Israel as the Nation State of the Jewish People*. Jerusalem: Bursi Publishers and Menachem Begin Heritage Center, 2017 (Hebrew).

Vitkon, Gideon. "Agricultural Land Management Policy in Israel." 11 *Mekarkein* (Real Estate) (2012) (Hebrew): 103.

Webman, Esther. "The Evolution of a Founding Myth: The Nakba and Its Fluctuating Meaning." In *Palestinian Collective Memory and National Identity*, edited by Meir Litvak, 27. New York: Palgrave Macmillan, 2009.

Weisman, Joshua. "Camouflaged Privatization of Land in Israel." 21 *Iyuney-Mishpat—Tel-Aviv Law Review* (1998) (Hebrew): 525.

———. "How Long Will the Ottoman Land Laws Govern Us?" 12 *Mishpatim—Hebrew University of Jerusalem Law Review* (1982) (Hebrew): 3.

———. "The Land Law, 1969: A Critical Analysis." 5 *Israel Law Review* (1970): 379.

———. "A Lease That Is Renewed Permanently: A Miracle Drug or Deceit." 29 *Karka (Land)—Journal of the JNF Land Policy and Land Use Research Institute* (1987) (Hebrew): 2.

———. "Long-Term Lease as a Substitute for Ownership." In *Memorial Book for Gad Tedeschi: Essays in Civil Law*, edited by Yitzhak England et al., 211. Jerusalem: Sacher Institute, Hebrew University of Jerusalem, 1996 (Hebrew).

———. *Principal Features of the Israel Land Law 1969*. London: British Institute of International and Comparative Law, 1972.

———. *Property Law—General Part*. Jerusalem: Sacher Institute, Hebrew University of Jerusalem, 1993 (Hebrew).

———. "Restrictions on the Acquisition of Land by Aliens." 28 *Am. J. of Comp. Law* (1980): 39.

Weissner, Sigfried. "Indigenous Self-Determination, Culture and Land: A Reassessment in Light of the 2007 UN Declaration on the Rights of Indigenous Peoples." In *Indigenous Rights in the Age of the UN Declaration*, edited by Elvira Pulitano, 31. Cambridge: Cambridge University Press, 2012.

Weitz, Joseph. *The History of the Covenant between the Government of Israel and the Jewish National Fund*. Jerusalem: Central Bureau of the Jewish National Fund, 1960 (Hebrew).

Whynes, David K., and Roger A. Bowles. *The Economic Theory of the State*. New York: St. Martin's, 1981.

Williams, Colin, and Anthony D. Smith. "The National Construction of Social Space." 7 *Progress in Geography* (1983): 502.

Yacobi, Haim. "Planning Control and Spatial Protest: The Case of the Jewish-Arab Town of Lydd/Lod." In *Mixed Towns, Trapped Communities*, edited by Daniel Monterescu and Dan Rabinowitz, 135. Abingdon: Routledge, 2016.

Yadin, Uri. "Reception and Rejection of English Law in Israel." 11 *International and Comparative Law Quarterly* (1962): 59.

Yahel, Havatzelet. "Land Disputes between the Negev Bedouin and Israel." 11 *Israel Studies* (2006): 1.

———. "The Policy of the Israeli Government and State Authorities regarding the Negev Bedouin: 1947–1989." PhD Diss., Hebrew University of Jerusalem, 2015 (Hebrew).

Yahel, Havatzelet, et al. "Are the Negev Bedouin an Indigenous People? Fabricating Palestinian History." 19 *Middle East Quarterly* (2012): 3.
Yakobson, Alexander, and Amnon Rubinstein. *Israel and the Family of Nations: The Jewish Nation-State and Human Rights*. Translated by Ruth Morris and Ruchie Avital. Abingdon: Routledge, 2009. First published 2003, Tel Aviv.
Yozgof-Auerbach, Nicola, and Arnon Soffer. *Between Judaization and Lost Galilee: The Case of Upper Nazareth in the Years 1956–2016*. Haifa: Chaikin Chair for Geostrategy, University of Haifa, 2016 (Hebrew).
Zamir, Eyal. *Law, Psychology, and Morality: The Role of Loss Aversion*. Oxford: Oxford University Press, 2015.
Zeltner, Wladimir Zeev. "Reflections of the Contracts Law (General Part), 5733–1973." 1 *Tel Aviv U. Stud. L.* (1975): 153.
Zilbershats, Yaffa. "The Right of the Majority to Choose Residence." 6 *Mishpat Umimshal* (Law and Government)—*Haifa University Law Review* (2001) (Hebrew): 87.
Zilbershats, Yaffa, and Nimra Goren-Amitai. *Position Paper: Return of Palestinian Refugees to the State of Israel*, edited by Ruth Gavison. Jerusalem: Metzilah Center for Zionist, Jewish, Liberal and Humanist Thought, 2011.
Ziv, Neta, and Chen Tirosh. "The Legal Struggle against the Classification of Candidates for Community Settlements: A Catch in a Drowning and Boring Network." In *Gated Communities*, edited by Amnon Lehavi, 311. Tel Aviv: Buchman Faculty Law Series, Tel Aviv University, 2010 (Hebrew).

## News and Media

Abu Toameh, Khalid. "Abbas: Palestinians Won't Accept Jewish State." *Jerusalem Post*, March 4, 2015, http://www.jpost.com/Middle-East/Abbas-Palestinians-wont-accept-Jewish-state-Islamization-of-struggle-in-Mideast-392910.
Ahronheim, Anna. "Defense Ministry Presents Plans for Two Additional IDF Bases in the Negev." *Jerusalem Post*, November 13, 2017, http://www.jpost.com/Israel-News/Defense-Ministry-presents-plans-for-two-additional-IDF-bases-in-the-Negev-514126.
Azulay, Moran. "Kahlon Demands Israel Land Administration Portfolio." *Ynet-News*, January 12, 2015, https://www.ynetnews.com/articles/0,7340,L-4614404,00.html.
Bachner, Michael. "Retired High Court Judge Urges Ex-colleagues to Overrule Nation-State Law." *Times of Israel*, July 31, 2018, https://www.timesofisrael.com/retired-high-court-judge-urges-ex-colleagues-to-overrule-nation-state-law/.
Basok, Moti. "Government Approved the Transfer of Israel Lands Authority and the Planning Administration to the Treasury." *The Marker*, May 19, 2015 (Hebrew), https://www.themarker.com/news/1.2640198.
Ben-David, Rickey. "Israel Inaugurates Chinese-Run Haifa Port Terminal, in Likely Boost for Economy." *Times of Israel*, September 2, 2021, https://www.timesofisrael.com/israel-inaugurates-new-haifa-port-terminal-in-expected-boost-for-economy/.
Ben-Ozer, Tamar. "Bedouin Join Druze in High Court Petitions against Nation-State Law." *Jerusalem Post*, August 5, 2018, https://www.jpost.com/Israel-News/Bedouins-join-Druze-in-High-Court-petitions-against-Nation-State-Law-564193.
Ben-Yishay, Ron. "The 'Lab' Uncovering Cross-border Tunnels from Gaza." *Ynet*, December 12, 2017, https://www.ynetnews.com/articles/0,7340,L-5055087,00.html.

Bob, Yonah Jeremy. "ACRI: Ruling by Top Court Might be Insufficient for Mixed-Housing." *Jerusalem Post*, August 16, 2017, http://www.jpost.com/Israel-News/ACRI-Ruling-by-top-court-might-be-insufficient-for-mixed-housing-502540.

———. "High Court Drops the Ball on Jewish Nation-State Law—Analysis." *Jerusalem Post*, November 19, 2019, https://www.jpost.com/Israel-News/High-Court-drops-the-ball-on-Jewish-Nation-State-law-analysis-608296.

———. "Supreme Court Gets More Conservative with Appointment of Two New Justices." *Jerusalem Post*, February 22, 2018, https://www.jpost.com/israel-news/supreme-court-gets-more-conservative-with-appointment-of-two-new-justices-543418.

Bousso, Nimrod. "After 52 Years, Jewish National Fund Divorcing Israel Lands Administration." *Haaretz*, June 30, 2013, http://www.haaretz.com/israel-news/business/.premium-1.532730.

———. "Everyone Is Going to Lose from the Separation between JNF Lands and the State." *The Marker*, July 6, 2013 (Hebrew), https://www.themarker.com/realestate/1.2064095.

———. "The Transformation of the Moshav: From Chicken Coops to Mansions." *Haaretz*, June 26, 2015, http://www.haaretz.com/israel-news/business/real-estate/.premium-1.663002.

Chudy, Ori. "Israeli Arabs Do Not Cooperate with Lotteries for Residential Flats ('*Mehir Lamishtaken*')." *Globes*, September 25, 2017 (Hebrew), https://www.globes.co.il/news/article.aspx?did=1001205920.

———. "3,000 Homes Approved for Tzrifin Base." *Globes*, December 4, 2017, http://www.globes.co.il/en/article-3000-homes-approved-on-former-tzrifin-base-1001214373.

Cohen, Adi. "As Israel Grows More Crowded, State Plans Incentives for More Underground Building." *Haaretz*, May 2, 2019, https://www.haaretz.com/israel-news/.premium-as-israel-grows-more-crowded-state-plans-incentives-for-more-underground-building-1.7189758.

———. "Israel's Novel Solution to Housing Shortage: Build Underground." *Haaretz*, March 17, 2021, https://www.haaretz.com/israel-news/business/.premium-israel-s-novel-solution-to-housing-shortage-build-underground-1.9624899.

———. "Shopping Malls and Underground Streets: The Plan to Solve the Problem of Overcrowding." *The Marker*, May 2, 2019 (Hebrew), https://www.themarker.com/realestate/.premium-1.7189228.

Darel, Yael. "The Defense Plan Promised by the Ministry of Interior Has Been Stuck for Two Years." *Calcalist*, July 15, 2014 (Hebrew), https://www.calcalist.co.il/real_estate/articles/0,7340,L-3636080,00.html.

———. "It's Over: Jewish National Fund and Israel Finally Agree to Part Ways." *Ynet*, February 1, 2015, http://www.ynetnews.com/articles/0,7340,L-4620833,00.html.

Editorial. "The Israeli High Court's Strange Views about Equality: A Panel Actually Ruled That an Entity That Declares That It Discriminates Can Be among Israel's Decision-Makers." *Haaretz*, July 4, 2018, https://www.haaretz.com/opinion/the-israeli-high-court-s-strange-views-about-equality-1.6242391.

Eichner, Itamar, and Asaf Zagrizak. "Gov't Unveils Infrastructure Investment Super-program." *YNetNews*, September 3, 2017, https://www.ynetnews.com/articles/0,7340,L-5011351,00.html.

Elis, Niv. "Cabinet Approves Relocating IDF Bases, Clearing Land for Real Estate." *Jerusalem Post*, January 4, 2015, https://www.jpost.com/israel-news/cabinet-approves-relocating-idf-bases-clearing-land-for-real-estate-386644.

———. "Israeli Politicians Protest China's Bright Foods Purchase of Tnuva." *Jerusalem Post*, May 23, 2014, http://www.jpost.com/Business/Business-News/Israeli-politicians-protest-Chinas-Bright-Foods-purchase-of-Tnuva-353153.

Elis, Niv, and Sharon Udasin. "Lapid Calls to Nationalize 'Corrupt' KKL-JNF." *Jerusalem Post*, February 11, 2015, http://www.jpost.com/Israel-News/Lapid-calls-to-nationalize-corrupt-KKL-JNF-390652.

Eshed, Eli. "The Solution to the Housing Crisis: Living under the Ground." *Makor Rishon*, March 13, 2015 (Hebrew), http://www.nrg.co.il/online/55/ART2/683/343.html.

Freidman, Ron. "JNF Assembly Approves Land Swap in Disputed Vote." *Jerusalem Post*, June 23, 2009, http://www.jpost.com/Israel/JNF-assembly-approves-land-swap-in-disputed-vote.

Gazit, Amitai. "Rehabilitation after Decades: The Legal Advisor Approves Illegal Construction in Arab Communities." *Calcalist*, July 4, 2017 (Hebrew), https://www.calcalist.co.il/real_estate/articles/0,7340,L-3716424,00.html.

Ghert-Zand, Renee. "Underground Cemetery Project Looks to the Past for the Graveyard of the Future." *Times of Israel*, November 14, 2017, https://www.timesofisrael.com/underground-cemetery-project-looks-to-the-past-for-the-graveyard-of-the-future/.

Greenberg, Sara. "Netanyahu's Adviser to 'Post': Nation-State Law Critics are Misinformed." *Jerusalem Post*, August 6, 2018, https://www.jpost.com/Opinion/PMs-adviser-to-Post-Jewish-Nation-State-law-critics-are-misinformed-564267.

Harkov, Lahav. "Bayit Yehudi's Yogev in Hot Water over High Court Bulldozer Comments." *Jerusalem Post*, July 29, 2015, https://www.jpost.com/Israel-News/Politics-And-Diplomacy/Left-calls-Right-wing-criticism-of-High-Court-criminal-410485.

———. "The Fiercest Warrior against Judicial Activism." *Jerusalem Post*, November 29, 2017, https://www.jpost.com/Diplomatic-Conference/The-fiercest-warrior-against-judicial-activism-515595.

———. "Netanyahu, Levin Push for Dramatic Judiciary Restructuring." *Jerusalem Post*, April 15, 2018, https://www.jpost.com/Israel-News/Top-Likud-minister-Well-even-go-to-election-to-limit-Supreme-Court-549850.

Hasson, Ayala. "A Dunam Here and a Dunam There." *Weekly Diary Program, Channel 1*, May 7, 2010 (Hebrew), https://www.youtube.com/watch?v=N3p7ysvP03E.

Hasson, Nir. "The Dead Sea: A Dramatic Look at Israel's Endangered Natural Wonder." *Haaretz*, March 1, 2016, https://www.haaretz.com/st/c/prod/global/deadsea/eng/5/.

Hay, Shahar. "Knesset Committee Approves Override Power Over High Court." *Ynet-News*, June 5, 2018, https://www.ynetnews.com/articles/0,7340,L-5252771,00.html.

Hovel, Revital. "Former Prime Minister Ehud Olmert Convicted of Accepting Bribes in Holyland Case." *Haaretz*, March 31, 2014, https://www.haaretz.com/israel-news/1.582901.

Hovel, Revital, and Noa Shpigel. "Israel's Justice Minister Warns of 'An Earthquake' if Top Court Kills Nation-State Law." *Haaretz*, August 5, 2018, https://www.haaretz.com/israel-news/.premium-justice-minister-warns-of-earthquake-if-court-kills-nation-state-law-1.6343122.

Israeli Public Broadcasting Corporation (Kan 11). "The High Court Hears Petitions against the Nation State Law." *Kan11 New*, December 22, 2020, https://www.youtube.com/watch?v=RFozxsh5uLE.

Itiel, Yoav, and Ashkenazi Eli. "The New Member of Kibbutz Sdot Yam: Muhammad from Kafr Qara," *Walla-New*, June 22, 2021 (Hebrew).

Keinon, Herb, and Lahav Harkov. "PM to Push Basic Law That Will Define Israel as 'Jewish State.'" *Jerusalem Post*, May 1, 2014, http://www.jpost.com/Diplomacy-and-Politics/PM-to-push-Basic-Law-that-will-define-Israel-as-Jewish-state-351057.

Khoury, Jack. "Israel Promised to Build Its First Modern Arab City since 1948. Here's What Came of It." *Haaretz*, October 17, 2017, https://www.haaretz.com/israel-news/.premium.MAGAZINE-israel-vowed-to-build-its-first-modern-arab-city-since-48-then-nothing-1.5457042.

Klein Leichman, Abigail. "High-Speed Tel Aviv–Jerusalem Rail Coming Down the Track." *Israel 21C*, March 22, 2017, https://www.israel21c.org/high-speed-tel-aviv-jerusalem-rail-coming-down-the-track/.

Landers, Israel. "The Emma Berger Law." *Davar*, October 15, 1980 (Hebrew).

Lavi, Zvi. "Laws for the Protection of State Lands from Invaders and Strangers—Approved." *Davar*, January 16, 1980 (Hebrew).

Lis, Jonathan. "Israel Passes Law Meant to Crack Down on Illegal Building in Arab Communities." *Haaretz*, April 5, 2017, https://www.haaretz.com/israel-news/.premium-israel-passes-law-cracking-down-on-illegal-building-in-arab-communities-1.5457966.

———. "Israel's Governing Coalition to Advance Nation-State Bill That Subordinates Democracy to Judaism." *Haaretz*, December 18, 2017, https://www.haaretz.com/israel-news/.premium-coalition-to-advance-nation-state-bill-that-subordinates-democracy-to-judaism-1.5628953.

Meiri, Baruch. "A New Law Will Prevent the Sale of Land in Israel to Foreigners." *Ma'ariv*, September 16, 1980 (Hebrew).

Melnitcki, Gili. "Ending Earthquake Proofing Program Leaves 1 Million Israeli Homes at Risk." *Haaretz*, July 7, 2019, https://www.haaretz.com/israel-news/business/ending-earthquake-proofing-program-leaves-1-million-israeli-homes-at-risk-1.7453984.

———. "Israel's Quake-Proofing Program Now Slated to End in 2022." *Haaretz*, November 7, 2019, https://www.haaretz.com/israel-news/.premium-israel-s-quake-proofing-program-now-slated-to-end-in-2022-1.8091901.

Mirovsky, Arik. "Israel Tops World in Increase in Housing Prices." *Haaretz*, March 13, 2017, https://www.haaretz.com/israel-news/1.776849.

Pincus, Walter. "U.S. Overseeing Mysterious Construction Project in Israel." *Washington Post*, November 28, 2012, https://www.washingtonpost.com/world/national-security/us-overseeing-mysterious-construction-project-in-israel/2012/11/28/e5682d8e-38b6-11e2-a263-foebffed2f15_story.html?utm_term=.ccf37bfde9d0.

Priel, Aharon. "A Public Committee Will Try to Prevent Sublease of Land." *Ma'ariv*, September 30, 1980 (Hebrew).

Pulwer, Sharon. "Supreme Court Clears Ehud Olmert of Main Corruption Charge in Holyland Case; Cuts Jail Term." *Haaretz*, December 29, 2015, https://www.haaretz.com/israel-news/1.694309.

Rasgon, Adam, and Udi Shaham. "Arabs on Land Day: We Won't Move; Israeli Arabs Set for General Strike, Protests on 40th Annual Land Day." *Jerusalem Post*, March 31, 2017, https://www.jpost.com/Arab-Israeli-Conflict/Arabs-on-Land-Day-We-wont-move-485730.

Raved, Ahiya. "Poll: 51% of Israeli Arabs Refuse to Recognize Israel as Jewish State." *Ynet-News*, July 3, 2018, https://www.ynetnews.com/articles/0,7340,L-5148927,00.html.

Rinat, Zafrir. "Are Things Finally Looking Up for the Dead Sea?" *Haaretz*, February 25, 2017, https://www.haaretz.com/israel-news/science/.premium-1.773631.

Sadeh, Shuki. "JNF Accused of Squandering Your Generosity." *Haaretz*, April 3, 2014, https://www.haaretz.com/israel-news/business/.premium-1.583680.
Sales, Ben. "First Arab Muslim Accepted as Kibbutz Member." *Jerusalem Post*, June 12, 2008, https://www.jpost.com/israel/first-arab-muslim-accepted-as-kibbutz-member.
Shaham, Udi. "New Law Stiffens Punishment for Construction Violations." *Jerusalem Post*, April 6, 2017, https://www.jpost.com/Israel-News/Politics-And-Diplomacy/New-law-stiffens-punishment-for-construction-violations-486234.
Shalita, Chen. "Nof Zion Buyer Believed to Be Bashir Al-Masri." *Jerusalem Post*, December 16, 2010 (Hebrew), https://www.jpost.com/Business/Globes/Nof-Zion-buyer-believed-to-be-Bashar-al-Masri.
Shany, Yuval. "Judicial Activism? It Depends Who You Ask." *Jerusalem Post*, June 26, 2019, https://www.jpost.com/Opinion/Judicial-activism-It-depends-who-you-ask-593196.
Soler, Shmuel. "Head of the Givat Ada Council: 'They Allocated Land to People Who . . . Went Abroad.'" *Ma'ariv*, November 4, 1962 (Hebrew).
Spiro, Amy. "High Court Rejects Petitions Seeking to Strike Down Nation-State Law," *Times of Israel*, July 8, 2021, https://www.timesofisrael.com/high-court-rejects-petitions-seeking-to-strike-down-nation-state-law/.
Staff, Davar. "Jews Lease Land and Sub-lease It to the Arabs." *Davar*, July 13, 1975 (Hebrew).
Staff, Economist. "Buying Farmland Abroad: Outsourcing's Third Wave." *Economist*, May 21, 2009, https://www.economist.com/international/2009/05/21/outsourcings-third-wave.
Staff, JPost.com. "Full Text of Netanyahu's Speech to 71st UN General Assembly." *Jerusalem Post*, September 23, 2016, https://www.jpost.com/Israel-News/Benjamin-Netanyahu/READ-Full-text-of-Netanyahus-speech-to-UN-General-Assembly-468500.
———. "Read the Full Jewish Nation-State Law." *Jerusalem Post*, July 19, 2018, https://www.jpost.com/Israel-News/Read-the-full-Jewish-Nation-State-Law-562923.
Staff, MEE. "Hamas in 2017: The Document in Full." *Middle East Eye*, May 2, 2017, http://www.middleeasteye.net/news/hamas-charter-1637794876.
Staff, PBS. "Public Interview." *Public Broadcasting Service (PBS)*, January 19, 2000, https://www.pbs.org/wgbh/commandingheights/shared/minitext/int_kennethbaker.html.
Staff, TOI. "Jerusalem–Tel Aviv Highway Reopens with New Tunnels, Bridge." *Times of Israel*, January 20, 2017, https://www.timesofisrael.com/jerusalem-tel-aviv-highway-reopens-with-new-tunnels-bridge/.
Staff, TOI, and Jacob Magid. "MKs Push Ahead with Bill Curbing High Court in West Bank Land Disputes." *Times of Israel*, May 28, 2018, https://www.timesofisrael.com/mks-push-ahead-with-bill-curbing-high-court-in-west-bank-land-disputes/.
Stub, Zev. "As Israel Looks to Solve Housing Crisis, Future of Tama 38 in Question." *Jerusalem Post*, July 12, 2021, https://www.jpost.com/israel-news/as-israel-looks-to-solve-housing-crisis-future-of-tama-38-in-question-673607.
Surkes, Sue. "Scientists: Noble Energy 'Grossly Underestimates' Gas Pollution Threat to Israel." *Times of Israel*, October 22, 2019, https://www.timesofisrael.com/noble-energy-grossly-underestimating-leviathan-gas-rig-pollution-scientists/.
Udasin, Sharon. "Israel Set to Regulate Sea's Legal Status." *Jerusalem Post*, August 7, 2017, https://www.jpost.com/Israel-News/Israel-set-to-regulate-its-seas-501725.
———. "Plans to Build 27,000 Hotel Rooms Receive Knesset Approval." *Jerusalem Post*, August 2, 2016, https://www.jpost.com/Israel-News/Plans-to-build-27000-hotel-rooms-likely-to-receive-Knesset-approval-462991.

Wootliff, Raoul. "Chief Justice to PM: Bill for 61 MKs to Overturn Rulings 'a Danger to Democracy.'" *Times of Israel*, April 29, 2018, https://www.timesofisrael.com/pm-chief-justice-end-meeting-without-agreement-on-bid-to-limit-supreme-court/.

Yanovsky, Roi. "State Comptroller Issues Scathing Report on KKL." *Ynet*, January 8, 2017, https://www.ynetnews.com/articles/0,7340,L-4909566,00.html.

Yefet, Nati. "Tel Aviv Light Rail Tunneling Begins." *Globes*, February 15, 2017, https://www.globes.co.il/en/article-red-line-tunneling-begins-1001177146.

Zarchin, Tomer. "Eichmann Trial Judge, Moshe Landau, Dies at 99." *Haaretz*, May 2, 2011, https://www.haaretz.com/1.5006533.

Zieve, Tamar. "Tens of Thousands Druze-Led Protest against Nation-State Law." *Jerusalem Post*, August 4, 2018, https://www.jpost.com/Israel-News/Tens-of-thousands-attend-Druze-protest-against-Nation-State-Law-564130.

# INDEX

*Page numbers in italics refer to figures and tables.*

abandoned property, of Palestinian refugees, 24–25
Abel (biblical character), 2
Abraham (biblical character), 6, 46
activism, judicial, 176, 184, 194, 195, 208; of Barak, 179, 209
Adalah, Legal Center for Arab Minority Rights, 139
Admati ("My Land"), 58
admissions committee, of small community settlements, 150; bills to change, 151
Afula, 150
Agnon, Shmuel Yosef, 95
agricultural land: conflicts with urban land and, 84–85; privatization of, 81–88; use for residential purposes, 86–87; Zionist movement and, 81, 89
agricultural purpose of lands, retention of, 82–84
Aharonov case, 182–84, 188–89
Akunas case, 112–13
allocation: of land resources, 145–56, 161; of state land for Arab settlements, 156
*Altneuland* (Old New Land) (Herzl), 45, 48–49, 56
American sources, reliance on, 177
apartment, time to build, 104
approval, of construction, 107–9
Arab and Jewish population, relationship between, 27–28, 31–32, 50–52, 130–36, 160, 207
Arab and Jewish Settlements, numbers and statistics, 158, *159*
Arab and Palestinian resistance, to Zionism, 50, 132
Arab leadership, 145
Arab minority, in Israel, 9, 27, 31, 51, 130; allocation of land resources to, 145, 207; growth rate of, 131; as indigenous, 143–44;

nationalism of, 132, 155; percentage of population of, 131
Arab National Movement, 28
Arab population core, cities with, 149
Arab settlements, 151, *159*, 207; independent planning initiatives in, 156; new, 157–58; real estate in, 156
Arara case, 157
Arbel, Edna, 58, 88
areas, of integration, 148–50
army: camps transfer to periphery of, 107; training grounds, 99
artificial islands, 115, 116
attachment, to place, 2–4
authority, given to Israel Lands Council by Knesset, 73
Avi-ezer case, 57
Avitan case, 152

Bader, Yohanan, 51, 53, 57
*Baker v. Carr*, 177
Balfour Declaration, 132
Barak, Aharon, 57–58, 110, 113, 134, 146–47; on expropriated land, 193, 194; Ganz case and, 185–89; judicial activism of, 179, 209; on property rights, 175, 183, 187–89
Barcelona Convention for the Protection of the Mediterranean Sea, 115
Basic Law: Human Dignity and Liberty, 130, 141, 178, 190–91, 195
Basic Law: Israel as the Nation-State of the Jewish People, 135, 148
Basic Law: Israel Lands, 29, 45, 52, 58–59, 75–76; socialism and, 205
Bedouin, 18, 143–44, 151–52
Begin, Menachem, 25
Beinish, Dorit, 48, 141
benefits: for farmers, 83–84; of LAA, 138
Ben-Gurion, David, 28–29, 51, 56

*245*

Beth-El communities, 53
BLM. *See* Bureau of Land Management, of US
Bob, Yonah Jeremy, 150
Boeing Decisions, 83
Boker case, 181–82
Bright Food Group, 54
British Mandate, 6–7, 14, 17, 18–19, 27–28; disengagement of judicial system from, 176; dual obligation and, 130; planning laws and, 102, 204
Brown, Brené, 102
*Brown v. Board of Education*, 146
building reinforcement (earthquakes), 108–9
buildings, incentives to reinforce, 108–10
built-up lands, in cities (*mulq*), 20
bureaucratic efficiency, 77–78, 103–4, 206
Bureau of Land Management, US (BLM), 62

Cain (biblical character), 2
Canada, 5
capital, human, 95
capitalist worldview, 203, 205, 209
Carmel tunnel, 111
cases: Aharonov, 182–84, 188–89; Akunas, 112–13; Arara, 157; Avi-ezer, 57; Avitan, 152; *Baker v. Carr*, 177; *Brown v. Board of Education*, 146; Dinar, 141; Dror, 48, 57–58, 61; Ganz, 185–89; Harel, 147; Holzman, 193; Horowitz, 194; Jabareen, 140–41; Ka'adan, 57, 134, 146, 148, 159; Karsik, 192; Mahul, 155, 157; *Marbury v. Madison*, 178; Mehadrin, 84–86; Museum of Tolerance, 141; New Discourse, 57, 82–83; Nusseibeh, 191; Rotman, 193; Sabach, 151; Sabith, 140; Saig, 150; Shawahna, 142; Al-Uqbi, 142, 144
caveat, registration of, 185–89
CEA. *See* Crown Estate Act
center and peripheral areas: divide between, 107, 110; gap between, 98, 206
Center for Human Dignity, 141
Central Bureau of Statistics, 160
central tenet, of Zionist movement, 49–50, 133–34
change, in designation of land, 86
"Changes in the Conditions of Leasing Land to Saturated Public Housing" (Israel Lands Council), 77

Cheshin, Mishael, 194
China, privatization in, 88
cities, with Arab population core, 149
claim, to indigenousness, 143–45
coastline: adjacent development, 116; limits of construction around, 108; Mediterranean, 115
Cohn, Haim, 25–26
collective estates (*moshavim*), 86, 150–51, 158
collectively-based allocation, of public resources, 145
colonizers, Jews as, 143
commercial land, 191
commercial land percentages, contrasted with residential land, 98
commission, to recommend release of absentee properties, 137
communal settlements (*Kibbutzim*), 58–59, 86, 150–51, 158
compensation: exemption of authorities from, 194, 195; for expropriation of land, 192–95; for land lost in War of Independence, 137, 160, 208; partial, 193
complex identity, of Israel, 203
concentration, of Arab population in urban settlements, 158, 161
condominium owners, coordination between, 109
conflicts: between agricultural and urban land, 84–85; between governmental institutions, 104; Israeli-Arab, 7, 132; between local and national planning, 103–4
conservatism, of Supreme Court, 186, 195
conservative approach, of Landau, M., 181
Constitution, Law and Justice Committee, of Knesset, 2, 25–26, 74
Constitution, US, 5–6, 190
constitutional: protection of property rights, 175, 180, 189–90; reviews of legislation, 178, 189–90; revolution, 178, 189–90, 193
construction: approval, 107–9; unplanned, 156
control, over rural areas, 158, 159, 162, 207
coordination, between condominium owners, 109
creativity, of judicial system, 176

criticism, of integration model, 145
crowding, 96–97
Crown Estate Act (CEA 1961), 63
Crusader Knights Palaces, 111
*Cujus est solum, ejus est usque ad coelum ed ad inferos* (land ownership extends from the ground down toward the center of the earth and up toward the sky), 112
cultivated plots (*miri*), 16, 17, *17*, 20
cultural importance, of land, 4–5
curb, of urban expansion, 107

Dead Sea, environmental problems and, 100
*Dearing Greatly* (Brown), 102
debate, over judicial role, 179, 203
Decision 1, of Israel Land Council, 75–76, 81
Declaration of Independence, Israel, 51, 143
degree of authority, granted to local government, 103–4
demand, for housing, 104–5, 110
Democratic Arc movement, 83
dense population, of Israel, 8
density caps, 107
departure, of Israel from English law, 176–77
desalination plants, for water, 106, 114
designation of agricultural land, change in, 86
developed: formally owned land (*raqabe*), 16, 17; lands growth rate of, 98
development, coastline-adjacent, 116
Development Authority, 24–25, 26, 35–36, 76, 137; lands controlled by, 204
Dgani, Ilan, 84
Diaspora Jewry, 30, 31, 32, 46, 133–34
Dinar case, 141
discrimination, racial, 5
disengagement, of judiciary from British Mandate system, 176
distribution, of private property rights in real estate, 153–54, 191
distributive approach, of justices, 189, 194
divide, between center and periphery, 107, 110
Dorner, Dalia, 140, 193
Doukhan, Moses, 7
Dror case, 48, 57–58, 61
dual obligation, of Israel, 130–34, 160, 207
duration of stay index, 111–12

economic orientation, of Israel, 55, 72–73, 195
EEZ. *See* Exclusive Economic Zone
efficiency, bureaucratic, 77–78, 103–4, 206
efficient use, of private land reserves, 156–57, 161
energy independence, 106
English equity law, 180, 183, 188, 195; departure of Israel from, 176–77
environmental awareness, increase in, 108
environmental problems, of use of Dead Sea, 100
equality: evaluation of, 152; land benefits and, 83, 205; modern conceptions of, 48
equitable rights, to land, 175, 180–81; "made in Israel" (*Tozeret Ha-Aretz*), 182–89; precedent of, 183
Eshkol, Levi, 29–30, 36, 51, 56, 204
Eshkol Committee, 28–30
estate (*Nahala*), 86
estates, collective (*moshavim*), 86, 150–51, 158
estoppel, 180–81, 185–88
Europe, 83, 96, 98, 178
European Court for Human Rights, 79
evaluation, of equality, 152
Exclusive Economic Zone (EEZ), 100, 114
exemption, of authorities from compensation, 194, 195
expanse, of scope of Israeli Supreme Court, 177
expropriation, of land, 154–55, 189–92, 209; compensation for, 192–95; justification for, 191; Supreme Court on, 193
extension, of lease period, 79

family ownership, long-term, 156
farmers, benefits for, 83–84
farmers, residential rights of, 87–88
Federal Land Policy and Management Act (1976) (US), 62–63
feeling, of ownership of lessees, 78
foreigners, 52, 53–54, 62
formal privatization, 75, 205; ILA and, 79; Knesset and, 79–80
Forum of the Heads of Israel's Large Cities, 88
Foundations of Law Act (1980), 176
Frankfurter, Felix, 177

## 248 | Index

Friedmann, Daniel, 179
*Future Vision of the Palestinian Arabs in Israel, The* (The National Committee for the Heads of the Arab Local Authorities in Israel), 26, 132

Galilee, 154; urban settlement in, 151–52
Ganz case, 185–89
gap, between center and peripheral areas, 98, 206
Gaza Strip, 53, 111, 132
geographic information systems (GIS), 98
geography, 5
GIS. *See* geographic information systems
globalization, 54
Goadby, Frederic, 7
good, public, 60, 75, 81
good faith, 188
Gordon, Aaron David, 49
government: control of land ideological motives for, 46, 88–89; Thatcher, 88
governmental institutions, conflicts between, 104
governmentally administered lands, 30
governmental systems, weakening of, 178
Granovsky, Abraham, 56
growth rate: of Arab minority, 131; of developed lands, 98; urban, 98–99

HaBayit HaYehudi party, 33
Haredi-Jewish population, 152
Harel case, 147
Hayut, Esther, 142
hazards, natural resources and, 100–101, 117
Herzl, Theodore, 45, 48–49, 56, 76, 210
high population growth, of Israel, 96–97, 101
high status, of Basic Law, 178
historical territory, 3
Holocaust, the, 133
Holy Land, the, 3, 6
Holzman case, 193
homeland, return of Jewish people to, 62
homogeneous population, preference for, 149, 152, 161
Horowitz case, 194
housing, demand, for, 104–5, 110

housing units, 76–77, 80, 104–5
human: activity land and, 2; capital, 95
Husseini, Amin al-, 141

identity: land and, 1–5, 89, 203, 210; national, 4, 8, 35
ideological: differences between justices, 194, 195; motives, for government control of land, 46, 88–89
IDF. *See* Israel Defense Forces
ILA. *See* Israel Lands Administration
IMP-MED. *See* Integrated Maritime Policy in the Mediterranean
incentives, to reinforce buildings, 108–10
increase: in environmental awareness, 108; in property price, 59
independence: of judicial system, 175, 177, 196, 208; legal, 8
independence, energy, 106
Independent Cities Forum case, 61
independent planning initiatives, in Arab settlements, 156
indigenous: Arab minority as, 143–44; peoples, 3
indigenousness, claim to, 143–45
inefficiency, of ILA, 59
inequality, socioeconomic, 159–60, 162, 208
inflation, 138
informal privatization, 74–75, 88–89, 205; milestones of, 76–77
infrastructure, 105–6, 206
innovation, 117
innovative judiciary, 175
Integrated Maritime Policy in the Mediterranean (IMP-MED), 115
integration, areas of, 148–50
integration model, 146, 149, 152, 157; criticism of, 145; resistance to, 161, 207; Supreme Court on, 146, 208
intensification, of judicial review, 177
internal claims, for restitution of refugee assets, 138–39, 160
interpretation, of previous legislation, 190, 195
Islamic Movement in Israel, 139, 141
islands, artificial, 115, 116
Israel. *See specific topics*

Israel Defense Forces (IDF), 137
Israeli: Bedouin, 18, 143, 144, 152; judicial system, 9, 140–43, 175–76; Ministry of Finance, 23; Parliament, 73
Israeli-Arab conflict, 7, 132
Israeli Arabs, religion of, 131–32
Israeli Arab Vision, 139
Israel Lands Administration (ILA), 25, 29, 31, 33, 52; formal privatization and, 79; inefficiency of, 59; land inventory of, 99; logo of, 82; lump sum payments to, 77, 88; Mehadrin Case and, 84–85
Israel Lands Administration Law, 76
Israel Lands Authority, 59–60, 61, 83, 85–86; logo of, 82
Israel Lands Council, 74, 78–79, 83, 87–88; authority given to by Knesset, 73; Decision 1 of, 75–76, 81; political power of ministry controlling, 73–74, 89n8; Supreme Court on, 73
Israel Maritime Plan, 116
Israel Ministry of Foreign Affairs, 117
Israel's Proclamation of Independence (*Megilat Ha-Atzmaut*), 130
Israel Survey, 115

Jabareen case, 140–41
Jabotinsky, Ze'ev, 49
Jerusalem, 99, 104, 141
Jewish and Arab Settlements, 158, *159*
Jewish and democratic, Israel as, 1, 9, 130–62, 203, 207–9
Jewish National Fund (JNF), 14–15, 27–30, 191, 204; privatization policy of, 33; return of land to administration of, 31, 32; swap of lands with other state lands and, 31, 33
Jewish Settlement, 148, *159*
Jewish state, 50–51, 142, 144, 160, 203
Jews, as colonizers, 143
JNF. *See* Jewish National Fund
JNF lands, nationalization, of, 31–32
Joubran, Salim, 151
Jubilee laws, 47
Jubilee Year (*Shnat haYovel*), 47
judicial: activism, 176, 184, 194, 195, 208–9; creativity, 176; legislation, 177; restraint, 189–92, 195–96, 209; review intensification of, 177; role debate over, 179, 203
judicial system: creativity of, 176; independence of, 175, 177, 196, 208
judiciary, innovative, 175
justices: distributive approach of, 189, 194; ideological differences between, 194, 195
justification, for expropriation, 191

Ka'adan case, 57, 134, 146, 148, 159
Kahlon, Moshe, 74
Kaplan, Eliezer, 138
Karra, George, 135–36
Karsik case, 192
*Kibbutzim*. *See* communal settlements
Knesset, 19, 25, 45, 58–59, 61; authority given to Israel Lands Council by, 73; building reinforcement and, 109; Constitution, Law and Justice Committee of, 138; formal privatization and, 79–80

LAA. *See* Land Acquisition Validation of Acts and Compensation Law
lack: of English sources on Israeli land law, 7; of treaties with neighbors regarding maritime space, 114
*al-Lajjun*, 140
land: built-up cities (*mulq*), 20; commercial, 191; controlled by Development Authority, 204; cultural importance of, 4–5; developed formally owned (*raqabe*), 16, *17*; development socialist worldview and, 55; as economic resource, 5; equitable rights to, 175; expropriation of, 154–55, 189–92, 209; as family property, 156; governmentally administered, 30; human activity and, 2; identity and, 1–5, 89, 203, 210; inventory by district, 21, *21*; inventory refugee, 35; in Ottoman law (*mulq*, *waqf*), 16, *17*; ownership by Arab population, 153–54; ownership personal liberty and, 5–6, 7; planning, 95–96; private ownership of, 4–6, 8, 9, 20, *20*, 21; as public good, 60; publicly owned municipal (*matruka*), 16, *17*; reserved for development, 61–62; rural non-agrarian (*mewat*), 16, *17*, *17*, 18, 19–20, 21; usage of, 23

Land Acquisition Validation of Acts and Compensation Law (LAA), 24–25, 137, 141; benefits of, 138
Landau, Leah, 15
Landau, Moshe, 15; conservative approach of, 181
land benefits, equality and, 83, 205
Land Day, 154
land inventory: of ILA, 99; public, 8, 27, 45, 72–73, 203, 205; refugee, 35
land law: democracy and, 3; identity and, 1–4; Muslim, 16
Land Law, 181, 185
"Land Law, 5729–1969 at First Sight, The" (Doukhan-Landau), 15
*Land Law of Palestine, The* (Goadby and Doukhan), 7
Land of Israel (*Eretz Israel*), 46, 81, 132–34
land ownership: public, 56–57, 59–61; underground, 113; urban, 153–54
land registry, registration in, 181, 185
land reserves, shortage, of, 99–100
land resources, allocation of, 145–56, 161
Land Settlement of Title Ordinance, 18–19
Lands (Expropriation) Ordinance (1943), 190–91
land title registration, 18
Lapid, Yair, 33
large size, of maritime space, 114
*Law and the Culture of Israel* (Mautner), 193, 194
Lawson, Frederick H., 6
leadership, Arab, 145
leadership of the Jewish settlement (*Yishuv*), 55
leasehold system, public, 75–76
lease Jubilee, rules on, 78
lease period, extension, of, 79
leasing, of agricultural lands as residences, 86; problems with system, 87–88
leasing market, secondary, 149
legal: independence, 8; regulation of underground space, 112–13
Legal Center for Arab Minority Rights, Adalah, 139
legislation, judicial, 177

length, of privatization process, 72–73
lessees, feeling of ownership of, 78
Leviticus, 47
limit: of authority of judiciary, 175; of construction around coastline, 108
limitation clause, 178
local: government degree of authority granted to, 103–4; planning system, 103, 117
local and national planning, conflicts between, 103–4
logo, of Israel Lands Administration (ILA), 82
long-term family ownership, 156
lump sum payments, to Israel Lands Administration, 77, 88

"made in Israel" (*Tozeret Ha-Aretz*) equitable rights, 182–89, 195
Mahul case, 155, 157
Makr (village), 154, 155
Mandate of the League of Nations, 19–20, 130
Mandatory Constitution, 180
*Marbury v. Madison*, 178
maritime space: large size of, 114; planning, 115–16; policy measures for, 116; use of, 113–17
market forces, 149, 152, 208
maturation, of Israel, 210
Mautner, Menachem, 179, 193, 194
Mediterranean coastline, 115
*Megiddo* Kibbutz, 140
Mehadrin case, 86; ILA and, 84–85
Mehadrin company, 84; offer of stock purchase, 85–86
memorial protest, of land expropriation, 155
Metula, 19
Mickiewicz, Adam, 3
milestones, of informal privatization, 76–77
Millennium Development Goals, of World Bank, 62
Ministry of Justice, 115
modern conceptions, of equality, 48
*moshavim*. *See* collective estates
Museum of Tolerance case, 141
Muslim land laws, 16

*Nahalot* (Estates) System, 86
*Nakba* (catastrophe), 133, 138–40
Naor, Miriam, 113, 144
narrowness, of Israel, 96, 101, 206
National Committee for Preferred Housing Compounds (NCPHC), 103
National Committee for the Heads of the Arab Local Authorities in Israel, 26
National Council for Planning and Building (NCPB), 102, 104, 105
National Economic Council, 107–8
national identity, 4, 8, 35
National Infrastructure Committee (NIC), 103, 105
nationalism, of Arab minority, 132, 155
nationalist dispositions, of Israeli Arabs, 131–32
nationalization, of JNF lands, 31–32
national-level planning bodies, 102–3
National Outline Plan for Construction, Development and Conservation (NOP 35), 106
National Outline Plans (NOPs), 102, 105–6, 112
National Water Carrier, 100
Nation-State Basic Law, 135–36, 142, 143–44, 147; Section 7 of, 148
natural: environment preservation of, 108, 110; gas reserve, 114; resources hazards and, 100–101, 117
Nazareth Illit, 149, 154
NCPB. *See* National Council for Planning and Building
NCPCH. *See* National Committee for Preferred Housing Compounds
needs: public, 60, 190–92; security, 106
Negev, 18, 100, 139–40, 144
Netanyahu, Benjamin, 32, 33, 74, 106, 135
networks, train, 105–6
new Arab settlements, 157–58
New Discourse Case, 57, 82–83
NIC. *See* National Infrastructure Committee
nongovernmental organizations (NGOs), 80
NOP 1, 112
NOP 35. *See* National Outline Plan for Construction, Development and Conservation

NOP 38, 108–10
NOP 40, 111; slowing of plan, 112
NOP 44, 151, 155
NOPs. *See* National Outline Plans
Numbers, book of, 47
Nusseibeh case, 191

*Old New Land (Altneuland)* (Herzl), 45, 48–49, 56
Olmert, Ehud, 33, 104
*Only Yesterday* (Agnon), 95
open spaces, 106
Ottoman: Empire, 6, 14, 15–16; land law, 15–17, *17*, 18–19, 22, 195, 204
Ottoman Land Code of 1858, 15, 16, 17, 204
ownership, of underground land, 113
ownership transfer, to non-Jews, 50, 52–53; prohibition of, 52, 55, 62

Palestine, 14, 23–24, 136, 204
Palestine Order in Council 1922, 176
Palestinian: national movement, 132; refugees property abandoned by, 24–25
*Pan Tadeusz* (Mickiewicz), 3
partial compensation, for expropriated lands, 193
past, struggle with, 203–4
patriarchal society, 47
peripheral areas, structural reinforcement in, 109
peripheral territories, of Israel, 96
"Permission to Transfer Ownership" (Basic Law), 76
place attachment, 2–4
planning: bodies national-level, 102–3; institutions, 102; laws British Mandate and, 102, 204; progress slow, 155, 161; system local, 103, 117; three-dimensional, 111–12
Planning and Building Law, 102, 190–93
plots, cultivated (*miri*), 16, 17, *17*, 20
policy decisions, technical, 74
policy measures, for maritime space, 116
political power, of ministry controlling Israel Lands Council, 73–74, 89n8
population: density of Israel, 97–98, 101; dispersion, 106–7
population, Haredi-Jewish, 152

## 252 | Index

Ports Authority, 114
precedent, of no equitable rights, 183
preference, of homogeneous population, 149, 152, 161
present absentees, 137, 140, 142, 154
preservation: of land for future generations, 61, 106; of natural environment, 108, 110
"preservation of laws" (Basic Law), 190
pressure on agricultural lands, urban, 81–82
previous legislation, interpretation of, 190, 195
private land: ownership, 4–6, 8, 9, 20, 20, 21; reserves efficient use of, 156–57, 161
private ownership, of land, 4–6, 8, 9, 20, 20, 21; in Ottoman law (*mulq, waqf*), 16, *17*
privatization: of agricultural land, 81–88; in China, 88; formal, 75, 79–80, 205; informal, 74–75, 76–77, 88–89, 205; policy of JNF, 33; UK initiatives, 88; of urban public lands, 31, 36, 58, 72–73, 75–80, 203, 205–6; of US, 36
problems: with leasing system, 87–88; with water, 100–101
profiteering, 56
profits, of urbanization, 83–85
prohibition, of land ownership by foreigners, 52, 55, 62
property price, increase in, 59
property rights, constitutional protection of, 175, 180, 189–90
protection, of private property, 46, 190, 194–95
protection of property rights, constitutional, 175, 180, 189–90
public: good, 60, 75, 81; land inventory, 8, 27, 45, 72–73, 203, 205; land ownership, 56–57, 59–61; leasehold system, 75–76; needs, 60, 190–92; trust in Supreme Court, 180
publicly owned municipal lands (*matruka*), 16, *17*
"public need," 191
public trust, in Supreme Court, 180
*Purse and the Sword, The* (Friedmann), 179

racial discrimination, 5
Raz-Dror, Ofer, 151
real estate, 6, 156, 187; distribution, of private property rights in, 153–54, 191

"redeeming the wilderness," 29, 33, 48
refugees, 23–24, 52, 133, 136
registration: of caveat, 185–89; in land registry, 181, 185
relationship: between Arab and Jewish populations, 160, 207; between transferor transferee and, 184, 188–89
release of absentee properties, commission to recommend, 137
reliance, on American sources, 177
religion, of Israeli Arabs, 131–32
religious faith (*Halakhah*), 48
renewal projects, urban, 5, 107
reserve, natural gas, 114
residential land percentages, contrasted with commercial land, 98
residential rights, of farmers, 87–88
resistance: to integration model, 161, 207; to Zionism, 50, 132
restitution, of internal refugee property, 160, 192, 204, 207; internal claims for, 138–39, 160
retention, of agricultural purpose of lands, 82–84
return: of Jewish people to homeland, 62; of JNF land to JNF administration, 31, 32; right of, 136
reviews of legislation, constitutional, 178, 189–90
revolution, constitutional, 178, 189–90, 193
right: of contract holder to land over creditors, 182–83, 188–89; of return, 136
Rotman case, 193
Rubinstein, Elyakim, 26, 85, 134, 141, 144; on Harel case, 147
rules, on lease Jubilee, 78
rural areas, control over, 158, 159, 162, 207
rural non-agrarian land (*mewat*), 16, 17, *17*, 18, 19–20, *20*; ownership of, 21
rural settlements, between Arab and Jewish population, 158, *159*
Russia, 62

Sabach case, 151
Sabith case, 140
sacred spaces, 3

Saig case, 150
Sapir, Pinhas, 29
secondary leasing market, 149
security: needs, 106; threats, 99
"separate but equal," 146–47, 152, 161, 209
separation model, 145, 152, 157, 161, 207
settlements: Arab, 151, 156, 157–58, *159*, 207; cooperative, 82; Jewish, 148, *159*
Shaked, Ayelet, 48, 135, 179
Shawahna case, 142
shortage, of land reserves, 99–100
SII. *See* Standards Institution of Israel
slow planning progress, 155, 161
small size, of Israel, 7, 95–96, 101, 117–18, 203; necessity of creativity and, 206–7
social: stratification, 5; unit, 47
socialism to market economy, transition from, 58–59, 205
socialist worldview, 55–56, 59, 62–63, 87, 203, 205; land development and, 205
socioeconomic: index of Central Bureau of Statistics, 160, 208; inequality, 159–60, 162, 208; status of different populations, 153
solar power, 100
spaces: open, 106; sacred, 3
spread, urban, 97–100, 106
Standards Institution of Israel (SII), 108
state, Jewish, 50–51, 142, 144, 160, 203
state of flux, of identity of Israel, 209–10
State of Israel, 19, 21, 27, 32; ideological transformation of, 62; land development and, 117; mixing populations and, 152–53, 207–8; socialism and, 56; transfer of refugee lands to, 24, 35, 136–37, 204
state-owned lands, 20, *20*, 204
state sovereignty, 96
status of different populations, socioeconomic, 153
Strasberg-Cohen, Tova, 183–84
*Strategic Plan for Housing for the Years 2017-2040, The* (Raz-Dror and Kost), 151
stratification, social, 5
structural reinforcement, in peripheral areas, 109
struggle, with past, 203–4
subsurface space. *See* underground

Supreme Court, Israel, 18, 26, 45, 56–58, 61; conservatism of, 186, 195; expanse of scope of, 177; on expropriated land, 193; on integration of populations, 146, 208; on Israel Lands Council, 73; public trust in, 180; on registration of caveats, 186; restitution of refugee land and, 140–42; restraint of, 189–92, 195–96, 209
Supreme Court, US, 5–6, 178, 191
Supreme Muslim Council, 141
swap, of JNF lands with other state lands, 31, 33

Tchernichovsky, Shaul, 1
technical policy decisions, 74
Technion, 116
Tel Aviv: light rail of, 111; metropolis of, 98, 191; Regional Court of, 85
territory, historical, 3
Thatcher government, 88
threats: of earthquakes, 101, 108–10, 117; security, 99
3D land parcels, as separate units, 112
three-dimensional planning, 111–12
time, to build apartments, 104
Torrens system, 18
training grounds, army, 99
train networks, 105–6
transfer: of army camps to periphery, 107; of JNF lands to government, 29, 204; of refugee lands to state, 24, 35, 136–37, 204
transferor and transferee, relationship between, 184, 188–89
transition, from socialism to market economy, 58–59, 205

UK. *See* United Kingdom
underground: expanse as solution to division of sovereignty, 111; land ownership of, 113; parking garages, 111; space use of, 110–13
UNDOP. *See* United Nations Conciliation Commission for Palestine
Union for Distributive Justice, 88
United Kingdom (UK), 79; privatization initiatives, 88

United Nations Conciliation Commission for Palestine (UNDOP), 23
United States (US), 5–6; BLM of, 62; Constitution of, 190; land privatization of, 36; Supreme Court of, 178, 191
units, housing, 76–77, 80, 104–5
Unna, Moshe, 138
unplanned construction, 156
Al-Uqbi case, 142, 144
urban: expansion curb of, 107; growth rates, 98–99; land ownership, 153–54; pressure on agricultural lands, 81–82; public lands privatization of, 31, 36, 58, 72–73, 75–80, 203, 205–6; renewal projects, 5, 107; settlement in Galilee, 151–52; settlements concentration of Arab population in, 158, 161; spread, 97–100, 106
urbanization, profits, of, 83–85
US. See United States
use: of agricultural land for residential purposes, 86–87; of maritime space, 113–17; of underground space, 110–13

Venezuela, 5
Verne, Jules, 113

Warhaftig, Zerach, 51
War of Independence, 9, 14, 23, 50, 133, 136; aftermath of, 139, 154, 207, 209; compensation for land lost in, 137, 160, 208
water: desalination plants, 106, 114; problems, 100–101
weakening, of other governmental systems, 178
Weisman, Joshua, 15–16, 78, 181–82, 204
Weitz, Joseph, 28
"White Papers" (Mandate Government), 28
World Bank, 62
worldview: capitalist, 203, 205, 209; socialist, 55–56, 59, 62–63, 87, 203, 205
World Zionist Organization, Settlement Division of, 147

"Zionism in the Twenty-First Century?" (Saposnik), 210
Zionist movement, 6, 21, 28, 31, 46–47; agricultural land and, 81, 89; central tenet of, 49–50, 133–34; Gordon on, 49; infinite ideal, 210; socialism and, 55–56, 205
*Zochrot* (Remembering), 139, 140

HAIM SANDBERG is a member of the Faculty of the Striks School of Law of the College of Management Academic Studies (COMAS). He teaches Property Law at the Law Faculties of COMAS, the Hebrew University of Jerusalem, and Tel Aviv University. He has published dozens of articles and three books on Israel's land law, among them *Land Title Settlement in Eretz-Israel and the State of Israel* and the *Commentary on Basic Law: Israel Lands* (both in Hebrew). His publications are frequently cited by Israeli courts. He is a member of the Israeli Bar, and for three decades he has advised governmental bodies, public institutions, and commercial firms in the fields of land law and land policy. Professor Sandberg was a member of the Israeli Council for Higher Education (CHE), and his name was officially published as a candidate for judge in the Israeli Supreme Court.

www.ingramcontent.com/pod-product-compliance
Lightning Source LLC
Chambersburg PA
CBHW020328240426
43665CB00044B/890